Maria H. Brons

SOCIETY, SECURITY, SOVEREIGNTY
AND THE STATE IN SOMALIA

From Statelessness to Statelessness?

International Books, 2001

The publication of this book was financially supported by the Faculty of Law of the University of Groningen, the University Library of Groningen and the Jurriaanse Foundation, Rotterdam

ISBN 90 5727 038 2

Cover design: Karel Oosting
Production: Trees Vulto
DTP: Hanneke Kossen
Printing: Drukkerij Haasbeek

Keywords: Somalia, State collapse and -formation, security, sovereignty

International Books, Alexander Numankade 17, 3572 KP Utrecht, the Netherlands
Tel. +31 30 2731840, fax +31 30 2733614, e-mail i-books@antenna.nl

Contents

Preface and Acknowledgements

This book is the result of a fifteen-year long engagement with the contemporary development of Somali politics. I first came to know about Somali society and state in a rather practical way. In 1986, I implemented a project for refugee women who had fled from Ethiopia to Somalia in the end of the 1970s. This was when I first began to ask questions about the political landscape of the Somali region, the different states, clans and political identities. Why were the refugees with whom I worked not integrated into Somali society, not really welcome? How did the state authorities deal with the refugee population, and how did they deal with expatriates coming from the West? How much freedom and security did the state provide to its citizens? Why was the political atmosphere so different in Hargeisa and in Mogadishu?

When I resumed my university education in Germany after this break in Somalia I continued to investigate Somali politics. I studied the regional conflict in the Somali part of the Horn of Africa – the roots of the crisis that had forced the women in my project to flee their homes. In my Masters thesis I investigated the mutual impact of international, regional and national security politics in and around Somalia.

The first steps towards the book that you now hold in your hands, towards the analysis of internal dynamics of the Somali conflict and the relation between state and society, were taken when I was given the opportunity to shift my research into this direction and to publish my findings. In this regard I am grateful to the Friedrich-Naumann Stiftung for approving a one-year grant, Deutscher Akademischer Austauschdienst for a six-month scholarship, and Deutsches Institut für Afrikakunde for accepting and financing my first two book publications. During this period of research I received every support from the Institute of Ethiopian Studies at Addis Ababa University in Ethiopia and the Scandinavian Institute of African Studies in Uppsala, Sweden.

My thanks also go to Prof. Dr. Rainer Tetzlaff, University of Hamburg in Germany who supported me in my research efforts, accepted me as a PhD student and, in March 1994, generously approved the transfer of my PhD project from Hamburg to Groningen in the Netherlands.

It was thanks to Prof. Dr. Martin Doornbos from the Institute of Social Studies in The Hague that I came to know about the research project on 'state-society relations and security studies in weak states' at the University of Groningen. Knowing my earlier work, he encouraged me to apply and – as a specialist in the politics of the Horn of Africa – Professor Doornbos became one of my promoters. Drawing on his profound knowledge of Somali history and contemporary politics, he critically observed and commented on my interpretation of the Somali experience. Looking back over seven years of support and friendship, I am very grateful to him.

Turning to my promoters at the University of Groningen, I had the pleasure of working under the supervision of the late Prof. Dr. Herman de Lange. His unconventional way of supervision inspired me and strengthened my confidence; like many others, I feel very sad that he was taken away from us so suddenly. A big vote of thanks goes out to all my colleagues at the department of Theory of Law in Groningen, in particular to Prof. Dr. Theo van den Hoogen from the Political Science section. From the very beginning of my five-year stay in Groningen he showed a keen interest in my research and supported me by providing literature, commenting on drafts, enabling me to teach, and supporting my requests to attend several international conferences. He took the burden of supervision during the time of illness of my first promoter.

I am also most grateful to Prof. Dr. John Griffiths, the Head of the Department of Theory of Law, who – without knowing much of my work at that point – offered to become my first supervisor and enabled me at a time of crisis to continue the PhD project. His critical remarks and serious reading sharpened my view and argumentation. His patience allowed me the necessary time to improve the book.

I was given the opportunity to be part of the Center of Development Studies in Groningen under the directorship of Prof. Dr. Caspar Schweigman. My colleagues in the 'state and society' section offered me a platform to present first findings and teach some of my material to students, and gave me the feeling of academic belonging, although my visits to the far North were rather irregular.

After leaving the University of Groningen, the University of Amsterdam became my academic home, where I was generously invited by Prof. Dr. Joke Schrijvers and Prof Dr. Ton Dietz as a guest researcher with INDRA/AGIDS. My colleagues in Amsterdam encouraged me in the final stages of the very last draft of the book and, at the same time, enabled me to explore new academic ground in the form of conference planning, research networking, teaching and editing. My special thanks go to Prof. Dr. Joke Schrijvers, Dr. Philomena

Essed, Prof. Dr. Georg Frerks, Margriet Poppema, the students of the 'Refugees in North and South' course and particularly to my dear colleague Marlie Hollands.

During all these fifteen years I have learned an immense amount from numerous discussions with Somali politicians, diplomats and academics in Bonn, Mogadishu, Uppsala, Stockholm, Addis Ababa and The Hague. I would not know where to begin and where to end naming all of them. In particular I would like to mention my friend and co-authoress of other publications, Amina Warsame.

With regard to the finishing touch of the book I would like to thank Paula Bownas for proofreading assistance, Koos van Wieringen for drawing the maps and my supervisors and members of the reading committee for their patience.

I would never have come so far without the support of my family, friends and neighbors. First and foremost are my parents who, from the very beginning, encouraged my sister and me to learn hard and discover new grounds, seizing opportunities that they had never been offered in their own educational lives. Not only as parents but also as grandparents they have been the cornerstones of support on which I can always count. My two girls, Norika and Johanna, were born into the PhD project and will be among those who are most pleased as it comes to an end. Their loving kindness and affection nurture my happiness in life and have helped me through the difficult times. My husband, Prof. Dr. Mohamed Salih, is the source of strength, optimism and encouragement in my life. His care, patience and readiness to support me by providing me with the latest literature, discussing developments in the Horn, questioning my argumentation, solving numerous computer problems, caring for the babies at night, cooking, and so on, helped me to finish the project in an acceptable time frame.

Thank you all.

I dedicate this book to my parents Gertrud and Heinrich, to my girls, Norika and Johanna, and to my nephews, Jos and Bruno.

Maria Brons,
The Hague, December 2000

Maps

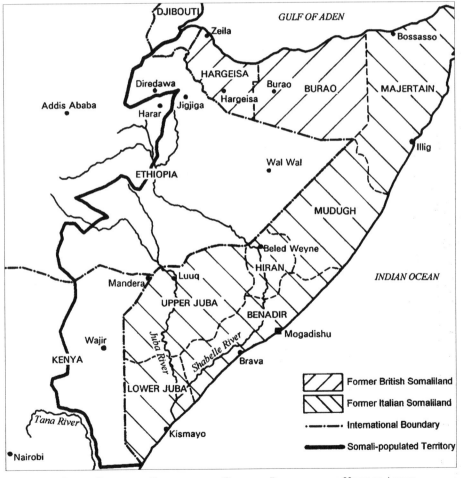

MAP 1   SOMALI POPULATED TERRITORY AND COLONIAL BORDERS IN THE HORN OF AFRICA

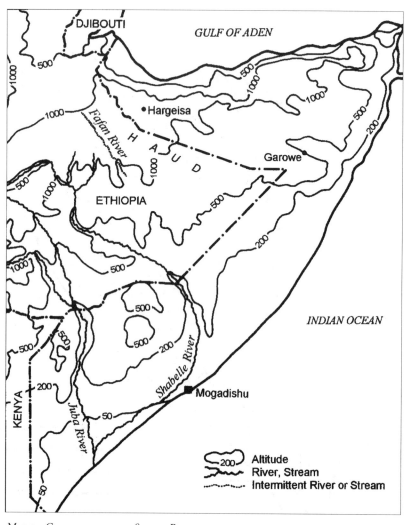

MAP 2   GEOGRAPHY OF THE SOMALI REGION

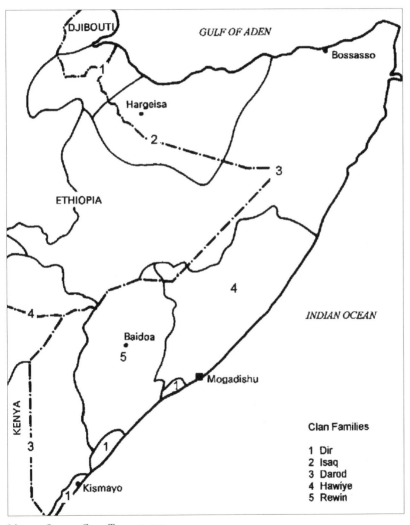

MAP 3 SOMALI CLAN TERRITORIES

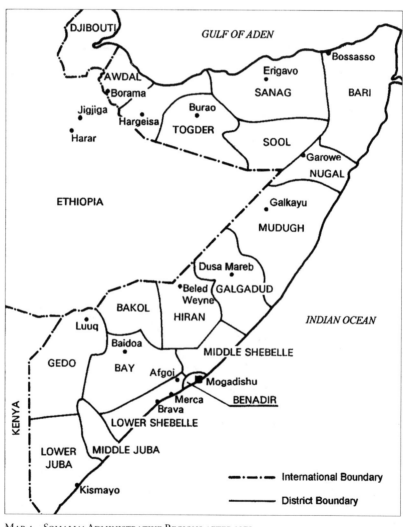

MAP 4   SOMALIA: ADMINISTRATIVE REGIONS AFTER 1975

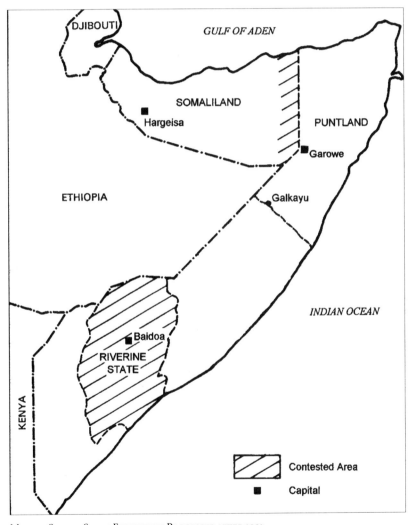

MAP 5   SOMALI STATE FORMATION PROCESSES AFTER 1991

Diagram 1

Somali Clan Structure

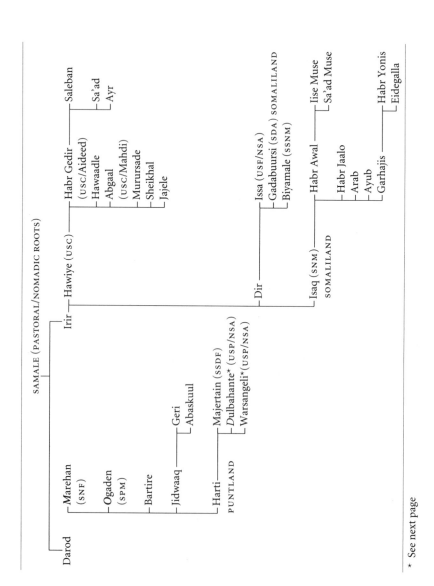

* See next page

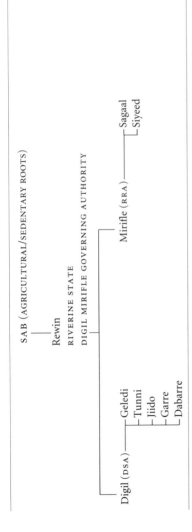

SAB (AGRICULTURAL/SEDENTARY ROOTS)

Rewin
RIVERINE STATE
DIGIL MIRIFLE GOVERNING AUTHORITY

Digil (DSA) — Geledi, Tunni, Jiido, Garre, Dabarre

Mirifle (RRA) — Sagaal, Siyeed

There are obviously more sub-clans and lineages than the ones listed above. This diagram includes those clans/lineages that are mentioned in the text.

MOD: Clan power base of Siyad Barre
(SNM): Abbreviation of politico-military faction
PUNTLAND: Clan background of state formation processes
⋆ Divided loyalty between Puntland and Somaliland

Abbreviations

ARRA	Administration for Refugee/Returnee Affairs
BMA	British Military Administration
COGWA	Coalition for Grassroots Women Organisations, Mogadishu
DSA	Digil Salvation Army
HDMS	Hisbia Dhigale Mirifle Somaaliyeed; renamed in 1957 to Hisbia Dastur Mustaqil al-Sumal, Somali Independent Constitutional Party
IGAD	Inter-Governmental Agency for Development
MI	Military Intelligence
MOD faction	Marehan/Ogaden/Dulbahante faction
NEGAAD	Women Umbrella Organisation, Hargeisa
NER	North Eastern Region
NRC	National Refugee Commission
NSA	Northern Somali Alliance (USP and USF)
NSC	National Salvation Council (Sodere Initiative)
NSS	National Security Service
NUF	National United Front
OAU	Organization of African Unity
RRA	Rahanweyn Resistance Army
SALF	Somali Abbo Liberation Front
SDA	Somali Democratic Alliance (Gadabuursi)
SDM	Somali Democratic Movement
SNC	Somali National Congress
SNF	Somali National Front (Marehan)
SNL	Somaliland National League, since 1948 Somali National League
SNM	Somali National Movement (Isaq)
SOSAF	Somali Salvation Front (predecessor of SSDF)
SPM	Somali Patriotic Movement (Ogaden)
SRC	Supreme Revolutionary Council
SRSP	Somali Revolutionary Socialist Party
SRYO	Somali Revolutionary Youth Organization
SSDF	Somali Salvation Democratic Front (Majertain)
SWDO	Somali Women's Democratic Organization
SYL	Somali Youth League
UNDOS	United Nations Development Office for Somalia

UNHCR	United Nations High Commissioner for Refugees
UNITAF	United Task Force
UNOSOM	United Nations Operation Somalia
UNRISD	United Nations Research Institute for Social Development
USC	United Somali Congress (Hawiye)
USC/SNA	United Somali Congress/Somali National Alliance (Aideed)
USF	United Somali Front (Issa)
USP	United Somali Party (Dulbahante/Warsangeli)
WSLF	Western Somali Liberation Front

Glossary

abban system	the lineage of a caravan guide is basis for unhindered passage through alien clan territory
adoon	slaves
ahmadiya	name of Sufi order
aqil	title of elder
aqiyaarta	council of elders in the South
asabiyyah	tribal bonding
bakaaros	grain storages
barista hisbiga	party investigators
bilis	nobles within the village
boon	commoners within the village
boonka conference	Rewin clan conference in 1993
boqor	title for clan elder
dabarjebinta	military counter intelligence
dandaraawiya	name of Sufi order
daraawiish	fighters of Sayyed Mohammed Abdulle Hassan
dhalad	literally 'member by birth' agnates in Rewin clan
dhaqan	literally 'member by culture'/adopted Rewin clan members
dhasheego	flood recession farming
dhibaad	presents, utensils that the girl brings into the marriage
diya-paying group	blood money paying group
duq	village headman
gabaati	gift offered to girl's family after successful arrangement of marriage
garad	title for clan elder
golaha guurtida	council of elders, Somaliland state
golaha wakiillada	constituent assembly, Somaliland state
golaha xukuumadda	government or executive power, Somaliland state
gosha	identification of ex-slave lineages originating in East-African tribes with Somali clan lineage of ex-masters
guddiga malaqiiyada	committee of clan chiefs, Rewin state
guulwadayaal	party militias/victory pioneers
guur-haye	bodyguard daraawiish state
guurti	special conflict resolution committees appointed by shir

hangash (hayada nabadgelyada gaashaandhiga)
military intelligence
hanti-wadaagga 'ilmi ku disan

	literally 'sharing wealth based on wisdom', scientific socialism
heer	contract/customary law
hidid	lineage ties through marriage
jama'a	religious congregation
jiimo	irrigated riverbank farming
kadis	urban Islamic courts
khusuusi	council of elders in daraawiish state
koofiyada casta	military police
maarra weyn	official army in daraawiish state
mag-paying group	blood money paying group
malaq	title for clan elder
maxaa	Sab Somali language
maxkamada wareegta	mobile military court
may	Samale Somali language
meher	legally claimable payment promised to bride in case of husband's death or divorce
moryaan culture	lawless youngsters
qaadiriya	name of Sufi order
qaat	narcotic stimulant (also: qat, kat, khat, chad)
reer badiya	people of the bush, 'pure' Somali
reer goleed	people from the forest, discriminative against Sab
reer-beade	community at large, daraawiish state
salihiya	name of Sufi order (Mohammed Abdulle Hassan)
sayyed	religious title
seyla'iya	name of Somali Sufi order
sharia	Islamic law
sheegat	genealogical submission of smaller clan to the lineage of a bigger clan
sheikh	religious title
shir meetings	ad-hoc conflict resolution meetings
sultan	title for clan elder
tariiqa	literally 'path', 'way to God', Sufi orders
tin jileec	people with soft hair, 'pure' Somali
tol	patrilineal descent
ugaz	title for clan elder
uwaysiya	name of Somali Sufi order
wadaado	men of God
waranleh	warriors
yarad	bride wealth (men's lineage pays to woman's lineage)

CHAPTER 1

Introduction

Is the state in modern circumstances a necessary and inevitable form of social organization, one, which once it emerges in a given society, is a permanent fixture? This is the question that will be critically considered in this book. What is meant by the *state* in this context is a political entity comprising a variety of institutions, which exercise control over violence within particular territorial boundaries.

We will consider the specific case of Somalia, which has been without a *state* since 1991. The Somali state collapsed when, at the climax of the civil war at the beginning of 1991, president Siyad Barre, his family and select political entourage were left with no other option than to flee their residence 'Villa Somalia' in the capital Mogadishu. The numerous clan-affiliated factions which had collaborated to take control of most of the country and which finally won the battle for Mogadishu were not able to unite in forming a new government. As a result, the territory of the former Somali state was controlled by different military factions and fell apart, politically, into various territorial units. In 1998, as I finish writing this book, there are a number of different political entities on Somali territory, including the self-proclaimed Republic of Somaliland in the Northwest and the autonomous regional state of Puntland in the Northeast. There are also numerous locally governed political entities in the South, where different faction leaders exercise politico-military dominance over particular territories, whose boundaries remain unsettled. Sporadic fighting and political maneuvering continue up to the present time.

Although the institutions, which constituted the Somali *state* collapsed, the Somali people continued their life, albeit with patterns of existence other than state-driven socio-economic and political arrangements. Some parts of Somali society seem to have been able to manage quite well without the state. Others, which had suffered under state authority, have seen little improvement in the no-state situation. These phenomena challenge the assumed necessity of modern state institutions to social life.

The focus of the following study is the Somali experience as a society confronting the collapse of the modern state. Throughout the recent stateless years in Somalia political authority formation has taken different forms, which raises questions about the direction to be taken by future Somali state formation processes. Our empirical analysis of Somali state collapse and state(s) formation is intended as a contribution to the discussion of the modern state, its nature, purpose and future.

State-Centered Theories of Sovereignty and Security and its Critics

In recent years, the universal validity of the concept of the modern state, in the context of the political, social and economic realities of modern societies has been increasingly called into question. Critics call attention to two developments: a tendency towards global governance and trans-national loyalties and identities on the one hand; and, on the other hand, the increasing political importance of localized structures, reflected in sub-national loyalties and identities. The first trajectory refers mainly to the developed, Western world where the tendency of political and economic decision-making by trans-national bodies, such as witnessed in the context of the European Union Amsterdam Treaty, is widening (Held, 1995, Linklater, 1995). The second trajectory is developed in the context of weak or collapsing states in the Southern part of the world, particularly in Africa (Grindle, 1996; Olukashi and Laakso, 1996, Zartman, 1995). In the light of these developments, the question is often asked whether the state is still necessary, or whether the political institution of the modern state is damned to increasing insignificance. As Linklater (1995: p.178, p.193) notes:

> A myriad of factors are currently transforming political communities across the world and, as the century comes to an end, the time is indeed ripe for enunciating new principles of political life which break with the tyranny of the concept of the state. … The consequent failure to theorize the world outside the state has left the modern political imagination profoundly impoverished.

What, then, should be the starting point of our inquiry? The alternative to a state-centered analysis is to take society as a reference point. In this book, society is defined in a broad way as a conglomeration of people who tend to interact more with each other on social, cultural, economic and political dimensions than they do with those who are not members of the same society. Obviously, such a concept is indeterminate, both in the sense that one can speak both of European society and of French society, for example, and in the sense that the more marginal a member is, the greater his or her interaction with members of other societies. Unlike a state, a society does not necessarily have fixed or determinate geographic boundaries and if it does, these do not necessarily coincide with those of any particular state. Society is highly differentiated and a less coherent unit of analysis than the state. Unlike the state, it does not speak as an anthropomorphic entity (Waever, Buzan, Kelstrup, Lemaitre, 1993).

A society is characterized by social integration as well as social fragmentation. Social integration might derive internally from commonly perceived or transmitted ethnic roots, common descent or language. It might go along with political integration in cases where integrated state-society relations prevail. Externally-driven social integration might be stimulated by a commonly perceived enemy. Social fragmentation exists in various forms and multiple layers, such as gender, religion, clan, class and age. Segmentary lineage societies, such as Somali society (Lewis, 1961), can be extremely fragmented into tribes or clans. Nevertheless, close bonds of family and kinship are counterbalanced by strong individualism. The nomadic sector of Somali society, particularly, has an individualistic, egalitarian component. In addition, Somali society has undergone a transformation process whereby lineage fragmentation and the political perceptions of the individual as citizen have become molded into a sometimes contradictory and conflict-prone whole.

Society is continually shaped and re-shaped and is, finally, the product of decisions people make concerning when, how and with whom they interact (Howard, 1993). Social identity patterns, such as ethnic belonging, gender and historical precedent all influence this decision. I will assume that the prevailing and inherently dominant factor in determining people's choices and subsequently identities is the search for relative security.

In the study that follows, the search for security is thus considered the key factor determining political authority formation. Conventional theory in security studies is centered on the state, the dominant political authority in the contemporary world system:

> Realism's construction of the possibilities for political order, of the realm of
> politics, and thus of security yields both an object to secure (the territorially
> defined political community) and an agent to pursue this end (the state)
> (Williams and Krause, 1997: p.xiv).

Within such a framework, the institutions that make up a modern state are supposed to play the role of caretaker for a basically integrated society. The basic relation between *state* and *society*, the *raison d'être* of a state, is containment of violence. The principal concern of conventional security studies is the problem of how to contain or control violence, conflict or war between states. State security, however, is threatened not only by other states but also by violence from within society. Furthermore, violent conflict often evolves from state policies that threaten the security of its population. An approach to security studies that limits itself to the category of state, to peace and security between states, cannot grasp the multitude of phenomena of conflict and insecurity.

In contrast to the conventional approach to security studies a debate has developed that takes a critical perspective *vis-à-vis* the state-centric line of thought. According to the critical security approach, both the *object* ("the territorially defined political community", see the quotation above) and the *agent* ("the state") need to be scrutinized when defining the possibilities for political order, the realms of politics and of security.

Moving towards a society-centered analysis of political order involves re-thinking not only the role of the state, but also the related concept of sovereignty. When taking up Linklater's challenge to "theorize the world outside the state" (see p.26), we must therefore also theorize sovereignty independently from the state. We can do this by reconsidering the theoretical link between security and sovereignty as expressed in normative theories of state formation by consent, which trace the genesis of sovereign authority to consent given by members of society. According to the consent theory, sovereign authority is granted for and therefore conditional upon the provision of security to those who vest political authority in the 'sovereign'. The link between security and sovereignty, therefore, ultimately derives from the people who participate in building a society – the social unit in which the origin of sovereignty lies.

In the theoretical framework that I develop for the analysis of the Somali case I link the debate on security with that on sovereignty and state-formation. I assume that the political concept of sovereignty is not satisfactorily described as indivisible state sovereignty, but must be seen as divided between various security agents within and outside society. State formation can only be sustainable if the state as one institution among others proves to be the superior security-providing agency for society.

With these considerations in mind, an analysis of the Somali case – of a people that moved from statelessness, through state formation and collapse, back to statelessness and further to new kinds of political authority formation – can contribute to contemporary discussions about political community, state formation and the future of the state as the most prominent institution for political order. In the analysis that follows, I intend to draw on society-centered security studies, which consider the modern state framework as just one option for society in the search for relative security and for the investment of political authority and sovereignty. At the end of the analysis I will return to the question whether, in the light of the Somali experience, a shift in the security debate from the conventional to a critical security approach might prove promising.

The Collapse of the Somali State

A functional as well as an institutional definition of the state guides the analysis of the Somali experience that follows. The primary function of the state is considered to be security provision, and throughout the case study we will be asking how the Somali state performed in that function. In exercising this particular role, the ideal state both serves and is controlled by society.

Drawing on the Weberian definition of the state, Buzan (1991) suggests a triad of component parts of any state: (1) the idea of the state; (2) the physical base of the state, i.e. its territory and population; and (3) the institutional expression of the state. The first pillar of the state – the idea of a state – is reflected in its underlying political identity. "The notion of purpose is what distinguishes the idea of the state from its physical base and its institutions" (ibid.: p.69-70). Buzan refers, in this respect, both to different variants of nation-states, and to their organizing ideologies, such as political, economic, religious or social ideologies. With regard to the second component – the physical base of the state, including territorial borders, and the population, natural resources and man-made wealth within these borders – the size of its population is seen as more influential than the size of its territory in determining the permanence of a state. State territory is the most specific of the three state components, and the international system relies on territorial demarcations of states. State territory can be threatened by other states and/or by claims for independence or separatist movements within the state. The third component, the institutional expression of the state, comprises "the entire machinery of government, including its executive, legislative, administrative and judicial bodies, and the laws, procedures and norms by which they operate" (ibid.: p.82).

The Buzan triangle of state components enables us to develop a classification of states in terms of different threats and weaknesses. The ideology of the state, its territorial integrity, or its major institutions, can all be threatened. The state can be weak in its institutional framework (particularly with regard to control over the use of force), or in the cohesive idea, which should bind state and society, or because of an inappropriate population/territory ratio or unsettled territorial boundaries.

It is important not to reify the state as some kind of autonomous entity. In this context we read in Weber (1968):

Thus, for instance, one of the important aspects of the existence of a modern state, precisely as a complex of social interaction of individual persons, consists in the fact that the action of various individuals is oriented to the belief that it exists or should exist, thus that its acts and laws are valid in the

legal sense. ... A "state", for example, ceases to exist in a sociologically relevant sense whenever there is no longer a probability that certain kinds of
meaningfully oriented social action will take place (Ibid.: p.14, p.27).

It is people who bring a state to life or let it collapse, who exist before the state
and who finally determine whether a given political entity is considered a
state. In the Somali case the three constituent parts – the idea of the state, the
physical base of the state (territory and population), and the institutional expression of the state – all collapsed.

THE IDEA OF THE STATE

The idea of the state, reflecting its political identity and the bond between society and state, in other words, the leading ideology propagated by the Somali
state leadership, was, in retrospect, threefold.

First, the 'Greater Somalia' quest for the unification of all Somali-inhabited
territories in the Horn within one nation-state was a sacrosanct idea for the
early post-colonial state. After 1969, the socialist Somali state, too, relied on
the idea of 'Greater Somalia' to rally people behind its policies (Laitin and
Samatar, 1987). 'Greater Somalia' lost momentum after Somalia's defeat in the
Ethiopian-Somali war over the Ethiopian-Somali borders, known as the
Ogaden-war, in 1977/78.

Second, scientific socialism – *Hanti-wadaagga 'ilmi ku disan,* literally 'sharing
wealth based on wisdom' – was officially announced as the ideology of the
state on the first anniversary of the Revolution in 1970 (Lewis, 1988; Samatar,
1988). Together with it went the political goal of eradicating tribalism within
Somali society: people were no longer allowed to address each other as cousins
or brothers *(walaal),* but only as comrades *(jaale)*; the *aqil,* the head of a
clan-lineage and mediator between state and traditional political authority
during colonial times, was renamed *nabad doon,* literally meaning 'peace-
maker'. However, these socialist ideals, if ever a genuine goal, faded away with
the increasing decay of Somali state politics into coercion, ruthless state terrorism and the perfecting of sophisticated tactics of *divide and rule* based on
clan antagonisms (Africa Watch, 1990).

Third, the bond between Somali society and state was based on the perception
of Somalia in the way that it came to be portrayed, by Somali politicians as well

as by foreign and Somali academic analysts and political commentators, as an ethnically homogeneous nation of camel nomads.[1] In the ideological vacuum of the recent stateless years (since 1991) this perception has been increasingly challenged by Somali and non-Somali scholars, who stress the diversity within Somali society and who have unveiled the history of domination of nomadic Somali over sedentary Somali (Mohamed Salih and Wohlgemuth, 1994a; Ahmed, 1995a). The critique points out how the myth of Somali origin, which classifies the Somali people as being in between African and Arab (see Mukhtar, 1995; Kusow, 1995; Ahmed, 1995b), was politicized and became a tool of political power in the hands of clans with a nomadic background. The collapse of the state in 1991 revealed the fundamental crisis of Somali political and social identity, a crisis reflected in the breakdown of social conscience and the apocalyptic experiences of a cruel civil war.

STATE TERRITORY

The physical base of the Somali state, combining territory and population, also collapsed – if it ever really existed. It is widely recognized that state borders on the African continent often have little to do with underlying socio-geographic realities. This also applies to the Horn of Africa and the Somali region in particular. In colonial times the Somali region was divided amongst Italy (South, Central and Northeastern region), Britain (North and Southwest), France (Northwest) and Ethiopia (West). In 1960, the newly independent British Somaliland and the UN Trusteeship-territory under Italian administration united to form the Republic Somalia, while the Northern Frontier District stayed with Kenya,[2] the Ogaden, Eastern Hararghe and Bale regions remained part of Ethiopia and, in 1977, French Somaliland finally became Djibouti. The territorial base of the Somali state, therefore, never reflected the territorial base of Somali society or the Somali-inhabited areas in the Horn. This is where the origin of demands for a 'Greater Somalia' lies.

The physical base of the state generally refers to the legal definition of state territory in international law (Jackson and Rosberg, 1982). In this sense, and

---

1   One example of many is Laitin and Samatar (1987).

2   Kenya became independent in 1963. In a referendum shortly before independence, a majority in the Northern Frontier District, the Somali-inhabited areas in Northeastern Kenya, voted for integration into Somalia. British colonial authorities ignored the referendum (Farah, 1993).

despite its physical collapse it seems that the Somali state is still internationally recognized. Although there has been no central government in Somalia since 1991, the UN and other international organizations still consider the borders of the ex-Somali state as a reference point for their policies towards Somalia. The UN strategy, particularly during the UNOSOM operations, as well as the attitude of foreign governments towards the Somali question, is reflected in their reaction to the proclamation of independence by Somaliland (the Northwestern territory, former British Somaliland Protectorate) in May 1991 (Brons, 1993). Although external actors respect the existence of the 'Northern authorities' as legitimate political authorities, Somaliland still awaits international recognition. In spite of this anomaly, however, there is no doubt that the Somali state (1960-1991) collapsed territorially in 1991, with its population and territory divided into several entities.

Apart from the connotation of 'state-territory', territoriality in the Somali context has another dimension. The agro-pastoral and pastoral clans, in particular, move according to climatic conditions and the needs of their herds for water and pasture. Their territories are defined according to the pastoral way of life that has little to do with international law, whose rules of the game were set by colonial powers. Thus, for about a century, international borders have divided Somali clan territories. The lands of the Southern agricultural clans also stretch across international borders into Ethiopia. Yet – and this may be different from other cases in Africa – despite international borders, clan territories are very much integrated in the economic, social and political life of the Somali. The Somali conceptualization of territoriality as derived from geographic, economic and trading patterns also impacts on settlement patterns and social and political norms and perceptions. In terms of territoriality, one could speak today of three distinct territories in the Somali-inhabited areas of the Horn. (See maps 1 and 2). These are: (1) the Northwestern region including the 'Somali part' of Djibouti, Somaliland and the Northwestern part of the Somali 'region 5' in Ethiopia; (2) the South, stretching from the Somali-inhabited Northeastern Moyale district in Kenya in the West to the Southern edge of the Ethiopian region 5 in the North, up to the areas just beyond the Shabelle river in the East; and (3) the Central and Northeastern region making up the tip of the Horn and stretching into Southern Ethiopia. As will be shown later, these regions are political as well as economic units as a result of family/clan connections, pastoral movement and trade.

Although we will, of course, return to questions of territory in the rest of this study, these remarks should be sufficient to highlight some of the contradictions involved in a legal approach to Somali state-territory and the relative insignificance of state territorial boundaries for the life of the common Somali people.

STATE INSTITUTIONS

State institutions, which carried the executive, legislative and judicial powers of the Somali state, stopped functioning in 1991. Government employees, most of who were in one way or another related to the politically powerful clans dominating the Siyad Barre regime, fled from violence that was fuelled by emotions of hatred and revenge. Government offices, ministries, the National Bank, army and police, courts, postal services and educational institutions disintegrated. Indeed, not only did the state institutions cease to function, but also buildings and equipment were looted beyond recognition. Arms, money, office files, books, furniture, technical apparatus, telephones and wires, waterpipes, roofs, window-frames – everything was taken, sold or destroyed. The extreme devastation of the institutional framework of the Somali state must be taken into account when state reconstruction on Somali soil is discussed.

State territory, state institutions and various ideas/ideologies were expected to build the bond between Somali society and state, but collapsed and proved to have been weak social constructions all along. So what did survive? Life went on in Somalia in a situation of statelessness. Members of Somali society turned to alternative security arrangements, most of which had existed side by side or in conjunction with state institutions. If such security arrangements, rooted in the non-state social sphere, prove superior to those that a proto-state can provide, especially in the sensitive task of controlling the means of violence, then is it possible that Somalis might prefer to continue living without a conventional state institutional framework (Doornbos and Markakis, 1994)? Alternatively, is it possible that previously non-state institutions of security provision will be transformed into state institutions? Such a process would reflect a bottom-up dynamic of institution building and an essentially consensus-based attempt at state formation. A third scenario envisages a top-down state formation process (perhaps externally driven) that would bring (parts of) Somali society under state control.

Somali society is not static but flexible and rich in variety, that is reflected in categories of clan and class, in regional differences of economic production patterns, of language, tradition and history. In addition, Somali society today is divided between those who live abroad as international migrants and those who stayed at home in the region. This background gives rise to the question of who in Somali society is in favor of reconstituting a state, and what kind of a state. Military faction leaders, former civil servants, businessmen and traders, educated women, farmers in the South and nomads in the North, all have different and sometimes conflicting visions about structures and functions of a future Somali state.

In the light of the various options with which Somali society is confronted, I intend critically to evaluate the post-1991 attempts at and processes of state formation within the territory of ex-Somalia.

Objectives of the Study

This book is intended to provide a contribution to three interrelated fields of inquiry. Firstly, it offers an account of the impact of state formation, state collapse and renewed state formation processes on the Somali people, highlighting their heterogeneity rather than their homogeneity.[3] Findings are based on my own field research in the broader Somali region as well as in Nairobi and Addis Ababa during the years 1986, 1991/92 and 1996/97. The characterization of past and contemporary Somali society is based on a wealth of literature on Somali society, history and politics as well as on works, in particular those by Somali social scientists that reflect new trends in re-reading the past and analyzing the present. In this context, I have endeavored to include the literature, which reflects the 'fresh wind' blowing in Somali studies, breaking away from

---

3   Recent publications show how the image of homogeneity is sustained; if the farming communities are mentioned at all, they are portrayed as Somali minorities or as non-Somali. "In general, the Somali people share a common language (Somaale), religion (Islam), physical characteristics, and pastoral and agropastoral customs and traditions" (Adam, 1995: p.70). Again: "For centuries before the European colonial era, Somalia was a pastoral and nomadic society. Herders of camels, cattle and sheep lived in a world of 'egalitarian anarchy' where the main preoccupation of clan families was the well-being of the herd. With the exception of small Bantu communities along the Juba and Shebelle Rivers, there were no ethnic or religious minorities. It was a singular homogeneous culture that in theory should have come into the modern era in a cohesive and stable way. ... From the tenth century on, ethnic Somalis were dispersed throughout the Horn of Africa in a continuous search for forage and water for their herds. In the riverine area between the Juba and Shebelle, a small number practised maize and millet agriculture, and a small trading class along the coast maintained contact by sea with the Arab Peninsula" (Hirsch and Oakley, 1995: p.3).

stereotyped accounts of Somali society.[4] In this way I hope to contribute to the academic debate in the field of Somali studies.

The second field is that of critical security studies. The Somali experience, a case where open state collapse has taken place, offers a challenging opportunity for study in the light of the premises of critical security studies. This book is intended to make a contribution to this endeavor.

The third contribution, which this study hopes to give, is to the discussion concerning external intervention. By integrating a trans-national security-provision dimension into the analysis of Somali state-formation processes, it provides themes for a critical evaluation of the impact of external involvement on internal political processes in Somalia. I am referring not only to UN involvement in peacemaking, peace-enforcement and humanitarian intervention,[5] or to short-term emergency relief, but also to the long-term impact of international involvement. The awareness of international agencies and foreign governments needs to be raised with regard to the dangers of external involvement (including in the choice of participants for negotiations)[6] for the political balance of the no-state situation in Somalia.

Structure of the Book

Following this introduction, the book begins by developing an analytical framework that will guide the reader through the study of the Somali experience (chapter 2). The first part of chapter 2 elucidates two analytical approaches to state formation reflecting bottom-up and top-down dynamics and borrowing from the philosophical consent theory and the historical force theory of the origin of the state. The second part of the chapter focuses on a re-conceptualization of the term 'sovereignty'. Challenges to the paradigm of state sovereignty from within and beyond society are discussed, and the argument is made for an analytical shift from undivided state sovereignty to divided sover-

---

4 Among these are Ahmed (1995a) and Besteman and Cassanelli (1996). Not included are French, Italian, Arabic and non-translated Somali literature. German literature is used to a limited extent.

5 The UN intervention in Somalia is dealt with in Brons (1997).

6 Interview with Gian Paolo Aloi, the Head of the Local Administration Structures Unit at the United Nations Development Office for Somalia (UNDOS), Nairobi, 9 October 1997. He considered finding and choosing the 'right' interlocutors one of the most difficult tasks in the no-state situation in Somalia.

eignty beyond the state. The third part of the chapter concentrates on the term 'security' and the way it is conceptualized in conventional and in critical security studies. Security, it is argued, needs to be conceptualized broadly, looking beyond military/strategic considerations to include economic, social and environmental factors. Like 'sovereignty', it must also refer to sub-state and trans-state spheres that interact with the state. In this way, the linkages between local, national, regional and international security can be drawn. Conditions for sustainable state formation are seen to obtain where the state institutional framework is considered to be the *primus inter pares* option for the provision of security. The last part of chapter 2 summarizes the analytical framework and elucidates the methodology applied in the Somali case study.

Chapters 3 and 4 describe Somali society in a situation of statelessness. Chapter 3 provides an introduction to Somali geography, subsistence and economy, while chapter 4 concentrates on a description of Somali identity and society, in which reference is made to anthropological and historical material as well as to contemporary accounts of the characteristics of the Somali people.

In chapter 5, a link is established between theory and the specific case. Referring back to the methodological considerations at the end of chapter 2, I give an overview of relative security providing social arrangements that shows the various dimensions of (in)security which have been prominent in stateless Somali society.

Chapters 6 and 7 are taken up with the analysis of the Somali state(s). Chapter 6 looks at the impact of colonial state policies on Somali society and at Somali state formation attempts that developed in response to colonial occupation. Chapter 7 analyses the period since independence, including the independent Somali state (1960-1969), and the socialist state which was formed after the *coup d'état* in 1969, and which finally collapsed in January 1991. It addresses a number of questions: the degree of security, or insecurity, which these states provided to different parts of Somali society; the sources of sovereignty which the states could claim; and how other non-state security networks performed in reaction to state policies. The chapter then deals with the results of increasingly dictatorial state policies, leading to the development of political opposition in Somalia and to declining state authority. It describes the slide into open civil war, state collapse and ensuing statelessness.

Chapter 8 deals with the period of statelessness in Somalia from 1991 onwards. It examines the networks, which were activated in order to deal with violence and to secure survival, and economic and political stability. In the first part of the chapter, the political economy of continuous violence in the Southern areas, the weaknesses and strengths of sub-state mechanisms *vis-à-vis* this violence, and the performance of the international security network in the form of the UN involvement in Somalia are discussed. The second part of the chapter focuses on the processes of political authority formation that took place in the post-collapse years. The cases of Somaliland, the Digil Mirifle Governing Authority and Puntland are used to analyze perceptions and problems with regard to territoriality, the emergence of cohesive ideas and ideologies within these polities and the performance of political authorities with regard to the control of violence. This brings us back to the three pillars of the state – territory and population, idea, and institutions – and asks how the political/state authorities described in the chapter measure up in these areas.

In a concluding chapter (chapter 9), the findings deriving from the case study are linked back to the theoretical discussion in the early chapters of the book. Does the Somali experience offer insights that are relevant for the formulation of a critical approach to security studies and a theory of divided sovereignty? And – as theory and practice are considered mutually influencing – does a society-based theoretical approach to security and sovereignty provide a suitable framework for analyzing cases of hidden and open state collapse?

CHAPTER 2

Theoretical Framework:
State Formation, Sovereignty and Security

State Formation: Bottom-up Versus Top-Down

This chapter introduces two analytical approaches to state formation. State formation, in reality, is a long and multi-causal process that can only be recognized in retrospect. The two approaches that are discussed in this chapter – bottom-up and top-down – differ in the role that they ascribe to the members of a society *vis-à-vis* the emerging political authority or the state. The analytical focus therefore, is directed to this relationship in the process of state- or political authority formation.

The first approach to state formation emphasizes the bottom-up dynamics of political authority formation and is indebted to the philosophical consent or 'social contract' theory. Consent theory is basically normative. Although I do not intend to apply a normative approach to the case study of Somalia, my analysis does rely on an understanding of political order, which places society at center stage. Contract theory, similarly, departs from a bottom-up approach to political authority formation and in this regard offers an analytical point of orientation which is useful for empirical analysis. Consent theory does not assume an actual historical event, with people literally sitting under a tree and discussing how to overcome anarchy and install social order by establishing a permanent political authority. Nevertheless, as will be shown in the analysis of contemporary Somali political developments after the collapse of the central state, bottom-up approaches to state formation occurred that actually do resemble the *tree* scenario. That is why I decided to contrast the consent approach with the historically founded theories of state formation by force.

The second analytical approach emphasizes the top-down dynamics of state formation by force. Common to both approaches is the close linkage between the origins of state authority and violence. Where consent theory sees the foundation of political authority in mutual agreement by members of society to create and maintain instrument for security provision, force theory focuses on the, often, harsh reality of state formation by violent conquest. As a point of departure in developing an analytical framework to guide us through this book, I will briefly elaborate on both these approaches.

Bottom-Up State Formation

Consent theory (Sicker, 1991) is a philosophical construct in which society is considered the ultimate initiator of state formation, with containment of violence as the prime motivation. The political theory of the social contract developed by Thomas Hobbes (1588-1679) is particularly pertinent here, for the following reason. Hobbes went in search of the fundamental reason for the establishment of a political contract, a covenant wherein the individual members of society decide to relinquish their sovereign rights to a political authority. In that sense Hobbesian theory is basically society-centered. It differs in this respect from governmental contract theories where the relation between rulers and ruled, the control of state power and the establishment of a legitimate government are central.[1] Governmental contract theories reflect a state-centered approach. Hobbes, however, departs from the fundamental dynamics within society, describing "an agreement between individuals in a particular community to establish a political society, without necessarily specifying in the original agreement in whom political authority is to be vested or how it is to be exercised" (Sicker, 1991: p.79). Hobbesian contract theory thereby assists in identifying the fundamental factor linking society and state, or in other words, the basic function of a state for society.

Before further elucidating Hobbes' state-formation theory, it should be stressed that in both Western and Eastern philosophy thinkers before Hobbes had invoked the idea of a social contract.[2] In Plato's *Republic*, for instance,[3] we read:

> The idea is that although it's a fact of nature that doing wrong is good and having wrong done to one is bad, nevertheless the disadvantages of having it done to one outweigh the benefits of doing it. Consequently, once people have experienced both committing wrong and being at the receiving end of it, they see that the disadvantages are unavoidable and the benefits are unattainable: so they decide that the most profitable course is for them to enter into a contract with one another, guaranteeing that no wrong will be committed or received. They then set about making laws and decrees, and

---

1 A political philosopher who deals specifically with the governmental contract rather than the social contract is Montesquieu, *de l'Esprit des Lois*. Most contract theories include both the social and the governmental component.

2 I refer here to Sicker (1991) who mentions several examples in this context.

3 Plato, *Republic*, 358e-359a, translated by Waterfield (1998), p.46.

from then on they use the terms "legal" and "right" to describe anything which is enjoined by their code.

In another example from the time of antiquity, Kautilya's *Arthasastra* formulates a social contract theory for the genesis of the state:

> People suffering from anarchy, ..., first elected Manu, the Vaivasvata, to be their king; and allotted one-sixth of the grains grown and one-tenth of merchandise as sovereign dues. Fed by this payment, kings took upon themselves the responsibility of maintaining the safety and security of their subjects, and of being answerable for the sins of their subjects when the principle of levying just punishments and taxes has been violated (Kautilya, 1967 edition, quoted in Sicker, 1991: p.80)

In the tenth century, the Arab philosopher Al-Farabi expounded a social contract theory based on the "renunciation of rights". In a stateless or pre-state society the weak suffered from domination by the strong, which made life insecure and conflict-prone:

> The unsatisfactory nature of this mode of existence eventually drives [man] to join with others who find themselves in a similar predicament to seek a means of mutual protection. They therefore agree among themselves to renounce part of their inherent rights and autonomy, and to delegate them to a particular individual, who will act as the protector of the group, making him their sovereign ruler. This voluntary renunciation of rights, taken in the form of mutual vows and commitments, constitutes a compact between the people and the sovereign that establishes the state (Zaky, 1964: p.15-16, quoted in Sicker, 1991: p.82)

In the development of social contract theory, it was an early medieval writer, Manegold von Lautenbach in the eleventh century, who first stressed the conditions such an approach imposes upon state authority and society's obedience. Final sovereignty remains with the people and they can withdraw authority from the king if he turns out to be a tyrant threatening rather than providing security.[4]

---

4 "Manegold compared the tyrant king to a swineherd who was hired to attend to one's pigs, and who was discovered to be butchering them instead of caring for them. In such a case, there would be no question about whether the swineherd should be fired in disgrace, as there should be no question about the appropriate disposition of the tyrannical king" Sicker (1991: p.83).

Reconsidering Hobbesian Social Contract Theory

Hobbes developed his social contract theory in his major work, *Leviathan*, published in 1651.[5] Hobbes took as his starting point a state of nature in which individuals live according to their personal needs and desires, but continually threatened by others. The establishment of a sovereign political authority derives from the individual decisions to forego individual freedoms in exchange for a common rule of law that applies compulsorily to everybody. Only in this way can the insecurity of life in the state of nature be overcome. The cost of this security is the restriction of formerly limitless, but permanently threatened personal freedom, by accepting the authority of the sovereign. The legitimacy of sovereign authority, of the state, defined as the right of this authority to exist and the right to exercise political power, therefore derives ultimately from the authorization of individual members of society.

Hence for Hobbes the state is a human invention. The individual person – egoistic by nature, keen to satisfy short-term needs and desires, and as such following the 'law of nature' – should, according to Hobbes, act rationally to ensure the existence of a political order which safeguards him from the consequences of other people's egoistic tendencies. This "enlightened egoism" (Hoerster, 1989: p.109) leads to a willingness to be ruled by an autonomous political authority that is by laws that apply to everyone within society. The social contract allows people to live in a secure environment and thus enables them to pursue the fundamental interest of survival, which is the pre-condition to the satisfaction of all other interests.

Conditioning of State Authority

The sovereign in Hobbes' *Leviathan* should not, however, be seen as an absolute authority with regard to the exercise of coercion and oppression. Unconditional authority would always be legitimate and there would be no such

---

5   In order to understand Hobbes' approach, it is important to consider the historic-political circumstances in which he developed his theory. The experience of civil war during the reign of Charles I, which resulted in the execution of the king and the rule of the Commonwealth under Oliver Cromwell, were political developments driven by religious and political fanaticism. They created extreme political instability as well as personal, physical insecurity for the philosopher who was finally forced into exile in France for several years. These experiences guided Hobbes' pessimistic perception of human nature which is fundamental to his theory. See Meyers (1979); Plant (1991).

thing such as illegitimate authority.[6] According to the social contract theory, sovereign state power is established in order to safeguard a social order, which puts an end to the insecure conditions of a state of nature. A sovereign authority is only legitimate if the life and security of members of society are guaranteed. Only when the political authority satisfies these conditions are people obliged to render obedience to it. To quote Hobbes (1651/1985: p.272):

> The Obligation of Subjects to the Soveraign, is understood to last as long, and no longer, than the power lasteth, by which he is able to protect them. For the right men have by Nature to protect themselves, when none else can protect them, can by no Covenant be relinquished.

Thus, the authority, which is established through the consent of individuals, can claim sovereignty and legitimacy only as long as it can offer protection against insecurity. Sovereignty therefore derives from society and is but conditionally vested in a political authority. It is this idea of limited authority that is central to social contract theory.

Broadening the Security Agenda

In order further to elaborate on the linkage between security and sovereignty in Hobbes' social contract theory, we need to examine more closely the concept of 'security'. Does Hobbes specify the different factors which characterize insecurity and which should therefore be addressed by a sovereign authority? In fact, Hobbes is quite clear about the obligations of a sovereign authority towards its citizens:

> The office of the Soveraign, (be it a Monarch or an Assembly,) consisteth in the end, for which he was trusted with the Soveraign Power, namely the procuration of *the safety of the people*; to which he is obliged by the Law of Nature, and to render an account thereof to God, the Author of that Law, and to none but him. But by Safety here is not meant a bare Preservation, but also all other Contentments of life, which every man by lawfull Industry, without danger, or hurt to the Commonwealth, shall acquire to himselfe (Hobbes, 1651/1985: p.376).

Hobbes refers to a wide range of security needs: "those that are dearest to a man are his own life, & limbs; and in the next degree, (in most men,) those that

---

6   For the following argument I profited from Laclau and Zac (1994: pp.11-39).

concern conjugall affection; and after them riches and means of living"
(Hobbes, 1651/1985: pp.382/383). Formulated in the vocabulary of contemporary social science these include, first, the need for military/physical and political security, i.e. the absence of war and the political stability of the system in
order to avoid civil war or anarchy. Second comes personal security in the legal sense, i.e. the right to life and equal treatment before the law. This includes
basic civil rights not only in relation to other citizens, but also in relation to the
political authority as provider of security. Third, Hobbes stresses the security
needs of the family: social security and the provision of basic needs, such as
food, shelter, clothing, health and education. Fourth, if "riches" and "means
of living" are given a contemporary interpretation, then Hobbes includes not
only basic needs, but also economic security through the provision of an environment in which economic activity can prosper. Fifth, given our current
awareness of linkages between ecology and economy as well as between ecology and conflict, one would be obliged to add to the list of security needs the
need for environmental security and sustainability, incorporating the dimensions of insecurity deriving from ecological degradation and resource competition.

The inter-linkages between various dimensions of security have by now
been recognized, so that cause-effect relations have become part of an ongoing
debate.[7] For instance, military security (the absence of war and control of violence within society) may be considered basic to all other forms of security. Legal security can be considered as basic to political stability. Fundamental injustice woven into a political system may evoke violence and thus military
insecurity. Similarly, ecological and economic security is fundamental to political stability.

Sovereignty and Security beyond the State

For the argument developed in this book, the significance of Hobbes' political
theory lies not in his characterization of the sovereign authority, but in the way
he establishes a fundamental linkage between sovereignty, security and political authority/state formation. The defining factor of the Hobbesian *sovereign*
need not be related exclusively to the political institution defined as the *state*.
Sovereign authority can be vested in authority relations and structures within
society other than the state. It is the consent given by members of society in

---

7   Among others, see Wyn Jones (1996); Hjort af Ornas, Mohamed Salih (eds.) (1989).

vesting political authority in a sovereign, which is essential to the bottom-up dynamics discussed above.

Top-Down State Formation

In the formation of political authority by consent approach internal security is considered the prime determinant and the process is a bottom-up one. In the state formation by force approach it is the element of external violence and conquest that are central. State formation by force is a top-down process, which puts the militarily strong in an advantageous position from which to claim political authority.

State Formation and Leadership by Conquest and Domination

Referring to historical experience, Hume argues against the idea of state formation as a social contract:

> Almost all the governments that exist at present, or of which there remains any record in history, have been founded originally either on usurpation or conquest or both, without any pretence of a fair consent or voluntary subjection of the people (Hume, 1953: p.47, quoted in Sicker, 1991: p.68).

As Sicker points out, Oppenheimer (1975) also emphasizes state-formation by conquest:

> 'The state completely in its genesis, essentially and almost completely during the first stages of its existence, is a social institution, forced by a victorious group of men on a defeated group, with the sole purpose of regulating the dominion of the victorious group over the vanquished, and securing itself against revolt from within and attacks from abroad.' Oppenheimer insists that no primitive state known to history originated in any other manner, regardless of local traditions that may suggest otherwise. The relentless pattern of the past has been one of warlike tribes 'breaking through the boundaries of some less warlike people, settling down as nobility and founding its State.' (Sicker, 1991: p.70)

The top-down dynamic that is prevalent in state formation by conquest ascribes a passive role to society *vis-à-vis* the establishing of political authority. Sovereign authority does not derive from members of society rather political leadership is imposed on society.

Referring to state formation in segmentary societies, the 14th century Arab analyst Ibn Khaldun noted the predominance of particular clans or families in leadership positions:

> The constituent families of the larger society are not all equal, and one 'being more powerful than the rest, dominates and directs the others and finally absorbs them, thus forming an association which ensures victory over other peoples and states.' Within that leading family group there is bound to be one outstanding personality that dominates the group. 'That person will therefore be appointed as leader of the wider group, because of the domination enjoyed by his house over the others.' (Sicker, 1991: p.66-67)

The lineage structure of segmentary societies creates social cohesion based on family ties that might serve as a foundation for state formation by consent. However, the element of force is inherent in those processes of state formation where weaker clans are conquered and stronger clans or tribes claim leadership or political authority.

The analytical differentiation between bottom-up and top-down approaches helps in examining the relationship of power and legitimacy between rulers and ruled in historical processes that in retrospect are recognized as state formation processes. These historical processes can contain both, top-down and bottom-up elements.

Post-colonial State Formation: Spreading the Seeds of State Collapse

State-formation processes during the de-colonization of developing countries in the 1950s and 1960s were often externally driven and influenced by policies deriving from imperatives of the international system. Colonialism disrupted evolutionary processes of state formation that were underway in numerous societies in Africa and Asia. Other societies, including mostly pastoral, segmentary lineage societies, had never gone through the experience of state formation. In the process of de-colonization the newly independent countries inherited the colonial state framework and its underlying ideological assumptions. The new states thus embarked on a process of nation building in which the ideas and ideologies of the state either followed in the footsteps of their colonial predecessors, or shifted away from the capitalist political ideology towards the socialist, the second dominant political ideology in the post-colonial era.

The cold-war separation of the world into two competing systems, communist/socialist and capitalist influenced and to a certain extent molded the state formation processes of the early post-independent states in the developing world:

> To the extent that outside states continue to supply military goods and expertise in return for commodities, military alliance or both, the new states harbor powerful, unconstrained organizations that easily overshadow all other organizations within their territories. To the extent that outside states guarantee their boundaries, the managers of those military organizations exercise extraordinary power within them. The advantages of military power become enormous, the incentives to seize power over the state as a whole by means of that advantage very strong (Tilly, 1992: p.186).

The state-formation processes that evolved in the early post-colonial period were thus mostly top-down processes often driven by force rather than bottom-up processes driven by consent. In many cases, large sections of societies were victimized by their own, now independent state authorities, and were denied the chance to play an active part in political life as an expression of their sovereignty. Since external allies strengthened the state, it did not need to respond to challenges to its authority deriving from within society.

The changing international circumstances in the post cold-war era have made the artificiality of post-colonial state formation increasingly recognizable. With reduced external backing and with increasingly open challenges and competition from social forces within society, state authority has been weakened and, in some cases, collapsed. People claim a voice, and political space is increasingly emerging for state (re)formation processes founded on societal consent.

The discussion of bottom-up and top-down analytical approaches to political authority formation suggests that, in a sense, both approaches are reflected in contemporary post-colonial political processes. On the one hand, people are increasingly raising their voice, claiming the sovereign rights while, on the other hand, the rule of force often denies them a say and obstructs peoples' search for security.

Divided Sovereignty: Looking beyond the State

The idea of a modern, secular state, a state personified in a juridical body, originates in the social contract theories. "This 'Person' could, thus, be understood as the subject of sovereignty – a determinate structure of laws and institutions with a life and standing of its own" (Held, 1995: p.38). Theoretically the state is considered, both sovereign – i.e. entitled to rule – and autonomous –

i.e. possessing the political power to articulate and achieve policy goals independently (ibid.: p.100). The legal conception of state sovereignty is mainly based on a supreme rule of law in a geographically demarcated state territory. The state is considered a legal entity, recognized by international law, with the attributes of a defined territory, a permanent population, an effective government and independence or the right to enter into relations with other states (Jackson and Rosberg, 1982). This conception of state sovereignty is referred to as *de jure* sovereignty. State sovereignty is granted from outside, through recognition by other states and by the United Nations as the umbrella organization of all states in the world. In the international arena (that is, in the realm of inter-state relations), state and government are conceptualized as congruent, with governments acting as sovereign representatives of their states (Buzan, 1983). On this basis states are furnished with sovereignty via international recognition regardless of whether a government is internally legitimized (Jackson and Rosberg, 1982; Jackson, 1992).

In contrast to the legal conception of sovereignty is that of empirical, *de facto* sovereignty (Jackson and Rosberg, 1982). *De facto* sovereignty refers to the relationship between state and citizen, to the degree to which citizens are in a position to condition and determine the legitimacy, power and authority of the modern, secular state.

In a political crisis fundamental aspects of modern state sovereignty sometimes break down. The state is not in control of all of its territory; it is not considered the only authority that is entitled to use violence; it is not considered the exclusive referee with regard to rules and regulations defining social relations. State sovereignty cannot be taken for granted.[8] A state can continue to exist *de jure* by being accorded external sovereignty, whilst it ceases to exist as a *de facto* state (Jackson and Rosberg, 1982; Jackson, 1992). In

---

8   Migdal (1994: p.14). See also Held (1995: p.48-49): "(2) Control of the means of violence. The claim to hold a monopoly on force and the means of coercion (sustained by a standing army and the police) became possible only with the 'pacification' of peoples – the breaking down of rival centres of power and authority – in the nation-state. This element of the modern state was not fully attained until the nineteenth century, *and remained a fragile achievement in many countries.* (3) Impersonal structure of power. The idea of an impersonal and sovereign political order – that is, a legally circumscribed structure of power with supreme jurisdiction over a territory – could not prevail while political rights, obligations and duties were conceived as closely tied to religion and the claims of traditionally privileged groups. This matter remained in contention in Europe in the eighteenth and nineteenth centuries, *and still remains so in those countries today where the 'rule of law' is in question*" (emphasis added).

the literature, states in this kind of condition are referred to as 'quasi-states' (Jackson, 1990).

Political realities, such as competition between societal forces and state authority, or UN policies, which in some instances bypass state authority, challenge the applicability of the theoretical concept of state sovereignty. If political experience proves that we cannot assume internally undivided state sovereignty, then theoretical concepts must be reconsidered and eventually adapted in order to provide explanations.

Any conception of sovereignty, which interprets it as an illimitable and indivisible form of public power – entrenched securely in individual nation-states – is undermined. Sovereignty itself has to be conceived today as already divided among a number of agencies – national, regional and international – and limited by the very nature of this plurality (Held, 1995: p.135).

I will now elaborate on some alternative analyses of sovereignty, which challenge the conventional concept of undivided state sovereignty and instead consider sovereignty both divided and intrinsically linked to security provision. First, internal political challenges, which call the applicability of the theoretical concept of undivided sovereignty into question, and second, the international political dimension of divided sovereignty, that is reflected in the contradiction within international law and international intervention policy between a people-oriented world system approach and a state-oriented international system approach, will be dealt with.

Divided Sovereignty: The Internal Dimension

The idea of sovereignty 'beyond the state', is based on a society-centered approach to sovereignty. The state institutional framework is considered just one social organization or agency among others on the political stage, a conception of state that is referred to as the 'state-in-society perspective' (Migdal, 1994).

Although state leaders may seek to represent themselves as distinct from society and standing above it, the state is, in fact, yet another organization in society (Migdal, 1994: p.26).

The state-in-society approach derives from conflict theory.[9] Society is conceptualized as a dynamic body, composed of multiple spheres or arenas – 'arena' here to be understood as "a conceptual locus where significant struggles and accommodations occur among social forces" (Migdal, 1994: p.33). The individual member of society engages in one way or another in multiple social organizations. The driving motivation for social/political engagement is the need for a secure existence. In the ideal model, people bestow their sovereign rights to those social organizations, which offer access to sources of security. Yet, a relationship with a security-providing organization or body always implies the acceptance of a certain degree of domination. For clarification Migdal (1994: p.32) quotes Weber:

> A circle of people who are accustomed to obedience to the orders of leaders and who also have a personal interest in the continuance of the domination by virtue of their own participation in, and the benefits derived for them from, the domination, have divided among themselves the exercise of those functions which will serve the continuation of the domination and are holding themselves continuously ready for their exercise.

Consequently, authority – the legitimate right to exercise power – is furnished to the security-providing body and its leadership. A social organization or security-providing institution can be a natural social unit, such as the family, the clan, the ethnic group, the religious congregation or the village community which acts in a way as 'semi-autonomous' authority, setting, controlling and enforcing rules. In addition, constructed social units, such as trade unions, women's organizations, and associations of different kinds all are considered social organizations. The state, then, in its institutional manifestation, is simply one security-providing organization among others in society.

Sovereignty, as we concluded from the discussion of social contract theory, originally derives from people in the form of a conferment of authority upon the security-provider. Thus, following the state-in-society perspective, sovereignty can actually be divided among several security-providing agencies, social organizations and their respective leadership within a society.

Choices, Adaptive Strategies and Identities

Fundamental to the logic of the state-in-society perspective is the moment of choice. One might ask whether people ever have a real choice in terms of at-

---

9 The premise of conflict theory is that men are organisms and as such they must compete for access to the resources of life. Struggle for existence does not occur between isolated individuals but between groups, such as families, clans, classes, nations, races. As conflict between groups becomes stabilised, one may speak of the emergence of a structured society.

taching themselves to one social organization or another. The earlier discussion on state formation by force provides one argument against the idea of freedom of choice: Where political authority is imposed, choices are limited and may imply high risks. In a situation of extreme, sometimes life-threatening insecurity people do not choose for 'security', but for the option that inflicts the least 'insecurity'. Rather than choices based on free will, one might speak of adaptation mechanisms born of desperation. Even then, however, there remains a moment of choice, which is often experienced in a combination of flight of women, children and the elderly, and the active, violent engagement of men in liberation movements against the state or, more generally, against the oppressive political authority.[10] The human instinct for survival – the sense of security and insecurity – influences choices.

An identity refers to a constructed location in a social structure that involves an active process of identification (Laclau, 1994: p.1-3). Identities are basically conceptualized as multiple and flexible. One might argue that people do not identify primarily as individuals but as affiliates of a group.[11] In similar vein, one might argue that the question of individual choice does not arise with regard to natural social organizations: one is born into a family, a clan or ethnic group, into political, social and economic frameworks. However, ascribed identities, identities that are acquired by birth, still entail an element of flexibility that is reflected in the degree to which people consider these identities to define their social reality.

Gender plays a role in the context of choice and the flexibility of ascribed identities. In many societies, women find themselves confronted, after marriage, with divided identities, which can either be conflict-prone or bridge existing differences. A moment of choice derives from this constellation, which creates for women an option for emancipation from ascribed affiliations and for relatively independent rational choice directed towards security-provision.

It has been noted that even ascribed identities are sometimes flexibly applied within society. Here, I am not only referring to the discussion around 'imagined communities' (Anderson, 1983) and 'constructed identities' (Barth, 1969), and to historical accounts of shifting and shaping identities, but also and particularly to aspects of incorporation and re-construction of ethnic/

---

10 For more on choices taken by society, see Azarya (1988). By introducing the state-centric term 'disengagement' it is implicit that 'engagement' in non-state spheres is a viable option. Azarya refers to extreme cases of disengagement, flight and emigration, and links up with the Hirschman model of exit-voice options.

11 As argued in Chazan et al. (1988, pp.74-77).

clan identities as illustrated in anthropological accounts (Schlee, 1994). In many societies where ethnic or clan stratification prevails, possibilities exist for individuals in extreme situations of economic, social or legal insecurity to opt for a shift in identity in order to attach themselves to more secure social frameworks.

In our approach, the search for security is considered one of the most determining factors that shape a society. Search for security and the process of identification are closely linked. By referring to specific identities people link up to security arrangements that provide social, economic, political or other forms of safety, protection or belonging. Identity, in the context of the search for security, is often not a matter of free will but an adaptive strategy which people are forced to accept in order to safeguard their physical, economic or socio-political survival.

In sum, while keeping in mind political, cultural, social and economic constraints against 'free' choices, which operate in many societies, it is nonetheless justified to consider the rational individual, the citizen, as an analytical unit in the analysis of state-society interaction, sovereignty and state formation.

Integrated Domination, Dispersed Domination, Lost Domination

In the course of developing the state-in-society approach, Migdal (1994) asks whether particular social forces are capable of creating an integrated society-wide domination. He applies the concept of 'integrated domination' to signify the possibility of one social organization achieving prominence within society. I argue that if the state would assume this dominant position one can speak of a case of positive state sovereignty. An alternative scenario is that of 'dispersed domination', where multiple social forces dominate parts of society but no one social force is able to create a domination which encompasses society as a whole. "People's identities and moral codes remain remarkably diverse in such a society" (Migdal, 1994: p.27). In a society that is characterized by dispersed domination, the state's position is that of aspiring *primus inter pares*. Sovereignty is divided among several social forces.

What happens to state-society relations in a case of virtual state collapse or, in other words, in a case of lost domination? What is it that collapses? If we consider the state as being one social arrangement among others within society, this implies that not the whole socio-political structure within society collapses with the state. Society as an arena of social forces, being engaged in domination struggles and accommodation processes, continues to exist. Only the aspiring *primus inter pares* has gone.

Leaning on Migdal's approach to state-society relations as captured in the notion of a range from integrated to dispersed domination, the following definition of a weak state can be formulated: A state is weak once it loses out in the process of competition over security provision and domination to other, non-state organizations. The weak state tries to halt the process of vanishing domination by implementing coercive means. The use of coercive means by a state is therefore an indication of state weakness (Buzan, 1983/1991). The more coercive means a state employs, the weaker that state can be considered.

If the state is ill suited or too weak to provide security, other forces within society become strong (Migdal, 1988) in the sense that they can exercise dominance and are vested with authority based on their ability to offer means of survival. They thus can be considered sovereign political bodies backed and legitimized by a limited constituency that might be defined territorially or otherwise. People who accept the conditions of a social contract accordingly accept domination by a leader or group of leaders. Such leaders could then be perceived as sovereign authorities. Submitting to this form of authority-structure enables people to live a (relatively) secure life in a particular social setting, which might be localized in a non-state or in a sub-state scenario. According to the state-in-society approach, there are thus various parallel covenants at work. It can therefore be argued that sovereignty is divided rather than exclusively vested in the state.

STATE SOVEREIGNTY UNDER SCRUTINY AND PRESSURE: THE EXTERNAL DIMENSION

The sovereign status of a state is not only challenged internally but also externally. We saw above that the theoretical concept of state sovereignty has an internal and an external dimension, with the internal dimension linked primarily to aspects of society-state relations (*de facto* sovereignty), and the external dimension mainly to international legal aspects (*de jure* sovereignty). The *Westphalian* order that came into existence in 1648[12] introduced a system in which the world is divided into states; these were considered sovereign political units whose representatives were involved in international politics. Territorial integrity, the recognition of international borders as defining the outer limits

---

12 The Westphalian Order refers back to the 1648 peace of Westphalia, which ended the 30 years war in Germany and consisted in a number of peace treaties signed by European powers at the time in Muenster (see Held, 1995).

of state sovereignty, and an internationally respected rule of impermeability, or non-interference into internal affairs, remained the core aspects of an international system from 1648 until 1945, and "many of the assumptions underpinning it are still operative in international relations today" (Held, 1995: p.78).

The aspect of territorial integrity raises serious questions. In 1963, for instance, the Organization of African Unity (OAU) ratified the legality of international borders as inherited from colonial times (Cervenka, 1968). Although these borders usually bore little relation to socially and ethnically coherent units, this ratification was expected to prevent war and provide peace on the African continent. In fact, some state separatist movements claiming a state territory of their own have questioned these territorial demarcations. In other cases, territorial integrity broke down as the result of the collapse of empires, such as the Soviet Union, or, on a smaller scale, Ethiopia. The newly emerging states based their claims on the conditions laid down in international law.

The Rule of Non-interference: International Society versus World Society

However, it is another core aspect of state sovereignty, the rule of non-interference in internal affairs, which, in the 1990s, has particularly come under scrutiny and has been seriously challenged in several cases.[13] In its external dimension, state sovereignty legally extends to, and stops at, the state borders: no questions are asked about state policies within these borders. This aspect of the principle of state sovereignty is considered fundamental to an international civil society of states.

> The sovereignty of states gives rise to a claim to legal equality and to respect for this condition even by stronger powers. States enjoy self-determination and domestic jurisdiction and it behooves members of international society not to interfere in the domestic affairs of other states (Clark, 1991: p.36).

The concept of international society used here refers to inter-state relations, to the *security of states and security between states*. A contrasting concept is that of a world society or world order which focuses on the quality of relations between individual human beings. World order, therefore, refers to individuals, to the *security of individuals and security between individuals*. Thereby, these two concepts reflect the difficulties that arise when discussing security and

---

13 Deng (1993); Boutros-Ghali (1992) An Agenda for Peace, printed as appendix A in Roberts and Kingsbury (1993: pp.468-498).

sovereignty in relation to state and society. On the one hand, it is difficult to imagine a world without states. The state is considered an autonomous political authority in international relations. It is bestowed with sovereignty and must be secured against external and internal enemies as the dominant political order that can keep peace and prevent anarchy. On the other hand it happens that, in the process, autonomous rights of individuals become violated. National and international state order is no guarantee for people's security.

Despite the primacy of state sovereignty, people often acquire a legal and political space in the international arena, independent of the state. Individual people or groups are increasingly recognized as subjects of international law:

> It is generally accepted, for example, that persons as individuals are subjects of international law on the basis of such documents as the Charters of Nuremberg and Tokyo War Crimes Tribunals, The Universal Declaration of Human Rights (1948), the Covenant on Civil and Political Rights (1966), and the European Convention on Human Rights (1950) (Held, 1995: p.83).

War crimes are considered crimes against humanity and as such surpass the limitations of inter-state relations. Moreover, the differentiation between permissible and non-permissible war targets in international law makes a clear differentiation between state- and civilian institutions, protecting the latter against deliberate attack.

The emergence of an international humanitarian law – the link between human rights and international military intervention, in accordance with Chapter VII of the UN Charter – questions the very legitimacy of governments, violating human rights. It is argued that the people of the world should be acknowledged as the "true subjects of international law" rather than states, which represent the "formal subjects of international law" (Fieldings, 1994: p.7). A direct link should be established between the individual and an international human rights authority, which would have power over the violating state.[14]

Both the international society and the world order concepts underlie UN policy-making and lead to inevitable contradictions. The discussion concerning humanitarian intervention shows that the UN has been searching for modalities to legitimize its operations by referring to Chapter VII of the UN Charter. UN military interventions in the 1990s drew their justification from a direct link between the insecurity of individuals and regional peace and secu-

---

14 This argument is taken up by Cohen and Deng (1998) with special reference to internally displaced persons.

rity. At the same time, the conventional paradigm of state sovereignty is constantly reaffirmed by UN support for states, which have lost all credentials of *de facto* sovereignty.

THE WEAK STATE AND DIVIDED SOVEREIGNTY

In order to summarize the discussion on divided sovereignty let me conclude that in weak states, state sovereignty is challenged from two sides. Internally, state authority is often ignored by social forces within society as reflected by strategies of legal, social and/or economic withdrawal and disengagement (Azarya, 1988). In many societies customary legal systems operate in parallel with modern state-laws. Social security especially lies to a great extent in the hands of family or neighbourhood/community networks. Economic disengagement is expressed in informal market activities and criminal activities such as smuggling, bypassing state registration and taxation. One form of alternative political organization to the state comes in the form of liberation movements with their different goals, such as regional autonomy, separation and independence.

Within society, there are different sorts of security arrangements. In social contract terms: people enter into different covenants to meet their various needs for security. Although many such social relationships are given, such as religious belief, family and lineage or nationality, there remains, as we have seen, room for individual choice or adaptation.

Our discussion of divided sovereignty has also revealed that there are intra-society but also extra-society, international security arrangements, which enable people to bypass the state. Besides the indirect protection of human rights through international conventions, in the event of a state collapse the protection and security of individuals and groups are increasingly provided by UN organizations such as UNHCR, UNICEF, WFP and others, supported by a myriad of trans-national non-governmental organizations.[15] Hence, external challenges to state sovereignty come from international organizations, such as the United Nations Security Council, International Monetary Fund/World Bank and International Court of Justice, with regard to a state's political right of non-interference, economic independence and legal autonomy, respectively. Governments of aid-receiving countries generally retain steering and control

---

15 For more readings, see Prendergast (1996); Humanitarian Aid to Somalia Evaluation Report (1994); SIDA (1994).

mechanisms over non-governmental organizations (NGOs). Nevertheless, NGOs tend to occupy a fairly autonomous position in the operational fields of social security provision, humanitarian assistance, and education and in grassroots economic activities – particularly in cases of long-term, seemingly permanent involvement in a country or conflict region.

Linking the discussion of state sovereignty in this second part of the theoretical introduction to that of state formation in the beginning of the chapter leads to the conclusion that if a state is formed, fundamentally re-formed or kept alive by the use of force, it can be considered a weak state. It lacks *de facto* positive sovereignty and is often challenged by competitors in the struggle of social forces within society. If it responds positively to this challenge, tries to co-operate with other social organizations, grants social and political space to customary networks, and allows civil society to prosper, the relationship between *state* and *society*[16] can be mutually empowering and strengthening, leading eventually to relatively integrated state domination. If, on the other hand, the coercive means of a state authority predominate and state formation by force is followed by state rule by force, then sovereignty of the state will remain negative.

Extremely weak states are confronted with latent and eventually manifest collapse. This, in turn, leads to crisis situations in which the international community, in the form of the UN, finds itself obliged to intervene in one way or another. Such moves undermine *de jure* state sovereignty. In addition, in accordance with the state-in-society perspective, they can lead to competition between non-state and trans-state security-providers. Thus, international organizations in a sense enter the local societal arena for struggle over domination and accommodation.

The theoretical concept of state formation by consent, seen in the light of the state-in-society perspective, is reflected in a bottom-up approach to political authority formation. Consent could be understood as peaceful competition and co-operation between various social organizations and the state. The foregoing theoretical reflections have led us to see the state as one of many security-providing socio-political contracts. A theoretical shift away from a state monopoly of the provision of physical, legal and institutional security is driven by the recognition of tendencies towards increasing disengagement from the state and engagement in non-state security-providing organizations.

---

16 On the discussion whether so-called primordial, ethnic- or clan-based social organisations or associations could be considered agents of civil society, see Azarya (1992).

Furthermore, cases of hidden or open collapse of states did not necessarily involve a relapse into anarchy or a 'state of nature'.[17]

In a stateless context, the search for political authority formation is a delicate balancing act. In the absence of a *primus inter pares* state, internal competition of social forces over who will occupy the dominant position of state power and authority will be fierce. In addition, external involvement can negatively affect authority formation in two ways. In the first place, there might be significant pressure from the international system (based as it is on *de jure* state sovereignty), to reinstall a state that fits into the given system of sovereign states. This can seriously hamper state formation by consent. Secondly, as noted above, the fact that various international agencies are heavily involved in security provision effectively makes them yet another competitor with potential to upset the balance of the state formation process.

Theorising Security Beyond the State

ON SECURITY AND SECURITY STUDIES

Defining Security

Given the central position that the concept of security/insecurity occupies within the theoretical approaches to state formation and sovereignty discussed so far, we might ask whether security studies could furnish us with an appropriate analytical framework to express this centrality. Security refers in this connection to "the condition of being secure", as described by a conglomeration of terms such as "safety", "protection", "stability", "confidence" and "certainty" (Dillon, 1996: p.212). These synonyms of 'security' cover a wide range of factors: individual physical safety from other people; legal, economic and social protection; political and military stability; and certainty or confidence in the value-system in which the individual is embedded. The various dimensions of security of which people are in need were long ago elucidated in Hobbes' *Leviathan*. Of course, the "unavoidable normative dimension to se-

---

17 This is not to say that in some cases of open or hidden state collapse acts of brutal inhumane violence and widespread lawlessness do not occur. However, these may also occur in the name of state-law, at the hands of state organs.

curity" (Job, 1992) needs to be taken into consideration, hence Buzan's emphasis on "the *perception* of well-being of individuals and collectives" and "the assurance of the core values central to the *self-definition* of communities" (Buzan 1983/1991: pp.16.17).

Furthermore, it is worth stressing that 'security' is not a specific state of affairs. Dillon (1996: p.125) talks of the "fundamental duality of security": security and insecurity are two sides of the same coin, presenting one dynamic rather than two separate conditions. This has far-reaching implications for the theory of security.

> Modern usage, moreover, proposes that there is a state of affairs – insecurity – and the negation of that state of affairs – security – and by doing so thoroughly represses the complexity not only of the act of securing but also of the inextricable relation between security and insecurity. It offers, instead, a simple dialectic opposition together with the implied promise that insecurity can always be mastered in principal if not in current practice (ibid.: p.122).

Rather than hammering out the dialectics of (in)security by emphasizing the paradox of a state both providing and threatening security at the same time, the reality of the phenomenon is better grasped in terms of a dynamics of (in)security.[18]

> The radical ambivalence of (in)security is consequently not a paradox. Neither is it a contradiction to be resolved through more careful securing. This ambivalence is inescapable and it provides the very dynamic behind the way in which security operates as a generative principle of formation for the production of political order (ibid.: p.127).

In sum, the idea that the social condition can change from insecurity to security misses the point. A term, which better pinpoints the multitude of securities in a way that expresses the dynamics of security, is 'relative (in)security'. A political, military, social or economic situation can only be considered 'relatively less insecure', never 'secure'. The dynamics of (in)security can be understood as the process by which political order is produced.

---

18 According to Dillon this is revealed in the Greek word for 'security', *Asphaleia,* which literally means 'not insecure'. "Hence the privative *asphaleia* is to avoid falling, error, failure, or mistake. It is to make something stand, steadfastness, assured from danger, safe, steady, fortified, to be furnished with a firm foundation, to be certain, or sure" (ibid.: p.124).

Early Critics of Conventional Security Studies

Security studies, as one discipline within the study of international relations, conventionally focus on threats to security rather than on the provision of security. Threats to security emanate from states and are directed towards states.

The international dimension of security points to the state, the territorially defined sovereign guardian of internal law and order, as the object to be secured. It is taken for granted, in other words, the rule of non-interference prohibits to question, whether the state indeed operates as the guardian of security for the political community within its territory. In the international system it is the state whose security is threatened and it is the strengthening of national security that stands central.

However, critical voices had already been raised in connection with the controversy around nuclear deterrence, claiming that the threat deriving from nuclear weapons could not be conceptualized in terms of a state-centric analytical framework (Deudney, 1995; Russett and Starr, 1992). It was people rather than particular states that were threatened by nuclear weapons. Similar arguments were put forward in the context of increasing awareness of the global environmental crisis (Russett and Starr, 1992; Thomas, 1992; Weizsäcker, 1994). Threats emanating from water and air pollution, climate change and ozone depletion posed a global threat to humankind rather than a threat to particular states and their citizens.

Another dimension is provided by the focus on a North-South dichotomy in nuclear, environmental and economic (in)security (Thomas, 1987; Wyn Jones, 1996). Until very recently, states exercising control over nuclear weapons were all powers in the Northern hemisphere. While states in the South had no control over the use of nuclear weapons, their populations were equally threatened by nuclear fall-out.

Another North-South dichotomy is expressed by the fact that the economic well being (i.e. security) of the developed world is achieved at the cost of depletion of primary resources and of global environmental pollution. These factors lead to increasing ecological and economic insecurity, scarcity of resources and resulting causes of conflict, particularly in the developing world. In the words of Wyn Jones (1996: p.203):

> Furthermore, radical understandings of global politics suggest that those few developed states which do indeed provide their citizens with a good deal of security (however defined) can only do so because of their dominant, privileged position within the global economy. However, the very structure of this global economy creates and reinforces the gross disparities of wealth, the environmental degradation, and the class, ethnic and gender

inequalities, which are the source of insecurity in the South. In other words, the relative security of the inhabitants in the North is purchased at the price of chronic insecurity for the vast majority of the world population.

Although the end of the cold war period is often said to have brought about a major shift in thinking about security, in retrospect it is clear that the state-centric approach to security had been challenged long before this:

> There had already been plenty of signs of discontent about Cold War conceptions of 'national' and 'international' security by the early 1980s, if not earlier, among proponents of alternative defense, peace research, and the many supporters of global civil society committed to nonviolence, human rights, environmental sustainability, and so on (Booth, 1997: p.85).

One approach, which takes as a focus of analysis the specific dimensions of security for so-called third world states, or more generally for weak states, is the insecurity-dilemma approach. In the following paragraphs the genesis and main arguments of this approach are discussed, followed by critical reflections on its shortcomings.[19]

Weak States and 'National Security'

The struggle for power between states in general, and the superpower competition over zones of political/ideological influence in particular, has been the focus of security studies during the last few decades. In conventional security studies, states are perceived as single actors in the political world arena (Bull, 1969; Wight, 1978; Morgenthau, 1973; Waltz, 1979; Keohane, 1986). Their internal sovereignty is not questioned. The term 'national security' is distinctively defined with regard to external threats from other states. In this context the theory of the security dilemma emerged, a theory, which seemed satisfactorily to explain the international political arena. As Job (1992b: p.17) delineates the concept:

> Operating in conditions of anarchy, states by seeking to advance their individual national securities (through policies of arming, deterrence, and alliance), create and sustain an international environment of decreased relative security for themselves and for the collective of states. The security

---

19 In the presentation of the insecurity-dilemma approach, which follows, I refer mainly to Job (1992a).

dilemma, therefore, hinges on the external threat conditions that states experience and on the results of their efforts, as unitary state actors, to meet these threats.

Examining the term 'national security' in the context of weak states, Buzan (1991) argues that only the *physical territorial base of the state* may be well enough defined to constitute a clear object of 'national security' in the traditional understanding of the term. The other two major pillars of the state that we considered in the introduction, the *idea of the state* and the *institutional expression of the state* are too unstable.

Territory may indeed be the most stable and concrete pillar of weak states. However, this applies more to the *de jure* than to the *de facto* dimension of stability. A case in point is the fact that although, at the 1963 OAU summit, the heads of the African post-colonial states argued to refrain from reopening border questions in their relations with neighboring states, this did not imply that these borders did not pose problems of social and political cohesion for the newly formed states.[20] In the weak state context, therefore, the relevance of the territorial dimension for defining 'national security' is only valid within the premises of the conventional approach to security, which focuses on external threats between states.

Buzan (1983/1991) was among the first to point out that the security of a weak state is not primarily externally but rather internally threatened. While the security of strong states is concerned with protection from outside threats or interference, security of weak states is mainly concerned with responding to domestic threats posed by social forces, individuals or groups which are in one way or another opposed to state-authority.

Developing the Insecurity-Dilemma Approach

Instead of a 'security dilemma', Job (1992b: p.18) argues that one could better speak of the 'insecurity dilemma' with which weak states are confronted:

---

20 The fact that the only security which weak states can claim with any confidence is their territorial integrity (externally granted sovereignty), provided a reason for the OAU – which represents the conglomerate of African governments i.e. power holders rather than the African people – to emphasise the territorial integrity of their member states. I believe it is for this reason, guided by the security interests of weak states' governments, and not some "almost amazing equanimity" (Holsti, 1992: p.56) that these states have accepted their inherited boundaries.

What results in such a contentious environment is better characterized as an insecurity dilemma i.e., the consequence of the competition of the various forces in society being (1) less effective security for all or certain sectors of the population, (2) less effective capacity of centralized state institutions to provide services and order, and (3) increased vulnerability of the state and its people to influence, intervention, and control by outside actors, be they other states, communal groups, or multinational corporations.

Another critical approach to the meaning of 'national security' in the context of weak states focuses on the imperative of 'international security' rooted in the desire to uphold a balance between power-blocks (Held, 1995: p.113-120). In order to achieve this goal, external support to weak states or client-states is provided by dominant powers or patron-states, mostly in the form of military aid for the protection of the state, coupled with development aid for improving the economic/social security of the citizens. However, externally-provided military strengthening of 'weak' states often leads to an internal use of coercion in the name of safeguarding 'national security', which in most cases violates basic human rights (Hatchard, 1993; Africa Watch, 1990). Reference to threatened 'national security' legitimizes the use of violence against society itself. We came across this earlier when discussing top-down state formation: the strengthening of weak, internally illegitimate states leads to the perpetuation of internal conflict and insecurity. Pinpointing this phenomenon, Jackson (1992) speaks of "turning Hobbes on his head".

> Instead of states or alliances defending their populations against external threats, international society is underwriting the national security of states, whether or not they convert it into domestic security for their citizens. ... What the assumptions and values of classical security theory have difficulty accommodating is not only a domestically threatening sovereign – as Buzan (1983a) and Berki (1986) point out – but one which is inaugurated and survives primarily, if not almost entirely, by the indulgence of the international system (ibid.: p.93-94).[21]

---

21 Jackson (1992) refers to Buzan (1983) and Berki (1986). His argument leans on earlier works of Jackson and Rosberg including their widely quoted article, "Why Africa's weak states persist: the empirical and the juridical in statehood", in which the authors elaborated the external factor of territoriality as legitimacy for African states and the actual irrelevance of legitimacy from within African societies.

Job (1992: p.18) summarizes the findings of the insecurity-dilemma approach as follows:

> Thus, the assumptions of the traditional security dilemma metaphor are violated – states are preoccupied with internal rather than external security, and weak states have a guaranteed existence in what is supposedly an anarchic international environment.

The achievement of the proponents of the insecurity-dilemma approach lies in their critical analysis of the concepts underlying traditional security studies. However, although the insecurity-dilemma approach points to significant contradictions between security studies theory and the contemporary political experience of weak states, its vocabulary and basic premises remain statically attached to the conventional security studies framework.

Critique of the Insecurity-Dilemma Approach

One reason for this lack of innovative strength in the insecurity-dilemma approach lies in its failure to go beyond the state as organizing principle. The state is critically examined at the level of national politics, but the global or trans-state level is considered exclusively as *inter*-national, and the sub-state level, the "competition of the various forces in society" (Job, 1992: p.18), as a threat to the state.[22] Accordingly, most authors attribute the 'crisis' or 'dilemma' to the state.[23] State sovereignty is taken for granted and the dilemma is conceived in terms of a diminishing degree of state autonomy.

Another limitation of the insecurity-dilemma approach is the narrow definition applied to 'security'. As Job (1992: p.16) argues:

> Security can be defined as involving some or all social, economic, political, military and physical (including ecological and environmental) concerns.

---

22 Another example of this from Holsti (1992: pp.54-55): "Political loyalties tend to remain primordial rather than national. All of these conditions confront governments that already suffer from debilitating political and economic problems. To them are added intercommunal strife, armed protests against government suppression, gross social inequalities, secession movements, and ethnically based rebellions. In these circumstances, the state apparatus must spend a disproportionate amount of time and energy brokering or mediating deals between ethnic/linguistic/religious groups. In an unfortunate number of cases, even where good intentions come into play, they fail."

23 This point is expressed in titles such as "The Security Predicament *of the Third World State*" (Ayoob 1992), and Job (1992b), "The Insecurity Dilemma *of the State*".

Further complications are brought to bear by debating whether the long-
or short-term considerations of these sectoral components of security de-
serve priority. For most analysts in the security studies field, the matter is
relatively straightforward. Security is about political-military threats in the
short term.

The shortsightedness of this approach can be demonstrated, for instance, by
recalling the immense impact which the internationally designed economic
programs of structural adjustment have had on the increased political insecurity of weak states, as a result of a decrease of social security. In UN circles, too,
the interconnectedness of various security dimensions has been recognized.
    We live in an age of interdependence – whether it is in areas like environ-
ment, refugees, drugs, trade or jobs. The idea of collective security has
grown beyond military matters to embrace political, economic, social and
cultural developments (Eliasson, 1994).

Although it is not easy to frame a theory that incorporates all these diverse but
interconnected elements, such difficulties should not lead us to ignore them,
or to treat them as less relevant, or to artificially keep them out of the theoretical framework. According to the UNDP's Human Development Report (1994:
p.3) the concept of security has for too long been defined in the categories of
inter-state conflict, security of borders and the concentration on military
means in order to protect the state's security. Although military security can
be basic to other dimensions of security – military insecurity, or in other
words war, impacts negatively on all other dimensions of insecurity – the re-
verse dynamics also need to be acknowledged and integrated into a holistic approach within the discipline of security studies.
    Thus, although the insecurity-dilemma approach does take into account
the specific conditions of weak states, of states in the developing world, it
nevertheless fails to go beyond the conventional, state-centric and militarily
oriented paradigm of security studies.

CRITICAL SECURITY STUDIES

A line of thought which challenges us to go beyond the state-centered strategic
perception of security studies, and which has been developing more explicitly
since the mid 1990s, is critical security studies. According to Booth (1997: p.107):
    The idea (or more precisely the label) is only of recent coinage (May 1994),
    and because it has been the focus of only a couple of academic papers, crit-

ics should not expect too much too soon. The subject is being worked out; it is presently at the takeoff stage, waiting to happen, in some ways comparable to strategic studies in the mid-1950s, when the subject was a handful of books in search of an academic label.

The three main features of critical security studies are: First, a revised perception of the role and capability of the state; Second, a focus on the individual and on society at large as prime object of security; Third, a shift away from the military dimension of security as the only reference point of security studies. Critical security studies thus calls for a re-examination of contemporary security discourse (Dolby, 1997: p.24).

Turning, first, to the revised perception of the state with regard to security, Booth (1997: p.106) notes:

Critical security studies begin in a rejection of traditional security theory. The approach rejects, in particular, the definition of politics that places the state and its sovereignty at the center of the subject; the moral authority of states; the belief that the state is and should be the key guardian of peoples' security.

However, although the state is questioned as the prime referent of security and critical security studies tries to "theorize the world outside the state" (Linklater, 1995), the state remains in place as one prominent factor in the realm of organized violence. As Williams and Krause (1997: p.xvi) put it:

From a critical perspective, state action is flexible and capable of reorientation, and analyzing state policy need not therefore be tantamount to embracing the statist assumptions of orthodox conceptions.

The second characteristic feature of critical security studies is that the individual rather than the state is made the prime object of security. As noted earlier, in my interpretation of contract theories, the idea of a covenant basically rests on the premise of the individual's search for security: the individual as object of security was thus already inherent in early contract theories. In theory, sovereign rights originally lie with the individual. Our consideration of external challenges to state sovereignty showed further that direct links between the individual, as right-bearing entity, and international law have been made in the form of conventions such as the International Declaration of Human Rights.

A second relevant point, once it is the individual's security rather than state security that is focused upon, is that the state potentially threatens its citizens' security. This point was made in the early contract theories as well as in the historically rooted theories of state formation by force.

A third consideration had already been raised by early critics to strategic studies: the impact on the individual security of nuclear, environmental and other threats which exceed state borders, and the underlying perception of world society as distinct from international society. As Krause and Williams (1997: pp.45-46) note:

> Each of these three threads of arguments challenges the vision of sovereignty underlying the neo-realist conception of security. In the first case, the claims of sovereignty must be limited by the more basic rights claims of individual persons. In the second, the state as a source of threat to citizens themselves, and the disjuncture between state and society, is highlighted. In the third, narrow conceptions of national interest and state sovereignty are seen to limit our ability to deal with security issues whose source and solution stand beyond statist structures and assumptions. Making the individual the object of security provides the conceptual shift that allows these perspectives to take their place as central elements of any comprehensive understanding of security.

Referring back to the original *raison d'être* of the state – i.e. the provision of security to society – several authors claim a confusion of 'means' and 'ends', emphasizing that the state is nothing but the means to the end of security for society, for the individual. Booth (1991: p.320) adds:

> It is illogical therefore to privilege the security of the means as opposed to the security of the ends.

Linking the international, the national and the internal realm of politics, and stressing the need for these empirical inter-linkages also to be reflected in theory building, Jackson (1992: p.94) argues:

> Finally, this revisionist reasoning also has general implications for the character of international relations theory. It suggests that any attempt to focus exclusively on national security – the state – and ignore domestic and personal security – the individual – is myopic. The state is not an end; it is only a means. Individuals and their well-being is the end. Just as international politics are not a separate world but merely external facets of sovereign states with connection to domestic politics via statesmen who are simultaneously obliged to look both outwards and inwards, by the same token international relations theory must be considered part of political theory and not separate from it. In conclusion, there is only one theory of security that must address both sides of the equation.

The third feature that characterizes critical security studies and distinguishes it from critical insecurity-dilemma approaches is the recognition that it is essential to include dimensions of security other than the military dimension in the study of security. My earlier criticism of the limitations of the insecurity-dilemma approach in this respect finds support in Booth (1997). Clarifying the place of the military aspect of security in the field of critical security studies, Booth (ibid.: p.107) states:

> Critical security studies, as just described do not – should not – ignore or play down the state and the military dimensions of world politics. ... There is an important place in critical security studies for the study of the threat and use of military force, but the study of (military) strategy should no longer be synonymous with security studies, as was the case in Cold War International Relations, and as some still want to maintain it. ... Military strategy is a subject area within critical security studies, but it is only one aspect – although sometimes a crucial one – of a wide agenda and one with security referents other than the state (which hitherto has given strategic studies their meaning).

Critical security studies is still in the process of developing specific features, premises and methods, and – at the moment – its scholars are primarily questioning conventional paradigms rather than providing ready answers to fill the declared gaps in security studies. The critical security studies literature that has been published in the last few years, however, give important support to the perspective on sovereignty, security and the state elaborated in this chapter.

The Somali Case: Theoretical Concept and Method

Against the background of the discussion presented so far, a conceptual framework can be developed which provides us with the necessary tools for analyzing the Somali experience. It is worth stressing at this point that the process of developing an analytical framework includes reflection on theory and method that is influenced by in-depth knowledge of a specific case or area. Thus, shaping an analytical framework is a dynamic process whereby reconceptualization of theoretical concepts and understanding and interpretation of a case-experience are mutually enriching.

In trying to conceptualize security beyond the state I start with the fundamental linkage between security, sovereignty and the individual. In order to structure the analysis of the Somali case I introduce a model of relative-security providing social arrangements, which reflects the basic conclusions of the earlier theoretical considerations. The model of relative security providing social arrangements consists of two dimensions: (1) three levels of security-provision; and (2) six varieties of (in)security.

Turning first to the three levels of (in)security (sub-state, state and trans-state), my approach assumes that people enter simultaneously into a number of various and shifting security arrangements. There are three levels at which security arrangements can be distinguished: the sub-state, the state and the trans-state levels. Second, six varieties of relative (in)security are identified which together cover most aspects of a society's security needs. These are legal, social, economic, environmental, political and military/physical security. Each variety can be considered on each of the three levels of security-provision. Legal security refers to the laws on which a polity is based. Social security includes access to health and education as well as social well-being and belonging. Economic security considers the ways in which production and trade function. Environmental security looks at adaptation mechanisms and policies directed towards natural resources. Political security comprises most importantly political stability as reflected in stable mechanisms of political decision-making and transfer of power, while military/physical security refers to control mechanisms over, and access to, means of violence.

The analytical framework of relative security will be our guide through the Somali case study that describes various security providing institutions that operate among the Somali people. Although I try to provide a comprehensive account of the different aspects of security provision, special attention is given to three groups: traders, farmers, and women.

These population groups are of particular relevance for the following reasons. First, trade is, apart from subsistence agriculture and pastoralism, the most relevant economic sector in Somalia, as the country cannot survive without the export of livestock and agricultural cash crop and the import of food and consumer commodities. The business class is financially very strong and influential. In a sense, options for peace or war, outbreak or control of violence depend on the attitude of the trading sector *vis-à-vis* political/state authority. Second, because of the scarcity of fertile land in the otherwise arid Somali region, the struggle over control and exploitation of land is one of the main causes of the ongoing Somali conflict. If effectively cultivated by Somali farmers, this land could make a substantial contribution to food security of the sedentary as well as pastoral population. Without a satisfying solution to the land issue that recognizes the rights of the sedentary farming communities, there will be no sustainable peace and political stability in Somalia. Third, women play a central role in Somali society, particularly after state collapse. Women contribute to social security provision, economic reconstruction and political reconciliation. However, their factual contribution to society is not reflected politically. The specific focus on women is centered on options that are available to women in order to reconcile the traditional with the modern in Somali society.

A dynamic perspective is taken in that the analysis of security providing institutions is located within the Somali historical sequence from pre-colonial *stateless* society through the colonial and post-colonial *state* and then back to the condition of *statelessness*. The last chapter of the book then discusses recent *state formation processes* that took place during the 1990s in some regions within the territory of ex-Somalia.

The complex question whether Somali society can be regarded as stateless before the advent of European colonialism in the late 19th century is discussed at length in chapter 6. The attribution of statelessness to the post-1991 situation is also problematic: In depicting the post-1991 situation as stateless, I mean that there is no Somali state based on the premises according to which Somalia was founded in 1960. In this sense, the contemporary situation in the Somali region can be characterized as one of statelessness. Functioning non-state social structures in Somalia are shaped by the earlier period of statelessness in that the security-providing institutions now operative are similar to (and apparently descent from) those in operation in the earlier period.

The middle segment in the sequence refers to the time when a state or states (colonial, anti-colonial, and post-colonial) provided relative security to Somali people. The analysis of the Somali state(s) focuses on the impact of state structure and policies on the security of Somali people. It is shown that the Somali *state* featured more as a threat than a protector to an increasing number of its citizens. That is why I find it useful to apply the following four aspects of state policy-making that mark threats which emanate directly or indirectly from the state.

– Lack of stable mechanisms for the transfer of political power, and resulting threat of political violence;
– Domestic law making and enforcement in conflict with protection of broad civic liberties;
– The state's external security policies;
– Direct political action by the state against individuals or groups (Buzan, 1983: p.24-25).

Security is conceived as a dynamic force. A permanent search for security is under way in all different spheres of societal life, which – in the end – can at best result in *less insecurity*. This applies to the private sphere, as conceptualized in social life or economy and business, as well as to the public sphere where arrangements for establishing political stability or reducing and controlling violence are made and continuously adapted to changing circumstances. Hence, when referring to various dimensions of (in)security within Somali society, it is the dynamic aspect of (in)security, the ebb and flow of social life, which is expressed by adding the *(in)* to *security*.

Before beginning our description and analysis of security provision, however, an introduction to the geography, subsistence and economy of the Somali people is given in the next chapter. I emphasize the variations in environmental and economic insecurity with which the Somali people are confronted and to which they adapted in different ways. This chapter is followed by an account of Somali identity and society. Together, these chapters provide the necessary background knowledge for our consideration of the Somali experience with state formation.

CHAPTER 3

Geography, Subsistence and Economy

Insecurity begins with conditions found in the natural environment of a people and their adaptation to it. This chapter describes the physical features of the Somali-inhabited area in the Horn of Africa region and the social structure that had arisen to deal with geography and climate, and it gives an overview of the economic activities of Somali society.

We will see how close the linkage is between environmental and economic insecurity: The fragile environment requires sophisticated and vulnerable economic adaptive strategies. And the economic strategies of the Somali people take place within an integrated Somali economy, which does not respect state borders. The discussion cannot be limited to the territory of ex-Somalia, according to the borders of 1960, but must include all Somali-inhabited areas in the Horn (see map 1), in order to show the linkages, which existed long before any international borders were drawn and continue to operate today.

Topography and Climate

The Somali people live in the eastern-most part of continental Africa, known as the Horn of Africa, bordering the Gulf of Aden and the Indian Ocean. The area stretches about 250 kilometers South and 1250 kilometers North of the equator, roughly between the 41st and the 51st degree of Eastern longitude. The coastline runs along the Red Sea in the North and continues southward along the Indian Ocean to approximately the Tana River, which forms the Southwestern limit of the Somali population. In total, the Somali coastline is a little more than 3000 km long. To the West the branches of the Ethiopian highlands form the limit of Somali expansion. The Somali-inhabited area in the Horn comprises about 900,000 km^2, of which 637,600 km^2 make up the Somalia state territory, as it existed from 1st July 1960 to the end of January 1991. The remaining Somali-inhabited areas form parts of Djibouti, Ethiopia and Kenya, which have borders with Somalia of 58 km, 1,626 km and 682 km, respectively.

Somali population figures are a matter of guesswork. The civil war that ravaged the country since the mid-1980s, counted a large number of people killed in combat, violent attack of civilians and famine victims throughout the 1990s. Internal displacement, flight and migration dominate the population development. In mid-1996, aid and relief agencies estimated the population of Somalia to be 6.0 to 6.5 million people, based on the number of persons being fed by aid programs. An additional 2.5 to 3.0 million Somali live in neighboring countries. A considerable number of Somali migrants/refugees live in other East African countries, in the Gulf states, in North America and Canada, and in Europe, particularly in Italy, Britain, the Netherlands, Germany and the Scandinavian countries.

The Somali region (see map 2) is dominated by savanna scrubland and arid to semi-arid climatic conditions.[1] Northern and Southern Somalia share essentially the same geographic patterns of arid maritime plains and coastal dunes, followed inland by semi-arid plains of thorns and steppes, and finally grassy plains in the area leading to the Ogaden region across the Ethiopian border, and the trans-Juba region in the Northeastern province of Kenya. In the Northern region one can identify three main zones which are (1) the *Guban* or burnt land (*gub* = to burn), a hot semi-desert stretching from the coastal plains up to the sand dunes, which offers little pasture; (2) dry mountainous forest, further inland, including frankincense and myrrh trees, and the *Ogo* or plateau land, a thorn-covered area with sometimes extensive pasture; (3) the *Haud* grass plains which provide excellent grazing. The *Haud* area receives some rainwater during brief but recurrent rainy seasons. "Its water resources are not extensive though grass is abundant during the rainy season. It is in the *Haud* area that one finds some of the best grasses of the region such as the *dar* and *dihe*. The *Haud* is a very extensive zone stretching from Northern Somalia through the Ogaden as far as Mudug and upper Shabelle areas of Southern Somalia along the Ethiopian-Somalia borders" (Ayele, 1980: p.295-7). In the North there are no permanent rivers, only some seasonal rivers (*tug*), small temporary lakes, and underground watercourses.

The main difference between the North and the South is the existence of two big rivers, the *Shabelle* and the *Juba,* in the Southern Somali region.

Of the two the Shabelle to the North is 1250 miles [=2,012 km] long and its water portage fluctuates between 100 and 500 cubic meters per second depending on the rain conditions in the Ethiopian Highlands from where it originates. The Juba, also rising from the Ethiopian Highlands, is 1030 miles

---

1   In this description of the geography and climate of the Somali region I rely especially on the works of Lewis (1961, 1965); Kaplan et al. (1969); Ayele (1980); Samatar (1989).

[=1,658 km] and navigable. The water portage has been reported to be as much as 800 to 1000 cubic meters per second at its peak periods. These two rivers have so far given the Somali people the only areas of cultivation and stockbreeding (ibid.).

During good rains the Shabelle ends its journey in swamps between the towns of Brava and Jilib, while the Juba River enters the Indian Ocean in the town of Kismayo.

The Southern region, as described by Ayele, can be divided into five different zones:[2]

1 *Bala'd*: shifting sand-banks along the shore, corresponding to the *Guban* in the North;

2 *Arra'd*: white land of hills and plains of consolidated sand, which continues the first zone inland;

3 *Arra gudud*: red flinty sand steppes, covered mainly with acacia;

4 *Arra mado*: black alluvial soil rich in humus lying along the rivers Shabelle and Juba

5 *Doi*: Many thousands of square kilometers of red lands between the Juba and Shabelle providing the richest pastures of Somalia. The *Doi* is roughly similar to the *Haud* of the North.

The Somali differentiate between four seasons, two wet and two dry: *Gu* (long rainy season) lasting from April to July, *Hagaa* (dry) from July to October, *Dayr* (the small rains) from October to December and *Jilaal* (long dry season) lasting from December to April. Lewis (1961: p.42) explains that for the Northern pastoralists it is also common to divide the year into two halves – *Gu* and *Jilaal*, or *Doog* (fresh grazing) and *Abaar* (drought), or *Daaq* (grazing) and *Aroor* (watering) – as the two seasonal poles about which their lives revolve.

High temperatures (ranging from 20 °C to 40 °C, and averaging 30 °C) coupled with the monsoon winds[3] cause rapid evaporation of rainwater that has a negative impact on the recharging and level of groundwater. Rainfall is relatively low: most of Somalia gets less than 500 mm of rain annually. Along the coast of the Gulf of Aden, the annual rainfall has been measured at 100 mm; the same applies to enclaves in the Northeastern region. Around 500 mm annual

---

2 Ibid., referring to Lewis (1955: p.59; 1961: p.31).

3 December to February: Northeast monsoon wind, with moderate temperatures in the North and very hot in the South; May to October: Southwest monsoon, torrid in the North and hot in the South; hot and humid periods in between monsoons.

rainfall is more common in the Kismayo area in the South extending along the coast into Kenya along the coast, an area which is characterized by humid savanna in the inter-riverine area between Juba and Shabelle, and also in a few mountainous places in the North around Erigavo and Sheikh and in the area stretching from Gebiley to Jijiga.

The level of rainfall in Somalia and in the Ethiopian Highlands determines the seasonal availability of water resources, including the water-level of the Shabelle and the Juba, the occasional appearance of seasonal rivers such as the *Tug Jerer* and *Tug Fafan* and temporary lakes in the *Haud* in Southeastern Ethiopia (map 1), the productivity of wells, and the amount of water storage in artificial water basins. The high degree of variability of rainfall (Awad and Boothman, 1975: p.8; Samatar, 1989: p.16) in this extremely harsh environment makes access to water one of the most challenging objects of adaptive strategies.

Economy

Contrary to the view that the vast majority of Somali are nomads, figures from 1983[4] count just 52.5% of the population as nomads, 19.9% as settled farmers and 27.6% as non-agricultural. Compared with figures from 1975, the nomadic population fell by 6.2% and settled farmers by 1.9%, while the non-agrarian population rose by 8.1%.

THE AGRARIAN SECTOR: FARMING AND PASTORALISM

The agrarian sector is made up of pastoralists/nomads, agro-pastoralists and farmers. Generally, the difference between pastoralism and agro-pastoralism is defined as follows (Bovin, 1990: p.30):

> The term *pastoral production system* is used to describe an economic system in which the herding of domestic ruminant animals on open bush land is the dominant economic activity. 50% or more of the household gross revenue, i.e. the value of marketed plus subsistence production, comes from animals or animal related activities, or where more than 15% of the house

---

4 Statistisches Bundesamt (1988). Note, however, that these figures refer to the Republic of Somalia. Most Somali in Ethiopia and Kenya are agro-pastoralists. In Djibouti the number of Somali involved in non-agricultural activities (trade, administration etc.) is much higher (ibid.: table 7.2, p.39).

food energy consumption consists of milk or milk products, produced within the household. The *agro-pastoral production system* is a system in which more than 50% of the household income comes from farming, and 10-15% from pastoralism.

In parts of the Northwest and West (Ethiopia), where, in years with good rains, seasonal rivers offer opportunities for cultivation, agro-pastoralism is dominant. In the South, by far the most fertile region in Somalia, one finds not only agro-pastoralists but also farmers who are engaged exclusively in cereal production and horticulture. This also applies to the Southwestern part of the Somali-inhabited region that lies in Ethiopia. The Northeastern and Central regions (including those within Ethiopia), with the highest temperatures and lowest rainfall, are predominantly inhabited by nomads/pastoralists.

Farming in the Northwest

There is thus an area in the Northwest where rain-fed cultivation is practiced, although its agricultural capacity is not at all comparable to the richness of the soil in the South. The Northwestern farmland stretches from Hargeisa westward to Gebiley and further to Borama and extends across the Ethiopian-Somali border up to the area around Jijiga, where particularly the area between the seasonal rivers *Tug Jerer* and *Tug Fafan* is cultivated in the rainy seasons. Sorghum and maize are the main crops that can be cultivated under the climatic conditions of the area; limited horticulture (onions, tomatoes) is also practiced. For the Gebiley district, Samatar (1989: p.137) estimates that about 30% of the population are peasants who also keep some animals. The figure is similar for the Jijiga/Kabrebeya area. The area under cultivation constitutes about 30% of the land, with some 50-60% used exclusively by pastoralists for grazing (Brons, 1992: p.1-16). Besides maize and sorghum, limited amounts of wheat, *teff*, barley and sweet potatoes are also cultivated.

Qaat farming has played a role in the Gebiley area – somewhat rudimentarily in the late 1960s, and increasingly since the late 1970s. The leaves of the Qaat tree (*catha edulis*) contain a mild stimulant, which is very popular among Somali men throughout the Horn. It is mostly grown on the fertile Harar plateau, Northwest of Jijiga, but the plant can adapt to a wide range of ecological conditions and is less sensitive to rainfall variations than sorghum or maize (Samatar, 1989: p.134-47). *Qaat* became increasingly important as a cash crop for farmers of the Northwest during the late 1970s and early 1980s. Vast areas of arable land were allocated to the crop, and tractors and hired laborers were introduced to work what became large *Qaat* farms. In spring 1984, the consumption, import and cultivation of *Qaat* were prohibited and the Somali government destroyed all *Qaat* farms.[5] During the wars of 1981-88 and 1988-90 in the North, not only *Qaat* tree plantations but also citrus plantations were destroyed, along with wells, pumps and generators and other farming equipment (Africa Watch, 1990). After the civil war, the use and trade of *Qaat* were reintroduced, and agricultural production revived in the North-western areas (Save the Children Fund UK, 1993).

Farming in the South

The Southern inter-riverine areas are the only parts of the Somali region in which water is continuously and readily available. Rain-fed and irrigated agriculture and cattle-pastoralism are therefore concentrated in these areas. Cereals, fruits and vegetables from the inter-riverine areas are traded as far away as Mandera (Kenya) and Dolo (Ethiopia).

In the South, access to fertile and agriculturally productive land is a key factor determining the level of economic security. It is difficult to assess the contemporary level of agricultural production in the South because of ongoing civil war in that part of Somalia. Before 1990, wealth derived from the land in the form of cash-crop plantations where tropical fruits (particularly bananas but also grapefruits, papaya and mango) were harvested, as well as in the form of domestic food production, the cultivation of cereals such as sorghum and maize, horticulture, cattle-breeding and poultry (Statistisches Bundesamt, 1988; Kaplan, 1969). Bananas were produced on large-scale plantations in the Lower Shabelle and Lower and Central Juba regions, particularly for export to Italy, while other food-stuffs supplied the urban markets in the big cities, especially Mogadishu (*Xamar*). In addition, sugarcane and cotton were produced and processed.

Pastoralism in the Central and Northern Areas

In the Central and Northeastern zone, the climatic and topographic conditions make pastoralism the most efficient adaptive strategy. Camels and goats

---

5   For more on government policies on *qaat*, see chapter 5. Warsame (1997: p.28) lists other spellings of *qaat*: *qat, kat, khat, chad*.

are suited to dry-land and semi-desert conditions: a variety of camel species are kept by the Somali pastoralists in the different topological zones, each specifically adapted to particular types of vegetation cover, water resources, soil characteristics and climatic conditions.[6] The pastoral way of life is structured around seasonal migratory patterns determined by rainfall and pasture. In the wet seasons – the long (*gu,* April to July) and the short (*dayr,* October to December) rains – pastoralists can move with all their animals, camels, sheep and goats and sometimes also cattle into arid zones where grass is plenty and water holes and seasonal rivers are filled: to the *Haud* in the West and the *Doi* in the Southwest. In the dry season – the short *Hagaa* season (July to October) and the long *Jilaal* (December to April) – watering the animals requires daily access to wells and pastoralists move their herds to the Northern *Ogo* and Southern *Arra gudud.*

During the dry season most families split into two groups (Lewis, 1965: p.8-9). Herders, mostly unmarried youngsters, such as brothers and cousins of the owner, stay behind on pastureland and come to the home wells about once a month to satisfy the less frequent but more substantial watering needs of the camels (Rirash, 1988). Women (wives, daughters, unmarried sisters), small children and the elderly, move together with the burden camels and the smaller stock close to the home wells. Because of their migratory lifestyle, pastoral families live in easily movable tents (*reer*), a number of which make up a settlement. Women and young girls not only take care of the smaller animals (goats and sheep which graze close to the hamlets) but are also responsible for building and moving the tents, milking, and collecting firewood and water.

In the North and East, where there are no permanent water resources and the availability of water in temporary rivers and lakes depends on the length and intensity of rainfall, the quality and accessibility of wells plays an important role in social organization. Control over wells is of crucial importance for the survival of animals and people. Violent conflict can break out, if particular clans disregard customary water rights of other clans.[7] The water issue thus determines not only economic but also social and political relations between pastoral groups. In the *Guban, Ogo* and *Haud,* the seasonal availability of water resources differs greatly. In the *Ogo* and *Haud,* relatively deeply water wells are dug and form the home-wells of particular clans who come there in the dry

---

6 Rirash (1988: pp.53-66). Rirash discusses the specific knowledge of Somali camel pastoralists of adaptive strategies and how this knowledge is passed on to the next generation in poetry and songs.

7 For more details on the Somali clan system, see the following chapter.

seasons. Further into the *Haud* there are no permanent watering places and therefore no home-wells to supply the large amounts of water needed by camels. In the *Guban*, although it is very hot and dry particularly between June and September, groundwater is relatively easily available from shallow wells (Lewis, 1965: p.2), as it collects in the mountain ridges behind the *Guban:*

> Only where water is not freely available, and where the expenditure of much labor and effort is required before it can be used, are exclusive rights asserted and maintained, if necessary, by force. And while in the general nomadic flux there is no rigid localization of pastoral groups and no appreciable development of ties to locality, the 'home-wells' regularly frequented in the dry seasons, and the trading settlements which spring up all over Somaliland wherever people congregate even temporarily around water, provide some check to a more random pattern of pastoral mobility (ibid.: p.9).

Somali nomads have always been in contact with towns, villages and settled communities. Some are engaged in trade, exchanging milk, meat, hides and skins for grain, salt, sugar and tea, and other commodities such as clothes, medicine and household utensils. Towns also act as market centers for livestock, where pastoralists make contact with livestock-trading middlemen or brokers.[8] Caravan routes from the Ethiopian Highlands to the Red Sea were largely dominated and controlled by camel pastoralists.

Natural disasters such as the repeated periods of drought in 1964/65, 1970-74 and 1983-86 impoverished many pastoralists. Not only did many animals starve to death, but the animal-grain price ratio also turned to their disadvantage.[9] During times of drought, the conditions of most animals, particularly cattle, sheep and goats, deteriorate; they therefore fetch lower prices at market. At the same time, many people are obliged to sell their animals, pushing prices down even further. Grain prices, on the other hand, increase dramatically in times of drought. More animals have to be sold than the herd balance actually allows, thus damaging the long-term pastoral basis. One of the short-term survival strategies in such periods of crisis consists of temporarily settling close to town with a few animals, and managing the household needs

---

8 On the importance of Jijiga for the Somali pastoralists, see Brons (1992: pp.10-13). In the 1920s the Somali pastoralists called Jijiga 'La'a': the shining spot which attracts the eye from afar (Echete, 1988).

9 Similar predicaments of pastoralists in the Sudan and Kenya are described by Mohamed Salih (1988: pp.19-29), and by Hjort af Ornäs (1989: p.67).

through petty-trade and (very) small-scale farming.[10] With increased household income, money can be saved to purchase more animals.

Besides the problems of natural disasters, Somali pastoralists have suffered during the last three decades from man-made policies, which, in combination, created an increasingly insecure environment. The establishment of international borders politicized nomadic areas: although these borders are largely ignored by Somali pastoralists in their seasonal migrations, economic, social and political/military insecurity have all increased as a result of the division of Somali territory into different states.

PRODUCTION AND INDUSTRIAL DEVELOPMENT IN THE COASTAL AREAS

Fishing

The Indian Ocean offers considerable potential for fishing. The main fishing area is on the Northeastern coast between Ras Asir and Xaafun, but all communities along the coast are involved in fishing. Partly due to the absence of a marketing infrastructure within the Somali region (which would have to be adapted to climatic conditions), but mostly due to the refusal of the pastoral Somali population to eat fish, the consumption of fish is very limited. Only the population in the coastal towns of Kismayo, Merca, Brava, Bossasso, Berbera, Zeila, and, to a limited extent, the urban population of Mogadishu and the surrounding Benadir district regularly eat fish. Most fishing is coastal, done by traditional boats, the *dhows*. In 1974, with Soviet support, a Somali deep-sea fishing fleet was established. Although this co-operation ended in 1977 with the departure of all Soviet advisors, the Somali deep-fishing fleet of freezing trawlers and prawn trawlers grew to fourteen ships. Of these, nine were registered in 1980 with a gross tonnage of 100-499; five were registered in 1984 with a gross registered tonnage of 500-999 (Statistisches Bundesamt Wiesbaden, 1988: p.44-45). However, 1988 statistics (ibid.) show that the actual catch never surpassed 10% of the catch potential of 200,000 tons. Some fish-processing factories were established in the early 1970s, such as the canning industry in

---

10 Field research observations in Jijiga in 1991. Numerous studies exist on adaptive strategies of pastoralists in crisis situations in other parts of Africa: see, e.g., Dietz (1987), Bovin and Manger (1990), Mohamed Salih (1992).

Las Khoreh, Candala and Mogadishu (Marchal, 1996: p.61), but most of these were closed down because of a lack of spare parts and inadequate maintenance. Exactly what happened to the Somali deep-sea shipping fleet following the 1991 state-collapse is not known, although Marchal (1996: p.65) mentions seven ships, which apparently continued to be used for commercial purpose. Nowadays, fish and sea fruit (lobster) export across the Red Sea is on the rise particularly in the Northeastern port of Bossasso (ibid.).

Salt, Frankincense and Leather

There are a number of other activities, which play some economic role in the region. Salt production occurs in several places along the Red Sea coast. At the very tip of the Horn there are small-scale date plantations. The forest-belt of the Northern mountains that link to the coastal area, has frankincense trees whose gum is harvested and exported to the Gulf states, France and China (Farah, 1994). In 1985, Somalia claimed to be the world's largest producer of incense with 2000 tons per annum (Statistisches Bundesamt, 1988). Gum collection is often an additional source of income for pastoralists in the Northern region.

There is a large leather tannery in the coastal town of Brava about 250 km South of Mogadishu. Before the collapse of the central state, high quality hides and skins, in particular from goats, were usually exported. In Brava, a sophisticated leather processing industry is in place, in private hands, with local craftsmen producing sandals, bags, belts, chairs, etc. which are sold all over the Somali region. Another, more industrialized, modern tannery, leather dyeing and shoe factory (mainly producing army boots) is located in Mogadishu. Several handicraft centers for shoe and handbag production – most of them with family connections to Brava – are located in the harbor area in Old Mogadishu, using not only local leather but also imported materials such as plastics for their production. What happened to these industries under civil war conditions is difficult to assess. What is known is that most of the families involved in the leather producing and processing business belong to marginalized clans and fled the capital.

Other Industries

The Somali region has seen very little industrial development; what development there has been is mostly concentrated in and around Mogadishu. Most of these industrial facilities were damaged in the civil war, although it is difficult to assess the extent of the damage. An oil refinery was built, with a capacity of 300,000 tons per annum, but productivity fluctuated, as it was dependent on the import of crude oil.[11] Although electric power stations were built in the years 1975 to 1985 and energy output tripled, the bulk of the region's electricity supply derives from diesel generators. Statistics for 1985 show that in Somalia, a total of 11,345 people were employed by 175 factories in various branches, including the food processing and beverage industry, leather and textiles, furniture, printing, chemicals, processing of stones and soils, and metal production and processing. These statistics, however, include only those companies with more than five employees and do not cover industrial processing in the informal sector. The basic fact is that, throughout the 1970s and 1980s, industrial development remained severely limited and inadequate, and the policy of import-substitution failed to reduce dependence on imports. Following local agricultural and pastoral production, it is not industry but trade, which represents the second most important sector of the Somali economy.

TRADE

Since ancient times, the Somali people have been heavily involved in trading. The patterns of intra-regional and import-export trade demonstrate the flexibility of the Somali people in securing their economic needs, relying on networks which do not fit in the framework of a 'national' economy.

In terms of the international import-export trade, import commodities include agricultural products such as rice, spices, sugar and dates, as well as consumer commodities, clothes, cosmetics, household equipment, construction materials and spare parts, including oil and other petroleum products. According to statistics published in 1988 (Statistisches Bundesamt, 1988), imports into Somalia originated mainly from the EU (US$ 162.3 m, of which no less than US$ 97.8 m from Italy, US$ 19.5 m from Germany, a further US$ 19.5 m from Belgium, the Netherlands and Luxembourg, and US$ 12.2 m from Great Britain and Ireland). The other main exporters to Somalia were the USA (US$ 63.1 m), Saudi Arabia (US$ 47.1 m) and Bahrain (US$ 24.2 m).

Export commodities include pastoral products such as livestock on the hoof, hides and skins, as well as frankincense, and agricultural products, pri-

---

11 The following data are taken from Statistisches Bundesamt (1988).

marily bananas. In the 1980s, the main export destination was Saudi Arabia, although export rates fluctuated as a result of import restrictions on livestock because of rinderpest (1980: US$ 92.7 m, 1985: US$ 38.4 m). The second most important Somali export-trading partners were Italy (1985: US$ 20.6 m) and Yemen Arab Republic (1985: US$ 18.0 m), followed by Egypt (US$ 6.7 m), United Arab Emirates (US$ 6.2 m), China (US$ 4.9 m) and Hong Kong (US$ 4.4 m).

As far as intra-regional trade is concerned, three geographical zones can be distinguished, with profound differences in their local/regional market orientation: the South, the Northwest, and the Northeast (map 1). International borders are not taken into account in the day-to-day business of economic and trading activities in the Somali region, reflecting the characteristic Somali disregard for externally imposed concepts of territoriality.

The Northwestern Trading Zone

The principal trading zone in terms of both the exchange of local products and the history of import-export trade is the Northwestern Somali region. Here, farming products from the fertile and agriculturally rich Harar plateau in Ethiopia have long been, and are still, traded for pastoral products from the Somali lowlands (Brons, 1992: p.3-13). The products purchased include different types of grain, such as sorghum, barley and maize, vegetables, fruits, groundnuts, oil-seeds and oil, coffee, tea, honey and *Qaat*. The Somali who engage in this trade are in contact with Oromo farmers who inhabit the wider Harar plateau as well as with Harari townspeople. The current international borders have very limited meaning and are relatively recent compared to the long commercial tradition of the people in this area. Main trading centers and towns in this geo-economic setting are Dire-Dawa, Harar, Fugnanbira, Jijiga, Degehbur and, relatively recently, Hartisheik refugee camp[12] in Ethiopia, and Borama, Gebiley and Hargeisa in Somaliland. The towns in the Ethiopian Ogaden, such as Kabrebeya and Wardher, are also linked to this commercial complex, although mainly via Jijiga. For an understanding of the contemporary socio-political reality of the Northwestern Somali-inhabited area it is important to be aware of these trading networks. These were established long ago, have undergone slight alterations and adaptations to new political cir-

---

12 For details of the Hartisheik economic phenomenon, see chapter 7, p.204.

cumstances, but are still functioning and make up the basic economic reality of the region today.

In one of his early books on Somaliland the British anthropologist Lewis describes the character of towns in relatively remote pastoral areas (Lewis, 1961: p.90-95). His description is still generally valid:

> The villages (*tuulo*) and towns (*magaalo*), which are the centers of trade, are widely scattered and vary greatly in size... Town populations fluctuate with the seasons. The number of their inhabitants is generally greatest in the dry months when they attract nomads from the interior as temporary settlers, In the rainy season the movement is away from the urban centers when temporary town-dwellers are drawn out with their stock to the pastures. ... The pastoralists who thus form a transitory element in towns live for the most part in their nomadic huts (*aqal*) erected on the periphery of the urban centers. The more permanent townsmen who are occupied as shop-keepers, livestock merchants, importers and exporters, petrol retailers and mechanics, and government officials, etc., live mainly in stone (*daar*) or mud and wattle houses (*'ariish*), and now, to some extent in government-constructed brick dwellings. ... The majority of Northern Somali towns are of recent formation, and, inhabited mainly by Somali, have little or no sense of corporate identity as urban centers. ... For in towns the tendency for people of the same lineage to live side by side where they settle is still strong. ...Towns are primarily the markets for the interior and to an important degree are the centers of pastoral politics. Town and interior form one economic and political system in which the same structural principles govern social relations ...

Historical sources[13] reveal the existence not only of local and intra-regional exchange but also of external trade as early as the first few centuries A D.

At the turn of the era [300 BC to AD 500], several significant trading emporia existed along the Southern shores of the Gulf of Aden, the most significant of these being at Malao (present-day Berbera). Other commercial sites included Mundu (modern Heys) and Mosyllon (probably near modern Bossasso). A goodly variety of commodities were imported at these locations, such as clothing, drinking vessels, iron wares, and Roman coins. A lesser range of goods passed into the outward bound trade – mainly raw

---

13 For the interpretation of Arab sources, I refer to the article of Mukhtar (1995). Other historical sources on Northwestern Somali trade include Barker (1842), Burton (1856) and Paulitschke (1888).

materials, in particular myrrh from Malao and frankincense from Mundo and Mosyllon. Tortoise shell also was a valued product of those coasts (Ehret, 1995: p.241).

Merchants from pre-Islamic Arabia, Persia, India and Yemen visited Somali ports. Some of them stayed there permanently, intermarried with Somali and to a great extent shaped the history of coastal towns.

The Southern Trading Zone

In the South, agricultural production developed along the rivers Juba/Genale and Shabelle far into the generally pastoral lands. However, the majority of fresh agricultural produce originates from the Bardere area along the Juba and from the intensive farming areas stretching towards the Indian Ocean coast (Central and Lower Shabelle and Central and Lower Juba regions). The farmers and agro-pastoralists in the rich inter-riverine area supply Somali pastoralists with agricultural products, in particular grain. Again cross-border trade is very common, the Southern trading complex stretching far into Kenya in the South and Ethiopia in the North. South of the Juba river. Somali pastoralist territory extends into the Northeastern province of Kenya (Mandera, Wajir and Garissa district). Towns located on the roads leading into Kenya represent important trading centers for Somali pastoralists and traders. The most important of these are Mandera, on the Ethiopian-Somali-Kenyan triangle, El Wak, Wajir and Libol. Towards Ethiopia the roads from Luuq to Dolo on the Ethiopian-Somali border and further North to Bogol Manyo and Lama Shilindi in Ethiopia, and the road from Beled Weyne to Ferfer (border town) further North to Mustahil and Kellafo in Ethiopia geographically define the Southern trading zone. Other towns in the Somali central region, such as El Dhere, Dhusamareb, Abduwak, and others, are also important pastoral trading centers supplied by the Southern agricultural zone.

Apart from intro-regional exchange, the export trade is an important feature of this zone and, as in the Northwestern zone, has a long tradition. Historical records[14] speak of the existence of the trading centers of Mogadishu,

---

14 Mukhtar refers here to Abu 'Abdalla Muhammad Ibn Muhammad al-Idrisi, Kitabu Nuzhat al-Mushtaq fi Ikhtiraq al-Afaq, MS. British Museum supplement 685, or 4636. The supplement is entitled: Mukhtasar Nuzhat al-Mushtaq fi Ikhtiraq al-Afaq. See Mukhtar (1995: p.6).

Merca and Brava which were commercially linked to the trading centers on today's Tanzanian coast, particularly the city-states of Kilwa and Zansibar:

Al Idrisi (1100-1166), in his *Nuzhat*, described the commercial coastal centers of Southern Somalia – Marka, Barawa, and Mogadishu. In addition, he reported the rise of inland trade between the coastal centers and the hinterland, such as the caravan routes originating from Sarman, Luuq, Bardhera, Buur Hakaba just to mention some. ... With regard to Mogadishu, he mentioned that it was a significant port in the region, and one of its various roles was that of a link between the East and West trading centers for Indian Ocean products (Mukhtar, 1995: p.6).

The Northeastern Trading Zone

The Northeast, which forms the very edge of the Horn, is a relatively isolated region. It is predominantly pastoral – apart from fishing on the coastlines – and is therefore dependent on the import of fresh products from outside the region. The Northeast is not well connected by land to agricultural areas. The South-North road links Mogadishu via Beled Weyne and Dhusamareb to Galcaio and further to Garowe and splits there, one way continuing to Las Anod, Burao and Hargeisa, and the other linking the Northeastern towns of Garowe, Qardho and the harbor town Bossasso. However, both the road to Somaliland and that to the Southern region are long. Furthermore, there are no direct links into the Ethiopian Ogaden. The region is therefore largely oriented towards over-seas import of commodities. Food imports into the region are obtained mainly through shipments from Kismayo to Bossasso, and through imports from Yemen. From ancient times, the Northeastern region has been called *Puntland*.[15] One of the earliest mentions of Puntland dates back to the reign of Mentuhotep III (2019-2007 BC) of Egypt, when the kingdom of Punt was raided several times (Marchal, 1996: p.10). Like other parts of the Somali coastline, the Northeastern ports historically developed trading links with Indian and Arab merchants.

In Bender Kassem, Bender Khor, Bender Merayo and Caluula Indians and Arabs were settled and exported to Bombay and other ports: gum was sent to Bombay, dried fish to the Indian coast and shark fins and tails were sent

---

15 The regional state, which, in July 1998, was proclaimed in the Northeast, was given the name 'Puntland'. Ancient identities are brought back into political identity formation, which is one factor in state formation.

via India to China, while many of the imports were similarly brought in by Banyan [Indian] traders (ibid.: p.11).

Bossasso harbor town went through a period of neglect during most of the three decades of independent Somali government; the capital Mogadishu and the Northwestern port of Berbera were favored instead, the latter partly because of its military significance (deep-sea harbor facilities had been built in Berbera in 1973). It was only during the last few years of the Barre regime that the government invested in the development of facilities in Bossasso, seemingly in order to make up for the increasingly unstable situation in the Northwest and to win the sympathies of the Northeastern population. In recent years, Bossasso has experienced a revival, with booming market and trading activities (*Horn of Africa Bulletin* 9/2, 1997).

In summary, it is important to stress that Somali economic and trading zones are defined by ecological and economic dynamics, which developed long before international borders were drawn. Despite the fact that these borders divide the Somali region into different state territories and therefore in theory require the application of international trade laws, the old trading patterns in fact persist. Their vibrant existence militates against conceptualizing the Somali economy as a 'national' economy of the Somali territorial state of 1960. With reference to Somali financial markets, this conclusion is supported by Marchal (1996: p.105):

> In fact, what should be understood is that the Somali currency is not only circulating inside Somalia. It may appear as very strange that a country without state apparatus, or a central Bank, is still able to make its currency used by neighboring markets. The explanation lies again in the Somali trade networks which are able to supply a large part of the region's five markets in Ethiopia and marginally Djibouti and Northeast Kenya. It is not uncommon to hear that some traders have gone as far as Godey to get SoSh [Somali Shilling].

The Somali people have had to cope with a high degree of environmental insecurity. Naturally harsh climatic conditions coupled with unpredictable disasters such as drought or flooding, have put important constraints on families' strategies for survival. The variety of economic and trading activities described in this chapter show that the Somali have adapted in a range of flexible ways in order to face the challenge of environmental insecurity. Centuries-old coping strategies and networks have developed over time and have adapted to changing circumstances. The economic security of Somali society is dependent on keeping these strategies and networks operational.

CHAPTER 4

Identity and Society

In this chapter I characterize Somali society in terms of various identities. Identities in Somali society have often been politicized. There is a political aspect to identity, which is inherent in the segmentary lineage society of the Somali people. However, it is not only tribal or clan identity, but also religious and mythical identity, which become increasingly politicized when confronted with processes of modern state formation.

We focus first on the basic divide between the nomadic and the settled Somali – a divide which is reflected in two distinct ways of thinking about the question of Somali origin, and which has a discriminatory connotation, which still affects Somali society and politics, determining to some extent power relations and conflict. The protagonists of the Somali state have propagated the nomadic as the national identity, and state policies have marginalized the sedentary Somali, both economically and politically. In this context, knowledge of both the myths and the historical findings related to Somali origin is a basic condition for understanding, firstly, the depth and ideological genesis of the Somali conflict and, secondly, the contemporary challenges to state formation.

The second form of identity we will examine is religious identity, especially the unifying and dividing aspects of Somali Islam. Religious identity became particularly politicized during the anti-colonial struggle in the early 20th century when, on the one hand, Muslim Somali identity was used as a unifying factor against Christian domination and, on the other hand, early Somali nationalism failed partly because of the dividing forces within the Somali religious identity. The role and authority of religious men as silent diplomats of peace, surpassing clan limitations, is contrasted with the political role of the clan elders, in the context of their contemporary role in the reconciliation process after the civil war (Mubarak, 1997).

The third form of identity to be discussed is clan identity. Clan membership is an ascribed identity but the Somali clan system was traditionally quite flexible in this regard. Clan identity always had a political connotation, particularly in stateless nomadic society. Since state formation clan identity has become increasingly politicized and violently expressed. Against this background, I believe it is important to recognize that today the clan divide as such is not the core factor of the Somali crisis of state formation: it is rather competition over resources and over the power which is seen as safeguarding access to these resources that is expressed in competitive clan labels. By looking more closely at the reconciliatory potentials of the clan system, the flexibility within it, and the identities which exist apart from the clan, I intend to lay the foundation for an understanding of contemporary *state-* or rather *political authority-*formation by consent which will be presented towards the end of the book.

Nomadism and Sedentarism: Somali Identity in Crisis

MYTH AND HISTORY OF ORIGIN: ARAB AND AFRICAN

The Somali are considered part of the Cushitic language family to which the Afar, the Oromo, the Beja and Saho also belong. The dominant myth of origin is built upon the Arabian ancestry of the Somali. According to this myth, "ultimately all Somali genealogies go back to Arabian origins, to the Prophet's lineage of *Quraysh* and those of his companions" (Lewis, 1961: p.11). There are differing opinions about the actual line of descent from Arabia. One is that the pastoral clan families trace their descent from an ancestor called *Samale* while the agricultural clan families, the Digil and Mirifle, are descendants of an ancestor called *Sab*. In this myth of origin, all Somali are descended from a cousin of the Prophet Mohammed, Aqiil Abuu Taalib. (Lewis claims that the Isaq trace their descent from Aqiil's brother Ali Abuu Talib who married the Prophet's daughter Fatima.)[1]

There is a second set of narratives of Somali origin that refers to the story of the man in the tree, the charismatic ancestor who came from Arabia and married a Somali girl, thus founding the patrilineal descent line originating in Arabia. According to Luling (1988) and Mansur (1995), this narrative is rooted in old African mythology and was fitted into the new belief system after the conversion of the Somali to Islam. This interpretation of the myth, then, asserts a historically African origin of the Somali.

---

1   According to Lewis (1961: p.12), Abuu Taalib of Quraysh died at Mekka in AD 620. The pastoral Somali clans Darod, Dir and Hawiye claim descent from his son Aqiil, but the Isaq claim descent from another of his sons, Ali who married Prophet Mohammed's daughter Fatima.

Most of the Eastern Cushitic people, the Afar, Borana and Guji Oromo and the Darod and Hawiye Somali refer to a similar legend, in which a local girl discovers a stranger with extraordinary powers (in the Somali case, the Arab progenitor) in a tree. Only after being promised both the girl to marry and the submission of the local people – often in the gesture of descending from the tree on the back of a local – does the stranger agree to come down. In the belief system of these groups, some trees are considered sacred. The man in the tree is equated with the man from the sky or the sky-God *Waaq*, which in the Oromo language means sky as well as God. According to Mansur (ibid.: p.120):

> This name is still used to mean God by the Oromo, Konso, Burji, Haddiya, Tasmai, Dasenech, Arbore, Elmolo, Bayso, Rendille, Dahalo, and Somali, all of whom speak Eastern Cushitic languages except the Dahalo. ... Needless to say, the old religion is adapted to reflect the hegemony of the new in that the ancestral home of the ancestor is in Arabia, the headquarters of Islam. Nonetheless, the ensuing myth is a living testimony to the syncretistic powers of African traditions.[2]

SOMALI EXPANSION IN THE HORN

Along with the myth of Arabian descent goes the portrayal of early Somali history as the "story of the great Somali expansion from the North" (Lewis, 1965: p.18). According to this oral tradition, the arrival from Arabia of Sheik Ismail Jabarti around the 10th or 11th century, the expansion of his descendants, the Darod and, about two centuries later, the arrival from Arabia of Sheik Isaq whose descendants settled West of the Darod, marked the beginning of the southward migration of the Somali.

Fortunately, oral records are on the whole sufficiently abundant and consistent in their essentials, to enable the broad outlines of the Somali expan-

---

2   Mansur (ibid.: p.120) provides us with another example of a Somali tradition a rite called *Kur* or *Madaxshub,* performed during the last months of pregnancy, which evidences an African Somali origin: "The invited women pour abundant oil on the pregnant woman's head, invoking Eve or Fatima, the daughter of the prophet, in order to safeguard the woman during delivery. This rite is not a part of Islam; it has its roots in the cult of the goddess of fertility and maternity practiced by the Borana women in the same way and for the same purposes. Here Fatima is a covering name for the ancient goddess Ateta, as the Arabian descendant was for the heavenly origin." Aves (1987: pp.88-89), too, mentions several spiritual practices, such as the zaar-, bebo- or mingis-customs, which make up part of the Somali tradition of sorcery.

sion to be traced with what is probably a considerable degree of accuracy. Certainly the evidence at present available leaves no doubt that the gradual expansion over the last ten centuries of the Hamitic Somali from the shores of the Gulf of Aden to the plains of Northern Kenya is one of the most sustained, and in its effects, far-reaching movements of population in the history of North-East Africa (ibid.).

According to Lewis, the Somali moved from the Northeast into the Horn, not only occupying empty land but also pushing the Oromo into what is today Ethiopia, and the Zanj population (consisting of Bantu sedentary people along the two rivers, and the coastal hunters and gatherers of the Boni people) further South. The question remains where the other Somali clans come from.

The Hawiye is the first Somali clan that was mentioned by an Arab geographer in the 13th century. Another, oral, tradition speaks of Somali Digil having settled in the Shabelle area even before that time (ibid.: p.24). These accounts, together with the incorporation and transformation of African mythology and customs into the dominant myth of Arab descent of the Somali, tend to suggest that the oral records of Somali origin to which Lewis refers, may be more mythical than historical. Pastoral Somali oral tradition claims an agnatic descent, exclusively in the male line. It is historical fact that Arab immigrants intermarried with Somali and several generations later created their own lineages within the Somali clan system. However, a strict descent from Arabia would imply that at the time of the arrival of the first such immigrants there were no Somali (men) already inhabiting the area (Schlee, 1994: p.225).

Historical and linguistic analyses[3] (Kusow, 1995: p.81-106) reveal the origin of the Somali to have been in the Southern fertile zone. From there, stimulated by population pressure and facilitated by the introduction of the camel, Somali began in about the 6th century to move towards the harsh environment of the central, northern and northeastern regions. According to Kusow (1995), this is when camel pastoralism became widespread in the Somali peninsula. Nomadic migration patterns were established and enabled the population of the vast, hot and dry thornbush savanna plains. Over generations, the offspring of early nomads built their own pastoral clan-families. This development was met by the advent of Islam about two centuries later. Somali adopted the Islamic religion and reconciled it with their earlier belief systems.

---

3 Kusow (1995) refers in his analysis among others to the work of Lewis (1966), Turton (1975), Hersi (1977) and Ali (1985).

In the process, Somali genealogy was linked to Arabian ancestry representing the superior, dominant culture at the time.

Critics of the Arab origin theory[4] argue that the nomadic clans, which had by then spread throughout the Somali Horn, and especially the Darod, who claimed to be the 'original' clan, used the link to Arabian ancestry, the dominant political culture of the time, in order to assert political dominance over other Somali clans.[5] In academic circles a reconsideration of the Arab origin theory is underway.[6] Historical, archaeological and linguistic research points to the possibility that the Somali people originated in the fertile Southern region of the Horn, that is, in Africa.

The interpretation that was common for decades in Somali studies, suggests that the very name Somali, or more correctly *Soomaali*, originates in the nomadic pastoral tradition, in which the words *soo* and *maal* mean 'go milk', with an implicit reference to the camel, thus strengthening the claims of the camel pastoralists as the 'real' Somali. An alternative linguistic interpretation, however, rests on the meaning of *sa-maal* in the Southern region, in particular among the Rewin people, where *sa* literally means cow and *maal* translates to milk, indicating that Somali originally were a cattle culture (Kusow, 1995). This interpretation would provide evidence for the theory that Somali people originate in the inter-riverine fertile region. However, the dominant popular history of Somali migration denies any historical importance to the Rewin,

---

4 On this point, see particularly Mukhtar (1995).

5 "The closer one is to the household of the Prophet of Islam, the greater chance one has to be a leader of a non-Arab Muslim community. The case of the Somali Arabised clans is, therefore, identical to the Sadah of Southeast Asian Muslims, the Mawlanas of Islamic India, the Bani Ma'qils of Egypt, or the Yemeni tribes of Northern Sudan, who each invented their own myth of descent from Prophet Muhammad's tribe, in order to dominate the position of leadership in their respective areas." (Mukhtar, 1995: pp.18-19).

6 Schlee comments on scholarly acceptance of the claim of Arab origin: "It is this recent migration of Northern and central Somali to the South and South-west, in combination with their pious traditions to have originated at Mecca and Medina, that misled a whole generation of scholars into believing that the Somali as such originated in the North and have moved from there into the rest of the Horn, replacing an earlier population for which the Oromo (Galla) are the most likely candidates. Not only the more general historians (e.g. Low 1963: 321) but also the best specialists (e.g. Huntingford 1955: 19; 1963: 65-6; I. M. Lewis 1955: 45; 1980: 22-3) have succumbed to this error. There is no way to reconcile this erroneous view with the evidence of historical linguistics or cultural history and one wonders why it took so long to die." (Schlee, 1994: pp.43-44).

focusing instead on pastoral North-South migration and the claim of Arab ancestry.

More research is needed on the issue of the Southern contribution to early Somali history and the linked discussion on the Somali origin and migration. Whatever the case as far as origin is concerned, Somali culture can certainly be considered a hybrid of Arab and African elements rather than a pure form of either one.

THE CRISIS OF SOMALI IDENTITY

Somali society has long been portrayed as a homogeneous society speaking one language, sharing one religion and practicing one culture and tradition (see, among others, Touval, 1963; Adam, 1995; Hirsch and Oakley, 1995). It has been characterized as individualistic, egalitarian, and anarchic with regard to institutionalization and authority (Laitin and Samatar, 1987: p.42). All these are supposed to be elements of Somali 'pastoral democracy'.[7] Those who did not fit this description have been considered a minority and to a certain extent not as 'real' Somali (Lewis, 1965: p.6). This applies not only to the Somali Bantu population, who even today are considered alien to Somali society (Besteman, 1995), but to a lesser degree to the *Sab* division within the Somali clan genealogy as a whole. According to Lewis (1965: pp.5-7):

> The distinction between the speech of the Digil and Rahanweyn and their more nomadic countrymen to their North and South is one feature of the wider cultural, geographic and historical primary division in the Somali nation between the 'Samale' or Somali proper and the Sab. The former make up the bulk of the nation, and their name (Samale) has come to include the Sab, perhaps in the same fashion as the word 'English' is applied by foreigners to all the inhabitants of the British Isles.

What is important to understand in this context is the politicization of the issue of Somali origin. Generally speaking the *Sab*, the settled Somali, many of whom have more African features, were at times and to a certain extent still are considered inferior by the *Samale*, the nomadic Somali people who claim to be the original Somali and, with that, claim a right to cultural and political domination.

---

7 The title of the famous anthropological analysis of the Northern Somali clans by Lewis (1961).

Ethnic homogeneity has been idealized as a core characteristic of Somali national identity. However, it was the numerically and politically dominant pastoral groups who provided the image of Somalia as the land of the nomad. The idea of the state – which, as we saw earlier, forms one of the three pillars of the state[8] – was centered around nomadic life and tradition. The camel became a kind of symbol of the Somali state, as expressed traditionally in Somali poetry. As Mansur (1995: p.112) comments:

In 1960 Somalia became a republic, and this new nation was symbolically compared to either a favorite she-camel called Maandeeq which gave abundant milk to the people, or to a herd of camels looted by thieves but later retrieved by the owner.

In this process of political idealization of the nomadic, some 40% of the overall population were marginalized – that is, the people in the inter-riverine areas in the South and those along the coast, consisting mainly of farmers, coastal fishing communities, and the outcast communities of blacksmiths, shoemakers and leather-tanners (*midgaan, tumaal, yibir*) (see Lewis, 1961: p.196). The idea of the state put forward by the dominant clans at independence, and kept alive until recent years under the guise of Somali nationalism, could never appeal to these people who, in their social life, customs and culture as well as in their language and economic activities, are quite different from the Somali nomads.[9]

The collapse of a repressive and discriminatory state ideology opened the door to a process of coming to terms with the past, and provided opportunities for intellectual freedom of thought and expression. It opened up the necessary space to critically reconsider issues of Somali origin, history and identity.[10] Being a people without a state thus provided options for emancipation from the dominant version of national history and identity.

Islam: Somali Religious Identity

The vast majority of Somali (some 99%) are *Sunni* Muslim, almost exclusively of the *Shafi'ite* school. Although there are differences in religious interpretation amongst the Somali Muslim clergy, they all adhere to the Sunni *Shafi'ite*

---

8   See the Introduction for an explanation of Buzan's three pillars of the state.
9   See, among others, Declich (1995).
10 See Mohamed Salih and Wohlgemuth (1994); Sharif (1997); Eno (1997).

Islam, and Somali society does not suffer from any major schism within its Islamic orientation. Religious belief is considered one of the uniting factors within Somali society.

Even before Islam, relations between Somali and Arabs were intensive, predominantly through trade and commerce. Islam spread to the Horn of Africa at a very early stage. Most early Muslim migrants were looking for a political safe haven and economic opportunities, which they found in the Somali areas on the Northern coast along the Gulf of Aden and on the Southern Benadir coast (Mukhtar, 1995; Aves, 1987). In the *Kitab al Zanj*[11] records have been found showing that one of the most extensive waves of Muslim immigration to Somalia took place during the reign of Caliph Abdulmalik Ibn Marwan (685-705).[12] Mukhtar (1995: p.5) refers to other Arab sources, which show that "the Muslim migration grew tremendously from the rise of Islam to the tenth century AD". According to Aves (1987) and Lewis (1955/56), there have been eight major waves of Islamic immigration to Somalia, the most important originating from Arabia, Persia, Yemen and Oman.

DIFFERENTIATION ALONG SUFI ORDERS

There are various Sufi orders, or *tariiqa*,[13] in Somalia. The oldest *tariiqa* is the *Qaadiriya*, which was founded in the 12th century. In the 19th century two main Somali *tariiqa* developed within the *Qaadiriya* order: the *Seyla'iya* founded by Sheikh Abdarahman Seyla'i, and the *Uwaysiya* founded by Sheikh Uways Mahamud al Baraawi.[14] The other influential Sufi order is the *Ahmadiya* order, a reform movement founded in the 18th century in Mekka (Lewis, 1955/56, 1961). One major branch within the *Ahmadiya* is the *Salihiya tariiqa*, named after Sayyed Mahammad Saalih, and introduced in Somalia in the 1890s by Sheikh Isaaq. Another smaller *tariiqa* of the *Ahmadiya* branch is the *Dandaraawiya*, founded by Sayyed Muhammad al Dandaraawi in 1885.

---

11 The Kitab al Zanj is an Arabic source/document, which was discovered at Kismayo in 1923 and has been translated by Enrico Cerulli (1957): *Somalia: Scritti vari editi et inediti*, 1 (Rome).

12 Aves (1987) describes in detail the historical accounts of this particular immigration as well as of later immigrations into Somalia; see pp.63-67.

13 'Tariiqa' means 'path' in the sense of the way to God, to be followed in the quest for grace. See Lewis (1961: p.219).

14 Lewis (1961); and, with specific focus on the second, Kassim (1995).

By far the best-known leader of the *Salihiya* was Sayyed Mohammed Abdulle Hassan in the early 20th century. At the time, competition and conflict over religious interpretation increased and became politicized in the context of the anti-colonial struggle. At the culmination of religious competition between *Qaadiriya* and *Salihiya* Sheikh Uways Mahamud al Baraawi, the founder of the *Uwaysiya* branch of *Qaadiriya tariiqa*, was killed in 1909 by followers of Sayyed Mohammed Abdulle Hassan.[15]

Religious congregations (*jama'a*) of the various *tariiqa* orders exist more in the fertile Southern region and less frequently in the North.[16] These are religious communities of brethren who live separately from other villages and are mostly self-sufficient. Clan divisions within the *jama'a* communities are of minor importance so that in times of conflict, such as during the colonial and religious wars in the early 20th century, they became safe havens for people from different clans. The Northern *tariiqa*, however, are more attached to the pastoral setting and therefore less independent from lineage affiliation. Lewis (1961: p.223) notes in this context:

> Although *tariiqa* affiliation thus unites men of different and often opposed lineage-groups, in opposition to members of other *tariiqas*, such religious solidarity is always ultimately subordinated to lineage ties. Common *tariiqa* allegiance cannot withstand, in a situation of lineage conflict, the demands of rival agnatic interest.

Within the *tariiqa* orders, the religious lineage, or so-called chains of blessing which list the "successive heads of the order through whom illumination is traced" (ibid.) provide the counterpart to clan affiliation outside the orders. For the common people, *tariiqa* affiliation is a matter of personal choice.

IMPARTIAL MEN OF GOD: THE *WADAADO*

Apart from the *tariiqa* communities with their distinct and independent religious character, Somali (pastoral) society generally makes a distinction between *wadaado*, men of God, and *waranleh*, warriors (Lewis, 1980). Men of God are devoted to religion, have substantial knowledge of the *Sharia*, the Koran and the traditions of the Prophet. The *wadaado* have the title of *Aw* added

---

15 For more on the religious and political impact of the *Salihiya* and Sheikh Mohamed Abdulle Hassan, see chapter 6.

16 For the North see Lewis (1961: pp.96-100); for the South see Mukhtar (1996).

to their name, but acquiring the title of Sheikh involves more intense and authentic (Arabic) knowledge of Islam (Lewis, 1961, 1955/56). A *wadaad* is responsible for teaching in Koranic schools, for prayers, religious feasts or processions, and for religious jurisprudence – particularly in the countryside away from towns where *Kadis* fulfil these functions. The men of God, *wadaado* or Sheikhs do not involve themselves directly in conflict resolution, but act as facilitators who try to convince conflicting parties to enter negotiations and give their blessing to the process and to the eventual agreement reached by the opposing sides. Although *wadaado* and Sheikhs live within their respective communities, rather than as members of a *jama'a tariiqa*, and in that sense are more closely linked to their clan affiliation, they usually earn the highest respect as men of God and are considered impartial.

The Clan System

The clan system is considered one of the most distinctive features of Somali social organization and polity. According to Lewis (1961: p.4) the term clanship refers to "corporate agnatic identity at all levels of political cleavage". Clan affiliation is interwoven with social, economic and political life of the Somali. In *A Pastoral Democracy*, the classic study of Northern Somali pastoralists, Lewis (ibid.: p.2) outlines the significance of the clan system for an understanding of Somali politics:

It is of the first importance to appreciate that a Somali genealogy is not a mere family tree recording the historical descent and connections of a particular individual or group. Whatever its historical significance, in the sphere of politics its importance lies in the fact that it represents the social divisions of people into corporate political groups. By reference to his ancestors, a man's relations with others are defined, and his position in Somali society as a whole determined. Thus an understanding of the political relations between groups requires a knowledge of their genealogical relationships. ... At the same time, the range of agnatic relationship recognized on one occasion need not be the same as that on another, so that the corporate kinship group in which an individual has political status varies with the context.

Basic Clan Divisions

The Somali clan system has two main lineage lines, the Samale and the Sab. (See diagram 1). In genealogical diagrams,[17] the Darod and Irir (Hawiye, Dir and Isaq) clan families belong to Samale whereas the Rewin clan family belongs to Sab. The differentiation between these two groups is reflected in the two major primary production/settlement patterns – the nomadic pastoralism of the Samale and the settled farming of the Sab. This major distinction among the Somali, between nomads and farmers, Samale and Sab, is also reflected linguistically: the Northern and central Somali pastoralists speak *Maxaa* Somali, whereas the Southern Somali agriculturists speak *May* Somali. The differences are not merely dialectical: the two are as different as, for instance, Spanish and Portuguese.[18]

Despite the fact that Somali people are found in five different states (Djibouti, Somaliland, Somalia, Ethiopia and Kenya), the Somali region is a sociopolitical and socio-economic unit (see map 1 and 3). The clan territories are units of social organization in their own right, which are geographically and historically conceptualized by the Somali, in particular by the pastoral Somali clan families, according to customary pasture and water rights.[19] Two points are relevant in this context: first, clan territorial units existed long before the emergence of any state borders; second, the existence and political meaning of modern state borders was recognized by the affected clans at a relatively late stage (Markakis, 1987).

In describing clan territory, I use state borders rather than the Somali perceptions of clan territory. For the analysis of the relationship of the Somali to the various states which they encountered since colonialism (before independence: British, French and Italian colonial states and the Ethiopian state; after independence: Somalia, Kenya, Djibouti, Ethiopia) it is relevant to know which clans find and/or found themselves citizens of two or more different states (map 1 and 3). The (in)security of the Somali clans and the (in)stability of the respective states are affected by the fact that the Somali people as a whole are divided by international state borders.[20] From the point of view of political

---

17 In drawing diagram 1 on the Somali clan structure I restricted the provided information on clan and lineage names to those that are mentioned in the book. My sources on Somali genealogy are Lewis (1965, 1994), Samatar (1988) and Mansur (1995).

18 Mentioned by Lewis (1965: p.5).

19 Lewis (1961), particularly pp.31-55.

analysis, therefore, it seems acceptable and even helpful to refer to state borders in the course of describing clan territories.

TERRITORIAL DISTRIBUTION OF SOMALI CLANS[21]

In terms of social organization, Somali society is considered a segmentary lineage society with clan membership determined by patrilineal descent *(tol)*. The inner structure of the Somali clan system can be described as a huge lineage web, whereby, through generations, the ties of common ancestry forge the basis of both alliances and oppositions.

Somali usually identify themselves as members of even more inclusive entities, beginning with their extended family and extending outward through their blood-money paying group (*diya* in Arabic; *mag* in Somali) and sub-clan up to the clan-family level. Regarding the genealogical chart of the Isaq clan family, a person might identify himself as *I am from the Jibril, Abokor, Isaaq, Sa'ad Muse.*[22] "Within this series of diffuse attachments, his most binding and most frequently mobilized loyalty is to his '*diya*-paying group' " (Lewis, 1965: p.11). Most protection, such as social security and economic co-operation derive from that level of clan affiliation. It is the basic juridical and political unit of Somali segmentary society, where compensation for crimes against another lineage is settled – including blood money in cases of homicide – and most po-

---

20 The establishment of an international border through Somali territory also affected Ethiopian state security, particularly when a war evolved between Somalia and Ethiopia in 1977/78 over the Somali inhabited areas. The same is true, although less dramatically, of the Kenyan-Somali dispute in the 1960s. See Markakis (1987); Matthies (1977); Al-Safi (1995). The fact that the Djibouti population is made up of Somali-Issa and Afar also poses a serious threat to the security of the Djibouti state in the 1990s. See Fenet (1983). Mohamed Salih (1999) mentions that of the 350,000 Djibouti inhabitants, 35% are Afar and 65% Somali, the number of Somali rising because of recent refugee flows from Somalia/Somaliland caused by the civil war. However, these 'sub-cases' of the Somali problem go beyond the scope of this book and must await another, separate study. The analysis of Somali state formation/state collapse in this book focuses on the state(s) of Somalia/Somaliland.

21 British anthropologist I. M. Lewis wrote extensively about the Somali clan system in: *A Pastoral Democracy* (1961), *A History of Somaliland* (1965), and *Blood and Bone* (1994) where selected articles from four decades are collected in one book.

22 I rely here on fieldwork in Hartisheik, Ethiopia, in January – May 1991 and refer to Bryden, (1994).

litical coalitions are concluded. Members are united "in joint responsibility towards outsiders" (Adam, 1995: p.20). These outsiders can be lineages within the same clan family or lineages – on the *diya*-paying level – from other clan families. For the settled communities in the South, however, 'joint responsibility towards outsiders' operates largely at the village level rather than at the *diya*-paying level.

In political analysis one tends to conceptualize the clan system from the clan downward to the extended family. This is because the clan and sub-clan levels of clan segmentation are the most important indicators of political identification. Diagram 1 shows the clan affiliation of contemporary Somali political/military factions, such as that of the SSDF (Somali Salvation Democratic Front), located in the clan structure as the *Darod, Harti, Majertain*. The diagram also points to the clan support for recent state-formation processes that can be identified on the level of the clan family (such as the Isaq in the case of Somaliland) or the sub-clan (such as the Gadabuursi in the case of Somaliland). Nevertheless, political division can also extend further down to the *diya*-paying level, such as in the case of the Dulbahante lineages in their divided loyalty to the Somaliland and the Puntland state, respectively.[23]

Traditional Clan Territories

The original territorial distribution of the Somali clans has been transformed during recent decades and is no longer as distinct as it was at the end of the 19th century. Still, in the contemporary political setting clans do claim specific territories, which refer back to traditional rights of access and control (see map 3).

The Sab, or Rewin,[24] with their main sub-groups Digil and Mirifle, are cultivators who live in settled communities in the inter-riverine areas between the

---

23 These remarks anticipate the discussion of the contemporary political situation in Somalia in chapter 7. As my intention is to outline the clan system not in a strictly anthropological manner but in respect to its repercussions on Somali politics I find it useful to note already here the linkages between clan affiliation, territory and contemporary political developments.

24 In the literature, the Rewin are mostly called Rahanweyn. In the Southern Somali language the settled agricultural people call themselves Rewin, whereas in the Northern Somali language they are called Rahanweyn. According to Helander (1997), the first term refers to the claimed ancestor of all Rewin clans, a certain Ma'ad or Mohammed Reewin whereas the second term refers to the tendency of the clan to integrate/adopt members of other clans, where '*raxan*' means crowd and '*weyn*' means big.

Shabelle and the Juba River. Their major town is Baidoa. The pastoral clans, the Samale, also have distinct territories, which are geographically defined by water sources, and pastureland that has been under customary use by particular clans at particular times of the year. The major cleavage within the Samale pastoral group (Mukhtar, 1997) is that between the Irir and the Darod (diagram 1). The Irir consists of the Hawiye, Dir and Isaq sub-clans, which are linked together by historical and blood ties.

The most widely spread clan family is the Darod. Their area stretches from the central Western Somali region, the Ogaden and Haud areas in today's Ethiopia, up through the Northeast right into the tip of the Horn. They are also found West of the Juba River in the pastoral area, which extends into Kenya's Northeastern district. The towns in these areas are Bossasso (Darod/Majertain), Gode (Darod/Ogaden) and Galcaio (half Darod/Majertain, half Hawiye).

One of the major sub-clans in the Darod clan-family is the Harti, subdivided into the Majertain, located in the Northeastern region, and the Dulbahante and Warsangeli located West of the Majertain, adjoining Isaq territory. Some of the Dulbahante and Warsangeli clans have strong linkages and intermarry with Isaq sub-clans, particularly in the Erigavo area.[25] Other Darod clans are the Ogaden, who inhabit the Western part of the Somali region in the Horn, which lies in Ethiopia. The Marehan clans are located across the Ethiopian-Somali border in an enclave, between the Ogaden and the Hawiye in the central region. The Bartire and Jidwaaq live in the Jijiga area linking them to the Gadabuursi and Isaq.

Turning to the Irir sub-groups, the Hawiye are situated mainly in the central Somali region, East and South of the Rewin. On the Eastern side they adjoin the Majertain (Darod), on the Northern side just before the Ethiopian-Somali border they adjoin the Marehan (Darod). Like the Darod, the Hawiye also live in territory West of the Juba, which extends into today's Kenya. The capital Mogadishu is considered to be in Hawiye land.

The Hawiye are split into Habr Gedir, whose territory stretches from Galcaio to Beled Weyne; the Hawaadle Southwest of Beled Weyne; the Abgaal and Murursade, located in and around Mogadishu and other lineages.

The Dir clans (diagram 1: Issa, Gadabuursi and Biyamale) are mainly concentrated in the Western part of the Northern region as well as in a few smaller enclaves in the Southern coastal areas around Merca and again South of Brava.

---

25 The Dulbahante are closely linked to the Habr Jaalo/Isaq, and the Warsangeli to the Habr Yonis/Isaq.

It has been suggested to me that neither the Issa nor the Gadabuursi or Biyamale clans feel strongly about a common Dir descent. In the literature, however, they are subsumed under the Dir clan family. The Issa occupy the Southern part of today's Djibouti including Djibouti town; further eastward, into Ethiopia, the area up to Dire-Dawa; and the Northwestern tip of what is today Somaliland, where the coastal town Zeila is situated. The Gadabuursi live in the adjacent territory to the South in Somaliland, with Borama as their major town, and across into Ethiopia. The Biyamale are found in the Southern coastal region (see map 3).

The Isaq inhabit the Northwestern region, where Hargeisa, today's capital of Somaliland, and the harbor town Berbera are both located. Another Isaq town is Burao. Isaq territory extends into the Haud plains of Ethiopia.

The major Isaq clans are the Habr Awal, around Hargeisa; Habr Yonis, South of Burao and along the Dulbahante/Warsangeli (Darod) territory in the East; Habr Jaalo, East of Berbera and Burao; and the smaller Eidegalla and Arab South/Southeast of Hargeisa.

The Rewin clan is divided into two branches, the Digil and the Mirifle (Mukhtar and Kusow, 1993). The Mirifle are settled around the central and Western inter-riverine region and are further divided into two main groups, the Sagaal (the nine) and the Siyeed (the eight). The Digil are divided into seven clans known as the Toddobadi aw Dighil, including Geledi, Tunni, Jiido, Garre, Dabarre. As Mukhtar and Kusow (1993, p.6) illustrate, there are also, associated with the Digil/Mirifle clan structure:

> Groups with more Asiatic or Negroid features within the *Dighil/Mirifle* clans, among which are the *Banadiris*, the *Jareer* and the *Bajunis*, mostly merchants, fishermen, hunting and cultivators, who inhabit the coastal strip (Banadir) on the banks of Jubba and Shabelle valleys and the Southern Islands of the Indian Ocean.

Influence of Migration Patterns on Clan Distribution

The geographical allocation underlying the clan structure as presented above reflects the strongholds and the traditional locations of the different Somali clans. However, clan distribution underwent transformation during the last four decades. People have always traveled and settled elsewhere for business or for education, or have migrated to other areas within and outside the Horn. Marriage into another clan sometimes also involves migration. Furthermore, there have been larger-scale factors that have altered the territorial distribution of clan-families since independence in 1960.

Firstly, there was a wave of migration to Mogadishu on the eve of independence in 1960. Even before independence, a civil servant stratum had developed in Mogadishu, which accommodated members of different clans. Mogadishu was also the center of the Somali modern educational system, hosting the only national university, the teacher-training center and several vocational training institutes. Bilateral and multilateral foreign aid organizations, including UN agencies and numerous non-governmental organizations working in Somalia, had their headquarters in the capital and attracted Somali as counterparts. Mogadishu underwent a rapid urban growth, its population increasing from 121,000 in 1963 to 223,000 in 1970 and more than 1 million in 1980 (Kaplan, 1969: p.58; Marchal, 1996: p.25). During the 1970s Mogadishu became a multi-clan town where it was impossible to identify one district with one clan (Marchal, 1996).

Secondly, during the 1973/75 *Dabadheer* drought and the subsequent bad years at the end of the 1970s and first half of the 1980s, life for pastoralists in the countryside became increasingly difficult. More than 100,000 nomadic drought-victims were resettled in the inter-riverine areas or on the coast, imposing on them an adaptation to the lifestyle of farmers or of fishermen.[26] These resettlement programs were far from successful. Nevertheless, they had lasting implications for internal migration of nomadic/pastoral clans into the territory of the Rewin people and the coastal communities. Once the climatic conditions had improved, the heads of the nomadic families moved back to their pastures while women and children often stayed behind in the settlements. Both through the resettlement programs and through independent migration, many pastoralists moved to environmentally more secure and promising areas in the South.

As the drought intensified the crisis of the pastoral economy pastoralists began to search for better economic conditions in towns. Again, Mogadishu proved attractive, particularly to young male pastoralists. The economic and infrastructure decay of local towns and big villages with regard to public services and general living conditions meant that everybody wanted to go to the capital city.[27] Once there, the pastoralists linked up with their kinsmen. By the mid-1980s, however, life in Mogadishu had also changed, as a result of cuts in public services related to IMF programs, and the increasing corruption and

---

26 Janzen (1984); of particular interest here is map no.5 "Nomadenansiedlungen, Ausbildungszentren für Nomaden und Flüchtlingslager".
27 Research experience in 1986.

mismanagement of food-aid distribution under an increasingly repressive regime.

The newcomers affected this urban geography not so much in the center of the town but surely in its peripheries. These new settlers were reinforcing this process as they started to meet in the coffee places owned by their kinsmen, to buy from the shops belonging to their clan and so on (Marchal, 1996: p.40).

Thirdly, internal migration in the Somali region was exacerbated by the refugee crisis, which developed after the defeat of Somalia in the 1977/78 Somali-Ethiopian war (the Ogaden war). The political aim of this war was to incorporate the Somali inhabited areas of Southern Ethiopia into the Somali state (Brons, 1990). These were mainly Darod territories, although Isaq and Dir in the Jijiga/Haud areas, and Hawiye and Oromo in the Southwestern areas were also affected. The Somali response to the war differed from clan to clan and from community to community (Brons, Doornbos and Mohamed Salih, 1995). Most ethnic Somali fled across the border from Ethiopia into Somalia; some stayed behind in their hometowns and territories. Again, family security strategies often dictated that wives and children should be safely looked after in refugee-camps while the men continued fighting, trading or herding, crossing back and forth over international borders and frontlines.

Most of the Somali refugees arriving in Somalia came from the Darod clan-family. The first refugee-camps were opened in 1979, among them the Qorioley camps in the Lower Shabelle region with a refugee population of 68,000.[28] More camps followed in the early 1980s. Of these, twelve were located in the South on the Juba River at Luuq and Garba Harre, with a population of 453,500. Four on the Shabelle river at Jalalagsi, and eight at Beled Weyne, with a total population of 378,500; and nine in the Northwest around Hargeisa and Borama, with a population of 395,500.[29] In 1981, the Somali government estimated that 1.3 million refugees were living in camps, with a further 200,000 scattered in cities and towns. These figures were almost certainly inflated, however, in order to receive more food aid from international donors which then could be diverted to other drought victims, to local markets or to army barracks (Brons et al., 1993).

---

28 The author worked and conducted research in one of the Qorioley refugee-camps from March to October 1986.

29 Sources: Janzen (1984); for the refugee population figures National Geographic (1981); for the number of camps and locations, various UNHCR reports.

What is important in the context of internal migration is that the pattern of pastoral population moving into agricultural areas continued and intensified. Through drought-related pastoral migration into Southern fertile areas, and war/refugee-related migration, pastoralists predominantly from the Darod clan-family settled in the fertile South, the Rewin territories, and in the few cultivable Isaq areas in the Northwest. In a few cases the local economy of refugee-camp areas boomed due to an improvement of infrastructure, an influx of food-aid, increased numbers of (often international) medical staff in local towns and the purchasing power and consumer demands of huge refugee populations.[30] Nevertheless, the dominant perception among the local population was that they received unequal treatment in comparison to the refugees[31] particularly when parcels of land began to be distributed to refugees for cultivation.[32] The local Southern (Rewin/Hawiye) and Northern (Isaq) population felt unequally treated compared to the refugees, a perception that was explained by congruent clan affiliation of the government leadership and the refugee population.

The various migration waves of Darod clan-family members into the resource-rich territories of other clans in both the South and the North since the early 1970s, and Darod occupation of land belonging to other clans, which was backed by the Darod-dominated government, led increasingly to conflict. As will be shown in chapter 7, the land issue was one of the main factors motivating political opposition in the early 1980s. Immigrant occupation of land is still one of the major causes of ongoing conflict in Southern Somalia today.

Variation and Flexibility within the Clan System

There is a fundamental difference in the way that the settled agro-pastoral communities of the inter-riverine areas and the pastoral clans perceive clan-affiliation or, in other words, a difference in the level of importance of patri-

---

30 I refer here to the case of Qorioley, where a small town of a few thousand inhabitants was joined by a refugee population of almost 70,000. In 1986, Qorioley was a big vibrant market place.

31 "One unforeseen outcome of these policies and the international response was that the in-camp population began to be better off than the national rural population in terms of health services, food, and water supply and lately in terms of education as well." Wood (1984: p.64).

32 Information during research in 1986.

lineal descent for the structuring of their socio-political and economic reality. For the pastoral clans, the Samale, the primary perception of social reality is constructed along patrilineal clan affiliation as it defines the rights, duties and securities of people in the social, political and economic sphere.

For the settled communities, the Sab in the Southern region, the importance of clan structure must be seen in relation to the importance of the village. People are attached to the land or territory that they inhabit. Territorial affiliation is reflected in the names of sub-clans such as *Reer Bay* (people of the Bay), *Reer Dhooboy* (people of the *Dhooboy*), *Reer Ghedo* (people of the other side of the Juba river), *Reer Maanyo* (people of the sea) (Mukhtar, 1997: p.49). In that sense, clan and territorial location often overlaps. Helander (1997: pp.138-40) provides a comprehensive account of the significance of village and clan among the Rewin, in particular the Hubeer clan.

The importance of clanship for the *Rahanweyn* is limited to a few important functions. It provides members with an overall security in times of conflict, and it provides a system for handling blood-compensation. However, beyond that, clanship is not the chief regulatory principle of social affairs that it generally tends to be in other parts of Somalia. A *Rahanweyn* individual will primarily turn to his or her village for support in everyday affairs. It is also the village that seems to provide people with a sense of identity. It is within the mixed-clan environment of a village or town that a person's status and prestige is settled by one's ability to live up to the obligations that are imposed in lateral networks for labor sharing and other forms of co-operation.

The two categories of village and clan may overlap. Although the larger terrain in which a village is located is prescribed as belonging to certain clans, land and other agricultural assets are linked to the village rather than to the clan. Most large villages and small towns host settlers from different clans and frequently also from non-related clans. There is also a custom among the Rewin to integrate newcomers into Rewin clan structure, the so-called *sheegat* system.[33] A basically open clan system offers security to inter-marrying members of other clans in the form of access to cultivable land (see Lewis, 1965: p.13) or personal safety and freedom from persecution. This characteristic of the settled Somali communities explains the meaning of the name given to the Rewin by the pastoral groups – *Rahanweyn,* literally the large crowd. This refers to

---

33 More about the '*sheegat*' phenomenon below.

the various male clan-affiliates that have been integrated into the Rewin clan structure (Lewis, 1965: p.13-14).

For the pastoral Somali marriage was usually conducted outside the primary lineage and very often outside the clan itself. Mohamed-Abdi Mohamed (1997) suggests that a distance of seven to ten degrees of kinship between two prospective spouses is ideal. Lewis (1994: p.51), claims that a transformation took place due to the civil war experiences:

> ... in areas formerly characterized by clan heterogeneity, with people of different clans living together harmoniously and inter-marrying, marriage outside one's own clan became the exception rather than, as formerly, the rule. Indeed, in the devastated capital, Mogadishu, women who had married outside their own clan found themselves at a serious disadvantage, they and their children being disowned and left unprotected by both sets of kin. Insecurity required maximum clan solidarity, including now clan endogamy rather than exogamy.

For the settled agro-pastoral Rewin clan in the South, traditional marriages are mostly conducted within the village, within the primary lineage or even the extended family. While patrilateral parallel cousin marriage is not considered desirable by pastoral Somali and is almost considered incest, it is preferred and is very common among the settled Somali clans in the inter-riverine areas.[34]

Although the Somali clan system is organized through patrilineal descent *(tol)* and political life is dominated by it, Somali society does recognize linkages between clans based on other principles. There are three important non-patrilineal clan relations:

1 *Hidid*, referring to the significance of matrilineal family;
2 *Sheegat*, referring to the incorporation of smaller clans into stronger ones; and
3 *Gosha*, referring to the adoption of lineage-identity by originally non-Somali groups.

In the pre civil-war period, intermarriage between different clans was frequent (Lewis, 1994). Marriage in the pastoral setting established relationships between lineages, laying a basis for general co-operation and opportunities to secure preference in employment or in trade. This encourages a wide spread of affinal ties. Often, the basis of lineage coalition is the husband's lineage in rela-

---

34 Lewis (1994: p. 52); Merryman (1996). The role of marriage within the Somali clan-structure is elaborated below.

tion to his wife's father's lineage. Women retain contact with their natal families throughout their lives, and the matrilineal connection provides social and
economic ties of support in times of crisis although, in the political realm,
patrilineal descent remains the decisive factor. Nevertheless, marital linkages
to other clans are important political instruments for peace making.

In peacemaking and the settlement of disputes between hostile lineages,
affines are regarded as ideal mediators and often sent on peace-making
deputations because of their dual affiliation. Here they join with 'men of religion', who whatever their lineage, are regarded ideally as neutral in lineage
politics (Lewis, 1994: p.48-49).

The practices of polygamy increase the flexibility of the clan system. Also children of a divorced couple remain members of a wider network of relatives. Although inter-clan marriage is no longer common because of the extreme
politicization of clan affiliation and the rise of clan-related violence, women
still play a role in narrowing clan differences.[35]

As noted above, the clan system includes *sheegat* relations (*sheeganaya*, literally 'I call', 'I tell', 'I claim') where small or weak clans relate to bigger,
stronger clans by genealogically submitting themselves to the forefather of the
more powerful clan, that is, calling this forefather their own (Schlee, 1995).
Adoption of members of other clans is specific to the Rewin clans (Helander,
1997), with adopted members tending to become fully integrated into their
host communities.

Most *sheegat*-arrangements derive from marriage whereby the man mar-
ries into the clan of his bride and adopts her father's clan affiliation. New
sheegat members of the clan are obliged to contribute to *diya*-payment, for being a member of the *diya*-paying group is a condition for gaining rights of access to farmland. Unlike pastoral marriage relations where both husband and
wife remain members of their own lineage (in the case of the wife, her father's
lineage), marriage within and into the Rewin clan enables full clan integration
for both men and women. It is, however, difficult to tell "at what stage these
changes shift from being a matter of political convenience into being regarded
as an integrated aspect of personal identity" (ibid.: p.137). Ties to the original
clan are maintained in the context of inheritance claims, and sometimes also
in *diya*-payment demands. And for some generations at least, children learn
their 'real' genealogy rather than that of the host-clan.

---

35 See Olsson (1994: pp.73-75); Gassem (1994; particularly p.vi-vii).

Gosha[36] describes the practice in Southern Somalia in which ex-slaves of Somali landowners identify with the clan of their former masters and genealogically relate to this clan rather than to their own original (East-African) tribe. This is reflected, for example, in their settlement pattern. Only when intra-clan conflict occurs is reference made to the original ancestor. The contemporary generations of the *Gosha* want to be identified within the Somali clan system and aim at full integration and acceptance as Somali (Besteman, 1995).

CLAN, CONFLICT AND RECONCILIATION

At all levels of lineage segmentation, alliances (*heer* contracts) can be made and splits occur. In this context, Adam (1995) speaks of "series of concentric and interconnected circles, with kaleidoscopic and diffuse attachments". Conflict mainly occurs between *diya*-paying groups within one clan or between two clans. Positive and negative relations interweave the Somali clan system, which is used dynamically by adapting alliances to different circumstances in a given setting. It is also important to differentiate between types of conflict. Conflict between pastoral clans mostly occurs over control of grazing territories, problems with the common exploitation of water sources, particularly deep wells, and criminal activities such as looting of livestock. Conflicts in areas where agro-pastoralists and farmers meet tend to involve land disputes, infringement of grazing reserves, a destruction of parts of the harvest by livestock, and occupation of (possibly abandoned) farmland.[37] Finally there are (contemporary) political conflicts which are often intertwined with clan conflict over resources, sometimes refer to historically transmitted traditional mistrust, suspicion or stories of betrayal, or simply exploit the common conceptualization of socio-political bonding along clan allegiance for purely political purposes. Clan affiliation is used as a tool in politics for mobilizing sup-

---

36 Besteman (1995: p.44): "Gosha is glossed as 'dense jungle' and denotes the forested banks of the Jubba River stretching from above Kismayo to below Saakow. The geographical term gosha has been extended to refer to the people who live in the Gosha."

37 Conflict over the rightful occupation and usage of pasture- or farmland is often rooted in contradictions between customary rights and claims based on state policy or laws. The civil war caused major displacement throughout the region and thereby further complicated claims from different sides. Allocation of land to refugees and/or internally displaced for camp-sites and for farming/cultivation is yet another factor which may lead to conflict.

port. This can occur at the highest level of clan-family, such as Isaq against Darod. But, it is just as likely to occur at almost any other level of segmentation (see diagram 1).[38] In other clans similar situations can be observed.

For the most common types of conflict, an *ad hoc* meeting of clan elders, the so-called *shir*-council, is called in order to solve disputes, decide on criminal accusations, or end violent conflict between rival clans. In pre-state/stateless Somali society the informal *shir*-council is considered the fundamental institution of government (Lewis, 1961: pp.198-99).

The ad hoc council disposes of the collective business of a group. *Heer* contracts are promulgated within *diya*-paying groups and between them, or they are rescinded; peace treaties are made, the decision to unite against another group is taken and attack planned with the appointment of a battle leader; all these and other matters are dealt with by the *shir*. Similarly, councils apportion and collect compensation received by, or due from a lineage. They sometimes arrange also for the settlement of debts incurred collectively in trade. ... In the dry season, the construction and maintenance of wells and the regulation of watering are considered; and in all seasons movement to new grazing areas is debated.

However, it should be stressed that the *shir* is not an institution of continuous jurisdiction, but an *ad hoc* gathering responding to particular needs. In case of conflict, special committees are formed at *shir*-council meetings; they take up residence at the affected location until the conflict is solved, a compromise found, or a follow-up meeting agreed upon. These are called *guurti* and are considered the highest traditional authority. The *guurti* council of elders can be called at the local or regional level, but also – as happened in contemporary Somaliland (see chapter 8) – at the national level.

Sultans lead the clans and larger sub-clans. There are various titles in use in different regions of Somalia and at different levels of clan segmentation, such as *Ugaz, Garad, Sultan, Boqor, Malaq*. Depending on the type of conflict and the parties involved, the *guurti* include elders of sub-clans or *diya*-paying groups either from within one clan, or of different clans. In principle, the position of Sultan was hereditary in the lineage of its founder. As Lewis (1961: p.209) observes: "Succession is normally by primo-geniture, although the of-

---

38 Such as Hawiye-Habr Gedir against Hawiye-Abgaal, as in the case of the split between the political factions of Mohamed Farah Aideed and Ali Mahdi Mohamed during the first half of the 1990s, or Hawiye-Habr Gedir-Saleban against Hawiye-Habr Gedir-Ayr as in the case of the split within the Aideed faction that occurred in late 1998.

fice may be tied to a particular uterine group and the Sultan required to be born of a woman of a particular clan." Farah and Lewis (1993: p. 18) however, also give evidence of the relatively open but proscribed access to the position of a traditional leader:

> Membership of a strong group and inherited status may increase the influence and status of some aspiring elders. However, factors that determine successful leadership are generally open and attainable to potential candidates. Personal qualities and fortunes, including wealth, political acumen, strength and courage; cultural values such as expertise in traditional law and religious knowledge, generosity, fairness and impartiality, probity; seniority and skill in oral poetry and oral discourse in general, all constitute ideals that are associated with distinguished traditional leaders.

Somali conflict resolution mechanisms are embedded in the clan structure. Councils of elders are flexible in composition as well as in purpose and time framing. The type of conflict – be it of a political, economic, criminal or personal, intro-family nature – determines the composition of the council. Reconciliatory meetings may last for a few days, or for several months. Clan elders committees are established in response to conflict. Clan elders have neither conflict prevention mechanisms nor conflict resolution-enforcement instruments at their disposal.[39]

Conflicts over resources, over pasture/water in the nomadic setting, and over land in the rural setting, pose special challenges to the impartiality of clan-elders. Pastureland as such is not privately owned but grazing rights are allocated to clan lineages according to customary rights and seasonal conditions.[40] Water-wells or reservoirs, the so-called *berkas*, might have been built and controlled by wealthy families, but reciprocity in the granting of watering rights in times of crisis is an unwritten pastoral law.

In the Southern, agriculturally rich inter-riverine areas, the situation is rather different. There, elders became very much involved in land-tenure politics and are therefore not considered independent peace-seekers by all communities or clans (de Waal, 1994). The clan-elder is usually the village-elder and thus the local authority with regard to the adjudication of land disputes.

---

39 Lewis (1961: p.206) points out that a Sultan, the head of a clan family, has no emissaries or soldiers to enable him to enforce his rulings.

40 During the last decade changes have occurred involving privatisation of grazing land, fencing etc. For the Ethiopian-Somali region see Tilahun et al. (1994); for Somaliland/the Northwestern region see Warsame (forthcoming).

Clan-elders are often among the most influential landowners, making them personally more involved in conflicts than is the case with their nomadic counterparts.

Flexibility and Multitude of Somali Identities

Our characterization of Somali society and identity has emphasized the multiplicity and flexibility of identities, and has highlighted reconciliatory as well as conflict-prone aspects of this situation. Besides those identities discussed there are other forms of social identification which express flexibility in social exchange. In addition to clan it is economic and educational assets, age, gender and religious learning that define the social status of a Somali in his/her community. Age groups, for example, play an important role for both men and women in social and economic life, based, for instance, in neighborhood or school friendships.[41] And village communities create special bonds between people, including those of different lineage affiliation.

Identities, which derive from production patterns (pastoralism and sedentarism), religious identities and clan identities are basically distinct but do overlap. Members of specific clans, sub-clans or lineages usually belong to the same *tariiqa* and are involved in the same productive activity. However, individuals may refer to their paternal or maternal lineage network, to their neighborhood or village network, or education or gender-related network depending on the social setting and specific needs (Simons, 1995). Shaping and shifting coalitions is one integral factor of Somali social life, and the possibility for choice and adaptation is another. One can say that Somali society is a complex of interwoven and interdependent strands, in which (patrilineal) clan-affiliation is the dominant but not necessarily the decisive security network.

---

41 These aspects were stressed in interviews with Sadia Muse Ahmed and Amina Mahamoud Warsame in Addis Ababa, November 1997. See also Simons (1995).

CHAPTER 5

(In)Security Arrangements in *Stateless* Somali Society

In the previous chapter I described Somali society, highlighting the major divide between the settled and the pastoral population and the role of religion and clan. In this chapter I will elaborate on the various kinds of security arrangements that are rooted in the clan system, the village communities and in the Islamic and customary legal system. I will do this by asking how legal, social, economic and environmental security needs were met in the stateless Somali society. Where did political stability derive from and how was control of the use of force implemented before there was a Somali state? The social arrangements that provide security will be presented in terms of the analytic structure developed at the end of the theoretical discussion in chapter 1 (see p.68-71), specifically in the context of the *stateless* level of security provision. Chapter 6 will deal with the question of the extent to which the stateless security structure of Somali society was affected by the imposition of the colonial state.

I should emphasize the basically non-historical dimension of the three levels of security provision – (1) *sub-state/stateless*, (2) *state* and (3) *trans-state*. In this chapter I refer to the pre-colonial and in that sense to the *stateless* level of security provision, structures of provision of various dimensions of security in Somali society before the establishment of a Somali state. However, these structures did not disappear after the introduction of state institutions. *Stateless* thus refers to the non-state realm of security provision which, after the imposition of colonial rule and later after the formation of an independent Somali state in 1960, continued to afford non-state sources of security for Somali people.

First, however, we must tackle the question of whether the term 'stateless' can be justifiably attributed to the Somali people before (European) colonialism.[1]

Historical Reconsideration of Statelessness

Prior to colonial occupation, Somali society consisted of several nomadic groups organized along kinship lines: the Isaq, Dir, Hawiye and Darod clans. Somali clans occupied and used specific grazing grounds and water points, and controlled trading routes that crossed their territories. The agricultural communities along the rivers Shabelle and Juba were mostly organized as chiefdoms, with a strong sedentary and religious character. These communities, members of the larger Rewin clan family, were virtually surrounded by pastoral groups, and contact between these two groups was often characterized by conflict.

The coastal communities were heavily intermixed with Arab, Persian, Indian, Portugese and Swaheli merchants, some of whom intermarried with Somali people and, as mentioned above, appear in the clan-genealogy with their own clan names such as *Reer Xamar* (i.e. the people of Mogadishu). "Most coastal historians agree that the Banadir coast was the first Swahili settlement on the East African coast settled around the 9th and 10th centuries. ... The Swahili culture that evolved in this coast was the result of the contact between this Arab-Islamic civilization on the coast with the Bantu culture of the hinterland" (Kassim, 1995: p.30). (City)state formation took place in several locations in the Horn from about the 13th century onwards. These were mostly sultanates or emirates built around commercial centers and locations of religious learning, such as the ancient trading town of Harar and ports such as Zeila on the Red Sea and Brava and Mogadishu on the Indian Ocean (see map 1).

With regard to Mogadishu, which in Arab chronicles is addressed as the city of Islam, 'Dar al-Islam', Mukhtar (1995: p.7) quotes the 13th century Arab historian Ibn Battuta:

> The titles used by the rulers of Mogadishu and their assistants were either Arabic (e.g. *Sheikh*, head of a state; *Qadi*, judge; *Amir*, military leader) or Persian (e.g., *Wazir*, political assistant). From Ibn Battuta's account, we learn about the tremendous development of the Islamic judicial system, government, and educational institutions in the Somali sultanates of the Benadir coast, where a judiciary council – including the Qadi, the Wazir, the private secretary of the Sultan and four of the chief Amirs – sat weekly to hear complaints of the public. ... He reported also that Somali Muslim centers placed great importance on education.

---

1 At a conference in Leeds in September 1997, Nurrudin Farah argued that the Somali were not stateless before the establishment of European colonial states, but had city states from which the nomadic population remained excluded. He argued that the so-called 'people from the bush' were excluded from the power-centre Mogadishu and that this split within Somali society between the nomads outside and the urban dwellers inside the political power centre is one of the main causes of the present conflict. The nomads are on his view now reclaiming access to political power by occupying Mogadishu (Farah, 1997).

With an increasing Somali population, these towns began using Somali languages in the 15th and 16th century, but never completely lost their cultural heritage (Declich, 1995).

Other state-like political entities existed in the fertile Southern region. The Ajuran sultanate emerged in the Lower Shabelle area stretching up to the coast to Mogadishu. Lewis records:

> Under a hereditary dynasty, the Ajuran consolidated their position as the masters of the fertile reaches of the lower Shabelle basin and established a commercial connection with the port of Mogadishu where some of their own clansmen were also settled. The fortunes of this Ajuran Sultanate thus appear to have been closely linked with those of Mogadishu, and the Ajuran reached the summit of their power in the late fifteenth or early sixteenth century when Mogadishu was ruled by the Muzaffar dynasty, an aristocracy related to the Ajuran if not actually of Ajuran stock (Lewis, 1965: p.24).

A third case of (city) state formation in which Somali became involved was the Muslim sultanate of Ifat in the 13th and 14th century. This was located in the area around Adal, Harar and Zeila, bordering and eventually stretching into the Northwestern Somali region. Early in the 14th century, the Sultan of Ifat waged a war against Christian Abyssinia in which Somali apparently took part. Lewis (1965: p.25) observes:

> This crushing defeat, and Sa'd ad-Din's martyrdom, for his death soon came to be regarded in this light, took place in the reign of the Abyssinian Negus Yeshaq (1414-29) and it is in the songs celebrating his victories over the Muslims that the name 'Somali' is first recorded.

About 200 years later, in the 16th century, the Kingdom of Adal regained strength under Ahmed Ibrahim al-Ghazi, or Ahmed Gran (1506-1543). He attacked Abyssinia in a holy war and succeeded in penetrating northward up to Lake Tana, where his men were finally heavily defeated by Abyssinian troops supported by the Portugese. Somali, mostly from the Darod clan family, were involved as warriors (*waranleh*) (Lewis, 1965), although they never were fully integrated as subjects of the kingdom. According to Lewis (1961: p.207), "The state's existence was constantly threatened by its egalitarian Somali population." The role of the Somali in the Adal Kingdom is best characterized as that of religiously motivated mercenaries.

Other smaller Muslim sultanates existed along the Somali coast at about the same time, such as in the Northeastern Horn around Bossasso and in the Southern port towns of Merca and Brava. In these (city) states, the process of formation of political authority and institutions was originally led by (Arab,

Persian, Swaheli) Muslim immigrants who intermarried with the local Somali population and, in subsequent generations, built their own lineages which became integrated into the Somali clan structure. These are found in the Sab/ Digil/Tunni line of descent in Somali genealogy (see diagram 1).

Whether these early (city) states can indeed be considered Somali, or whether they were rather of a Somali-alien character, is a very delicate matter. This is especially so since the question of Somali identity and early history has now reached the point where marginalizing tendencies in the studies of Somali history are beginning to be openly discussed.[2] There are certain connotations to being a pure Somali, which means of nomadic descent from the Samale branch, with specific racial features such as soft hair, tall thin bodies and thin noses. The sedentary branch of Somali genealogy, the Sab – particularly the Digil/Tunni branch – have been considered to be of non-Somali or at least less-Somali origin (Besteman, 1995; Helander, 1996). These ideas are not a throwback to the distant past but are still relevant in contemporary Somali life, where it would still be almost impossible for a Samale-Somali girl to marry a Sab-Somali man.

What can be said about Somali involvement in the life of these early (city) states is that sedentary Somali, farmers, traders or craftsmen seem to have integrated quite easily into the emerging authority structure as new opportunities for improving economic security arose. The sedentary farming population in the Southern region, the Rewin had increasing economic contact with and involvement in the Benadir sultanates. Trading activities flourished between the villages and towns along the Juba and the ports of Mogadishu and Merca.[3] Again in the South, a vibrant Islamic history is recorded for the sedentary Somali populations. Somali Sheikhs are reported to have been influential citizens of these (city) states (Kassim, 1995). Religion provided social stability and a feeling of certainty and belonging. Some scholars argue that Islam was able to take firmer root in the South, promoting unity and harmony among the sedentary clans, whereas in the North, among the pastoral Somali, the Arab factor of *Asabiyyah* (tribal bonding) remained dominant, with its char-

---

2   See chapter 4 above. See also the proceedings of the International Somali Studies Association Meeting in Worcester, 1993: Adam and Ford (1997); Mohamed Salih and Wohlgemuth (1994a).

3   Mukhtar (1995: p.10) notes: "The hinterland towns and cities established a commercial network linking the ports to the markets of East Africa, Abyssinia, and as far as ports in the North. Among the most important inland market towns were Luq and Bardhere on the Jubba River; Sarman, Baydhowa (Baidoa), and Bur Hakaba in the central interriver plain; and Awdhegle and Afgoye on the lower Shabelle River."

acteristically divisive rather than unifying effects (Mukhtar, 1995). Although this interpretation remains speculative, it is true to this day that the sedentary Somali clans have an integrative approach towards clan affiliation and accord a high value to communal identity. The nomadic Somali clans, on the other hand, seem to have had looser and more sporadic ties with the early states as caravan traders or as (mercenary) warriors, as described above (p.117) in the case of Ahmed Gran.

In summary, political processes of (city) state formation took place in the Somali region before, and increasingly under, the influence of Muslim immigration and subsequent religious conversion. These developments emerged partly out of the need for political stability and order that arose out of booming economies with increasing commercial activity and production in towns such as Merca, Mogadishu, Zeila and Harar in the centuries before European colonial occupation.

In particular Somali coastal communities (such as *Rer Baraawe, Rer Xamar*) and to a lesser degree Somali farming communities were integrated into these (city) states and transformed in their inner structure and organization. The nomadic Somali were less involved in the politics, economy and social make-up of these sultanates or chiefdoms. Before the colonial period, there were no signs of a Somali state formation, which would have united the nomadic and sedentary populations under one political authority. If there was anything akin to permanent institutions, a relatively reliable control over the means of violence or a perception of territorial unity – in short the assets of a state in the Weberian understanding – it was limited to local (city) state formations. Pre-colonial Somali sedentary society cannot be characterized as entirely stateless. However, the (city) states were by nature localized; they rapidly dissolved as integrative political structures with the advent of and confrontation with European colonial occupation. With all this in mind, I would suggest that the sedentary Somali population could be considered as living partly in a proto-state and partly in a pre-state society, while pre-colonial nomadic Somali society can be considered stateless.

Relative Security-Providing Social Arrangements: The Stateless Level

When we look in the following paragraphs at legal, social, economic, environmental, political and military/physical security-providing arrangements, both, past and present social reality, are reflected in the presentation. At this point, however, it is not my ambition to examine for each case to what extent these various social arrangements from the pre-state or stateless period have survived into the present, post-(central) state times. Issues of survival, transformation and revival of pre-state/stateless security provision will recur throughout the analysis. My priority here lies in generally categorizing sources of security for Somali society, with a particular focus on women, traders and farmers, as they developed in the non-state situation.

LEGAL (IN)SECURITY

Both customary and *sharia* law are used in conflict resolution, encompassing legal issues deriving from resource-competition over land, pasture or water, family affairs, criminal offences and compensation payments. Customary law is deeply intertwined with the clan system in the sense that descent (*tol*) and contract (*heer*) complement each other in one security-providing structure within Somali society (Lewis, 1961; Schlee, 1995). *Heer* refers to accords between clans, sub-clans or lineages. It can be described as an unwritten but formal political contract including the statement of common responsibilities and norms of conduct as well as fixed penalties for crimes. Lewis once characterized *heer* as a sort of social contract, which did not lead to the establishment of a state (Lewis, 1961: p.3).

A fundamental difference between *sharia* and customary law lies in the point that, in the former, the perpetrator is personally held responsible, whereas, in the latter, the lineage as a whole takes over the responsibility for the committed crime. Blood money (*diya*) payment rests on the understanding that the clan compensates for a homicide committed by one of its members. The perception of collective responsibility often leads to acts of revenge that are in turn directed against a clan as a whole. This is a major factor in the dynamics of violence that unfolds in crisis situations. In pre-colonial times permanent legal courts headed by *Kadis* existed in villages and towns, whereas in the (pastoral) countryside, most legal affairs were handled by *wadaado* or by sheikhs (see chapter 4).

In examining the legal status of women in pre-state Somali society[4] I intend to focus on a few main issues: inheritance, marriage, divorce and custody over children of broken marriages. Some detail is useful at this point in preparation for the later analysis of Somali state policies in the context of the introduction

---

4 I am grateful to Sadia Muse Ahmed and Amina Mahamoud Warsame for their insights in these matters.

and implementation of the 1975 family law. In the resolution of family conflicts it is often difficult to recognize whether customary or *Sharia* law, or a
mixture of both, is being applied; sometimes a supposedly Islamic law turns
out to be Somali custom rather than a religious rule.

In pre-colonial times, daughters generally inherited half what sons received. Girls could not inherit camels or land. If a family had only daughters,
part of the heritage was given to the father's brother. With regard to marriage,
the legal union of the couple before a Sheikh gives the husband right over the
children born out of the union and children do not assume the lineage affiliation of their mother. In return for the anticipated wealth of children, the
man's lineage pays bride-wealth (*yarad*)[5] to the lineage or clan of the girl. This
payment is negotiated pursuant to customary law and claims for the return of
bride-wealth are outside the jurisdiction of Islamic courts. This situation is
different for the *meher* payment, which is legalized by a man of religion. *Meher*
usually comprises a certain number of livestock or money, which is promised
to the girl by her future husband's family as a sort of insurance. It is not paid
immediately but only in circumstances such as death of the husband or divorce initiated by the husband. It is only the *meher*, which can legally be
claimed by women before an Islamic Court.

Men had the power of initiating divorce under Islamic Law. Still, divorce
was not very frequent as customary law functioned as a parallel framework of
obligations in family matters.

The legal setting for women in stateless Somali society was manifested in an
unequal relation *vis-à-vis* men. However, under normal circumstances within
a marriage, women did have some possibilities for maneuver. Checks and balances were provided through the clan network: mistreating a woman who had
married into another clan, for instance, reflected badly on the male clan and
did not go unnoticed by either party. Similarly, women were protected from
rape and other form of externally committed violence.

SOCIAL (IN)SECURITY

Forms of social security, such as support to families in times of crisis, natural
disaster, drought, death of animals and harvest failure, derive from the *diya*-
paying unit within the Somali clan system. In a reciprocal, unwritten agree-

---

5   Somali terminology with regard to bride-wealth and other kinds of payments differs from region to region.

ment pastoralists give animals as a gift to hard-hit families, or offer their wells and pasture to them, in the expectation that, if the same should happen to them, help will be returned in the same way. Agreements over child-care are also handled at the level of the *diya*-paying unit or extended family. Children of drought-affected pastoralists may stay with their relatives in town for a couple of years, or even permanently, and town children can be sent out to their nomadic family during the rich rainy season (Lewis, 1961).

In the villages where agriculture or agro-pastoralism prevails, the village community or neighborhood assumes many social security functions. Material support in times of crisis, labor-sharing agreements in order most efficiently to cultivate and harvest the fields, and the village community provides other forms of co-operation. Clan affiliation as such plays a relatively insignificant role (Helander, 1996, 1997), except in legal affairs, such as inheritance or conflict management over grazing access, where people relate to the *diya*-paying unit as a support and conflict resolution framework.

There is another aspect to social security, beyond material support itself: the feeling of certainty or confidence, socio-political arrangements that give people the psychological comfort of belonging and identity. Village and lineage made up the socio-political context of identity before there was any idea of a Somali national identity. For the sedentary Somali, socio-psychological security derived from the village community, which combined common land, common labor and common worship, together securing the material and spiritual survival of the people.[6] Religious education by the Sheikhs of Koran schools played a significant role in socializing the young, thus laying the ground for an age-group solidarity among women as well as men across clan affiliation. Among the pastoral Somali, social obligations, status and prestige, and with these a sense of certainty of belonging, were all provided by the lineage. There is an interesting differentiation to be made here between patrilineal and matrilineal lineages. Whereas a man might present himself as strong, confident and self-assured towards his father's family, and derive his prestige and status from that affiliation, it is to the mother's side and particularly the mother's brother that he could turn for social support.[7]

---

6 Helander (1997) p.140: "Village life among the Rahanweyn tends to have ideals of its own, often influenced by and coached in an idiom of religion. Village life is dominated by principles of good neighbourliness and inter-clan solidarity rather than the assertion of clanship ties. In fact, in many settings of everyday life in a Rahanweyn village it would be considered rude to, at least openly, treat the members of one's own lineage differently than other villagers."

ECONOMIC (IN)SECURITY

Pastoral migration – in accordance with customary rules, in response to sea-sonal change, and as a coping strategy in periods of natural disaster – forms the cornerstone of pastoral economic security (Lewis, 1961). The pastoral clans are not directly attached to land. Economic security is reflected in the strength, the number and composition of the herd. Security can be threatened if access to grazing lands is restricted. However, in the original, nomadic production structure of the Samale, land itself had no value for the pastoral clans.[8] An-other aspect of economic security for pastoralists is access to local, regional and international markets. In pre-colonial times, this involved clan co-opera-tion, and as such could become a source of extreme insecurity when inter-clan relations were strained (Samatar, 1989; Markakis, 1989). The *abban* system, whereby the lineage of the guide of a caravan was the basis for the unhindered passage of people and merchandise through alien clan territory (for a commis-sion fee), generally shaped the security framework for trade.

With regard to agricultural production in the Southern region, economic security-patterns were centered on a village-oriented system of land-right al-location. The village orientation overlapped to a certain extent with clan af-filiation as the territory of a village mostly belonged to one particular clan. The history of migration and the practice of co-optation of newcomers or settlers from other clans, and inter-marriage relations – not only women who are in-tegrated in their husband's lineage, but also husbands finding refuge in their wife's lineages or families (Marchal, 1996), all, provided the settled Somali communities with a basically integrative, community- rather than clan-ori-ented approach to economic security patterns.

In order to lay the basis for an analysis of the land law policies of the Somali state in the 1970s and 1980s, I will briefly sketch the pre-colonial land alloca-

---

7   Mohamed, Mohamed-Abdi (1997: p.153): "In fact, a mans relationship with his father's side of the family (reer adeer) and the one with his mother's side (reer abti) are very different. When dealing with the paternal family, he will always have to show that he is strong, virile, ready to do anything to defend his clan; when dealing with the ma-ternal side, in particular, his uncle, his mother's brother, he will be able to let himself go, express his feelings and his doubts, or ask for advice. As far as his in-laws are con-cerned, he shows them respect and never reveals his problems."

8   Land speculation and occupation by 'nomadic' clans in the South followed the in-troduction of a plantation economy by the Italian colonisers. Since then it developed into a complete disruption of the original land-tenure tradition in the inter-riverine areas. More about land policies in chapter 7.

tion system in the South. The allocation of usufructuary rights on land was decided by the *duq*, the village headman, in consultation with the council of elders, the *aqiyaarta* (Menkhaus, 1996). However, once a plot was given to a family in the village, it usually stayed within that family. According to Menkhaus (ibid. p.137):

> [O]nce farming rights were issued to a villager for a specific plot, he was generally free to sharecrop, loan, sell, or give the land to others without first seeking the approval of the *aqiyaarta*, unless such a transaction involved individuals from outside the village. Customary land tenure also permitted the inheritance of land rights, which became the principal means of acquiring farmland.

There were three different types of agriculture practiced by the population living in the Juba river-valley: (1) irrigated riverbank farming (*jiimo*), primarily of vegetables, fruit bushes and trees; (2) flood-recession farming (*dhasheego*), including vegetables, sesame and maize; and (3) rain-fed cultivation. The *dhasheego* plots were distributed by the village elder in strips, from the edges to the center of the riverbanks, so that every family could continue cultivating with decreasing water levels. The variety of soil usage combined with two water sources – the river floods and rain – and a sophisticated canalization system made a variety of cultivation systems possible and gave relatively high food security throughout the year, even if one of the water-sources failed. Furthermore, there were many wild fruits and roots as well as fish from the river, which were available in harsh drought periods. The riverine farmers also built *bakaaros* where grain reserves were stored for times of crisis.

Another option for enhancing economic security was migration, which was quite common among the Rewin in the South (Helander 1996, 1997). This included migration of single members of a family to other villages in the wider region who, given the widespread and open clan network, could always rely on kinsmen for initial support. The *sheegat* of single persons has to be understood in this context. In times of severe crisis, such as war or drought, it also happened that a whole village migrated to another location.

Economic security patterns in stateless Somali society were thus as diverse as the land and the people themselves. Access to resources was organized in different ways in the nomadic and sedentary settings. The inter-riverine areas were relatively self-sufficient in food (Menkhaus, 1996), whilst for the pastoralists, exchange of goods with farmers, as well as trading and/or looting, played a more significant role (Lewis, 1961, 1994).

ENVIRONMENTAL (IN)SECURITY

In terms of environmental security, the arid and semi-arid climate of the Somali region poses particular problems of adaptation and sustainability. People dealt with that environment, in particular with their inland water resources, such as seasonal rivers and wells, with their coastal waters and fishing stocks and with the limited fertile soil. They applied adaptation mechanisms that guaranteed sustainability in as much as this was possible in the face of unpredictable natural threats to environmental security, such as drought or flooding. Neither overgrazing nor overfishing represented serious problems on the eve of colonial occupation.

POLITICAL (IN)SECURITY

Political (in)security is understood here in the sense of political (in)stability. In this context, the source of political authority and its transfer to subsequent generations of leadership are central. As we have seen, in pre-colonial times political authority within the communities lay with the elders and the traditional heads of clans and lineages, the Sultans (e.g. *Garad, Ugaz, Boqor, Malaq*). Clan elders dealt with legal issues and economic resource allocation as well as with political conflict. Various councils of elders, *guurti* or *aqiyaarta* reconciled conflicts within the village community or between pastoral lineages. These were the sources of political stability for the community or lineage.

In the pastoral setting, meetings of political decision-making bodies were generally open to every adult male member of the lineage/clan (Farah and Lewis, 1993). However, political weight was attributed to age, wealth, knowledge of customary and religious law and oral poetry. There were certain families, which continuously supplied the core leadership of clans or lineages, thus providing yet another aspect of relative political stability. Nonetheless, participation in *shir* meeting was flexible and composition of membership was adapted to the specific kind of conflict (e.g. over access to wells, raiding of livestock, homicide) as well as to the clan- or lineage-level of the parties involved (Lewis, 1961: p.240-65).

The political structure of the Southern sedentary community was, in comparison to the pastoral setting, much more permanent but still not rigidly institutionalized. With regard to access to political decision-making and holding of political office, the Rewin did not differentiate between agnates (*dhalad*, literally member by birth) and adopted members (*dhaqan*, literally member by culture) of the community (Helander, 1996). A difference which was noticed among the Hubeer, and which might also apply to other sections within the Rewin and other sedentary clans, was that between commoners (*boon*) and nobles (*bilis*) within the village. These categories were not clearly defined but seemed to make a differentiation between people from *gosha* or Boran-Oromo descent and other village inhabitants. The category commoner also included "destitute and marginalized remnants of other Rahanweyn clans" (Helander, 1996: p.51-52). The village leadership, the clan elder's council, was elected from the nobles.

Military/Physical (In)Security

Military/physical (in)security refers to (in)security deriving from those accorded the task of exercising and controlling violent means of coercion. In the pastoral society, it was mainly the young men, the warriors (*waranleh*) – who went out with the herds to far-away pastureland and became involved in violent conflicts at well-sites. They had the responsibility of controlling and defending clan-territory and wells; the age-related behavior expected of them by their lineage or wider family was to show strength and pride and to acquire or maintain honor in defending the lineage, if necessary to death. That is one reason why it was young men (*waranleh*) who were responsible for outbreaks of violence, for instance in raiding the livestock of other clans, looting animals, or attacking caravans which were passing through clan territory.

The elders of the clan or village and, as facilitators, the religious men, the *wadaado* and sheikhs, were considered responsible for mediating peace and thereby securing stability and protection in the local or regional setting after conflict had occurred. As noted earlier, there were no specific mechanisms for conflict prevention or for resolution enforcement, and conflict resolution always depended on the goodwill and/or respect of the warriors towards their clan-elders and the clergy.

Violence was not only used in defense of resources or in order to increase control over resources, but also as a way of claiming political strength and power, and thereby determining political status (Lewis, 1961: p.240). Among pastoral people, outbreak of violence became related to the clan and, as indicated above, conflict resolution and compensation was seen as the responsibility of the clan rather than the individual. As such, violence between various segments within or between clans had not only a protection component, but also a power-regulation component.

With regard to the settled Somali communities, their experience with violence was largely through their conflict-ridden relationships with surrounding pastoral groups. Pastoral groups subjected inter-riverine villages to repeated raids and attacks. The nature of pastoral society and the pastoralists' feeling of superiority over the farming communities were the main assets of pastoral Somali in relation to sedentary Somali who, in terms of military organization, were relatively weak and inexperienced. The general attitude towards violence seems to have been rather different within the settled communities, which consisted of conglomerations of clans who were dependent on co-operation and relatively unified in their common locality and religion (Helander, 1997). According to Lewis (1961: p.242), in his characterization of Northern Somali pastoral society, the specific pastoral attitude towards violence had two main roots:

> In these circumstances, the ease with which individuals and groups resort to violence within the Muslim community and contrary to the principles of Islam has to be viewed in the ecological context of acute competition for sparse resources, and in the abrogation of individual responsibility through group loyalties.

Hence, "acute competition for sparse resources" and "abrogation of individual responsibility through group loyalties" made up the main differences in relation to the other Somali, who lived in a socio-economic environment, which provided relative food security (Menkhaus, 1996) and a strong attachment to Islamic norms of social life. According to Helander (1997), it was the performance of the individual measured against norms of community support and co-operation, which determined status and prestige, rather than honor gained in inter-clan warfare. In sum, military security, or attitudes towards and control over the use of violence, was one of the dividing issues within Somali society.

The table on page 128 shows the results of our discussion of security arrangements of *stateless* Somali society, classified according to the model of relative security introduced in chapter 2.

The following chapters will elaborate on the second, *state*-level of (in)security provision, and partly also on the third, *trans-state* level. In the course of the analysis that follows, we will refer regularly to the non-state security arrangements indicated on the table by asking to what extent they were affected by state policies. We will also discuss how the stateless social order re-emerged and adapted to new political circumstances after the collapse of the state. In this way, the analysis will prepare the ground for the final discussion of state formation processes in post-1991 Somali society.

RELATIVE SECURITY PROVIDING SOCIAL ARRANGEMENTS (I)

Variations of (In)Security Levels of Security Provision	1 Legal	2 Social (Incl. Access to Education)	3 Economic (Incl. Food Security)	4 Environmental	5 Political (Stability and Conflict Resolution)	6 Military/Physical (Control of the Use of Force)
A PRE-STATE STATELESS	customary law; *sharia* law	support by *diya*-paying group prevalent for pastoral people; village and community support for sedentary people age groups; Koran schools	clan arrangements on pasture/water; village arrangements on land-right allocation; trade based on *abban*-system; local market exchange between pastoral and farming products; export of livestock and frankincense; limited local production and craftsmanship	pastoral adaptation: seasonal migration determined by availability of water/pasture); agricultural adaptation to soil variation: differing cultivation systems and crops; in crisis: *sheegat* migration	in the pastoral setting: non-institutionalized ad-hoc meetings of male members of concerned clans or lineages (*shir*); for conflict resolution and important political decisions calling-up of council of clan elders (*guurti*); in the sedentary setting: relatively more permanent council of village elders (*aqiyaarta*) social differentiation between nobles and commoners	pastoral setting: limited control of elders over young warriors =defenders of clan assets and honor; widespread traditional inter-/intra-clan fighting; sedentary setting: relatively more control over use of force within village communities; relatively defenseless in cases of attacks from outside (raids by nomads)

CHAPTER 6

From *Stateless* to *State* Society:
The Legacy of European Colonization

The onset of colonization initiated a shift from a partly *pre-state*, partly *stateless*, to a *state* society. It introduced new (in)security arrangements in the form of colonial state institutions, laws and policies, which challenged, complemented, transformed and/or marginalized those known before. The colonial state structures that were established in the various parts of the Somali region laid the foundation for the political (in)stability and (in)security of the future independent Somali state. The genesis of the idea of a Somali (nation) state emerged through anti-colonial opposition.

This chapter is divided into three parts, of which the first provides a chronology of political events during European colonization with an emphasis on territorial aspects. I refer in this part to all of the Somali-inhabited areas in the Horn (see map 1) and the way these were divided among the several colonial powers.

The second part presents an analysis of one early Somali anti-colonial attempt at state formation that was located in the Northeastern Somali region. The establishment of colonial rule gave rise to a reaction from certain parts of *stateless* Somali society in which mechanisms rooted in the nomadic socio-political context led to the formation of a political authority structure which, in some ways, showed *state* features. Here, Somali state formation is conceptualized neither within a nationalist framework (as an attempt to create a Somali nation-state), nor in terms of *de jure* state sovereignty (which, under colonial rule, did not lie with Somali political authorities). Rather, a *de facto* perspective is adopted, using the approach of the three main pillars, which are perceived as conditions for calling a social construct a *state* – (1) territory, (2) institutions, and (3) idea. I refer back to the Buzan-triangle as described in the introduction. The following questions are asked: (1) Did the Somali polities as described reflect an internally relatively integrated and defined territory? Was this territory accepted by external, neighboring political authorities? (2) Was institutionalization under way, particularly with regard to control over means of violence? (3) Did an idea of the state emerge, providing a bond of political identity? Further, referring to our distinction between bottom-up and top-down state formation dynamics, we will consider whether people within this

polity perceived the political authority as a relatively well-performing organization providing security (bottom-up dynamics), or as a leadership imposed
by force (top-down dynamics). The failure to transform the polity described
into an anti-colonial process of nation-state formation reveals contradictions
within the formulation of an idea of the Somali state. These are relevant in the
wider context of Somali nationalism both past and present.

The third part of the chapter then examines the impacts of these two political developments – the imposition of colonial rule in the Somali region and
the Somali anti-colonial response – on the overall security of Somali society,
taking military, economic, social and political aspects of (in)security into
account. In this part, I mainly refer to the two colonial territories that later, in
1960, formed the independent Somali state, namely the British Protectorate
Somaliland in the Northwest and Italian Somaliland in the central and Southern regions.[1] Finally, at the end of the chapter, I provide a summary of the
Somali state's colonial heritage on the eve of independence, using the categories of territory, institutions and idea.

Colonial Occupation of the Somali Region

Although several foreign powers showed interest in it during the 19th century,
the Somali region never played more than a secondary role for the powers involved in colonial occupation.

EGYPTIAN INTERESTS

It was Egypt, in co-operation with and supported by Great Britain, which first
aspired to secure access to the sources of the river Nile. Since one of these
sources was located in Ethiopia, at Lake Tana, the Egyptians decided upon a
strategy of encirclement (Rubenson, 1991: pp.288-410), and it was in line with
this strategy that, in 1869, they occupied the harbor towns of Zeila and Berbera

---

1   French Somaliland, today's Djibouti, the Northern Frontier District in the British
East-Africa Protectorate, in today's Kenya, and the Somali-inhabited areas in Southern
Ethiopia are referred to in the context of territorial partition of the Somali region, but
not in the analysis of the impact of the colonial state on Somali society's security arrangements. The reason for this is that the focus of the latter analysis lies on the Somali
state(s) and not on the Somali region as a whole.

on the Northern Somali coast. From 1875 to 1884, Egyptian rule was established further inland, including the trading center and religious place of learning Harar.[2]

Great Britain had signed a protection treaty with one of the Northern Somali clans as early as 1827 and had taken possession of Aden at about the same time. However, there were no permanent British representatives in the Northern Somali towns of Zeila and Berbera until 1839. The British post on the Somali coast became more interesting with the opening of the Suez Canal in 1868. In 1873, Khedive Ismail of Egypt was given administrative responsibility for the Red Sea and Indian Ocean coasts as far South as Mogadishu by the Sultan of Turkey.[3] By mid-1875, Britain and Egypt had sorted out their differences on the Egyptian presence in Berbera and Zeila, albeit at considerable expense to Khedive Ismail – an expense that he hoped to recover many times over through exploitation of the hinterland, starting with the commercial center of Harar (Rubenson, 1991: p.310). At that time, British interests did not conflict with the Egyptian presence in the same area (Lewis, 1965). Indeed, in 1877, Britain signed a treaty in Alexandria, which guaranteed privileged status to British citizens all along the coast, and in the Harar hinterland (Petrides, 1983: p.23). It was only after the British occupation of Egypt in 1882, and the Mahdist uprising in Anglo-Egyptian occupied Sudan, that the Egyptians withdrew from their Somali territories and a power vacuum was created. This motivated the British and the Ethiopians to claim the territory as being under their jurisdiction. In 1884 and 1886, the British government signed protection treaties with the Issa, Gadabuursi, and Isaq sub-clans Garhajis, Habr Jaalo and Habr

---

2 In this strategic context, other advances on Somali territory were planned. "…[Khedive Ismail] was launching his grand attempt to gain control over all territory between the Nile and the Indian Ocean. … The orders issued on 17 and 18 September 1875 included instructions to Gordon Pasha to open a route from Albert Nyanza and Victoria to the mouth of the Juba River on the Indian Ocean; to McKillop Pasha to sail for the Juba, establish a permanent military colony there, explore the coast and the river, and advance some detachments into the hinterland; to Radwan Pasha and Abd al-Razik Bey to accompany McKillop and facilitate his mission; to Gamali Pasha to maintain peace and order at Berbera; …" As things turned out, Gordon found it impossible to undertake the march to the coast, and McKillop had to be recalled from Kismayu and Brava when the British government decided to uphold the claims of the Sultan of Zanzibar to the Benadir coast. (Rubenson, 1991: p.317).

3 After the Turkish occupation of Egypt in 1518 the Red Sea coast was claimed by the Ottoman Empire. In 1558, small Turkish detachments landed at Massawa and Zeila (Petrides, 1983).

Awal (Lewis, 1965: p.46), and in July 1887 the Protectorate of British Somaliland was officially inaugurated.

Ethiopia, Britain and France: Dividing Somali Territory

The Ethiopian claim to Somali territory was officially raised by Emperor Menelik in the so-called Circular Letter of 1891 (Rubenson, 1991: p.316). In the letter, large parts of Somali territory, including the lands of Somali clans who had signed protection treaties with Britain and France, were theoretically included in Ethiopian territory. Earlier, in 1887, Abyssinian forces had conquered the town of Harar, and Ras Makonnen[4] had been appointed governor. From Harar, Ras Makonnen's forces sporadically raided the Northern Somali lands of the Issa, Gadabuursi and Habr Awal, and the land of the Somali of the Haud and Ogaden to the East and Southeast (Lewis, 1965: p.55).

Ethiopia did not control these Somali territories permanently – it made its presence felt in Jijiga town but not further South or East (Echete, 1988). But although the Ethiopian presence consisted only of infrequent raids on livestock and intermittent fighting with Somali nomads, nonetheless, Ethiopia's territorial claims conflicted with those not only of Britain but also of France.

The French presence in the region dated back to 1859, when they obtained the cession of the port of Obok. However, it was not until 1881, when a French-Ethiopian trading company was initiated in Obok, that the French made their presence felt (Lewis, 1965: p.41). An increasing Anglo-French rivalry, coupled with the need for a secure stopover seaport on the way to France's new acquisitions in Madagascar and China, made a permanent French presence indispensable. In that sense, a major factor motivating both France and Britain to establish a protectorate or colony in the Northern Somali region was their imperialist competitiveness. Finally, in 1888, an Anglo-French agreement was reached which defined the borders between the two protectorates as lying between Zeila and Djibouti.

---

4   Ras Makonnen was the cousin of Emperor Menelik (who was then still King of Shoa), and the father of the later Emperor Haile Selassie.

THE ITALIAN BLUEPRINT FOR THE SOMALI REGION

Until 1892, the Sultan of Zanzibar occupied the Southern Benadir region, including the ports of Brava, Merca and Mogadishu, but subcontracted it to the Imperial British East Africa Company (Sheik-Abdi, 1993). By 1888, Italian trading companies had begun to sign protection treaties with Somali clans along the Indian Ocean coast – the Majertain Sultans of Obbia and Alula. In 1892, Italian trading companies took over the rights to exploit and administer the Zanzibari possessions at the Benadir coast, while the British kept the area South of the River Juba, Jubaland, which remained part of the British East Africa Protectorate until 1924.

The Italian interest in the Somali Indian Ocean coast and the British willingness to accept Italian colonial activity in this area – in contrast to their attitude about a decade earlier with regard to Egyptian Khedive Ismail's plans – have to be seen in a broader regional context. Emperor Yohannis of Ethiopia disputed the Egyptian possessions in the area of Bogos, including the port of Massawa (in today's Eritrea). When the Mahdist war in Sudan forced the Egyptian rulers to give up these territories, similar to their possessions in the Somali Zeila/Berbera/Harar triangle in 1884, a power vacuum was created. The British, who had by then occupied Egypt, claimed the right to decide what should be done with both these areas. Although King Menelik of Shoa was able successfully to occupy the Harar area in 1887, and the adjacent Somali areas of the Haud and Ogaden, and Southern regions up to Luuq, in the early 1890s, Massawa, was not to fall into Ethiopian hands. Britain pledged support to the Italians to occupy Massawa, which they "allegedly did not want to leave to the barbarians (read Abyssinians [Ethiopians]) or to a rival power (read France)" (Rubenson, 1991: p.362). In 1885, therefore, the Italians landed at Massawa and took over the former Egyptian possessions.[5]

It was against a background of power rivalry between King Yohannis of Tigrai, who then held the title of King of Kings / Emperor of Ethiopia, and King Menelik of Shoa, and in the context of Mahdist attacks into Northern Ethiopian territory and the violent spread of Italian control in the ex-Egyptian possessions, that King Menelik began negotiations with Italy which finally led to the Treaty of Wichale or Ucciali. By the time the treaty was signed, in 1889, Yohannis had died and Menelik had obtained the title King of Kings, becoming the new Emperor of Ethiopia. These developments put him in a position of

---

5   Soon afterwards, in 1886, followed the battle of *Dogali*, at which Italian forces were first defeated by Abyssinia. See: Beyene et al. (1988).

strength. In the Amharic reading of the treaty, Menelik "*could, had the right or authority to*, request the good offices of the Italian government in matters of foreign relations, if or when he so wanted" (Rubenson, 1991: p.386). The Italians, however, claimed to have acquired a protectorate over Ethiopia. Diplomatic infighting over this issue (one of many at the Berlin Conference of 1884/85), continued throughout the first half of the 1890s (ibid.: pp.389-98). It was this that led Emperor Menelik to write the Circular Letter of 1891. In the letter he characterized Ethiopia as "a Christian island surrounded by a sea of pagans" and claimed as Ethiopian territories, not the Italian occupations in the North, but Southern areas stretching far into Somali territory, including French and British occupied areas. The Italians continued to promote their claim of a *de jure* Italian protectorate over Ethiopia, and acted as if there was a *de facto* protectorate. Without Menelik's knowledge, they signed treaties with Britain in 1891 and 1894 over the British-Italian borders. Finally, Emperor Menelik's termination of the Wichale treaty in 1894 and Italy's persistence in its claims led to the battle of Adwa in 1896. The Ethiopian troops were victorious and proved that a unified Ethiopian state was a reality to be reckoned with.[6] The defeat left Italy humiliated as an imperial European power.

The importance of this historical background lies in the impact, which the Italian vision of controlling the whole of Ethiopia from the Red Sea coast of Eritrea to the Indian Ocean had on its policy in the Somali territories. It was this vision that motivated Italian advances on the Somali Indian Ocean coast in the first place; after the defeat of Adwa in 1896, the Somali possessions became even more important for Italy. Since the first protection treaties with Majertain sultans had been signed in 1889, other Somali had signed treaties with Italian representatives of the Filonardi Company. However, the Italians were often confronted with resistance from the Somali, such as in Merca in 1893 and in Lafole in 1896. Nonetheless, by 1896 the Filonardi Company had stations in Adale (Itala), Brava, Merca, Mogadishu, Warsheik and Luuq. After the Benadir Company had run into bankruptcy, Italy finally decided in 1905 on direct administration of their colony, *Somalia Italiana* (Pankhurst, 1950).

---

6   "At the crucial moment, Minilik commanded the loyalty of every important chief in the country. Old enemies or rivals such as Ras Mikael of Wello and Nigus Tekle Haymanot of Gojjam were present at Adwa, together with Mekonnin (who might have excused himself with the problem of the security of Harer) and the great men of the North. In fact the two most important Tigrean allies of the Italians, Ras Sibhat and Dejjazmach Hagos Teferi, defected to the Ethiopian side with 600 men only two weeks before the battle of Adwa. … Behind the leaders was this feeling of attachment to 'country and king'" (Rubenson, 1991: p.405).

The Demarcation of International Borders in Somali Territory

The Adwa victory changed the attitudes of all imperial powers towards Ethiopia. This was reflected in treaties concluded in the following years by Britain, France and Italy with Ethiopia in order to demarcate boundaries and spheres of influence in the Somali region.[7] In 1897, France and Ethiopia agreed on the borders of French Somaliland, with Emperor Menelik stepping back from the claims presented in his Circular Letter of 1891. French theoretical claims were doubled, and the territory under actual control, which "never exceeded 5 to 10 kilometers in depth, secured by Lagarde's force of 34 'gendarmes' (mostly local) and an equal number of customs and administration 'officials'" (Petrides, 1983: p.17-20), was trebled. According to Petrides, Ethiopian territory was given to France on the condition that it would be returned in the case of French withdrawal from the region. Ethiopia and France also agreed on the construction of a railway from Djibouti, the capital of French Somaliland, to the Ethiopian hinterland (the railway finally reached Addis Ababa in 1917) and other trade agreements, which secured Ethiopian import-export access.[8]

The British-Ethiopian negotiations were more complicated. The Ethiopian side asserted the claims of the Circular Letter, while the British argued from the standpoint of the Anglo-Italian protocol of 1894 and their protection treaties with Somali clans. The 1894 treaty, however, could not be applied, as Ethiopia had not been party to it. Furthermore, no actual British control/protection could be proven in the areas of the protectorate claimed by Emperor Menelik. In addition, the Somali question was for the British of secondary importance to the Sudanese issue, which also had to be discussed with Ethiopia. According to Lewis (1965: p.58) "the possibility of abandoning the Somaliland Protectorate altogether had already been raised". Britain finally agreed on a compromise border lying approximately between the two claimed borders,[9] and thus gave up the Haud areas to Ethiopia. An annex to the negotiations noted that those Somali who might become Ethiopian subjects because of eventual boundary adjustments were to be treated well and assured of "orderly government" (Lewis, 1965: p.59). The British government thus betrayed the Somali[10] in their promise of protection.

---

7   On this issue in detail including numerous maps, see Petrides (1983).
8   Dire-Dawa, the important Ethiopian trading town in the Southeast, was established in the course of the railway construction.
9   See map in Petrides (1983: pp.26-27).

Italy and Ethiopia also began boundary negotiations in 1897, although neither power could seriously claim to be in effective control of the Somali-inhabited areas, which they were determined to divide into spheres of influence and control. The Ethiopian troops under Ras Makonnen had repeatedly raided Somali nomads far into the Ogaden, but one could not speak of permanent Ethiopian outposts or even towns in this area; Jijiga had just been founded in 1891 (Echete, 1988). For the Italian protectorate a similar situation prevailed (Petrides, 1983: p.40):

> What Nerazzini described in 1897 to Emperor Menelik (who knew better) as "our possessions in the South" was, in fact, a thin administrative line along the coastal part of the so-called 'sultanates' of Miggiurtina, Nogal, Obbia and Benadir; a line about 1000 kilometers long and not more than 10 to 5 kilometers deep; behind it, a mass of desert, a hot and empty land which was still terra ingnota.

The first three sultanates mentioned here were certainly hot desert and may have seemed to be empty to those not venturing into the hinterland, given the characteristic mobility of the nomadic lifestyle. However, in the Benadir hinterland, which had seen several expeditions by Italians and other Europeans (Lewis, 1965), farming communities inhabiting the fertile lands particularly along the Juba and Shabelle rivers made some attempt to resist Italian colonialism. It was not until about 1920 that Italy effectively administered its colony. In 1897, the Italian delegate and the Ethiopian authorities agreed on a section of boundary between River Shabelle and intersection 48.8 by drawing a straight line on the so-called *Habenicht* map.[11] However, dissatisfaction with the extent of losses on the Italian side (in particular the location of the town Luuq in Ethiopian territory) made the Italian government reluctant to ratify this boundary agreement. Fighting between Ethiopian and Italian troops near Baidoa in December 1907 brought the issue back to the negotiating table and, in the summer of 1908, a boundary convention was signed and ratified by both parties. In 1911, the actual demarcation of the border began, but was interrupted and then never continued – a failing for which different schools of thought blame either the Ethiopians (Lewis, 1965: p.89) or the Italians (Petrides, 1983: p.48-50). The non-demarcation finally led to the Wal-Wal incident that triggered off the Italian fascist invasion of Ethiopia in 1935.

---

10 *The Betrayal of the Somali* (Fitzgibbon, 1982) provides a Somali perspective on these events.

11 For a detailed description of the negotiations, see Petrides (1983: p.32-33).

Reaction to Colonial Domination: Attempts at Formation of a Somali State

In reaction to the imposition of British colonial rule in Northern Somalia, an anti-colonial struggle began, led by Sayyed Mohammed Abdulle Hassan. In the early days of his public life, Mohammed Abdulle Hassan was primarily motivated to spread *Salihiya* religious belief among the Somali. After his visit to Mekka, where he received the title of *Sayyed*,[12] he opened a *Salihiya tariiqa* center of learning in Berbera. His movement developed into a political anti-colonial struggle culminating in 1905 when he was granted control over a specific territory in Northeastern Somalia by British and Italian colonial authorities.[13] It is against this background that we will discuss events under the leadership of Sayyed Mohammed Abdulle Hassan as an attempted Somali state formation process.

Territory, Institutions and Ideology: A *DARAAWIISH*-STATE?[14]

As indicated above, our analysis of Mohammad Abdulle Hassan's polity in the framework of a 'state in formation process' will rely on the Buzan triangle which defines the three pillars which constitute the commonly applied perception of a *state*: territory; institutional framework, and the idea or ideology of a state. We will also keep in mind the alternative dynamics of state formation – by consent and/or by force.

As far as territory is concerned, as we have seen, Mohammed Abdulle Hassan was "assigned a territory of his own under Italian protection" (Touval, 1963: p.54). The Italian colonial power assigned territory in the Northeastern Somali region to fall under the Sayyed's control. Although *de jure* the territory remained under the Italian flag, and Sayyed Mohamed Abdulle Hassan was

---

12 "He returned to the Somali country in 1895 crowned with two formidable achievements: the title of Haji – one who had made the pilgrimage, and that of Sayyid. The latter was more significant since it bestowed on Maxammad the respect and acknowledgement reserved only for the specially learned and heaven-empowered few of the Moslem clergy" (Samatar, 1988: p.28).

13 Jardine (1923): for the text of the treaty, see pp.156-58. Also on this issue, see Samatar (1982); Touval (1963).

14 *Daraawiish* (somalised Arabic) or *derwish* (English) are members of an order of Muslim religious fundamentalists.

installed as procurator of the Italian Government, *de facto* he was granted full political authority over these territories. Not only the British and Italian governments but also the Sultans and clan elders of the adjacent clan territories gave their approval to the territorial agreement. The Illig Agreement, signed on 5 March 1905, reads as follows:

> Seyyid Mohammed bin Abdulla is authorized by the Italian Government to establish for him and his people a fixed residence at the point most convenient for communication with the sea, between Ras Garad and Ras Gabbe. This also with the approval of Yussuf Ali and of Sultan Osman Mahmoud. ... The government of the tribes subject to him in the interior shall remain in the hands of Seyyid Mohammed, and shall be exercised with justice and equity. Moreover, he shall provide for the security of the roads and the safety of the caravans.[15]

Although *de jure* state sovereignty remained with the Italian colonial state, one could argue that Mohammed Abdulle Hassan hereby gained 'external' recognition of political authority over a particular territory and its people.[16]

In terms of institutional framework, Samatar (1982: p.119-20) lists the following categories that emerged under Mohammed Abdulle Hassan's leadership: the council of elders (*Khusuusi*), the official army (*Maarra-Weyn*), bodyguards (*Gaar-Haye*) and the community at large (*Reer-Beade*). The council of elders, however, did not have independent powers (Samatar, 1988) and the central power of the polity remained with the Sayyed, developing an autocratic rule, which incorporated both religious jurisdiction and political authority (Lewis, 1961: p.227). From 1905 to 1909, a period of relative peace, the use of violence was monopolized and controlled by armed forces under his leadership. The Sayyed's government was responsible for providing a secure environment for livestock grazing and trading activities (Jardine, 1923). The majority of the warriors who followed the Sayyed's theocratic/autocratic leadership came from the Darod clan, but other Somali clans were represented too. Although the size and clan composition of the army was very fluid over the years and over the seasons, it was the Sayyed's purpose to institutionalize his fighting forces.[17]

---

15 Jardine (1923: p.157). For full text, ibid.: pp.156-58.
16 The Italian and British concessions turned out to be of temporary nature. Particularly after the end of the First World War the colonial powers launched a huge military campaign that finally led to the breakdown of the *daraawiish* movement.

In considering the question of the idea of the state, one has to differentiate between the ideology which bound the *daraawiish* movement under Mohammed Abdulle Hassan, and the idea of a Somali state as it became expressed in the Sayyed's poetry and which created around him the aura of the founding father of Somali nationalism. The unifying ideology of his followers, the identity beyond clan affiliation had both a religious and a political component. As members of the *Salihiya jama'a*, this unity was conceived of in religious terms (Doornbos, 1975; see also chapter 4). If one considers the polity of Mohammed Abdulle Hassan as an embryonic theocratic state in a formation process within the territorial boundaries granted to him in the Illig Agreement, one might interpret the religious component as a consent component.[18]

The political component of identity beyond clan affiliation lay in his autocratic rule, where power was concentrated in one person. Lewis (1961: p.227) notes, "amongst his followers, who came from many different clans, lineages and diya-paying groups, he strove to replace clan and contractual allegiance by devotion to himself". Thus, devotion to a religious leader became intermingled with fear of his dictatorial rule. He "demanded unflinching loyalty to himself alone" (Doornbos, 1975: p.28) and "it is generally accepted that he ended his career as a tyrannical opponent of all who refused to accept his rule" (Lewis, 1961: p.227). In this light the Sayyed's attempts at state formation were driven by force.

THE FAILURE TO UNITE THE SOMALI POLITY THROUGH ANTI-COLONIAL STRUGGLE

When considering the idea of a state in a wider, pan-Somali context, several contradictions arise. The strength and charisma of Mohammed Abdulle Hassan (Jardine, 1923) lay in his unstinting pride at being Somali, which is reflected in his poetry with its strong anti-colonial and Somali national themes (Samatar, 1982). In this context, he created an idea of a state, which appealed to a pan-Somali, Muslim identity. The reasons for the Somali lack of consensus on the Sayyed's anti-colonial and pan-Somali ideas are not simple to de-

---

17 Non-clan institutionalisation was symbolised by the fact that the fighters wore uniforms of white robes and turbans (Lewis, 1961: p.227) and were accordingly called *Maarra-weyn*, literally big clothes.

18 However, this was challenged in 1909 when the Sayyed lost his religious title and was excommunicated from the *Salihiya* order (see Lewis, 1961; Doornbos, 1975; Samatar, 1988).

fine, but three factors particularly militated against his idea of Somali nationalism and made a consensus on anti-colonial state-formation impossible.

The first of these is the clan factor. Mohammed Abdulle Hassan came from a nomadic Somali background (he had an Ogaden father and Dulbahante mother), and most of his followers came from the Darod clan family. Although he appealed for religious unity within his movement, he continued to use clan politics – combining descent and contract (*tol* and *heer*) with descent and marriage (*tol* and *hidid*)[19] – as a tool for securing and extending his power base. One of the reasons why Mohammed Abdulle Hassan's movement did not mature into a united Somali anti-colonial struggle (and eventually into an evolving Somali state) was the fact that his policies remained clan attached and thus fragmented. His forces' violent revolt against colonial foreign rule was not only directed against the Ethiopians and the British but also against collaborators on the Somali side. These included the trading community in Berbera and other Northern Somali towns (Burao, Hargeisa), as well as those Somali who filled the positions of *aqils*: Somali elders who operated as the representatives of British indirect rule and had become a sort of colonial civil servants (see chapter 5). In this process, earlier inter-clan rivalries, such as those between Isaq and Ogaden over passage rights and the control of trading routes (Markakis, 1989), gained another dimension. Somali clans were divided into pro- and anti-colonial. The Somali clans who came out of this account as pro-colonial or anti-*daraawiish* were ruthlessly punished by repeated raiding and looting attacks and even massacres of whole nomadic settlements and villages, where neither women nor children were spared.

A second major factor for Mohammed Abdulle Hassan's failure was the competition between the different Sufi orders, the *tariiqa*. As mentioned earlier (see chapter 4), the *Qaadiriya* order of Sunni Islam was prevalent among the Somali until Mohammed Abdulle Hassan introduced the *Salihiya tariiqa*. The Sayyed began his career as a religious leader of the *Salihiya* and his fundamentalist attitude never allowed differences in religious teaching to be overcome to the benefit of Somali political unity. Religiously motivated conflict went so far that when Sheikh Uways Mahamud al-Baraawi (1847-1909), a reli-

---

19 See chapter 4. Lewis (1961: p.227) refers to both *heer* and *hidid* in the following passage: "Externally he made full use of kinship ties to summon support and applied his influence as a mediator to further his cause. Where he was not sufficiently strong to demand allegiance and failed to succeed by persuasion, he forged affinal links by marrying women of the groups concerned. In his lifetime he contracted over twelve marriages."

gious scholar and spiritual and political leader from the Southern coastal town of Brava, severely criticized Mohammed Abdulle Hassan's policies, he was killed by the latter's *daraawiish* fighters (Kassim, 1995).

Thirdly, the clan factor and religious differences overlapped with differing colonial experiences and, accordingly, different ways of dealing with the colonial occupying powers, the British in the North and the Italians along the Indian Ocean coast. Mohammed Abdulle Hassan's movement was embedded in the nomadic culture of Northern Somali society. Somali in the South, in particular the Rewin in the fertile inter-riverine lands, were confronted with other forms of oppression, such as slavery, which had already existed in pre-European-colonial times. Anti-slavery campaigns, such as that led by Nassib Buunto, transformed themselves into anti-colonial uprisings, as in the *Gosha* revolt of 1890-1907 (Mukhtar, 1996). Resistance was directed against Italian colonial landlords and Somali landlords (Marchal, 1996), who both had their farms cultivated by Somali slaves. The Southern anti-colonial/anti-slavery movement was embedded in the *Qaadiriya* religious movement, which had established several *jama'a* villages, settled religious communities, which were self-sufficient cultivators. Mukhtar (1996: p.547) emphasizes the importance of these villages for the anti-slavery and anti-colonial upheavals in the South:

> These centers became safe havens for runaway slaves and outcasts, giving them a fresh start and helping them to integrate into the religious and economic life of the region. The centers also enabled destitute people to acquire land and earn a living while also practicing their faith. Jama'a centers were actually a means by which the Somalis could evade the colonial forced-labor regime. In brief, these communities played a tremendous social and economic role and led most the Southern resistance at the time.

In short the diverse experiences and interests of Northern and Southern Somali made them victims as well as collaborators of the colonial regimes. Sayyed Mohammed Abdulle Hassan failed to turn his political ideas of Somali nationalism and anti-colonialism, as expressed in his poetry, into political practice. Clan divisions and religious fanaticism worked against the development of pan-Somali state formation by consent, while for a pan-Somali state formation by force, the *daraawiish* forces were not strong enough (Doornbos, 1975).

Transforming (In)Security Patterns

Colonial rule and the Somali political response influenced various dimensions of security for the Somali people. My intention here is not to analyze specific colonial policy measures, but to provide an overview by highlighting certain general features of transforming (in)security patterns: militarization and warfare, economic transformation, social inequality and changes in the legal-political framework. As mentioned in the introduction to this chapter, I will mainly refer in the following discussion to the British and Italian colonial territories, as these were the building blocks of the later independent Somali state.

In order to provide an overview of the main political developments in these two territories from the time of the early colonial occupation until 1960, let me first turn to Italian Somaliland. In the early colonial period, basically two Italian trading companies were the caretakers of Italian interest in its Somali territories. This changed after the Mussolini government came to power in 1923. After that, the Italian state expanded military control over its Somali possessions and invested in the establishment of a colonial armed force. In 1935/36, these forces invaded Ethiopia. During the Italian occupation of Ethiopia, the Somali-inhabited areas in the Southern Ethiopian region were administered together with the Italian Somaliland colony under the name *Somalia Italiana*. For a few months during the Second World War Italy also occupied the British Protectorate Somaliland.

In 1941, Allied Forces under British command defeated the Italians, thereby liberating Ethiopia and the Italian Somaliland colony and re-instating British rule in its Somaliland Protectorate. The Somali-inhabited regions in Ethiopia and the former Italian Somaliland colony came under British Military Administration (BMA). An agreement between Ethiopian Emperor Haile Selassie and the British government provided for the continuation of British Military Administration of the Somali inhabited areas until 1948, and, for the Haud grazing grounds on the Ethiopian-British Somaliland border, until 1954 (map 2).

In ex-Italian Somaliland, British Military Administration continued until 1950, when the territory was declared a UN-trusteeship for the period of ten years after which it was planned to be given independence. Under the permanent control of a UN committee, the Italian government was given administrative responsibility over the trusteeship territory. On 1 July 1960, the territory became independent.

The British Protectorate Somaliland underwent relatively less dramatic changes. After 1920, when the *daraawiish* forces were finally defeated and Sayyed Mohammad Abdulle Hassan had died, the territory did not experience major changes until 1940, when Italy occupied the British possessions for a few months. In 1941 the Allied Forces defeated Italy and liberated all Italian occupied areas in the Horn. In anticipation of the independence of the Southern UN-trusteeship territory Somaliland in 1960, a group of outstanding Somali political personalities in the British Protectorate urged the British government to grant it independence in order to let it join with the South and form an independent Somali state. Independence was granted to the British Protectorate Somaliland on 26 June 1960. On 1 July 1960, ex-British Somaliland and ex-Italian Somaliland united and became the independent Republic of Somalia (Brons, 1993).

Externally-rooted Militarization of the Somali Region

Although the Somali region, and in particular the nomadic areas, have always known clan-driven feuds and warfare, the colonial occupation and division of territory between the various imperial powers made the region more prone to violence and insecurity. Continuous external military engagement in the region involved Somali on opposing sides and increased the conflict potential of Somali society. Furthermore, it confronted Somali for the first time with modern warfare strategies.

Insecurity Caused by Anti-Colonial Warfare

The establishment of a British Protectorate in the Northwestern Somali region provoked conflict with Sayyed Mohammed Abdulle Hassan. This led to two major battles in 1901/1902 and 1904 and – following a period of appeasement after 1905 – to air-bombardment of the *daraawiish* strongholds and the final breakdown of the movement in 1920. In the course of these twenty years, Britain's credibility as protector was seriously damaged. The British protection treaties failed to provide security to people in Somali towns and settlements in the colony, which suffered from *daraawiish* attacks. Mohammed Abdulle Hassan's anti-colonial message, enhanced by his high religious authority as a *Sayyed*, raised doubts among some Somali about British authority. This is exemplified by the changing composition of colonial troops in the expeditions against *daraawiish* forces. Although they had initially used mainly native Somali, the colonial authorities had to base the last two expeditions exclusively on non-Somali British subjects, because of the increasing unreliability of the Somali troops (Hamilton, 1911: p.112). Somali loyalties towards the British administration were split, adding another dimension to intro-Somali conflict patterns. The British formula of governance using Somali elders collapsed in the face of Somali anti-colonial state formation dynamics. Only violent repression using foreign colonial troops finally secured the continuation of British rule in Northern Somaliland.

The *daraawiish* wars also affected Somali territories under Italian 'protection' in the Northeast. Majertain clans were divided in their reaction to the movement of Mohammed Abdulle Hassan (Pankhurst, 1950). The 1905 Illig Agreement, which had been mediated by Italy (Sheik-Abdi, 1993), pacified the region for some time. In general, the Majertain Sultanates seem to have continued their political business relatively independently of the Italian colonial state. It was not until 1927 that a military campaign ended the semi-autonomous status claimed by the Sultans of Obbia and Majertain (Kaplan, 1969). The Italian colonial occupation of central and Southern territories was also answered by anti-colonial uprisings such as the Gosha revolt.

Political and Military Transformation under Italian Rule (1923-41)

In 1923, the Italian government under Mussolini reactivated its policy in the Somali colony. A colonial armed force, the *corpo zaptie,* was created which later came to be at the forefront of the invasion of Ethiopia. The restructuring of military force in the Somali colony was motivated by the long-term goal of preparing for the occupation of Ethiopia. From about 1930, Italy infiltrated the Ethiopian-Somali Ogaden, which was facilitated by the non-demarcation of the border, the lack of Ethiopian administrative control over the Southern, Somali-inhabited territory, and sympathy and support among some of the (Darod) Somali for the liberation of their kinsmen from Ethiopian rule.[20]

In 1935, Italy used a confrontation between Ethiopian and Italian-Somali troops at Wal-Wal, a station obviously within Ethiopian and not Italian territory (Petrides, 1983), as the pretext to occupy Ethiopia – a kind of late revenge for Adwa (1896) and a fulfillment of Italy's long-term ambitions for the Horn region.

In the war against Ethiopia, the Somali colonial troops eagerly fought against their traditional enemy. Six thousand Somali Zaptie served loyally under Graziani and their Italian commanders. In the entire campaign, over 40,000 Somali participated, many as porters and laborers (Kaplan, 1969: p.393).

---

20 Pankhurst (1950: p.119) also writes of Somali tribesmen of the Ethiopian Ogaden who defended the country against the Italian invasion, resisted the Italians at the Wal-Wal station in 1934, and took part in guerilla activities against the invaders.

Between 1936 and 1941, Ethiopia came under Italian rule. The Somali-inhabited territories were annexed to the Italian Somaliland colony and *Somalia Italiana* was born. Apart from the Somali living under French rule in Djibouti, and those in the British-Kenyan Northern Frontier District, the mainland Somali region was administratively united under Italian colonial rule. This briefly included the Protectorate British Somaliland that was occupied by Italy in 1940.

In 1941, the victory of the Allied Forces over Italy in the Horn of Africa liberated the Somali people from fascist Italian rule, but it did not bring them immediate freedom. The administrative, political and territorial structure of governance of the Somali-inhabited territories remained largely unchanged. *Somalia Italiana* was dead but the British Military Administration (BMA) retained authority over the territories until 1950, when a UN trusteeship territory under Italian administration was established in ex-Italian Somaliland.

In the two wars fought by the colonial powers in the Somali region (the 1935 Italian invasion of Ethiopia and the 1941 World War II battles in the Horn) Somali had fought against Somali. To the inter-clan conflict and warfare, which had existed in pre-colonial times, and the conflict during early colonialism, had been added another new layer.

ECONOMIC AND SOCIAL (IN)SECURITY PATTERNS UNDER COLONIALISM

The imposition of colonial states on Somali territory at the turn of the century did not divide a politically, socially or economically unified Somali region into five parts, but it did bring international boundaries cutting across various clan territories, pastoral grazing grounds and trading zones.[21]

Pastoral Migration and Trade in the Northern Region

The splitting of clan territory implied a division of grazing lands for Somali pastoralists and increased economic insecurity in the region – this had in fact been foreseen by the British authorities when handing over the Haud grazing lands in the Northwestern Somali region to Ethiopia in 1897.[22] However, be-

---

21 See map 1 and 3, chapter 3 pp.71-76 for trading zones and chapter 4 pp.91-95 for territorial distribution of clans.

cause of the lack of permanent control of the hinterlands in all the protectorates, as well as in the Ethiopian Southeastern region, nomadic migration was
not always seriously restricted.

One source of economic as well as physical insecurity was livestock raids by
Ethiopian troops against Somali pastoralists. The exploitation of the Somali
hinterland and extraction of resources by coercive means were the prime characteristics of Ethiopian state expansion.[23] The development of garrison towns
such as Jijiga on the outskirts of the Somali region (Echete, 1988) must be seen
in the context of logistical needs for the purposes of exploitation and state
control. Nevertheless, the development of these towns, in particular Jijiga, had
a positive impact on the trading relations of Somali pastoralists.

The British claimed to have based their protectorate on the provision of security to Somali clans. However, although feigning a kind of state formation
by consent, they did not fulfill their supposed promises. Ethiopian attacks
were not only directed against Ogaden clan territory, but also towards the East
where the British claimed sovereignty. Neither British control nor British protection reached far into the pastoral hinterland. The final Anglo-Ethiopian
boundaries were not fixed until 1897, and even then clans under British protection continued to be affected by Ethiopian attacks.

It was the *Sayyed* who responded to these specific security needs of Somali
nomads. The *daraawiish* forces executed counter-attacks against Ethiopian
troops, even going as far as storming the Ethiopian military station at Jijiga
where they successfully reclaimed looted stock (Samatar, 1982; Sheik-Abdi,
1993) – actions, which undoubtedly increased Mohammed Abdulle Hassan's
popularity among the clans affected.

In the British Northern region, livestock trade through Berbera had be-
come increasingly developed (Samatar, 1989); beneficiary was foremost the
Berbera trading community, which consisted mainly of Indians, Arabs and
Somali middlemen.[24] During the conflict between the *daraawish* forces and

---

22 "...the third annex to the [Anglo-Ethiopian] treaty which stipulated that the clans
on each side of the new British protectorate frontier should have access to the grazing
areas and 'nearer wells' both within and outside the British sphere; during such migratory movements they were to be under the jurisdiction of the appropriate territorial
authority" (Lewis, (1965: p.60).

23 Samatar (1982: p.110), notes that in the last decade of the 19th century over 100,000
head of cattle, 200,000 camels and about 600,000 sheep and goats were taken from
Somali nomads in the Ogaden region.

24 The Somali businessmen in Berbera were in the majority from the Isaq/Habr Awal/
Iise Muse; see Marchal (1996).

the British colonial state, trade was seriously hampered and came to a temporary standstill because caravans were attacked and looted (Touval, 1963). The whole region was in a state of emergency, with conditions for trade unpredictable and insecure.

Although livestock export did not play a major role in the pastoral economy until the late 1930s, a shift from pure subsistence nomadism to trade emerged at the time of early European colonialism. The increase in water wells and veterinary services during the late colonial rule had a tremendous impact on the economic activities of the pastoralists and their herd-management arrangements. The establishment of livestock traders and middlemen among the Somali community also dates from this time (Samatar, 1989). It is difficult to assess the extent to which international borders crossing clan territory actually affected people's economic security, migratory and trading mobility. The integration of Somali territory in *Somalia Italiana* after the Italian occupation of Ethiopia in 1936 might have made pastoral movement and trading activities less insecure. However, unsettled borders and the military campaigns in the Horn during the Second World War impacted negatively on pastoral migration and trade. Instability continued until independence and beyond.

Impact of Colonial Rule on Southern Trading and Farming Communities

The Italian companies during the early colonial period – Filonardi (1893-1896) and Benadir (1896-1905) – established a monopoly over exports, customs and tariff regulations, which had a highly negative impact on the Arab/Persian/Indian/Somali business and trading communities in Mogadishu and other market centers in the South. The question of control over the ports was of particular importance for the local population of Somali, Arab and Indian traders.

The Banadir ports played a significant role in the region's external and internal trade. They supplied the hinterland with imported commodities as well as providing markets for livestock and major local products. Moreover, it was in these coastal towns that cottage industries like weaving and knitting the Banadiri cloth, the manufacture of utensils and tools flourished, and trader communities were established. It was essential to defend such economic resources, and the Banadir revolt (1888-1910), though religious in origin, was motivated by economic factors (Mukhtar, 1996: p.545).

Trading patterns, which had been established, transformed and adapted through the centuries along the Southern Benadir coast, were threatened by the policies of the Filonardi and Benadir companies and, from 1905 on, by direct Italian colonial rule. The socio-economic framework of the Southern region, marked by sedentary farming communities, Arab and Somali land-owners and slave laborers, pastoralists and traders, was shaken in the early 20th century, but not yet fundamentally transformed.

During that time, slaves escaping from plantations in the Shabelle region found refuge in the then dense forest along the River Juba and founded agri-cultural communities (Menkhaus, 1996). Other ex-slave Bantu-speaking farming communities were settling along the Shabelle, some in the *jama'* vil-lages mentioned above. The ex-slave farming communities, the Gosha or Jareer people, saw their initially insecure situation, subject to permanent threats of nomads raiding their villages, eventually improve with the arrival of European colonial control of the region (Besteman, 1995).

The Italian colonial government was (initially) in favor of the abolition of slavery and of the implementation of the Brussels slavery convention of 1890. Not only Arabs but also Somali landlords owned plantations and were de-pendent on slave labor.[25] Some Somali clan elders, therefore, resisted the Ital-ian colonial occupation. Many Somali landowners gave up agricultural pro-duction after the changes of 1890. In the end, the anti-slavery convention had very little impact; slavery and forced labor of Somali people continued and, under fascist Italian rule, was promoted and increased in scale.

With the advent of colonial administration, discrimination based on the differing racial features of the Somali people (see chapter 3) became to a cer-tain extent officially acknowledged. In British Jubaland,[26] Somali descending from the *Samale* genealogy wanted their supposed superiority over the Afri-can Somali to be recognized by being classified as non-'natives'. Claiming Arab origin, they were finally registered in the colonial administration as non-African which meant for them non-farming and non-slave (Besteman, 1995). The way in which the pastoral Somali categorized their own society into, on the one hand, the people of the bush (*reer badiya*) and people with soft hair (*tin jileec*), signifying the pure Somali (Samale) and, on the other hand, people from the forest (*reer goleed*) and slaves (*adoon*), being non or less Somali (Sab), became the officially accepted norm.[27]

---

25 According to Marchal (1996), around 4,000 slaves per annum were imported in Benadir during the 1870s.

26 Western Jubaland was under British rule until 1924, after which it became incorpo-rated into Italian Somaliland.

27 See diagram 1 and chapter 4.

In the years 1910-20 there were only a few attempts made to establish Italian plantations in the fertile regions. Shortage of labor was the most urgent problem as nomads would not farm and the farming communities were relatively self-sufficient and therefore not permanently dependent on income deriving from plantation labor. Attempts to bring in *Kikuyu* farmers or immigrants from the Italian homeland failed.

The impact of colonial rule in the Southern farmlands on matters such as land rights or transformation of cultivation patterns increased after 1923. Italian agricultural policies were dominated by the *kolonya* system (Menkhaus, 1996; Pankhurst, 1950). This entailed the expropriation of land of the highest quality from local villagers, without compensation, and forced relocation and conscription of villagers. Whole villages were relocated onto plantation sites. Meager rations, low pay, forced marriages and brutal punishments are reported from the *kolonya* times.

> For a first offence of disobedience or indiscipline fifty lashes with a hippopotamus-hide whip was a common award, and for a second offence the victim was strung up for several hours on a gallows, with his toes just clear of the ground, suspended by chains attached to wooden billets under his armpits and with his hands handcuffed behind his back (Pankhurst, 1950: p.139).

The fact that the best land, as well as capital and labor were moved out of food crop production into cash-crop monoculture led to food shortages from 1938 through 1942 (Menkhaus, 1996: p.143). Food security, as one marker for economic security, improved in the South only in the mid-1940s.

When, after 1941, the British Military Administration redirected plantation production to food crops, conscripted labor, officially called compulsory rotating labor, was used again (Menkhaus, 1996; Pankhurst, 1950). However, from the time in 1950 when ex-Italian Somaliland began to be administered under UN-trusteeship by Italy, coercion of labor and expropriation of land were no longer possible, as a UN body carefully controlled policies in the territory. The economic security of the farming communities significantly improved as small-scale subsistence farming centered on village communities regained its position as the foremost agricultural production pattern. During the trusteeship period many small-scale projects were launched and educational and health facilities improved.

PATTERNS OF TRANSFORMING THE LEGAL-POLITICAL ORDER

In the British Protectorate the British legal system was introduced. In the Italian-administered South (colony and latter trust territory) Italian civil and penal codes were in effect. According to Kaplan (1969: p.200):

> The pre-independence colonial court structures attempted as much as possible, to make use of the Islamic and customary systems. Somali *sharia* and customary courts were allowed to flourish and were given specific areas of jurisdiction by the colonial governments.

While the *stateless* and the *state* legal systems could function in a parallel and sometimes overlapping manner, the introduction of political institutions by the colonial states was to evoke more contradictions.

The Emergence of Civil Administration

Colonial administration in both the British and the Italian territories used a sort of indirect rule. In the Southern sedentary areas the *Sultan* was generally considered the link between the people and the colonial state. In the nomadic areas the *Aqil* became a paid middlemen, a civil servant, in the system of indirect rule (Lewis, 1961). Among the pastoral people, the Aqil was the representative of a lineage or diya-paying group. The promotion of the position of the lineage elder *vis-à-vis* the clan elder in pastoral areas marked a transformation in the power balance. The political authority of the head of the clans as it existed in the earlier stateless political system, became jeopardized. The inflation of titles of authority was a first step into the direction of divide and rule that until today haunts the Somali people. In addition, the Aqils became divided in their loyalties, torn between their clan-segment, in their position of elder, and the colonial state in their role as civil servant.

The Italian colonial administration was highly centralized with all posts of any importance held by Italians. Somali staffed the lower ranks of the police force and more than 40,000 served in the Italian colonial army during the invasion of Ethiopia (Kaplan, 1969). In 1941, the British Military Administration took over control and administration of the ex-Italian Somaliland colony. From then on, progress was made in the development of institutional structures in which Somali became increasingly involved. In the South, a British-led police force, the Somali Gendarmerie, was established, and training was provided to Somali to become members of the civil or police service. In the civil service, Italian appointed clan-chiefs (aqils) were gradually replaced and new District and Provincial Councils created.

In the British Protectorate the civil service was improved and the Aqil system became formalized in 1950. In 1946, the Protectorate Advisory Council was established with Somali representatives in each district. British Somaliland Scouts were the police force in the Protectorate. However, institutional development remained very limited until the mid-1950s.

The Political Genesis of a Somali National State Ideology

While in the early 20th century the idea of Somali nationalism found its first expression in Somali political poetry, such as that of Sayeed Mohammed Abdulle Hassan, in the 1940s Somali politicians lobbied through political diplomacy. As we shall see, however, they failed in preparing for the formation of a Somali national state, which would have united Somali society, all Somali-inhabited areas in the Horn, under the authority of one state.

Young Somali intellectuals from the North and the South had been discussing the formation of a Somali national state since the early 1940s. In the aftermath of the liberation of Italian-occupied Ethiopia by the Allies, the British Military Administration took control of the Somali territories in Ethiopia and the former Italian colony Somaliland, while retaining the protectorate in British Somaliland and the Somali-inhabited Northern Frontier District in the Kenyan colony. For the first time, almost all Somali people (the exceptions being those in French Somaliland) were governed by one colonial power. This stimulated ideas of Somali nationalism, whereby the optimal extension of a Somali nation-state would include all Somali-inhabited territories in the Horn.

The British first supported the Somali desire, thereby supporting the development of a political ideology emphasizing Somali nationalism. The ultimate goal was to transform the territory into an independent Somali nation-state. The Bevin plan of 1946, named after the British minister of foreign affairs at the time, promoted this idea, but failed to gain sufficient support. Political developments worked against Somali desires to form a nation state, which would include all Somali-inhabited areas. *De jure* claims of the Ethiopian state, and decisions of the UN over the plight of the Somali people of ex-Italian Somaliland, were among the decisive factors, which hampered the formation of a Somali national state in an ethnically defined territory (Touval, 1963; Petrides, 1983; Lewis, 1988). The idea of Greater Somalia remained alive among Somali political intellectuals, however, and influenced their pre- and post-independence formulation of policies.

Somalization of Modern Political Institutions and Organizations: Councils and Parties in the Pre-independent South and North

The Italian trusteeship administration was obliged by the UN to prepare the Southern territory for independence after one decade. An Italian Trusteeship Administration was set in place assisted by an international Advisory Council. In 1950, a Territorial Council was established whose 35 members included representatives from the traditional, pre-state political arena as well as from the slowly strengthening modern party scene (Kaplan, 1969: p.45). In 1954, elections took place for the Municipal Councils, which had been established in 48 towns and population centers. Their counterparts for the rural, nomadic areas, the District Councils, functioned less well: pre-state mechanisms of political representation were much better adapted to the conditions of nomadic migratory life and, in that light, the District Councils were a rather unnecessary addition. The first national elections were held in 1956 when a Legislative Assembly replaced the Territorial Council. Specific arrangements were made for the rural areas by introducing a clan voting system, whilst in the settled areas a secret ballot was used and universal male suffrage was applied.

The nomads met in some 600 *shirs*, traditional clan assemblies, and decided jointly on the candidate for whom all their votes would be cast. Clan leaders then informed the authorities of this decision and of the number of individual votes cast in the *shir*. Unfortunately, the total number of votes cast in the territory far outnumbered the estimated size of the actual electorate. This incident marred the Somali political image and left a residue of interparty distrust for a number of years, since the SYL, as the strongest party in the nomadic areas, was said by its opponents to have gained the most from the alleged irregularities (ibid.: p.46-47).

Various Somali parties emerged during the late 1940s transformed from associations or discussion clubs into political parties. They put different emphasis on the topics of state formation and independence. The Somali Youth League (SYL), which had been founded as the Somali Youth Club in 1943, had branches in all Somali territories by 1947, including the British-Kenyan Northern Frontier District, Ethiopia (Jijiga), British- and (ex)Italian Somaliland. Its constituency mainly derived from the Darod clan, which explains its widespread appeal in the region. The SYL's vision of Somalia was that of a nation in search of a state[28] including all five territories. It was here that the Greater Somalia idea – later represented in the national flag, a white star with five corners on a blue background – was most fervently nurtured. In the discussion about the future of ex-Italian Somaliland after 1941, the SYL supported a 10-year UN-trusteeship under British administration in the hope of eventually unifying all Somali territories then under British administration.

The second most relevant party in the South was the HDMS (*Hisbia Dhigale Mirifle Somaaliyeed*), representing the Digil/Mirifle clans of the Rewin. Having its roots in the National Benevolent Organization, a philanthropic movement of the 1920s, the HDMS was founded as a political party in 1947, and renamed itself in 1957 as Hisbia Dastur Mustaqil al-Sumal, the Somali Independent Constitutional Party (Mukhtar, 1996). In the context of the UN-trusteeship discussions, the Digil/Mirifle party had proposed a 30-year trusteeship under Italian administration, their proposal showing their fear of domination by the nomadic clans in a future independent state.

In 1947, the British Somaliland Protectorate introduced the Advisory Council. It consisted exclusively of people nominated by the British Protectorate Administration, such as Somali members of various clans, religious men and representatives of the Arab and Indian trading communities. The British Protectorate Administration had tried to balance clan representation in the Advisory Council (Lewis, 1961). However, civil servants were excluded from any direct political activities and political parties were considered illegal until 1959 (Laitin and Samatar, 1987). Given that only about 10% of the Somaliland population was urban, and that the protectorate administration was itself the major employer (Lewis, 1961), it was possible to keep the core of the younger Somali political leaders out of the realm of politics. The institutionalization of party politics therefore developed here much later than in the Italian-administered trust territory.

The Somaliland National League (from 1948, the Somali National League, SNL) came into being in 1935 (ibid.). Its members came mainly from the Isaq clan (Habr Yonis and Habr Awal/Iise Muse), with a minority from the Gadabuursi, Issa, Warsangeli and Dulbahante clans. Nationalist pan-Somali policies of the SNL were directed towards the unification of the Northern protectorate and the Southern trust territory, but not towards an integration of the Ethiopian Ogaden into a future Somali state (Markakis, 1991). Unlike the Somali Youth League, the Somali National League had no offices in Ethiopia.

---

28 The title of a book by Laitin and Samatar (1987).

The Somali Youth League had a Northern branch, most of whose members came from the Darod clans. The return of the Haud territory to Ethiopia in 1954[29] gave an impetus to the formation of the National United Front (NUF), made up of members from the Somali National League and the Somali Youth Club Northern branch. A fourth party, the United Somali Party (USP) was a Darod/Dulbahante and Warsangeli and Dir/Issa oriented party (Laitin and Samatar, 1987).

In 1957, the Legislative Council was established in the British Protectorate: all members were nominated. In 1958, 12 of the 29 members of the Legislative Council were elected in a first national election. As in the South, the election was by secret ballot in the urban centers and by acclamation by *shir* in the nomadic areas (Kaplan, 1969: p.50). In early 1960, new elections were held for 33 elected seats in the Legislative Council. These were the first elections in the British Protectorate with Somali parties involved. The Somali National League (SNL) won the majority of the seats (20) and its party leader, Mohamed Ibrahim Egal, became leader of the four-person cabinet. Twelve seats went to the United Somali Party and only one seat to the Somali Youth League Northern branch. By that time, Somali politicians in British Somaliland were urging the British government to give them independence in order to be able to join together with the South in forming an independent Somali state (Hall, 1961: p.27).

In preparation for the unification of the two territories, the Somali transitional government of the Southern trust-territory requested UN permission to establish a National Army prior to independence for protection of the still disputed frontiers. Permission was granted and the new 5000-strong Somali national army was created from a nucleus of the former British Somaliland Scouts and the paramilitary police of the trust territory in the South (Kaplan, 1969: p.394).

From Stateless to State Society: Colonial Heritage on the Eve of Independence

This chapter has reviewed the transformation of Somali society from a stateless *society* that had been politically structured by localized holders of power

---

29 During the Allied Forces war against Italy in Ethiopia/Somalia an agreement had been reached with Emperor Haile Selassie of Ethiopia, which kept part of the Ethiopian Haud area along the British Somaliland Protectorate border under British administration; see Petrides (1983). This area returned to Ethiopia in 1954.

and authority, to a *society ruled by colonial states*. It is clear that the introduction of state territorial boundaries and institutions and the implementation of colonial policies were a source of change in relative (in)security. As different factors impacted positively and negatively on Somali society, some groups, clans, professions, etc. profited and others suffered from colonial state policies. Furthermore, pre-state – now sub-state – security arrangements continued to exist in parallel to the structures that were imposed by the colonial powers, in ways that could be either complementary or conflict-prone.

I will conclude the analysis of the transformation of Somali society from a stateless to a state society by referring to the three factors, territory, institutions and idea of the state, that were defined as crucial for state formation.

First, the perception of territoriality changed. The introduction of international borders by colonial powers, splitting the Somali region into five parts, created a fact of international law with far-reaching implications. Somali people, clans, and communities were only marginally involved in this process through protection treaties. However, as became clear over time, the colonial powers did not consider these treaties with single Somali clans to be as binding as international border agreements. The concept of an undivided colonial state sovereignty was established, thus undermining the basic sovereignty of the Somali people that consisted *de facto* of divided sovereign political entities. The Somali concept of territoriality, reflecting the environmental conditions, economic adaptive strategies and socio-political structures of Somali society described earlier, was in effect completely ignored in the process of colonial partition. As will be shown in later chapters of this book, some of the contradictions that arose out of the imposition of colonial rule still haunt the Somali people.

One attempt to give political expression to a territorial entity, which came close to reconciling the Somali, clan-based and the European state-based concept of territoriality was the formation of a Somali polity under Sayyed Mohammed Abdulle Hassan. According to a *de jure* approach, the Sayyed's polity can be considered a sort of indirect rule, as the territory legally remained under British and Italian sovereignty. *De facto*, however, the Sayyed ignored these legal claims and challenged the colonial state sovereignty. In the line of argument on state formation as developed in this book, the case of the *daraawish* state will be particularly interesting when compared to processes of political authority formation in the Somali region that emerged after the 1991 state collapse.

Second, the introduction of new institutions that were rooted in the modern state system partly marginalized or decreased the actual power of political authorities of pre-state times, such as sultans and *khadis*. A central judiciary was introduced that referred to colonial laws of British and Italian origin and only partly to customary and sharia laws. The two legal systems, the *pre-state* and the *state* system, were not necessarily in conflict with each other, but the establishment of colonial state law introduced a perception of the superiority of the modern over the so-called traditional system.

Centralized colonial administration was likewise superimposed on localized clan- or village-rooted administrative patterns and structures. These political institutions claimed an undivided sovereign authority over the Somali people who, by then, had become Somali colonial subjects. With regard to control over the use of force, the establishment of colonial police and military units prepared the ground for the diminishing authority of the elders in clans and village communities. The merger of these units into a national army on the eve of independence paved the way for the development of strong instruments of coercive violence in the hands of future Somali state authorities.

Third, with regard to the development of an idea of the state that might have been able to bind the Somali people together on the eve of independence, the colonial heritage established a pattern of rising Somali political nationalism. This, however, did not necessarily reduce social fragmentation within Somali society. Instead, new layers of fragmentation were added through the colonial experience. The Somali people found themselves the subjects (future citizens) of five different states. They went through the experience of fighting in three wars against their own Somali kin – in the *daraawiish* war in 1900-1920; in the Italian-Ethiopian war in 1935/36; and in the World War II battles between Italy and the Allied Forces in 1941. Another aspect of social fragmentation that was consolidated rather than reduced through colonial policies was the rift between the nomadic Samale and the settled Sab populations. Colonial policies in the South sanctioned discrimination against settled, and particularly Somali-Bantu communities. These, then, were the most profound of the changes that accompanied the transformation of Somali society from a *stateless* to a *state* society.

CHAPTER 7

From State to Stateless Society: Three Decades of Experience with Somali State Rule

While chapter 5 discussed the prevailing security arrangements of Somali *stateless* society, chapter 6 described the profound changes that took place in the process of imposition of *colonial state structures* on Somali society. This chapter covers three decades (1960-1990/91) of *independent Somali state rule*. Broadly speaking, I shall depict developments from the rise and formation to the decline and collapse of the Somali state. In terms of the analytical perspective of this book, we are now dealing with transition from a *state* to a *stateless* situation.

The transformation from colonial to independent rule was formally completed when, on 26 June 1960, the Protectorate British Somaliland was declared an independent sovereign state. Five days later, on 1 July 1960, the UN-trusteeship over the formerly Italian Southern Somaliland ended, and the North and the South united to form the Republic of Somalia. The independent Somali state was initially governed by a democratic multi-party system, but in 1969 a military coup brought an end to civilian rule. The Supreme Revolutionary Council, under the leadership of Siyad Barre, established a socialist political system under military rule. Military rule was replaced in 1979 by presidential one-party rule.

In 1978, in the aftermath of the Somali military defeat by Ethiopia in the Ogaden war, the first political opposition movement was founded,-followed by others in 1981 and 1989. The first half of the 1980s was dominated politically by insurgence against the state by the Northern-based Somali National Movement (SNM) and, in reaction thereto, by increasingly coercive measures and a strategy of divide and rule on the government's part. By the mid-1980s the Somali state had degenerated into a brutal dictatorship. Open civil war began in 1988 in the Northwestern region, between SNM and government forces. It culminated in the mass-bombardment of the two major towns in the North and the flight of half a million Somali people into neighboring Ethiopia. The war then spread to the South, where several new opposition movements emerged and co-operated with the Northern SNM. The civil war reached its peak in 1990/91, when the fighting reached the capital, Mogadishu, forcing the remnants of president Siyad Barre's government to flee. The subsequent failure of the various opposition movements to agree on terms for the establishment of a post-Barre government finally led the country into statelessness.

It is important to recall here that a state is not understood as a concrete entity that either 'exists' or 'does not exist' in some simple sense. A state is manifested in a political authority structure that more or less effectively asserts sovereignty over a territorially defined entity, functions through an institutional framework, and propagates an idea or ideology that serves to bind population, territory and institutions. In the Somali case all three pillars of the state finally collapsed, so that we can say that the state disappeared as a political reality.

Focusing on the period of state power in Somalia, this chapter is divided chronologically in two. Part one deals with the 1960-1969 period of multiparty democracy. The purpose here is to provide some background to the conflict-prone patterns within Somali politics that were to have a long-term impact on political developments in the country. The territorial perceptions and ideology that underlay policy making and the framework of state institutions served as the foundation of arrangements that offered security to some while creating insecurity for others. Through the formulation and implementation of state policies, certain groups and clans elevated themselves into positions of privilege and marginalized others who were denied a fair share of political influence and economic benefits. This unequal development began immediately after independence and increased throughout the 1970s and 1980s. In examining these dynamics, I concentrate first on the reasons for the political instability of the democratic system and the way it became interwoven with clan politics. A second focus lies on the impact of external security policies and the role and prestige of the national army, both of which affected the availability of coercive means of violence in the hands of the government, finally leading to the military coup in 1969.

The second part of the chapter deals with the 21-year rule of the late president Siyad Barre. We will focus on those structures and policies of the Siyad Barre state that were threats to the security of its citizens, and describe the dynamics that evolved out of the interplay between state- and sub-state networks. These dynamics can be seen unfolding from unbalanced state policymaking, through the emergence of the first opposition movements, to an increasingly dictatorial leadership, and finally to the civil war that brought the Siyad Barre state to its knees and divided the Somali polity into clan domains. Threats emanating from the state can be categorized as follows (Buzan, 1983/91; see also chapter 2):

- lack of stable mechanisms for the transfer of political power and resulting threat of political violence;

- threats to broad civil liberties resulting from domestic law making and enforcement;
- external security policies;
- direct action by the state against individuals or groups.

This second part first deals with the political system under military and later one-party civilian rule, describing the slide towards dictatorship. I elaborate on the political instruments commonly known as national security laws that enabled the state authorities to persecute individuals and groups. Secondly, I will focus on the state's external policy; particularly the government's handling of superpower competition and of the Somali-Ethiopian war. Thirdly, I will examine how the head of state succeeded in strengthening his position in the aftermath of the war – developments that led to the formation of clan-related opposition. Next, I deal with the economic policies of the Barre government, and the re-emergence of the North-South division in the light of the formation of a Northern opposition movement. Discriminatory trade policies provoked various response mechanisms, which were based on sub-state security arrangements. Although the government's discriminatory land tenure policies and their impact on the farming communities in the inter-riverine areas did not lead to the formation of a Southern military opposition movement at that time, it is important for an understanding of post-Barre conflict dynamics to be aware of the background of the land issue. Finally, I highlight the impact of state policies on women, focusing first on the reform of family law and the foundation of women's organizations, and second on the increasing insecurity for women against the background of the evolving clan-patterned civil war in the country. In the last part of the chapter I focus on the countdown to state collapse, with the turn to open civil war in the North and the emergence of opposition movements in the South. The chapter ends with a discussion of the reasons behind the failure of post-Barre state formation.

It would be rather simplistic to identify the 'winners' and 'losers' of state policies exclusively in clan perspective. Similar analytical problems occur when looking at the population groups of traders, farmers and women. For instance, while the family law provided women with more rights *vis-à-vis* men, they still suffered from state policies as traders, farmers and/or members of clans, or as wives of men from other clans. Similarly, in the trading sector there have been businesspeople from all clans who benefited from the system and were among the quiet supporters of the late dictator – including those clans that were persecuted as sympathizers of opposition movements. The same applies to land tenure policies, where not only government-related clans but also clan elders from the farming communities became influential landlords. The analysis is therefore intended to reveal general patterns, which help us to understand the dynamics influencing Somali political development, right up to the present time.

The Mogadishu State 1960-1969: Patterns of Clan Domination and Marginalisation

On the eve of independence (see map 1), two parliaments existed side-by-side, one in the Northern Protectorate and the other in the Southern Trust Territory. The independent Somali state of 1960, in contrast, was a unitary republic based on parliamentary democracy (Kaplan, 1969). The new multi-party national assembly comprising 123 members (33 from the North and 90 from the South) constituted the center of political power. The president of the republic was titular head of state and elected by the members of the national assembly. He was responsible for choosing a prime minister who had then to secure a vote of confidence in the national assembly. In times of governmental crisis, the president had the power to dissolve the national assembly. The president was also the commander of the armed forces, and he signed all legislation and treaties. The term of the presidency was six years, with only two consecutive terms allowed. In case of the death or resignation of a president, the national assembly should elect a replacement within one month. Executive power was vested in a prime minister and council of ministers responsible to the unicameral national assembly. The size of the council of ministers was not specified. As well as ministers, there were deputy ministers who kept their seats in parliament. Secretariats supported the president, prime minister and ministers.

The constitution provided for an independent judiciary, whereby the supreme court could act as constitutional court, with two additional members, one appointed by the council of ministers and one elected by the national assembly. The jurisdiction of the constitutional court included questions concerning the conformity of legislation to the provisions of the constitution and to the principles of Islam, election disputes and impeachment cases. Although Islam was declared the official religion of the country and the main source of its laws, freedom of religious belief was one of the civil rights secured by the constitution, along with *habeas corpus*, and freedom of speech, press, association and petition.

Apart from elections to the national assembly, the only other elections to representative bodies were at the municipal level. For the eight regions and forty-seven districts, the minister of the interior appointed regional governors and district commissioners. Hence, politics became centralized in Mogadishu.

Shortcomings of Parliamentary Democracy in Clan-Political Practice

The constitution made no allowance for regional differences. Its drafters seriously considered neither federalism nor decentralization, although either system would have better reflected the political realities of Somali society. On the eve of independence the seeds of political instability had, as we saw in chapter 6, already been sown when political differences between North and South on the fundamental conditions of a union were suppressed rather than worked out openly. The Northern and Southern parliaments did not agree on the Act of Union, the very foundation of the formation of a united independent Somali state. On 1 July 1960, the interim government, headed by president Aden Abdulle Osman, decreed the unification of the two territories without having settled the outstanding differences. Northern-Somali politicians felt that they had been denied full participation in the constitutional development process. In the words of Laitin and Samatar (1987: p.70-71):

> Nearly all the preparatory work had been accomplished in the South, in negotiation with Italian officials, before the British agreed to grant independence to their protectorate in conjunction with Italian Somalia's schedule. Thus, Northern politicians only could make marginal effects on the constitutional draft, and there was considerable resentment in the North that the South had defined the political agenda.

The Italian model constitution was taken over virtually unchanged, without the necessary adaptations to the specific characteristics of Somali society. It was not only Northern (Isaq) politicians who raised concerns about the constitution. Even before the first elections to the territorial council in the Southern trust territory in 1956, the HDMS, the party representing the Southern Rewin, had argued for the adoption of a federal system of government as the only way of creating a harmonious Somali state (Mukhtar, 1996). The constitution was adopted by a referendum in 1961, but the overall results did not show an accurate picture: people in the North voted forcefully against the constitution, and separate referenda would have better reflected Somali opinion.[1]

The constitution provided no viable venue for the political expression of regional differences, and no problem-solving institutional framework. Later, in 1968, a National Advisory Council consisting of 300 delegates from munici-

---

1   According to Drysdale (1992), 72% of the people in Hargeisa voted against the constitution, as did 69% in Berbera, 66% in Burao, and 69% in Erigavo.

pal governments, labor unions and other organized interest groups was created in order to improve on direct popular participation in national affairs
(Kaplan, 1969). But this could not counterbalance the need for autonomous
regional political decision-making. The central political power formation
which had been inherited from colonial rule not only remained intact but
even increased as the Northern ex-protectorate capital Hargeisa became
marginalized, and all politics concentrated in the national capital Mogadishu.

The dynamics that developed out of this centralized, Southern-dominated
political structure can best be illustrated by a closer look into the characteristics and voting patterns of the political parties. The political parties fell into
three basic categories: the party that provided the majority throughout the
first decade of independence and was dominated by Southern clans; the minority opposition parties based on clan affiliation from the North and the
inter-riverine South; and thirdly a number of *ad hoc* parties which mush-
roomed before elections, sometimes with only one candidate and a constituency of a handful of voters deriving from lineage affiliation.

Throughout the nine years of parliamentary democracy the multi-party
democratic state structure deteriorated into a *de facto* one-party state. The opportunity for a place in government or in the wider state-bureaucracy could be
secured only if a politician elected to parliament became a member of that
party. This became the driving force of parliamentary dynamics in the early
post-independent era, and led inevitably to nepotism and corruption.

The party, which occupied this prime position, was the Somali Youth
League (SYL). As we saw in the previous chapter, the SYL was originally
Darod dominated, having emerged from the Somali Youth Club most of
whose members came from the Somali Police Corps in the period of British
Military Administration (Pankhurst, 1950). Nonetheless, the SYL acquired
the image of an integrative party. According to Nelson (1982: p.27), "its members made strong efforts to promote the concept of a common Somali nationality without regard for clan-divisions, going so far as to refuse to use their
clan names". SYL was not *per se* a clannish party, including members from
Hawiye, Dir, Isaq and Rewin besides the Darod hard core. Its program included a policy of nation building, the creation of a unified armed forces and
police corps, the establishment and improvement of educational facilities,
moderate Greater Somalia ambitions, economic liberalism and accommodation with non-Somali landowners – in general, a program of non-radical
modernization of Somali society. To what extent SYL's integrative strength
can be ascribed to its accommodating program, and to what extent to the opportunities for personal and clan enrichment, which arose from SYL membership, is open to speculation.

Especially during the first few years of independence, opposition parties whose emphases in their political programs varied according to different clan allegiance enlivened the political scene. These included the Somali National League (SNL) headed by Mohamed Ibrahim Egal, and the Somali Independent Constitutional Party (HDMS). The SNL constituency was drawn mainly from the Northern Isaq population, including ex-protectorate civil servants, members of the army and police force, and Isaq businessmen. In 1960, the SNL temporarily merged with the United Somali Party (USP), the minority Dir party from the North, to form a 'Northern coalition'. The perception of neglect and marginalisation that prevailed in the North immediately after independence was also reflected in the military and led to a coup attempt in the same year by Sandhurst-trained Northern Somali military.[2] In 1962, the Northern SNL-cabinet members, among them Egal, left a SYL-led coalition government in protest at Southern domination. In later years, however, the SNL became more accommodating towards the SYL position: there were two SYL/SNL coalition-governments before the coup in 1969 both headed by Egal as prime minister. He had left the SNL in 1962, and founded a party to oppose SYL/Southern dominance – the Somali National Congress (SNC). In 1964, however, he rejoined SNL. The Somali National Congress (SNC) became the party of former-SNL Isaq and former-SYL Hawiye, a coalition that united those who were increasingly disturbed by Darod-dominance in Somali politics, and which would be re-born some twenty years later.[3]

The *Hisbia Dastur Mustaquil al-Sumal* or Somali Independent Constitutional Party (HDMS) defined itself as a party expressing the interests of the settled farmers in the inter-riverine region. Like the SNL, it was anti-SYL. HDMS had been the only opposition force in the trust territory. The party remained an opposition party and never joined a coalition with SYL; rather, it became marginalized and oriented towards the specific interests of its constituency. In the 1960s it was "little more than an economic interest group" which nevertheless kept its "relative strength in every election until 1969" (Kaplan, 1969: p.221).

For the third category of party – those with a membership of just a few individuals – election dynamics led to the following political pattern. In order to

---

2   Within the Somali National Army there was a competitive mood between the ex-Italian and ex-British trained leadership. As the new government was Southern-dominated, the British trained "Sandhurst" group felt undermined in their status and influence within the Army (Kaplan, 1969; Lewis, 1965).

3   The Somali National Movement (SNM) of 1981 was originally founded by an Isaq/Hawiye coalition.

register as a party, individual candidates only needed the support of either 500 voters or of their clan, expressed through a vote of its *shir* (ibid: p.216). These minimal requirements, combined with the overall political influence of the majority SYL party, led to a mushrooming of mini-parties before each election. After the election, these parties would dissolve again and the individuals elected would defect to the major political party, the SYL, in order eventually to secure a position in government. These dynamics undermined the fundamentals of parliamentary democracy and helped transform the political landscape into a *de facto* one-party state.

The 1969 elections exemplify this trend in Somali party politics. In combined municipal and national assembly elections, 64 parties contested seats. After the elections, another 36 parliamentarians who abandoned their 'party' for the winning side joined the 73-strong SYL parliamentary group. In addition, the 11 members of the SNC formed a coalition with SYL, leaving only 3 seats in parliament to opposition parties.[4]

Parliamentarians perceived the central state framework as a source of opportunities and enrichment; in other words, the political system of parliamentary democracy became another layer in the personalized and/or clan-oriented arrangements of security provision. Government positions brought with them better access to educational facilities, such as scholarships abroad and places in the National Teacher Education Center in Afgoi (founded in 1963) or the University Institute of Somalia, which in 1960 was accorded university-status and attached to the University of Rome.[5] Notions such as 'public' property, impartiality towards citizen's rights and entitlements, and the responsibilities and political ethics accompanying these did not really develop. Within the dominant SYL party and with every cabinet to be formed, clan balancing became "a standard operating procedure in democratic Somalia, as government jobs necessarily meant representation for any clan" (Laitin and Samatar, 1987: p.70). The parliamentary system of power distribution seriously increased political instability and led finally to the military coup in 1969.

---

4   The political party scene also included other parties, which played a marginal role in the political developments we are considering. These were partly off-shoots of SYL, such as the Greater Somali League (GSL; since 1964 Somali Democratic Union, SDU), and the Popular Movement for Democratic Action (PMDA). Parties opposing SYL in national elections were the Somali African National Union (SANU), the Somali Liberal Youth Party, the Somali Socialist Party and the Umah Party.

5   The predecessor of the National University was the Higher Institute of Economy and Law, founded in 1954. Under the trusteeship administration a Teacher Training Institute had opened in 1953.

State political institutions did not penetrate society. Instead, non-state political structures penetrated the modern state. But only a minority of people
and lineages could link up with these Mogadishu-based state institutions by
having at least one member of the family positioned within the state apparatus. The majority of the Somali population remained detached from the modern state framework (Doornbos, 1993). The reasons for this were either geographical distance from the capital (the Northern urban population), a
marginalized status within the Somali clan system (the inter-riverine people,
close to the center but excluded), or continuous detachment from modern,
urban life (the pastoral people in the remote central and Northern regions).

Marginalisation was mainly felt with regard to the allocation of state investment in education, infrastructure and development projects. The success rate
of the policies formulated in the first (1963-1967) and the second (1968-1970)
development plans was generally very low (Kaplan, 1969), but if anything was
achieved it was mostly in Mogadishu and adjacent areas. This applies to medical and public health services, such as the allocation and staffing of hospitals
and the introduction of vaccination programs, to educational facilities, such
as the number of secondary schools (three in the North in 1965, six in the
South in 1964) and opportunities for higher education (teacher training centers in the North were only up to elementary level; the only university was in
Mogadishu, with Italian as the teaching medium); and to the emerging manu-
facturing and food-processing industry which was concentrated in and
around Mogadishu. With public investments concentrated in the South, the
North felt seriously neglected. This imbalance had its roots in pre-independence times, particularly with regard to the number of schools, hospitals and
roads, but there was no indication that state policies intended to correct this
imbalance by concentrating more investment in the Northern and central regions, remote from Mogadishu.

On the whole, a basically liberal policy left economic structures more or less
the way they were on the eve of independence (Samatar, 1988). Trade continued undisturbed by state interference. For the inter-riverine farmlands,
apart from the continuation of a liberalized plantation economy in the hands
of foreign investors and a few state farms run by army contingents, subsistence
agriculture experienced a benign neglect (Menkhaus, 1996).

The state also failed to offer a public social security system as an alternative
to sub-state mechanisms rooted in clan/family networks. As outlined above,
the state was perceived as simply an additional factor in the existing (pre-state/
stateless) security arrangements. Trans-state sources of security became incorporated into this structure as international agencies and bilateral creditors
acted as financiers of 'public' investments. They also acted, together with the

national army, as executing organ and as security provider in reaction to disasters such as the floods in 1961 in the South, and in fighting the drought-bred famine in the pastoral areas in 1965.

The independent Somali state was basically a liberal state with a wide range of theoretically guaranteed rights, and not a 'security' state or a police state. The legal system combined *Sharia* and customary law with modern state law so that traditional and modern legal security were just as intermingled as had been the case in pre-independent colonial times. In many respects, local and regional socio-political organizational structures continued to operate, creating a dispersed rather than an integrated domination over social control. Sovereignty *de facto* remained divided; *de jure*, however, it was ascribed to the government of the internationally recognized Somali state.

Territorial Perceptions and the Idea of The Somali State: Background to Darod Dominance

'Greater Somalia' was defined as the unification of all Somali-inhabited territories within the Horn into one Somali nation-state. It was symbolized in the national flag which showed a five-pointed white star on a light-blue background, referring to the five territories – British Somaliland, Italian Somaliland, French Somaliland, the Somali inhabited Bale/Ogaden/Haud regions in Southern Ethiopia, and the Northern Frontier District in the British Crown Colony Kenya. The post-1960 independent Somali state was portrayed as exercising a caretaker function for all those Somali territories, which were not (yet) under Somali political control. The majority of these territories were Darod-inhabited. Consequently, not only were the majority of Darod politicians eager to annex these territories into the independent state framework, and willing to use military means if political means failed in that endeavor; but thanks to the 'Greater Somalia' ideology they could claim in doing so to represent the majority of the Somali people. The 'Greater Somalia' ideology became a source of legitimacy for Darod political dominance. This was constitutionally reflected in the election law, which considered all Somali in the wider Somali region, including those residing in Ethiopia or Kenya, as Somali citizens with a right to vote. During election time, therefore, Somali crossed the border to vote.

Temporary migration was, in a way, nothing out of the ordinary as we saw in chapter 3: Somali pastoral economic activities and trade routes regularly cross international borders. The political and legal perception of state territory as developed in the idea of 'Greater Somalia' and promoted by the first independent Somali leadership reflected economic and social realities in Somali society.

However, the policy of ignoring the definition of state territory as derived from international law in the process of external policy-making and international diplomacy not only increased political and military insecurity in the region but also created a power imbalance within the independent Somali state.

In spite of having members from most clans, the Somali Youth League (SYL) remained a party dominated by Darod. It is difficult to count Somali people in a national census because of pastoral migration and innumerable opportunities for fraud. Nevertheless, it can be said with reasonable certainty that the Darod did not make up the majority of the inhabitants of the Somali Republic, although they might rightfully claim to be the clan occupying the largest territory in the Somali region (map 1). Within the boundaries of the independent Somali state, it was the Hawiye and the Rewin that accounted for the majority of the population.[6] In 1963, at a time when migration of nomadic clans into the inter-riverine region was still very modest (see chapter 4), statistics on the "Estimated regional distribution of population, Somali Republic" published by the Ministry of Health and Labor (see Kaplan, 1969: p.56), reveal that 21% of the population lived in Upper Juba (the inter-riverine Rewin lands), 23% in Benadir (Rewin/Hawiye including multi-clan Mogadishu), 10% in Hiran (mainly Hawiye), 26% in Hargeisa and Burao (the Isaq lands, with a Dir minority), 13% in Majertain and Mudug (Harti/Darod) and 7% in Lower Juba (mixed population of Rewin, Darod, Hawiye and Dir).

After unification the dominant Isaq political party from the North, the Somali National League (SNL), became a minority in Mogadishu. The SYL, in contrary, gained strength as the Dulbahante and Warsangeli clans, the Harti/Darod minority in ex-British Somaliland, joined the big sister party in the

---

6   With regard to population figures, Mukhtar and Kusow (1993: p.8) give the following information: "Census taking has been suppressed in Somalia, but the Italian government's annual report to the United Nation's Trusteeship Council in 1957 provided some interesting demographic figures, based on the six regions of the Italian territories before independence and the unification with the North. According to these figures, Upper Juba, mainly a Reewin country, had far higher population numbers than Mijurtinia and Mudug together, 362,234 and 223,773 respectively. The Benadir region had 387,600 and Lower Juba 113,449. However, it must be noted that large numbers of Dighil and Mirifle occupied what was then Benadir and Lower Juba. Given this, we can safely say that the population of the inter-riverine constitute roughly between 35-40% of the total Somali population. Since the 1957 census, SYL regimes from 1960 to 1969, and the military regime of Barre from 1969 to 1990 opposed any comprehensive census, except the 1974 census of which the results were suppressed."

South. HDMs in the South remained an opposition party but faced an over-whelmingly politically dominant Hawiye/Darod power-bloc.

The Greater Somalia idea of the state, which gave ideological backing to Darod dominance, was presented as representing the one voice of the Somali nation. In fact, however, it was already a controversial idea in Somali politics before and during the 1960s. As early as 1948, the HDMs, the Rewin party, had expressed fear of Samale domination after independence when it pleaded for a 30-year trusteeship under Italian administration. Policy-interests of Italian settlers and plantation owners were apparently considered less threatening and more likely to protect the interests of the farming population in Somalia than policies developed by pastoral dominated (SYL) Somali politicians.

The second group/clan opposing Somali unification as political priorities were the Isaq in the North. As much as the SNL had pushed for a timely inde-pendence of the protectorate from Britain in order to be able to join the trus-teeship territory and form the first independent Somali state, it adopted a modest position on the "Greater Somalia" issue and gave greater priority, first, to the economic development and socio-political integration of the Somali state and society in its 1960 form and, second, to peace with Kenya and Ethio-pia and stability in the region, than to pan-Somali unification. The short pe-riod of Egal-led government in 1968-69 was evidence of this political stand.

As a Northerner and former Somali National League leader, Egal was free of the clannish and political attachments that linked other leading Somali politicians to the Ogaden. In fact, he probably shared the feeling of many Northerners that preoccupation with the Ogaden was retarding develop-ment in other fields (Markakis, 1987: p.181).

The policies of the Egal-government led many Darod hard-liners to leave the SYL parliamentary faction in 1967/69.

EXTERNAL SECURITY POLICIES: INCREASING ROLE AND CAPABILITY OF THE NATIONAL ARMY

After independence, foreign policy concentrated on the 'Greater Somalia' ideal. Somali state authorities focused on two issues: on claiming the right of self-determination of the Somali nation,[7] and on the threat of an Ethiopian in-vasion, which would need the response of a strong Somali national army. The perception of threat was based on historical reference to the Circular Letter of Emperor Menelik of 1891 (see chapter 6). More broadly, there was a growing swell of anti-Christian sentiment, which focused on the Abyssinian and Christian European colonization of the Muslim Somali people. Modern Somali nationalism, which had in fact emerged as a political factor in the context of post World War II negotiations on the future of the Somali colonies, was attributed a historical dimension and justification by labeling 16th century Ahmed Gran (see chapter 5) and 19th century Mohammed Abdulle Hassan (see chapter 6) as 'national heroes'. Nationalism was further fuelled by Ethiopian state-policy in its Somali territories, which was marked by economic neglect and a political atmosphere of occupation (Markakis, 1987).

In their quest for a national army, the independent Somali state authorities approached the West. United States, Italy and Germany offered a tripartite aid program to train and arm 5,000-6,000 soldiers. In late 1963 Somalia rejected the western offer as quantitatively and qualitatively inadequate. The same year, the Somali government announced the acceptance of military assistance from the Soviet Union, which amounted to the equipping and training of a 10,000-strong armed force, including an air force and a small navy. Within a few years, the Somali army had developed into the fifth largest in Africa. In 1968, over 21% of the total national budget was allocated to defense (Kaplan, 1969). Military aid in the form of hardware, spare-parts, technical maintenance, logistical support (gasoline, oil lubricants etc.), military training, the conversion of the Berbera port into a deep-sea harbor, and financing of runways and army barracks, was all supplied by the Soviet Union.

Meanwhile, in a continuation of their activities since the time of the British Military Administration, western governments supported the Somali police force with equipment and training. Political obligations and remaining interests as ex-colonial powers had by the end of the 1960s turned into cold-war-driven policies of counterbalancing the Soviet influence in Somalia. The Somali government did its best to capitalize on the East-West conflict to improve its military capabilities *vis-à-vis* neighboring states.

Founded on the perception of 'a nation in search of a state' (Laitin and Samatar, 1987), Somali external policies led to a short war in 1963/64 with Kenya and to increasing unrest along the border with Ethiopia and in the Ethiopian Ogaden and Bale region throughout the 1960s. During the 1960s, Somali national security policy was primarily defined by external threats.[8] The early

---

7   The right of self-determination for the Somali people included also those living in the Northern Frontier district of Kenya. On the eve of Kenyan independence in 1963, a referendum was held regarding their preference for joining the Somali state or remaining in a future Kenyan state. When the result was a majority in favor of the former, it was quickly hushed-up (Farah, 1993).

post-independence state authorities were at that time not seriously threatened from within[9] and had not developed an extensive security apparatus. External aid to the military and the police force, however, furnished the state with a potential for violence, which could be put into use against either an external or an internal enemy.

During the first decade of independence the armed forces were often deployed in positive roles, which increased the people's trust in the army as protector. The national army was the only state institution that could claim to provide security to all Somali citizens. Its active role in response to natural disasters that struck the country in the 1960s, such as the flooding in 1961, the drought in 1965 and the water shortage in the Northeast complemented its protective function in relation to external threats in April 1969. The national army was assigned an ever-increasing role in nation building (Kaplan, 1969: p.395). In the context of regular public development programs, army units were operating experimental farms in the South (in order to popularize agriculture), working on government road-building programs, digging public wells in nomadic areas, and constructing military installations. The army provided jobs to a large number of people[10] who came from all regions of the country: these were relatively well-paid jobs with high social status. It was a combination of these factors on which General Mohamed Siyad Barre, the leader of the military coup in October 1969, was able to rely, and which created his early successes in rallying the people behind the revolution. In the words of Kaplan (1969: p.406):

> The Somali national Army had achieved more national importance than if it had been merely a customary symbol of national unity and virility. The army had become an increasingly powerful political factor among a people whose way of life was traditionally warlike. Moreover, the army's elite had become the national elite.

Thus, external support for the national security concerns of the government of the independent Somali state actually increased the insecurity-potential of the

---

8   Whether the threat of an Ethiopian invasion was a realistic scenario or merely a constructed "enemy vision" is not relevant here. Somali interests in annexing the Ethiopian-Somali territories were probably stronger than Ethiopia's interest in extending its state boundaries into the Somali Horn.

9   There were, however, unsuccessful military coup attempts by Northern army generals in 1961, and by Southern army generals in 1967.

10   10,000 soldiers relative to a population of some 2.7 million at the time (1968 estimate from Kaplan, 1969).

Somali people in a number of ways. Firstly, international insecurity within the region increased because of the military build-up of large armies in the Horn, on both the Somali (Soviet-supported) and the Ethiopian (American-supported) sides. The 'Greater Somalia' policy only became a military possibility once a strong Somali army was formed. The potential for waging war against Ethiopia implied a direct threat to Somali society, soldiers as well as civilians, on both sides of the border. Secondly, the concentration on military efforts diverted public expenditure away from civilian developmental policies; while this did not necessarily increase economic and social insecurity, it certainly did not improve the living standards of Somali society. The army's involvement in disaster relief and development projects hardly outweighed these tendencies. In the third place, potential insecurity was increased by the strengthening of the Darod-power bloc in the Somali political balance as Somali irredentism transformed itself from a political ideology of Somali nationalism into Somali government policy. Furnishing an already modestly Darod-dominated Somali state network with means of violence to be used either internally or externally, opened opportunities for a further marginalisation and suppression of other clans and political groups and parties within Somalia.

In sum, it is important to note that the road to what followed – a 21-year military dictatorship – was already paved in the first decade of independence.

The Siyad Barre Era 1969-1991: Maximising State-Security, Alienating Society and Fighting Opposition

From Popular Socialism to Autocratic Despotism

On 15 October 1969, President Abdirashid Ali Shermarke was assassinated by one of his bodyguards. This incident left both country and government in a political vacuum. The constitution provided for a situation of sudden death of the president but a few days later on 21 October, a group of army officers under the leadership of the commander of the armed forces, General Mohamed Siyad Barre, took advantage of the situation and staged a bloodless *coup d'état*. When leading politicians, including Prime Minister Egal, were put under house arrest or detained, and a Supreme Revolutionary Council (src) took over state leadership. The end had come for the largely inefficient parliamentary state. In general, this was welcomed by Somali society, since the national army had won the trust of many Somali as one of the few successful factors in Somali nation-building.

The predominant political objectives of the s r c were an elimination of clan rivalry that had produced corruption and nepotism in politics and society. Social, economic and cultural development oriented towards Somali national pride were to be fostered, aiming at the establishment of a Somali script,[11] a general *Somalisation* of the educational system and the elimination of illiteracy. Self-help and self-reliance, belief and pride in the abilities of the nation were all promulgated. These political objectives were considered to be directly linked to the ideology of scientific socialism.[12] While distinguishing itself sharply from the political orientation of the earlier governments, which were characterized as corrupt, clannish and capitalist, the military leadership sought to reconcile the new socialist political outlook with traditional values rooted in Somali society and in Islam. The concept of *zakat* (alms)[13] was transformed into socialist welfare for all, and scientific socialism translated as "sharing wealth based on wisdom".

> With this emphatic religious grounding, scientific socialism, Somali-style, known literally as "wealth-sharing based on wisdom" (hanti-wadaagga 'ilmi ku disan) is closely linked with such key concepts as "unity" or "togetherness" (waddajir), "self-reliance" (is ku kalsoonaan), and "self-help" (iskaa wab u qabso) (Lewis, 1994: p.151).

Popular participation was to be guided by socialist principles. All political parties were banned as expressions of clanism and an institutional structure of democratic centralism was introduced. Revolutionary Councils were established from the local and regional to the national level. The country was reorganized from eight provinces into sixteen regions, comprising sixty-four districts, with an additional fourteen districts in Mogadishu (see map 4). A District Commissioner headed each of these districts. Local orientation centers were meant to build the backbone of socialist society:

> Orientation centers with their public-spirited attendants, were intended to provide an approved alternative basis for social and political activities, indeed to replace the old lineage structure that the government sought to destroy. They represented the new nationalism based on friendship and patri-

---

11 It was not until 1973 that a written Somali language based on the Latin alphabet was finally introduced.

12 Until about the mid-1970s, a Somali-style socialism had strong popular appeal and could therefore be considered the binding "idea" of the Somali state. At a later stage of his rule Siyad Barre relied increasingly on "Greater Somalia" nationalism as the "idea" of the state.

13 The regular payment of *zakat*, literally alms, is one of the five pillars of Islam.

otism, not kinship, and were designed to form the nerve centers of the vibrant new revolutionary life. In some urban areas, they did appear to have become a focus of neighborhood social life in competition with that based on mosque or lineage association (officially banned) (ibid.: p.157).

Sub-state arrangements that had provided security, particularly in social, economic and legal spheres, throughout the early post-independence period became increasingly challenged, threatened or forbidden by state authorities under the Siyad Barre regime. The legal and political functions of clan elders, the *aqils*, were placed under increased state control. Clannism was officially banned and punished by death. There were attempts to sanitize social life of its clan foundations: marriage and funerals, for example, were to be organized by local orientation centers rather than by traditional authorities. In spite of these attempts, however, the state did not succeed in replacing non-state institutions, falling far short of what the clan network offered to society. Customary law and security arrangements rooted in the clan and family support system survived against all odds. In terms of legal security provision, Warsame (1997: p.48) notes:

> A large percentage of conflicts never passed beyond the local police station and were never referred to courts. When cases ended up in the courts, it was common for these cases to be 'taken out' of the courts by the elders of the two conflicting parties and solved according to tradition. In fact, in some instances, like family cases, Somalis prefer to settle them through traditional methods. It can cause embarrassment to the 'elders' and the other family members when such cases are taken to law courts.

Customary and state laws continued to be used in parallel, depending on the subject and the local circumstances of a particular case. However, customary law was not formally integrated into state law.

Each of the eighteen regions (see map 4) had a Regional Revolutionary Council, headed by a military governor as chairman and assisted by local military and police commanders, a regional National Security Service (NSS) chief and a representative of the President's political office, responsible for safeguarding socialist orientation. On the national level, a civilian Council of Secretaries assisted the SRC, the military leadership of the country. Key ministries such as those of defense, of the interior and of information and national guidance (responsible for state-propaganda or national thought control (Lewis, 1994: p.155) were headed by SRC members; other ministries or secretariats were given to civilians. The Supreme Court was abolished and a National Security Court established which was directly controlled by the SRC (Samatar,

1988). The head of state could overrule decisions of the National Security Court.

In 1976, the Somali Revolutionary Socialist Party (SRSP) was founded. This marked the beginning of the transfer from military to civil government. At the foundation congress some 3000 nominees from the military, the security forces and the administration participated, all known for their reliability and political commitment to the cause of scientific socialism. The Central Committee consisted of 74 members and was supposed to meet quarterly. Apart from the chairman, party secretary-general Mohamed Siyad Barre, the political bureau had four members. These were the three vice-presidents of the SRC and the head of the National Security Service (NSS) and Military Intelligence (MI). In the *Africa Contemporary Record* annual report for 1976/77, Legum notes (p.B326):

> thus, the transformation from a military to a civilian regime has been achieved without effectively disturbing the old leadership, while the powers of the president have, if anything, been widened.

The transformation from military to civilian government was completed in 1979 with the adoption of a new constitution. A civilian presidential system was established, and a widening of the political power base of the president became evident. The constitution was approved in a public referendum in August 1979, and in December of that year the first general elections in ten years were held. President Siyad Barre was sworn in on 27 January 1980 for his first six-year term under the new constitution (Legum, 1979/80: p.B306-7).

Although the constitution guaranteed religious freedom, freedom of press, speech and assembly, the right to work and to free education and the right to own private property, it basically reflected a political framework of one-party rule, which did not allow any opposition. Elections to a People's Assembly were to be held every five years, and first took place in December 1979, but all 171 candidates had been proposed by the SRSP and voting was simply a 'yes' or 'no' for the whole list. The President was to be proposed by the Central Committee of the party and elected by the People's Assembly for a term of six years; he was eligible for re-election. Presidential powers included appointments and dismissals of all senior public officials, including the President of the Supreme Court and the Attorney General. As commander of the armed forces and chair of the National Defense Council the president could declare war and proclaim emergency rule. In case of war or emergency Article 83 of the constitution stated "the president shall assume power over the whole country and those articles of the constitution which shall be incompatible with such a situation shall be suspended".

With the introduction of a constitutional political system, providing extensive executive authority to the president, Siyad Barre succeeded at both securing his internal power base and changing the outlook of his regime in order to make it more acceptable to western foreign powers.[14] The Ministry of Information and National Guidance, whose propaganda efforts characterized and praised him daily as father of the nation, presented President Siyad Barre's absolutist authoritarian rule as paternalistic. The reality was that under a civilian disguise all state powers – legislative, juridical and executive – were concentrated in one person. The presidential system introduced by the 1979 constitution transformed one-party rule into one-man rule. In effect, Siyad Barre became the personification of the state, an absolute authoritarian ruler in the sense of *l'état c'est moi.*[15]

As early as October 1980, the president invoked Article 83 and declared a state of emergency. The same month, he revived the institution of Supreme Revolutionary Council and instigated the creation of similar councils in all regions and districts. Under emergency rule the country returned to 1969-style military rule. It was not until March 1982 that emergency rule ended.[16] Even then, the core military leaders remained in key positions, and a real change from military to civilian leadership never took place.

The political institutions of the military state, which supposedly reflected the model of democratic centralism in political practice, left no significant room for stable mechanisms for the transfer of political power. State authority and domination relied on coercion rather than on fair competition between the various social forces operating within society. The state, therefore, was not a legitimized *primus inter pares* but, in its very foundations, was weak and prone to political instability.

---

14 This was particularly important after the shift of superpower politics in the Horn in 1977: the Somali-Ethiopian war had made the Soviet Union a close ally of Ethiopia and forced Somalia to look for allies in the West. See pp.179-184 in the following paragraph.

15 In this respect President Siyad Barre could be compared with Sayyed Mohammed Abdulle Hassan (see chapter 6). Both appealed to a Somali-unifying ideology beyond clan affiliation and both ended up by concentrating all powers in their own person as autocrats and, finally, as tyrants.

16 The same year, emergency rule was re-imposed in the Northern Region/Hargeisa in reaction to the foundation of one of the first opposition movements, the Somali National Movement (SNM), that was backed mostly by Isaq.

State-Security Laws and Institutions: The Tools for State Survival

The legal and institutional instruments of state coercion that secured the Siyad Barre government consisted of a combination of national security/state emergency laws and special units within the army, police and political apparatus. From the very beginning, in 1969/70, the state had a large capacity for violence and potential coercion. Both the army and the police were well trained and equipped by the Soviet Union and a number of Western-European and Arab countries.[17] Decrees issued in the early months after the coup by the Supreme Revolutionary Council provided the legal framework for putting these coercive means of social control into use for the sake of national security, i.e. for the sake of state security and ultimately state survival.

One of the first decrees to be enacted by the src in 1969 abolished the right of *habeas corpus*.[18] Other laws or decrees built the framework for institutions such as the National Security Court (law no.03 of 10 January 1970) and National Security Service (law no.14 of 15 February 1970). Special judicial powers were granted to the Supreme Revolutionary Council by law no.38 of 5 April 1972. Other institutions in the service of national security were the *Hangash* (*Hayada Nabadgelyada Gaashaandhiga*) or military intelligence, *Dabarjebinta* or military counter intelligence, *Koofiyad-casta* or military police (the red hats), *Barista Hisbiga*, or party investigators and *Guulwadayaal* or party militias (the victory pioneers).[19] In the early 1980s, the jurisdiction of a Mobile Military Court (*Maxkamada Wareegta*) that had originally been created as a military tribunal for the army was extended to include civilians (Africa Watch, 1990).

In the early years of military rule the state was not threatened from within, but was generally supported by a majority of Somali people. As Africa Watch (1990: p.26) noted in retrospect:

> Between 1971 and 1977, the political structure set up by President Barre and the economic policies he pursued produced mixed results. Many sectors of

---

17 Italy, Britain, West Germany, East Germany, Libya and Egypt were, to my knowledge, the most influential in this context.

18 "We cannot help but note, hereby, in a combination of shame and irony, that under European colonial rule, the ordinary Somali enjoyed the right to *Habeas Corpus* where as he has been arbitrarily deprived of such rights as a citizen by the regime as early as October, 1969 with Decree Law No.64" (Manifesto No.1, reprinted in Brons, 1993a/b: p.103).

19 Manifesto No.1 (15 May 1990) and Africa Watch (1990).

society were hostile to the rhetoric and the measures, political, economic and social, inspired by "scientific socialism", which they regarded as anathema to Islam. Many educated Somalis were particularly critical of the government's educational and economic policies. The ubiquitous security system, the clampdown on freedom of expression and the lack of any opportunities for political and civic activities were deeply unpopular. On the other hand, the emphasis on self-reliance generated a degree of genuine enthusiasm, spurred by mass propaganda techniques and myriad mass civic organizations sponsored and closely controlled by the state. It is important to keep in mind that these policies, in both a positive and negative sense, directly affected, for the most part, urban dwellers. It was not until the late 1970s and particularly, the 1980s, when the government began to implement its counter-insurgency tactics, that the rural population felt the full force of government policies.

The fact that the leading Isaq, Majertain, Hawiye politicians of the former government were not executed but held under continuous house-arrest could be taken as a sign of the src's confidence and relatively relaxed attitude towards political adversaries. Nonetheless, although the state leadership did not turn to openly despotic policies of threatening particular individuals or groups/clans in the early 1970s, from the very beginning the military state ruled through means of coercion.

A legal and institutional framework based on national security considerations built the foundation for increasing despotism in the 1980s. Political institutions for popular participation such as the Somali Revolutionary Youth Organization (sryo), the Somali Women's Democratic Organization (swdo), the Worker's Organization and the Victory Pioneers, were used as instruments of indirect control rather than for genuine participation.

> Since some members [of the victory pioneers] were popularly assumed to have had close links with the National Security Service, it was generally felt to be dangerous to ignore their appeals for "voluntary" co-operation in kind or cash to help with the latest campaign (Lewis, 1994: p.156).

This increasingly also applied to the Somali Revolutionary Socialist Party where internal opposition and discussion diminished throughout the 1980s. These years were marked by several reshuffles not only in the Party leadership but also in the Cabinet and the Political Bureau. The president made use not only of standard procedures such as early retirement and exchange of ministerial positions, but also of detentions without trial, death sentences, and the lengthy imprisonment of probable political adversaries.

Throughout the Siyad Barre era imprisonment, extra-juridical killings, torture and other widespread violations of human rights accompanied political control. These government tactics were recalled by the Manifesto Group, an initiative of more than one hundred prominent Somali men from politics, business and clergy, in a document called Manifesto No.1. The Manifesto was published in 1990 at a time when the country was deeply torn by civil war and the power base of the president had diminished to a minimum. Manifesto No.1 notes:

> In its twenty years rule, the present Regime has succeeded to have monopoly of power in the domains of politics, economy and security. In the process, the people lost all their basic freedoms and their role in the participation of the affairs of their own country. Well known to all is the regimes arbitrary practice of throwing thousands of innocent citizens to prison simply because they happened to comment on certain governmental policies or decision which seemed to them unjust and inefficient; worse still, others were jailed for mere suspicion of being members or sympathizers of the opposition. Thousands of citizens have suffered years of imprisonment under cruel living conditions without proper food, water, light, health care, bedding etc., for periods up to 17 years. Many have been tortured and others have died while still in detention without any formal charges or due process of law (Brons, 1991: p.102-3).

The early post-coup confidence in the military leadership and in the army as the only trustworthy national institution, was quickly overshadowed and was finally superseded by fear of the state in all walks of life, as state authorities monopolized political power and undermined any legal political opposition.

In the early 1970s, the military and political leadership represented a relative clan balance. Members of Isaq, Hawiye, and Darod sub-clans were to be found in the inner circle of political power. *Conditio sine qua non* for occupying a high political office was absolute personal loyalty to the head of state rather than a particular clan allegiance. However, this did not imply that an impartial citizen or socialist identity had replaced clan identity. Indeed, in spite of proclamations on the day of the *coup d'état* in 1969, there was never any genuine attempt to eradicate clanism. It was rather that political clan balancing, as it had been known from earlier times, was used by the Siyad Barre government during its first years in power.

With regard to clan affiliation at the state leadership level, the change from pre-1969 to post-1969 consisted broadly speaking of a shift from a Darod (Majertain)/Hawiye towards a Darod (Marehan/Ogaden/Dulbahante) alliance (see diagram 1). Particularly from the late 1970s, the state leadership relied on clan affiliation to retain control in the army and other state institutions, particularly the state security institutions. Members of these came predominantly from the Marehan, Siyad Barre's father's clan, the Ogaden, his mother's clan, and the Dulbahante, the clan of one of his sons-in-law. The faction on whom Siyad Barre's power rested thus came to be known as the MOD-faction. With regard to territorial considerations, it is important to note that the Marehan and Ogaden sub-clans of the Darod clan family are situated in the Somali-Ethiopian borderlands and that the Dulbahante border Isaq and Majertain territory in the Northern part of the country. By the early 1980s, the Marehan occupied most important government, party and army positions including the majority of the army troops in the Mogadishu region; all Red Brigade personal bodyguard troops of the President were Marehan.

In short, coercive state policies covered over the reality of diminishing legitimacy and were increasingly exerted following a clan rationale. These developments furthered alienation from the state. People were not free to express their views. NSS spies were all over the country. The political orientation of government employees was controlled by obligatory gatherings of their working units. Those who refused to sing the praise songs in honor of the president at the opening and closure of every meeting, risked detention. Faced by a police state that could be identified with a specific clan coalition, people trusted nobody but their closest relatives and lineage members.

The Interplay Between Somali Foreign and International Security Policies

We now turn to linkages between international security policies, Somali external security policies, and the impact of these on the Somali people. The argument made in chapter 2 that for a state that enjoys sovereignty deriving from the international system based on international law (*de jure* sovereignty), it is often external military, political or financial backing that provides the means of survival for a state that fundamentally lacks internal, *de facto* sovereignty, is relevant here. International security considerations and the security needs of a weak state complement each other, creating greater insecurity for people in the process.

Foreign Policy Orientation: Somalia as Partner of the Soviet Union

Already before Siyad Barre came to power in 1969, the Somali state had a large military potential at its disposal. Under Siyad Barre's political leadership this potential for the use of force became activated (1) against the internal enemy, supporting Barre's dictatorship; and (2) against the external enemy, when Somalia waged war against Ethiopia.

After 1969, there were basically two sets of external factors, which substantially supported the survival of the Somali state: the politics of superpower rivalry in the Horn, and international humanitarian aid to Ethiopian-Somali refugees. President Siyad Barre pursued a strategy of turning externally rooted policy-interests in Somalia to the advantage of his own personalized regime.

By shifting towards a socialist ideology in internal policy-formulations immediately after 1969, Siyad Barre sharpened the East-West confrontation in the Horn of Africa. At that time Ethiopia, under the reign of Emperor Haile Selassie, was a close client state of the United States (Lyons, 1986; Makinda, 1987). The Soviet Union, which had been involved in Somalia since 1963, welcomed the shift of Somali state ideology towards socialism as this opened an opportunity for stabilizing Soviet influence in the Horn and emphasizing its role as a global power in competition with the United States. This became particularly important after 1972, when a serious deterioration occurred in Soviet-Egyptian relations after the Egyptian president, Anwar El-Sadat, expelled Soviet military advisors and limited the harbor facilities for the Soviet military fleet. Somalia offered a viable alternative (Makinda, 1987; Porter, 1984). In addition, the shift of America's main military intelligence station in the region from Kagnew in Ethiopia/Eritrea to the Indian Ocean island of Diego Garcia necessitated an increased presence of the Soviet fleet in the Northwestern Indian Ocean and the Red Sea. Given the distance of its home harbors, Soviet interest concentrated on securing harbor facilities for its fleet. In 1972, the number of Soviet military personnel in Somalia raised considerably (reaching 2,500 by 1974), many of them moving directly from Egypt to Somalia (Patman, 1982; Makinda, 1987). In the same year, the modernization of facilities at Berbera began:

> The Berbera complex at one time encompassed a good-size deep-water port, barracks housing for over 1,000 personnel, a long-range high-frequency communications center that was apparently a key center of Soviet command and control in the Indian Ocean, a large petroleum storage area, and an airstrip more than 13,000 feet in length. Between late 1973 and 1976 the Soviet Union constructed a sophisticated handling and storage facility for conventional missiles at the Berbera site, the only one of its kind outside the USSR (Porter, 1982: p.52).

In a sense Siyad Barre also capitalized on Sino-Soviet rivalry (Olufemi, 1983/84). He engaged both the Soviet Union and China in Somalia, the former mainly in the military field of operations (hardware, software, training, logistics) and to a minor extent in industrialization projects (fish-processing industries), and the latter in infrastructure developments, the most important being the construction of the first (and to date the only) asphalt road linking the South to the North. In 1973, Chinese economic aid to Somalia surpassed that of the Soviet Union (ibid. also Patman, 1982). However, political and military co-operation with the Soviet Union was considered a priority and was sealed in 1974 with a bilateral contract of friendship and co-operation. The foundation of the Somali Revolutionary Socialist Party in 1976 was marked by the Soviet Union in the form of a generous extension of military aid to Somalia.[20]

Shifting Regional and Superpower Politics in the Horn and the Somali Defeat in the War against Ethiopia

The political landscape in the Horn of Africa changed dramatically when, in 1974, the Ethiopian revolution brought an end to the rule of Emperor Haile Selassie. In the two following years of Red Terror, the pro-Soviet oriented political clique around Mengistu Haile Mariam gained the upper hand in deciding on the political future of Ethiopia. In December 1976, the Soviet Union agreed to deliver military aid to Ethiopia (Steven, 1979), an agreement, which was extended in May 1977, after the Ethiopian leadership had expelled all American military advisors from the country a month earlier. Ethiopian-American relations that had been deteriorating since the revolution, declined still further with the beginning of the presidency of Jimmy Carter in January 1977, with its emphasis on human rights in American foreign policy. At about the same time, the Red Terror in Ethiopia reached its peak when Mengistu had the members of the rival political group around Taferi Bante murdered at a political meeting in February 1977.

The Soviet Union blueprint for the Horn of Africa (supported by Cuba) envisaged a socialist federation of Somalia, Southern Yemen and Ethiopia, a so-called 'pax Sovietica' that included the possibility of an autonomous status for Eritrea[21] as well as the Ogaden region (Garthoff, 1985). Cuban president

---

20 During the years 1974-1977 Soviet military aid amounted to a total of US$ 300 million (see Korn, 1986: p.18-19). There were at that time 1,678 Soviet military advisors in Somalia (see Makinda, 1987: p.119).

Fidel Castro and then foreign minister Alexander Podgorny traveled to Somalia and Ethiopia in March and April 1977 to canvass support for this political approach. It would have enabled the Soviet Union to keep its strategic investments in the Berbera deep-sea harbor in Somalia while gaining, in Ethiopia, an ally who could be considered economically and politically a much more influential and powerful partner on the African continent than Somalia.

At the same time, the Somali government was concerned with safeguarding a continuous Soviet military supply. Not only was the government increasingly supporting the guerrilla activities of the Western Somali Liberation Front[22] (wslf) in Southern Ethiopia, and even thinking of launching an attack against a weakened Ethiopia but also, in general, the government's strength depended on the army, and the army, even after thirteen years of military co-operation, still depended on Soviet logistical and technical assistance. In early 1977, therefore, the Somali government protested vehemently against Soviet military commitments to Ethiopia and expressed its concern that it would be impossible to maintain a Soviet military presence in both countries (Makinda, 1987). After having discussed with the new Ethiopian leadership in 1976 the possibility of an autonomous status for the (Somali) Ogaden region in Ethiopia, and after the Castro-Podgorny initiative had failed, Somalia strengthened the fighting power of the guerrillas of the Western Somali Liberation Front (wslf) and Somali and Abbo Liberation Front[23] (salf) and finally, in July 1977, regular troops of the Somali National Army joined the war. Since there had been signs from the United States as well as Saudi Arabia that military support would be forthcoming if Somalia were to break away from its Soviet ally (Garthoff, 1985; Makinda, 1987), it seems certain that Siyad Barre had again designed his policies at that critical time in terms of the rationality of superpower rivalry rationality. Although there were no concrete commitments from the side of the United States, Garthoff's (1985: p.637) assessment seems fair:

---

21 Eritrea, an ex-Italian colony had been annexed by the Ethiopian emperor in 1961, and since then, fought for independence.

22 The Western Somali Liberation Front emerged from protest movements by Somali clans in Southeastern Ethiopia. wslf was founded in 1970, and considered its range of action to be the Somali-inhabited areas in Ethiopia East of the Shabelle river (Markakis, 1987).

23 The Somali Abbo Liberation Front, founded in the early 1970s, took as its area of operation the Somali and partly Oromo inhabited areas west of the Shabelle river or Bale region (Markakis, 1987).

It is however, very likely that Siad and his colleagues believed the United States was so intent on squeezing out Soviet influence and building its own relations with Somalia by supplying arms that it would have little choice but to go along, even if reluctantly, with the Somali action. Certainly they saw the continued high-level re-affirmations of a positive American interest in military assistance throughout the escalating conflict in July as readiness to provide support.

However, the Somali government had overestimated their importance to American interests in the Horn. Strategically, the base on Diego Garcia covered American needs in the region. The loss of Ethiopia as a location for American stations in that regard was not considered serious, and the gain of Berbera less vital for the us than its loss would be for the Soviet Union. Although some claim that the Americans had ambitions of eventually arming the Somali and the Eritreans in order to involve the Soviet Union and Cuba in a costly war (see Makinda, 1987), this would have contravened the international legal framework of sovereignty and territorial integrity. Support for Somali nationalism (or, as some call it, irredentism) would have violated oau norms with regard to the sacrosanct nature of ex-colonial borders and would have been counterproductive for America's African policies in general. Somalia was not of such importance that America would have paid this high a price and taken such risks. That is probably the reason that, in early August, the American government declared that no military support would be given to Somalia because of Somali violations of oau norms and the security concerns for America's ally Kenya.

In October 1977, having first delivered arms to both parties, the Soviet Union made a final choice between supporting its long-standing ally Somalia or Ethiopia in the Ogaden war. The ussr stopped weapons deliveries to Somalia. In reaction to that, on 13 November, the Somali government ordered all Soviet and Cuban advisors to leave within 24 hours. About one week later the Soviet Union and Cuba began sending troops (more than 10,000 Cuban soldiers) and war equipment worth about us$ 1 billion (three times as much as the Americans had sent in the previous 25 years) via air and sea to Ethiopia. Contrary to its expectations the Somali government did not receive military aid from the West and finally, in March 1978, the Somali troops were forced to withdraw from the Ogaden. The only support from the us to Somalia was a warning given to the Soviet-Cuban troops not to cross into Somali state territory.

Thus Somali political calculations and expectations for capitalizing on superpower rivalry were dashed by the reluctance of the American government. Military aid to Somalia was only slowly forthcoming and was always accompanied by conditions that it could not be put to use in operations connected with the Ogaden issue. The Western Somali Liberation Front (wslf) and the Somali and Abbo Liberation Front (salf) were involved in sporadic border-skirmishes with Ethiopian troops throughout the first half of the 1980s; they received limited military and logistic support from the Mogadishu government and maintained offices in Mogadishu until about 1986/87.

After 1984, as a result of pressure from the American Congress not to agree to military aid to Somalia until guerrilla activities directed against Ethiopia had ended, the government had to change its attitude towards the Greater Somalia policy in order to secure its own survival. An agreement recognizing borders with Kenya was reached in 1984, and in 1988 initial peace talks between Ethiopian president Mengistu Haile Mariam and Somali president Siyad Barre resulted in confidence-building measures leading to a recognition of borders. The potential threat to the Somali state by external enemies was thereby reduced due to outside political pressure.

The American government was only interested in a strong and stable leadership in Somalia and did not take into account the extent to which it was strengthening the Somali state potential for violence against its own citizens. Although support of army and police remained modest, it helped secure the survival and functioning of the state-security apparatus. The international security policy considerations of the American and other western governments, and the security needs of the weakened Somali state leadership thus complemented each other, creating in the process more instability for the population in the conflict region.

The Aftermath of War

Stabilization of the Governmental MOD-Faction and the Foundation of the First Opposition Movements

The clan coalition within the Somali army that represented the president's power base was strengthened after the war. Several leading fighters from the Western Somali Liberation Front (wslf) were incorporated into the Somali National Army in 1978, increasing the coercive powers and political influence of the head of state. The majority of wslf and salf fighters stayed with their families in refugee-camps that were established in the Southern and Northern territories of Somalia in 1979.

In the aftermath of the defeat by Ethiopia in April 1978, Somali army officers of mainly Darod/Majertain clan affiliation staged a *coup* attempt. The failure of this attempt prompted the formation of an open opposition: officers who fled Somalia after the coup to seek political asylum in Ethiopia founded the Somali Salvation Front (SOSAF). In 1981, SOSAF and other groups founded the Somali Salvation Democratic Front (SSDF) (Legum, 1981/82). Although the majority of SSDF were made up of Harti Darod (Majertain, Warsangeli, and Dulbahante), the organization at that time also included Hawiye fighters, intellectuals, politicians and officers. The political program of SSDF had a strong Marxist rhetoric. Its main political objectives were the overthrow of Siyad Barre, Somali neutrality in international politics, the strengthening of relations with the Arab World and the commencement of peace talks with Ethiopia.

At the beginning of the 1980s, there were border clashes between Ethiopian army units and the Western Somali Liberation Front (WSLF), which at that time was launching sporadic attacks from Somali soil against Ethiopian targets. Ethiopian units captured two Somali villages. SSDF units in Ethiopian exile fought on the Ethiopian side, while WSLF forces whose members came originally from the Ogaden region in Ethiopia, received financial and material support from the Somali government.

The second opposition movement against the government of Siyad Barre was the Somali National Movement (SNM). It was founded in April 1981 in London, where the European office of the organization was established. The main headquarters of SNM, however, became Ethiopia, where SNM-members found political asylum. Members of the SNM came mainly from the Isaq clan in Northern Somalia, and partly from the Hawiye clan.

The establishment of an opposition movement in Northern Somalia was born of social, economic and political grievances over the continuous policy of Southern patronage combined with restrictive and increasingly coercive state-security policies in the aftermath of defeat in the Ogaden war. Support for the political aim of the Ogaden war – the forceful liberation of Somali from Ethiopian domination and eventual integration of the Ogaden region into the Somali state – had been very limited among the Northern Somali people.

In addition, the anti-religious attitude of the government rooted in the official ideology of scientific socialism that was rejected by large parts of the Somali population in the North as well as in the South. The SNM took up this issue in its program. "The Somali National Movement ... emphasizes its support for Islam, the traditional faith of the Somali people, which is felt to be undermined by Barre's secular state" (Legum, 1986/87: p.B410).

SNM's vision of external relations focused on an improvement in relations with the Arab world; this was considered a cornerstone for the foreign policy of any future Somali government. This concentration on the Arab states was born out of frustration at the enormous influence of the superpowers, USA and USSR, on Somali foreign policy at the time of SNM's foundation in 1981.

Political and some material support for the SNM were forthcoming from (ex-)Southern Yemen and Libya, and chiefly from Ethiopia (Salad Elmi, 1992). SNM used its bases in Ethiopia, located in the Haud area (map 1), for attacks on government installations in the North in and around Hargeisa and Burao, including the bombardment of military targets and the liberation of political prisoners (Legum, 1986/87). SNM anti-government activities continued sporadically throughout the first half of the 1980s.

Securing the State along Clan Lines: The Persecution of Majertain and Isaq Populations

In reaction to SSDF anti-government activities, parts of the Somali population and particularly those belonging to the Majertain clan in the Northeast were subjected to reprisals by the government. Africa Watch (1990: p.29) notes:

> The atrocities in the Mudug/Hiran region in 1978/81 have not been documented, partly because international human rights groups had not begun to focus on Somalia, and partly because when the abuses were taking place, there were not as many Somalis living abroad to publicize these developments. The pattern of abuses against Majertain civilians, concentrated mainly in Northeastern and Central Somalia, was a bitter foretaste of what was in store for the Issaks, the Ogaden and the Hawiye – extra-juridical executions, rape, the killing of livestock and the destruction of reservoirs. The government's scorched-earth policy was intended to deprive the SSDF of a civilian base of social and political support.

Soon afterwards, the Isaq population in the North of the country suffered from similar state security policies. Political and economic discrimination against the Northern region had been a regular occurrence since the early post-independence years and turned into open hostilities and clan-related state terrorism directed against Isaq people. After the foundation of SNM in 1981 and their first attacks on military installations in the Northern region reprisals began against Isaq in both the North and the South. From 1982 onward, in spite of the early reluctance of the civilian population to support the SNM, all Isaq were nonetheless suspected of being SNM-supporters and were punished accordingly. The Northern regional capital Hargeisa had the atmosphere of a town under military siege; special emergency regulations were put into effect and civilians were put under the jurisdiction of military tribunals and the military police.

The extraordinary powers given to the military and security forces under the state of emergency gave them unlimited power over the lives of civilians and led to violent excesses as a matter of policy (Africa Watch, 1990: p.8)

An Africa Watch report entitled "Somalia: A Government at War with its own People" (1990) provides shocking accounts of human rights abuses and reprisals against Isaq in the North. Somali civil servants from Southern or at least non-Isaq clans usually executed the harsh government policies in the North. This policy augmented hatred between clans and formed part of the president's strategy of divide and rule. These experiences encouraged many young Isaq men to join the SNM.

The State's Instrumentalisation of Refugee Policy

The defeat by Ethiopia in 1977/78 triggered off a huge flow of Somali-Ethiopian refugees into Somalia. This reached its peak in the early 1980s when an estimated 1.5 million[24] refugees were counted, enlarging the country's normal population of less than 4 million by almost 40% (Legum, 1980/81; see also chapter 4).

In terms of the political power balance within the army as well as with regard to economic considerations, the refugee crisis turned out to be a blessing in disguise for president Siyad Barre. Humanitarian and food aid to refugees in the aftermath of the Ethiopian-Somali war played an important part in the survival of the regime.

From 1979 onwards, UNHCR and numerous NGOs took up the refugee issue, bringing vast amounts of aid – food, medicine, and related equipment, transport facilities, such as trucks, cars and related spare parts, etc. – into the country. In 1980, US$ 132 million were channeled to Somalia through UNHCR, including US$ 66 million for food. Major donors were the United States, the

---

24 The estimate of 1.5 million refugees was contested by a UN survey in 1981, which came to an estimate of 600.000. UNHCR, finally agreed to use a planning estimate of 900.000. More than 90% of the refugees were women, and although post-war fighting in the Ogaden-region had ended by 1982, it was the insecure political as well as economic situation which led many men to leave their family in safe camps while they continuing their business of trading and herding.

European Community, Canada, China, Iraq, Saudi Arabia and Sweden. Food aid given in the context of UNHCR activities in the country made its way to the urban markets and impacted on local production.

The National Refugee Commission (NRC) was responsible for the placement of refugees and the national administration of aid. Housed in an impressive building in Mogadishu, a huge administrative body emerged, offering numerous opportunities for jobs in Mogadishu and in the regional headquarters of the NRC, as well as in each of the thirty-four refugee camps (Legum, 1981/82). In addition to steady public employment, the refugee sector also provided material support to those with good connections to the NRC administration. The majority of these state-controlled sources of income went to Darod clan-members, the clan not only of the core of the government (Marehan/Ogaden/Dulbahante) but also of the refugees themselves.[25] The NRC also became one of the largest public employers in the North after the establishment of refugee camps in 1979/80 gave positions to non-residents and/or non-Isaq (Africa Watch, 1990).

In this context one has to re-conceptualize the term 'refugee'. Ethiopian citizens of Somali ethnic origin had crossed international borders, fleeing from war and from a regime, which punished the Somali population for conspiracy during the war.[26] However, those who fled from Ethiopia mostly came from Darod clan territories. Refugee families – mainly women, children and the elderly – settled in camps in the South and in the North. They received food aid, basic health care and schooling, and were offered small-scale income-generating projects. In many ways the refugees, perceived as the government clique's 'own people',[27] were better off than the local population – the Isaq in the North and the Rewin in the South. In addition, the government took land

---

25 "Discrimination was obvious. Jobs were given, as a matter of priority, either to refugees or Southerners. Northern businessmen were 'encouraged' to pay money 'to help the refugees'. Otherwise, they faced the threat of arrest and having their business crippled. ... At Berbera, Isaak men who worked at the port were dismissed so that refugees could be hired in their place." (Interview with A. M. Hawsi Kirih, a businessman from Hargeisa, in London on July 9, 1989). "Every Isaak in a prominent government job was seconded by a refugee who, after a short while, would take over and be in command." (Interview with S. A. Mataan from Hargeisa, London, 17 August 1989, in Africa Watch, 1990: p.32-33.)

26 Not all Ethiopian-Somali had fought for the Greater Somalia cause, some being committed Ethiopian citizens. See Brons et al. (1995).

27 Fieldwork experience in 1986.

from local populations for refugee settlements/camps and for small-scale agricultural projects for refugees.

Northwestern Somalia had to accommodate a large number of refugees arriving from the Ogaden region in the immediate post-war period. In 1982, of 700,000 refugees from Ethiopia, 250,000 were sheltered in camps in the Northwestern region (Brons et al., 1993: p.26, table 2). Economic and social inequalities between the huge refugee population and the people living in these refugee-receiving areas and locations were sharpened by traditional clan animosities between Isaq and Ogaden Somali (Markakis, 1989). Against this background, the Isaq population in and around Hargeisa protested when land taken from residents was given to refugees, meaning that land traditionally belonging to the Isaq clan family came under the control of the Darod clan family. Pre-state perceptions of land ownership in the pastoral context relied on customary rights over the control and usage of land, pasture and water (see chapters 4 and 5). These conflicted with state perceptions and state laws that declared all land to be state-owned, thereby establishing the right of the government to determine the allocation of land including, in this context, allocation of land to refugees. The government was not perceived by the Isaq population in the North to be acting impartially in this matter, however, but was seen as being controlled and dominated by Darod clan interests.

In the South as well as in the North the local populations resented the wave of migration of mostly Darod people into 'their' areas (see map 3). In the Southern Rewin region this resentment towards government refugee policies did not find a political voice. In the Northwestern Isaq areas the SNM gained more and more support among the Isaq population. In response, Ogaden refugees were used as political spies by the government, and were armed and mobilized for anti-SNM attacks and, at a later stage, in the persecution of the Isaq civilian population (Africa Watch, 1990).

ECONOMY AND TRADE

Discriminatory State Policies

State policies in the economic and trading sector affected Somali society in different ways. Socialist policies favored the state *vis-à-vis* the private sector. The nationalization of foreign banks, the electricity company and several other industries and agricultural enterprises (state farms/plantations) created a number of employment opportunities for people connected to government circles.

Towards the end of the 1970s the parastatals faced stagnation and underproduction caused by miscalculations in government economic planning, shortage of skilled management and lack of new investments (Braun, 1992). In 1985 the state sector was drastically reformed and reduced according to an IMF structural adjustment program.[28] By that time, the refugee-related economy offered new opportunities for government-controlled employment.

In terms of the allocation of development aid and state investments, the North felt extremely neglected.[29] State expenditure in the economic sector, such as on infrastructure and the maintenance of government buildings, was lower than in colonial times under the British administration. In the industrial sector the only two big projects were a fish-processing plant in Las Qorey and a cement plant close to Berbera (Africa Watch: 1990). Smaller plants, mainly in the food-processing sector and some of them in private hands, were developed in the North. Civil service positions for Northerners remained scarce because of the centralization of government and administration in Mogadishu.

While the South saw the implementation of numerous agricultural projects, there was only one major agricultural project in the Northern region – the 'North West Region Agricultural Development Project' initiated in 1978, which concentrated on the area around Gebiley. It was supposed to improve the water availability for humans and animals, increase sorghum and maize production, and offer the availability of tractor- and bulldozer-services. The project, however, failed to address the real needs of the local farmers; it increased their dependency on government officials and made their situation rather insecure (Samatar, 1989). In 1983 a law was promulgated prohibiting the farming of *qaat*, which had become a viable cash crop in the Northwest in the late 1970s. Agro-pastoralists who had gone into the production of qaat as a relatively climate-independent and therefore reliable crop, and who had relied on the high prices and steady demand of qaat to secure their otherwise unpredictable income, suffered from these state policies.

While the state provided economic security mainly to those clans who had access to public employment in the government bureaucracy, state enterprises and in the refugee administration, it was mainly the Hawiye and the Isaq who dominated the two major centers of formal private commerce, Mogadishu in the South and Berbera in the North. The trading community in Northern So-

---

28 "Over 20% of state employees is the estimated number made redundant in the whole of Somalia" (Aves and Bechtold, 1987: p.160).
29 In a memorandum to the President dated March 30, 1982, 21, Isaq elders summarised Isaq grievances. Printed in *Africa Watch* (1990: p. 35-37).

malia[30] maintained intensive trading contacts with their Arab neighbors across the Red Sea, including North and South Yemen, Saudi Arabia and Oman. Industrial products, such as clothes, shoes, cosmetics, household utensils etc. were primarily imported through Berbera for resale in other parts of the country. Mogadishu, the capital, was the main import-export harbor in the South, particularly for the export of bananas and, to a lesser extent, livestock.

Saudi Arabia had long been the main importer of Somali livestock, 90% of which was exported via the deep-sea harbor Berbera.[31] The export of livestock and related products (hides and skins) accounted for about 80% (in 1980) and 93.9% (in 1982) of all export earnings. Throughout the socialist period and especially after economic liberalization in the early 1980s, the livestock sector remained basically in private hands. The government had tried in vain to gain control of the pastoral sector by resettlement and sedentarisation programs during the 1974 *dhabadeer* drought and by rangeland management projects in the Northern and Central regions (Samatar, 1989; Janzen, 1987). These had all largely failed to control the migration of pastoral herds and people and the production and marketing of livestock. In 1985, the Somali herd was estimated to number 40 million heads (making it one of the largest in Africa), with 4.2 million cattle, 6 million camels, 11 million sheep and 19 million goats.

It was in response to the formation of the Northern opposition movement, SNM, in 1982 that government policies in the economic sector became openly clannish, directed against Isaq businessmen in Mogadishu and threatening Hawiye businessmen in order to avoid the formation of an anti-government coalition. One of the ways in which many Isaq businessmen and women were disadvantaged in trade was in the issuing of licenses and credits (Africa Watch, 1990). During the first years of socialist transformation all import trade was brought under state control. This control was loosened toward the end of the 1970s, but in 1982, the "letter of credit" system was reintroduced in the South, and introduced for the first time in the North. Letters of Credit could only be obtained in Mogadishu. According to a memorandum that was written by Isaq elders, the legal entitlement for Northerners to receive Letters of Credit was restricted to a few commodities, and the administrative process was seriously hampered by government authorities in the capital. Underdeveloped communication and transportation links from the North to the South, where

---

30 Many of the big merchant families from the North, from the Isaq clan, were resident in Mogadishu.

31 See map of Livestock Export Routes in Somalia (Samatar, 1989 p.104).

the decision-making process was centralized and indeed monopolized, caused additional problems for the Northern businessmen.

In response to rising opposition, pastoralists, too, became the victims of discriminatory policies (Africa Watch 1990, Warsame, 1997). Water-wells were destroyed or poisoned and landmines caused victims among the pastoral population. Women were on their way to fetch water or firewood raped by government soldiers. Livestock was confiscated from Northern Somali pastoralists. "In fact many of these underpaid soldiers made it a habit to live off the nomads. The majority of the respondents, 70%, indicated looting by government soldiers as the major reason for animal losses" (Warsame, 1997: p.22). The transport of livestock to the export harbor of Berbera and to the regional capital Hargeisa was severely disrupted by countless military control posts on main access roads.

Sub-state Coping Mechanisms

Faced with government economic policies, which favored certain clans and discriminated against others, and in reaction to deteriorating economic conditions in the country, several coping mechanisms emerged at the sub-state level. Some Isaq from the North left to become migrant workers in the Gulf States. They used the so-called *franco valuta* system (Jamal, 1992) in order to send money home to their families. The SNM was financed in the same way (Clapham, 1990). The *franco valuta* system bypassed the official banks and official exchange rates by involving Somali merchants as middlemen between the migrant worker and his family in Somalia. Somali traders used the hard currency of the migrant worker in order to purchase consumer goods for informal import into Somalia. The family of the migrant worker received the remittances at free-market (black market) exchange rate. This system of trust relied heavily on the clan network. It avoided official state channels, with the result that the national bank lost control over a substantial proportion of the import trade. According to Jamal's characterization (1992: p.138) of the Somali formal urban economy, there was very little left of it anyway:

> The reality is that apart from government employees whose salaries are regulated, everybody else in the urban economy operates in the informal economy, which as opposed to the formal economy is essentially a free-market economy.

In the *franco valuta* system, the exchange rate was continuously adjusted to free-market conditions and devaluated, while the official exchange rate was not, leading to big discrepancies: in 1980, for example, the official rate was one third of the black market rate. The state tried to regain control by offering a higher exchange rate to remitted money, but this largely failed (Legum, 1981/82). As part of the IMF structural adjustment program, the government agreed to a substantial devaluation of the Somali shilling in order to encourage the channeling of remittances through its banking system, where they could be used for its own priorities.

> It has so far met with practically no success in capturing the remittances because (a) the free market always gives better rates and (b) the free market ensures safe delivery of money to the remotest corners in Somalia. The banks cannot match this, simply because there are no banks where potential customers and beneficiaries are (Jamal, 1992: p.148).

In livestock trade, government controls dictated that the total quantity of exports had to be reported officially, and earnings had to be remitted at the official exchange rate. According to Jamal (ibid.: p.140): "Two things happen: a considerable part of exports are traded unofficially and escape government control, and traders get to keep the difference between the official value of exports and the *franco valuta* value."

The analysis of state economic policies with their patterns of discrimination, particularly those directed against traders with Northern (Isaq) clan origin, reveal the dynamics of security provision that evolved out of these antagonistic state policies. Non-state structures became ever more important and in the process the state lost relevance for the economic life of those excluded groups/clans within Somali society. This dispersal of state control in the fields of trade and finance went hand in hand with the rise of opposition movements. The SNM, particularly, was financed through monetary transactions that bypassed the state and relied on clan connections. A mutually enforcing dynamic developed to the effect that the more state policies restricted economic activities in the North, the more SNM gained support within the Northwestern communities. The state retained coercive control but increasingly lost other aspects of *de facto* sovereignty in the Northwestern region.

THE IMPACT OF LAND TENURE POLICIES ON (IN)SECURITY PATTERNS IN THE SOUTHERN FARMING AREAS

The socialist government introduced land reform legislation, which put all land under state ownership. Registration of title became the only legal way to hold land. This meant that state law overruled customary land tenure rights, and local authorities such as clan and/or village elders could be sidelined in the process (Besteman, 1996). Instead, institutions such as the district agricultural officer, the district police, the regional ministry of agriculture and finally the national ministry of agriculture in Mogadishu took over formal control of land use (De Waal, 1994). The new law allowed individual leasing of land for up to 50 years; per family one farm could be registered, to a maximum of 30 hectares for irrigated land and 60 hectares for rain-fed land. The law also provided for the establishment of agricultural co-operatives, whereby a minimum of 30 members had to apply directly to the central Ministry of Agriculture, Department of Co-operatives, in the capital. In theory, the idea behind these co-operatives had been to allow "a lineage to register the entirety of its land and continue its customary tenure practices within those boundaries" (ibid.: p.40). However, in practice, both the land-registration requirements and the creation of co-operatives threatened and undermined the tenure security of local farmers.

Problems of Implementation of Land Registration for Small-scale Farmers

Most individual small-scale farmers (essentially from the Rewin, Digil/Mirifle clan-family) did not register their farms. One of the reasons for this was the high cost of the process. As Besteman (1996: p.41-42) notes, considering the low cash income of local small-scale farming families, the payments to witnesses and to the draftsman which were required, as well as unofficial gratuities and a possible trip to the capital Mogadishu to complete the process of registration, were too great an expense. Another reason lay in illiteracy and in the lack of familiarity with government bureaucracy and lack of political connections to facilitate the process. These obstacles implied additional payments and further expenses. And even if an individual local farmer tried to register his land, there was no guarantee that another 'owner' would not appear, who had given the responsible officers even bigger bribes (De Waal, 1994).

Land registration as such also implied the need for critical decisions by farming families. The rules of registration – such as one household being allowed to register only one farm – did not match the reality of the flexibility of farming in the fertile regions. The differing patterns of cultivation on different available soils (irrigated riverbank farming, flood-recession farming and rain-fed cultivation: see chapter 5), allowed farmers the flexibility to cope if one of the water sources failed. In optimal circumstances, one farming family would hold several plots in each of these qualitatively different and risk-related soils. Access rights were sub-contracted to other families or extended family members depending on the circumstances of the season. Women also had specific customary rights of access to land (Besteman, 1996). All these varieties of tenure arrangement disappeared with the introduction of the new land law. Situations within families became conflict-prone as only one owner could be registered for one farm or plot of land. Women/wives and younger brothers who were about to found their own nuclear family were seriously disadvantaged by the law, and officially written out of any right to land.

Social security in a sense of customarily codified rights of access to land and income of the various members of an extended family was thus seriously threatened. In addition, the social balance within a village often became disturbed as those who were better off with regard to connections or education did register their land, while others did not and had to face the insecurity of possibly being thrown off their farms. 'Strongmen' emerged, often village or lineage elders who suddenly became landowners, while others were turned into landless, dependent wage-laborers (de Waal, 1994: p.39; Menkhaus, 1996).

Environmental security also deteriorated, as land had to be cleared in order to continuously claim it; since capital to cultivate the land was often lacking, the soil cover was exposed to degradation (Besteman, 1996: p.45).

Food security was threatened not only because the land registration laws did not allow for flexible cultivation patterns, but also because of land claims and registrations by non-resident 'landowners' in accordance with state law, which overruled customary tenure rights. Government officials, civil servants and other people from a non-farming clan background but with good connections to the government registered land for the purpose of speculation rather than cultivation. Sometimes the original cultivator continued to work on the land, either without knowledge of the official transfer of ownership, or in permanent fear of being expelled from the land or of having the harvest claimed by an official who arrived at harvest time with a registration document.[32] Sometimes fenced plots 'owned' by absentee-landlords were left idle while the original farmers had to make their living out of the smaller leftover plots of land.

---

32 "Villagers at Buulo Nassiib recounted a familiar story of how a civil servant from Mogadishu visited them in 1986: 'He came with documents and claimed the land. Then there was a dispute, and the outcome is obvious. We went to the regional officials, but they said it was all documented'" (Menkhaus, 1996: p.147).

Shifting Ownership Patterns: State Farms and Land-Banking

Much of the best land was expropriated by the state for huge irrigated state farm projects, a developmental approach, which received much attention and considerable funding by external donor countries (Menkhaus, 1996; Janzen, 1987). This led to increased eviction of local farmers from the more fertile soils, with a resultant loss in their crisis-coping mechanisms. But the state farms often badly failed their economic targets. After a reorganization of state farms as part of the program of liberalization and IMF-guided agricultural policies after 1981, some areas saw an increase of production, but this was mainly in the export-oriented banana plantation industry[33] rather than in food production for local markets. Prices for agricultural products had been regulated during the socialist period but forced sales at fixed low prices were abolished in 1981. However, increases in local agricultural production which appeared in official statistics were the result of a shift from informal to formal, liberalized marketing structures, rather than an actual increase in local cereal production (Jamal, 1992). During the same period, it should be remembered, the country was being flooded with food-aid for refugees, which also found its way onto the local markets, impacting negatively on prices for locally produced cereals and masking the low local food production.

Apart from the impact on general food security, the expansion of state farms and irrigation projects affected the economic (in)security of local farmers in several ways. Of those who were expelled from their lands, few received any compensation payments. In this context, Menkhaus (1996: p.147) notes:

> During the 1970s and 1980s, the three major state farms established in the lower Juba – Fanoole Rice Farm, Mogambo Irrigation Project, and Juba Sugar Project – alienated over 16,327 hectares of some of the best land in the region. An estimated 5,200 hectares of this land were expropriated from actively cultivating smallholders without any compensation.

On the other hand, the registration of land by non-farming absentee civil servants, politicians and well-connected business people was often driven by insider information from the Ministry of Agriculture about sites of future irrigation schemes or extension of state farms, in expectation of compensation payments. For the Mogambo irrigation project, De Waal (1994: p.41) notes:

---

33 Janzen (1987) mentions that the privatisation of "SomalFruit" in 1983 reduced the state capital to 40% and increased banana production from 72,000 t to 110,000 t.

[The Mogambo project] was planned in the late 1970s as an ambitious irri-gated farm for the cultivation of rice. Work began in 1982 and 1986 com-pleted the first phase. This covered 2,300 hectares of prime farmland. The land was taken mostly from a string of Bantu villages, with 450 hectares taken from a Somalfruit plantation. The Central Bank of Kuwait paid the compensation, but while several large Harte landowners and Somalfruit were able to benefit from this, nothing reached the Bantu farmers. The set-tlers who came to work on the project were almost exclusively Marehan and Dulbahante (clans loyal to Siad Barre).

The Bardere Dam project on the river Juba, which was supposed to intensify existing irrigation schemes and provide about 85,000 hectares of irrigated lands in the middle Juba basin, became another object for land-banking dur-ing the 1980s. The project also aimed at delivering hydro-energy to the whole Juba-valley as well as to the capital Mogadishu.[34] Since the World Bank and EU were intensively involved in the planning, huge sums of compensation were expected. In the end, the Bardere Dam was never built because international donors became increasingly reluctant.

As a result of state land tenure policies the population structure of the inter-riverine lands changed.[35] Much land came to be occupied by Somali who did not originate in the inter-riverine lands. Not only absentee speculators of specific clans, but also their extended families profited from arrangements as 'settlers' in the inter-riverine region. However, they generally differed from the earlier migrants who had become integrated into the Rewin clan-structure through *shegaat*-relationships. The 'settlers' of the 1980s kept their own clan affiliation and occupied Rewin lands, rather than integrating into Rewin vil-lage communities. They were mostly Marehan/Ogaden/Dulbahante and sometimes Somali-Ethiopian refugees with Darod affiliation who managed to move out of refugee-camps into farms registered to them in the form of co-operatives. In this way, whole refugee villages came into existence in the Lower Shabelle area.[36]

---

34 Technical data of the project in planning: 75 m high dam wall; 4.8 billion cubic meter water reservoir capacity; 175,000 hectares all-year irrigation capacity; 105 mw electrical power capacity; estimated costs (for 1990) US$ 350-370 million (Janzen, 1987: p.31-32).

35 In chapter 4 we looked at migration patterns influencing clan-distribution. The land law was a major stimulus for the population drift into the fertile regions. Other reasons for migration were drought in pastoral areas in the mid-1970s and the refugee-crisis in 1979-1988 in the aftermath of the Ogaden war.

Women: Profiting from and Suffering under the Barre Regime

We will now take a closer look at the situation of women in the Siyad Barre era. When discussing pre-state social arrangements I referred to women's rights with particular reference to inheritance, marriage and divorce. We will now discuss whether changes took place in this context through the introduction of a new family law. We will also examine the impact of the Somali Women's Democratic Organization (swDO) and the Somali Women Research and Documentation Unit (swRDU) at the National University of Mogadishu on the women agenda. Finally, we will focus on the specific problems arising for women out of the tension that was created by anti-government opposition and by the government's coercive measures against these activities.

Changes in the Legal Position of Women

In order to modernize Somali society, Siyad Barre introduced in 1975 a new family law that, on the whole, was based on *sharia*, but with regard to property and inheritance introduced fundamental changes to the benefit of women.[37] The new law provided for equal property rights. Girls inherited an equal share with their brothers and in case of divorce property had to be shared equally between man and wife.

The divorce procedure itself became somewhat more woman-friendly, with specific cases outlined in the law under which a wife could apply for divorce. In theory law restricted the practice of polygamy. Marriage to a second wife was only allowed under specific conditions that had to be authorized by a family court. The new family law also provided for the punishment of men for domestic violence (Forni, 1980).

In connection with the introduction of the new law a whole range of social problems with regard to women's rights, which had not been acknowledged or openly discussed before, were brought to the surface, mostly by urban, educated women. However, as all civil rights were increasingly curtailed women's options for voice remained also very restricted. Progressive opinions were suppressed and conservative critique was brutally silenced. Ten Islamic

---

36 Field Research experience in the Shalambod/Qorioley area in 1986.
37 On women's rights in Somali pre-state/sub-state society, see the chapters 4 and 5.

Sheikhs were sentenced to death for opposing the new laws as non-Islamic and heretical.

In practice, the law was not applied in all strata of Somali society, and educated urban women profited more than their sisters in the countryside. The traditional legal system continued to be practiced in most parts of the country and only a few educated urban women succeeded in profiting from the new freedom and equality that was provided by the law. Women in the rural areas were often not even aware of all the aspects of the new family law and even those in urban areas could often be convinced by the male judges to follow the Islamic tradition, i.e. *sharia* laws.

The Somali Women Democratic Organization

The Somali Women Democratic Organization (SWDO) was founded in 1977 and became the women branch of the one year earlier established Somali Revolutionary Socialist Party.[38] Its mandate was "to propose, promote and initiate progressive policies and programs for the advancement of the Somali women" (SWDO, 1985: p.iv). In 1985, SWDO numbered 60,000 members (SWDO, 1985). Emphasizing the productive role of women as well as their reproductive role, the SWDO contributed to the increased participation of girls and women in education, businesses, and public administration. In a survey (ibid.: p.11) it is noted:

> In this nine-year period [1975-1984] the proportion of women in the public administration increased on average of 39.4% annually. In the ministries the average annual rate of increase was 37.14%, while in the autonomous agencies it was 45.3% annually. Indeed, this is a very spectacular increase.

The SWDO was an integral part of the socialist one-party system. In all government ministries it had a representative whose responsibility was to safeguard women's rights and see that no discrimination was practiced. SWDO had branches from the national to the local level; weekly meetings were held to build awareness of women's rights. SWDO representatives were involved as voluntary lawyers or advocates in courts on issues such as domestic violence

---

38 Before the 1969 coup, there existed an organisation called the Somali Women's Movement that had its roots in the independence movement of the 1940s. The organisation was mainly of a welfare nature and was led by the wives of leading politicians of the early post-independence period.

or divorce (Merryman, 1996). The organization campaigned for an increase of the number of girls in education,[39] pressed for an increase in the number of women judges and high political functionaries, and recommended a change in the land law with regard to women's ownership, arguing for joint titles for husband and wife in order to ensure rural women's effective access to land for cultivation (swdo, 1985: p.16).

However, members of swdo were not politically free; the party and other open and secret control mechanisms within the state framework strictly controlled them. In fact, it was not only subject to political control, it, itself, was and instrument of control.

The Somali Women Research and Documentation Unit

The establishment of the Women Research and Documentation Unit (swrdu) within the Somali Academy of Science and Art (somac) at the National University of Mogadishu in 1983 can be seen as the first step in laying the foundation for women's studies in Somalia. Although swrdu undertook several important studies on women's position within society the women researchers did not enjoy academic freedom. The state intervened in the choice of areas of research and open discussion of critical issues on policies regarding women was made impossible. The significance of the research center lay in training in gender awareness, encouragement of women students for the field of women studies and in the collection and documentation of oral literature on and by women.

The Impact of Political Instability on Women

Examining the political developments in those regions where political opposition movements grew stronger in the second half of the 1980s from a gender perspective reveals some specific problems that arose for women and that affected their position. In focusing on women, differentiation is of course necessary: their age and clan, their rural or urban background, all defined the ways in which women perceived and suffered from the effects of latent and then open civil war. The impact of political instability on women was mixed, on the

---

39 The policy of universal primary education (compulsory up to grade 8) had a positive impact on education for girls, although mostly in the urban areas.

one hand making life for women generally more insecure, on the other hand empowering women at the household level.

Through the clan antagonism that spread through Somali polity and society from the mid-1980s, women were torn between their own clan and that of their husband and children. Women living in mixed-clan marriages suffered from suspicion from both sides of the family. Women belonging to the clans that staged anti-government guerrilla actions were the least protected. Marriage patterns in the pastoral areas had been dominated by exogamy: marriages across the boundaries of clan families. Linking different clans, sub-clans or lineages by marital bonds had been part of the economic and political survival strategy of pastoral people (*hidid*). The more clan antagonism came to determine state policies and, in response, the formation of opposition after the mid-1980s, the more people turned to their closer clan relatives. This was reflected in a change in marriage patterns as endogamy now provided more security than exogamy (Warsame, 1997; Lewis, 1994).

One of the government strategies for discouraging support for the opposition was intimidation, violent attacks on and rape of women. Women in the nomadic areas were used to moving freely in order to collect water and firewood. Rape or other bodily harm had been rare in the past (Warsame, 1997). The government now suspected them of supplying food and acting as informants for snm units, and they were punished accordingly. The policy of punishing the civilian population seriously increased the insecurity of younger women, in particular, and restricted them from exercising their responsibilities within the larger family (Warsame, 1997; Africa Watch, 1990).

During the time of anti-government insurgency women's role within the family became stronger due to the fact that women took over tasks that were previously the domain of men. In rural-urban exchange it had usually been the men who were responsible for trading journeys, the *safars*. However, this became too dangerous, as men belonging to the Isaq clan were suspected of being members or sympathizers of the snm opposition and were detained by state officials. Pastoral women increasingly took over the trading in town. They did this not only because of the aspect of physical safety (women being less likely to be arrested by the police), but also because women were able to secure trade by using both their marital and their maternal family ties, making them more suitable for the task. As Warsame (ibid.) concludes, the position of women in socio-economic life was strengthened by this experience, giving them more decision-making power and access to environments that had previously been male-dominated.

Countdown to State Collapse

GOVERNMENT ATTEMPTS TO WEAKEN THE OPPOSITION

In 1986, the opposition groups SSDF and SNM both went through internal crises and splits. The majority of SSDF members belonged to the Harti Darod (Majertain, Warsangeli, Dulbahante). However, the organization at that time also included Hawiye fighters, intellectuals, politicians and officers. SNM, too, was not an exclusively Isaq organization but also incorporated Hawiye clan members, including the then vice-chairman, Ali Mohamed Ossobleh Wardigley. Siyad Barre is said to have interfered and orchestrated the conflict within the two movements. The president had offered amnesty to SSDF, and tried to reach a similar agreement with the SNM leaders (Salad Elmi, 1992). Some members of the SSDF movement accepted the amnesty and returned to Somalia, where most of them were integrated into the army. The remaining members of the SSDF moved to Kenya under the new leadership of Hassan Ali Mirreh.

For the SNM, it has been speculated that the Barre government approached both the Isaq and the Hawiye SNM leaders in order to convince them to withdraw from armed struggle. By the end of 1986, differences had emerged between Isaq and Hawiye, such as a disagreement about the under-representation of Hawiye in the central committee. These developments resulted in the breakaway of the Hawiye faction with its leader, Ali Wardigley:

> The skilful manipulator of clannism, dictator Barre, swiftly acted to preempt the Hawiya support for SNM by putting a wedge between the Chairman and the Vice Chairman that ended in the resignation of the Vice Chairman from his post in SNM and his departure for good with other leading Hawiya members in early 1987 (ibid.: p.24).

From then on, the SNM operated as an Isaq opposition. Under Ahmed Mohamed Silanyo, who was elected president in 1984 at the 4th SNM congress in Ethiopia, the religious-conservative approach changed into a secular-pragmatic one. He guided the SNM movement through times of increasing guerrilla activities and, after 1988, into open civil war against the Siyad Barre government.

THE TURN TO OPEN CIVIL WAR: THE NORTH

SNM's safe-haven in Ethiopia was threatened in 1988 when two years of peace talks between Siyad Barre and Mengistu Haile Mariam, president of Ethiopia, which had been under way since 1986, culminated in an agreement wherein the two governments pledged to stop supporting any political opposition directed against the neighboring country.

Confronted with an uncertain future with regard to military posts and retreat options, the SNM decided in May 1988 to launch major attacks on Burao (on 27 May) and Hargeisa (31 May), the two largest towns in Northern Somalia. "By July, ... it was clear that at least some areas of the towns of Hargeisa, Burao and Berbera had been captured by the SNM, and that government forces had begun a full scale military campaign to regain control of them" (Lewis, 1990: p.899). Air bombardment by government forces, supported by South African mercenary pilots,[40] destroyed SNM military and civilian targets in Northern Somalia, and left particularly the regional capital Hargeisa almost completely destroyed.

The SNM kept controlling Hargeisa until August 1988. Although the government succeeded in gaining the support of minority clans and their political movements in the North, the persistence of SNM units hindered the attempts of the Mogadishu government to regain full control over the North. After 1989 only the main cities, such as Hargeisa, Burao and Berbera, remained under government control.

The start of open war in 1988 with the bombardment of Hargeisa and Burao was an experience of extreme insecurity. About 50,000 people died and approximately 500,000 fled into the countryside, first towards and finally across the Ethiopian border. The war did tremendous damage to the Northern Somali economy and infrastructure. According to SNM sources, 80% of Hargeisa, 50% of Burao and 40% of Erigavo were damaged, while the harbor town Berbera suffered less. Journalists reported, "The totality and intensity of destruction in Northern Somalia is beyond description" (*New African*, May 1991).

Destruction, looting and the lying of mines was not only limited to the urban areas, but also extended into the rural areas. In the agricultural lands in the Northwest, equipment was destroyed or looted, and fields and fruit tree plantations uprooted. Wells were destroyed or poisoned. Besides the immediate impact of war on physical, economic and social security, three additional

---

40 According to Greenfield (1989), paid South African pilots did the job; see also Salad Elmi (1992).

factors threatened the security of the Northern Somali population: the loss of money transfers from Northern Somali migrant workers in the Gulf states as a consequence of the Gulf-war in 1990/91; a decrease in livestock exports via Berbera to the Arab countries; and drought in the Western and Eastern parts of the Northern region. All three put additional constraints on the survival of the local population (Holt and Lawrence, 1992).

The Refugee-Crisis: Sub-State and Trans-State Arrangements

Given this desperate situation, two strategies were followed. First, the urban population turned to their rural relatives, to whom they fled (Africa Watch, 1990; Warsame, 1997). Clan and family networks were the most immediate source of security. During the years of oppression by the Mogadishu government, clan affiliation had become increasingly important, as there seemed to be nobody else to trust. The SNM guerrilla-units were also structured according to Isaq sub-clan affiliation[41] and the SNM relied on civilian clan-networks for material support, safety and logistics, especially after 1988.

Faced with increasing food insecurity and continuous fighting in all Northern areas, during 1989/90 the second strategy was to seek refuge in neighboring Ethiopia. The total number of UNHCR-registered Somali refugees towards the end of 1990 was 381,369 (Brons et al., 1993). Figures for 1991 put the number of Somali refugees at about 473,170. As people fled to their respective clan areas across the border the UNHCR refugee camps reflected specific clan affiliations. This proved an effective way of ensuring the safety of all involved parties – the refugees, the people of the receiving areas, and the aid workers. The vast majority of refugees were Isaq (367,300) mainly from urban areas: they were located at the Harshin and Hartisheik refugee camps, about 75 km South-East of Jijiga, and at the Kamaboker, Daror and Rabasso camps near Aware, about 300 km South of Jijiga. Refugees of other clan origin were mainly Gadabuursi (105,170) who were settled in the refugee camps Arabi, Darwonaji and Taferi Ber about 50 km East of Jijiga. The Ayisha/Degehagog camp Northeast of Dire-Dawa hosted the Issa refugees (19,362).

Sub-state and trans-state networks of security provision (the latter under UNHCR mandate) complemented each other. Physical, legal, food and health security was delivered by international agencies. The status of refugee gave

---

41 1st regiment: Habr Jaalo, 2nd reg.: Habr Yonis, 3rd reg.: Eidegalla, 4th and 5th reg.: Habr Awal, according to *Indian Ocean Newsletter* (14 December 1991).

legal security and defined the rights of the camp inhabitants during their stay in Ethiopia. Physical security was provided by the camp administration, policing the area at night and preventing attacks on the refugees from Somali government units from across the border. Basic food and health facilities ensured the survival of the refugees. The distribution of food and water were a great challenge to the Ethiopian Administration of Refugee/Returnee Affairs (ARRA) and the UNHCR and meant a heavy burden on the receiving areas, in particular Jijiga town. To give an impression of the quantities involved, 800,000 liters of water per day were needed for Hartisheik refugee camp alone. Although logistic problems occurred in the process, the Northern Somali refugees nevertheless found a safe haven in Ethiopia, a meager but steady food and water supply and basic medical care. Social security in the sense of supporting each other with the management of rations and assisting female-headed households of widows or wives of fighters and old people with the problems caused by camp life derived mainly from existing family and/or clan relations. In the camps, women were relatively safe from rape and other forms of violence.[42]

A survey of Hartisheik refugee camp in 1991[43] revealed that most of the refugees (92.9% of questioned refugees) came from Hargeisa, the regional capital of Northern Somalia (Brons et al., 1993). The background of the refugees was therefore urban, many of them having been traders, employees in transport, or teachers. In Hartisheik they soon took initiatives to improve on their plight. Teachers among the refugees organized primary schooling for refugee children; some 12,000 pupils were involved, representing about 22.5% of the school-age children in the camp. Economic security, basically provided by UNHCR, was complemented by self-help activities to the extent that between 15% and 25% of the refugee population was, at the time of the survey, involved in some sort of income-generating activities. These were not initiated by aid agencies but by the people themselves.

It must also be mentioned that the refugees are highly differentiated; some managed to salvage their property, cash and a few belongings, while others have lost everything. Therefore, it is natural that some form of division of labor developed and after about 4 years of relatively stable settlement, some refugees became petty traders, and vendors of food, beverages, firewood and charcoal. There are also shoemakers, tailors, shops and small drug

---

42 In contrast to Somali refugee camps in Kenya. On human rights abuses in Kenyan refugee camps, see Omar and de Waal (1993); Adam and Ford (1997).

43 Fieldwork conducted by the author in Hartisheik refugee camp, March/April 1991.

store keepers and mechanics. Others are porters, man and animal-powered cart owners or sell their labor to those who are more fortunate (Brons et al., 1993: p.61).

A vast marketplace developed in Hartisheik where goods and fresh produce, including vegetables of Ethiopian and Somali origin, were traded. By mid-1991, economic security was coming from both sub-state and trans-state networks. The private banking sector thrived in Hartisheik. One could buy and sell not only Somali Shilling and Ethiopian Birr, but also American Dollars, Saudi Dinars and other currencies. Transactions were conducted within the camp, but also via family networks with relatives located in Addis Ababa and, after the first wave of temporary returnees to Hargeisa in summer 1991, with relatives who had begun reconstruction at home. Through relatives in the Ethiopian capital, connections for remittances were also established to Somali family members who, as refugees, were spread all over the world. There was also a thriving transport business using cars and mini-buses. There were regular connections to Jijiga, the town closest to the camp and the location of the aid agency's offices, shops and markets, among them the daily *qaat* market.

After the overthrow of the Mogadishu government and the end of the fighting, refugees began to return to their home areas, in the case of Hartisheik to Hargeisa. Often, the women and children stayed behind in the camps, while the men determined the security situation at home and began with reconstruction. Regular bus connections existed from Hartisheik refugee camp to Hargeisa city. For a long time, this was the only functioning transport link to the Northern Somali region, after the collapse of Somali airlines and the destruction of the airports. The strong linkages, contact and exchange with the home area, strengthened through trade and transport, compensated for the fact of living in a refugee camp, of residing temporarily in a foreign country.

With regard to political stability the Somali refugees in Hartisheik were active and innovative. A basic administrative structure was created which allowed the representatives of the refugees say in matters of camp policy. Refugee committees were formed at meetings held by elders, religious leaders, and clan and sub-clan heads in the presence of local government officials, ARRA, UNHCR and NGO representatives.

The executive committee is the highest organ of the refugee committees and is assisted by administration and the refugee population at large. The refugee committees organize people and maintain order during food distribution and also manage the informal education.... The committees resolve disputes and discuss the outstanding problems facing the refugee population. Members of the committees are provided with incentives in the form of cereals for the service they render and those who prove to be ineffective are replaced with the consent of the refugee community (Brons et al., 1993: p.61).

Political life in Hartisheik had an impact on political developments in the direction of state formation in the Northwest, culminating, on 18 May 1991, with the proclamation of the Republic of Somaliland, referring back to the ex-British Protectorate. (See further: chapter 8). One might argue that with regard to the overall Northern Somali/Somaliland population, the Hartisheik camp population was only of marginal significance. However, as already noted, Hartisheik housed the urban as well as the clan and political backbone of Northern Somalia – people with high human (education) and/or financial (trade and business) capital, people from the Isaq, the majority-clan in the North and an SNM political background.

GENESIS, POLICIES AND INNER CLEAVAGES OF SOUTHERN OPPOSITION MOVEMENTS

Hawiye fighting units had been active in the Central region (Mudug), first as part of the SSDF struggles of 1983-1986 and, after 1988, on their own. Salad Elmi (1992) mentions two guerrilla bases at Dhumoodle and at Hanan-Weilod which were made up of Hawiye (Habr Gedir/Saleban/ Sa'ad) fighters and whose numbers were swollen by defections from the armed forces. They coordinated their activities with the SNM Southern front. Thus, in September 1988, Darod/Harti and Hawiye fighters joined SNM for the following three reasons: "(1) to continue the struggle against the brutal dictatorship until the end; (2)to support SNM which stands for justice and symbolized the anti-dictatorial resistance so that it should not be defeated for ever and; (3) to contribute to the unification of the opposition" (ibid.: p.27).

The diplomatic moves of the Barre government – offering amnesty in order to split the opposition – left both the Darod/Harti and the Hawiye divided: there were those who refused to compromise, and continued their active opposition and guerrilla warfare, and those who, for the time being at least, came to a compromise with the government. The following extract reveals the pressure applied by the president on Hawiye businessmen in Mogadishu. Just as the town of Hargeisa was thought of as being located on Isaq territory, so the capital of Mogadishu – despite its multi-clan characteristics – was still considered to be located in Hawiye country:

After the destruction of Hargeysa by General Morgan's troops [in 1988], Siyaad Barre put the leading Hawiye businessmen in a plane and showed them Hargeysa: he used to say to the Abgaal and Murosade traders that Mogadishu was their goof (small garden, the word is typical in Abgaal dialect) but if they started opposition he was ready to destroy Mogadishu as he did for Hargeysa (Marchal, 1996: p.28).

Two main developments occurred as a result of the cleavages within the Southern Hawiye political community. First, in January 1989, mainly diaspora members of Hawiye founded the United Somali Congress (usc) in Rome, Italy. Second, in mid May 1990, the so-called 'Manifesto Group' emerged in Mogadishu, initiated to a large extent by influential Hawiye within the capital.

The Foundation of USC-Rome

usc-Rome was founded in January 1989. Ali Wardigley, of the Hawiye/Murursade sub-clan, who had left the snm in 1987, became Chairman (see diagram 1). Other prominent members, based in Mogadishu, were Ismail Jumaale Ossoble, a famous human rights lawyer from Hawiye/Abgaal sub-clan, and Ali Mahdi Mohamed from Hawiye/Habr Gedir/Saleban sub-clan. Other sub-clans attached to usc-Rome included Jajele, Sheikhal and Hawaadle (Compagnon, 1997). The usc published various position papers and held several meetings in Rome, Bonn and other diaspora centers. In its pamphlets usc strove for an extensively decentralized administration and a multi-party system. It called for a strict separation of legislative, executive and juridical power, advocated the complete abolition of the national security apparatus and the dismantling of the laws allowing its operation. In the economic field the usc promised to exert its main efforts on developing agriculture, livestock and fisheries. The usc leadership appealed directly to the snm for co-operation in an unprejudiced manner to realize the common goal of establishing a free and democratic Somalia.

For several reasons the usc made a very promising impression on outside observers. Its political program reached beyond the overthrow of the dictatorship. Its proximity to the Mogadishu government was another point in the sense that there were many secret usc supporters within or close to the government. Furthermore, some of its prominent members, such as the first post-independence president Aden Abdulle Osman, were believed to be politically well versed and widely respected within Somalia (Brons, 1991a). These factors proved to be of major importance in the course of events, which occurred when USC-Rome claimed the leadership of an interim government after the downfall of the Barre-government.

To insiders, the USC-Rome was perceived much more critically. It was considered initiated by

mostly young and middle class migrants, who converged to the founding congress from different parts of the world – primarily the Arab Gulf countries, Europe and North America, who formed the bulk of the delegates who were seized by their keen desire and compassion to see a movement of their clan to ascertain their identity and sense of belonging in a tribal climate where several clans had already their parties (Salad Elmi, 1992: p.27).

The Hawiye sub-clans represented by USC-Rome did not include the Habr Gedir/Sa'ad sub-clan which had fought against government forces in the Central region for many years, which was already very well linked to SNM and other fighting units and whose main military and political leader was Mohamed Farah Aideed. The rift between the guerrilla fighters, who risked their lives for the cause of overcoming dictatorship, and the politicians who merely talked about it in the comfort of a secure environment, became increasingly deep. Thus, although the foundation of an externally-based, Hawiye-dominated, opposition front initially seemed to stimulate and encourage the Hawiye population in Somalia and the Hawiye fighting units in the guerrilla war, resentments began to build when USC-Rome failed to get involved after the government retaliated against both civilians and fighters, with the same cruelty already known from the North.

There was an attempt to settle these differences within the Hawiye opposition at a USC congress held in May/June 1990 in the Ethiopian town of Mustahil, close to the Somali border. A USC delegation from abroad met with representatives from the Dhumoodle base and the Hanan-Weilod base, with guerrillas and activists from the Hiran, Galgudud and Mogadishu regions.

Action plans were drawn up to unify all these USC supporting factions and armed struggle streamlined from scattered groups and spontaneous sporadic actions into a unified comprehensive form with a centrally commanded force. The Hiran region was chosen to be the springboard of this main decisive new offensive (ibid.: p.30).

At the Mustahil congress, Mohamed Farah Aideed was elected chairman of USC. The SNM Southern Front also participated at this meeting. From that time on, one can confidently talk of a co-coordinated offensive by the USC and SNM. The war in the second half of 1990 marked the final downfall of the Siyad Barre government.

The Manifesto Initiative

In a timely parallel to increasing co-ordination of guerilla activities in the Northern and Central regions, a diplomatic initiative was launched in Mogadishu, when an open letter signed by more than 100 influential politicians from the old regime, businessmen and religious leaders was forwarded to president Siyad Barre on 15 May 1990. The document was called 'Manifesto No.1'. It was an appeal to the president to convene a national conference for reconciliation and salvation (*shirweynaha suluxa iyo badbaadinta ummadda*) based on the Somali traditional *shir* meetings which are based on compromise as a means to solve political, social and other problems between clans in conflict (see chapter 4). The Manifesto described the breakdown of the country and the impact of the civil war on society, the economy and national integrity. It stated that the continuation of the war would lead not only to the collapse of the economy but also to even more killing of the Somali population who already suffered great losses because of the war.

In clan terms (diagram 1), the Manifesto group was made up almost exclusively of Hawiye and Darod, with just a few token Isaq signatories. Among the Hawiye, the Abgaal and Habr Gedir were dominant (representing 27% and 46% of the Group, respectively); the Habr Gedir/Sa'ad, the sub-clan followers of Mohamed Farah Aideed, were significant by their virtual absence. The majority of the Manifesto Darod was Majertain (67.3%), the other strong sub-clan being the Dulbahante (14.3%) (Figures are from Compagnon, 1997).

Siyad Barre reacted to the Manifesto by arresting more than forty of its signatories, who were released only after considerable internal and external pressure. He relied blindly on the few state coercion measures, which were still available to him at that time, clutching onto the vestiges of a power, which had, in reality, long since deserted him. The diverse reactions of the opposition movements demonstrated the rift between military and political approaches within both the Hawiye and Darod clans. On the one hand there were the military leaders and their fighters in the countryside, the periphery of power. On the other hand there were (ex) politicians, businessmen and (ex) elite in the capital Mogadishu, the seat of central power, and the political exile abroad.

Thus, by mid-1990, the Southern opposition was crystallizing into two main segments: the Manifesto/usc-Rome group, on the one hand, with their prominent figures such as ex-politician Ali Mohamed Ossobleh Wardigley, businessman Ali Mahdi Mohamed, and the first president of independent Somalia, Aden Abdulle Osman; and on the other hand, the militarily strong usc/Aideed front, which was fighting alongside snm and some ssdf forces in the Central regions. The accord reached at Mustahil between the USC-Rome and the USC/Aideed wings of the Hawiye opposition was to be put on test.

The Somali Patriotic Movement: Ogaden Joining Anti-Government Struggle

Besides the SNM in the North and USC/Aideed in the Central regions, there was a third opposition movement and military force active in the Southern-most part of the country. The Somali Patriotic Movement (SPM) was established in 1989 as a military force, made up mainly of Ogaden who deserted from the Somali National Army during the military mutinies in the Lower Juba area led by Colonel Bashir Bililiqo. Many Ogaden had been integrated into the Somali National Army after the defeat in the Ethiopian-Somali war in 1977/78. The Ogaden formed one pillar of the MOD (Marehan-Ogaden-Dulbahante) coalition, which had backed Siyad Barre for decades. A reciprocal relationship developed between the Ogaden ex-fighters and their patron Siyad Barre: they owed him thanks for supporting their (ultimately unsuccessful) struggle, for hosting their families in refugee-camps and, at a later stage, for offering them a political position within Somalia, mainly in the Armed Forces;[44] while President Barre used them for enhancing his power base, for strengthening his army and eventually arming the Ogaden refugees in the North and mobilizing them in his fight against SNM insurgencies (Africa Watch, 1990).

However, as Barre relied increasingly on his own clansmen from the Marehan, his relation with the Ogaden became more and more uneasy. When they finally founded their own opposition movement, the SPM, they joined the struggle as a well-equipped and well-trained partner in co-operation with the USC/Aideed and SNM. SPM conducted its military activities in the Bakol and Bay regions, towards Mogadishu, while USC operations extended from the Central regions towards the capital. It was SPM forces, which captured the military air base at Ballidogle, 100 km West of Mogadishu, just days before Siyad Barre was ousted from Mogadishu on 26 January 1991 (Salad Elmi, 1992).

By autumn 1990, the various opposition groups, which were actively involved in military operations against the Barre regime, had agreed on joint military operations in order to lead a final, unified struggle against the Siyad Barre government. In October 1990, USC, SPM and SNM stated in a press com-

---

44 Fieldwork experience in 1986.

muniqué that, unlike the Manifesto group, they would not agree to any talks with the government. They opted instead for a military solution and made preliminary arrangements for power sharing in a post-Barre Somalia: this included Mohamed Farah Aideed (USC-Mustahil) becoming president, Abdurahman Ahmed Ali Tour (SNM) prime minister and Omar Jess (SPM) minister of defense.[45] By then, the civil war had spread over the whole country. While the SNM fought to gain full control over the Northern region, they supplied the USC and SPM fighters with ammunition and weapons to lead the final battle in the South. In November and December 1990, these groups gained control of more and more Southern territory and finally, in January 1991, USC fighters forced President Siyad Barre and his (by then, mainly Marehan) troops to flee Mogadishu. This is referred to as the first 'war of Mogadishu'.

BROKEN AGREEMENTS AND THE FAILURE OF POST-BARRE STATE-FORMATION

As long as Barre was the common enemy, the various opposition groups could rally behind the goal of bringing his regime to an end. This common agenda was reflected in strategic, financial and military co-operation on the battlefield, while the October 1990 accord between SNM, SPM and USC leadership also included political issues such as the delicate question of sharing power.

In terms of polity and territory, on the eve of the collapse of the Siyad Barre government the perception of a united Somali state territory still prevailed within the opposition movements. In January 1991, the SNM leadership was still committed to the establishment of a common transitional government of SNM, SPM and USC. Since these forces had been behind the military victory over the dictatorship (SNM having claimed its first victories in 1988, and USC and SPM leading battles in the Central and Southern regions since 1988 and 1989, respectively) they could claim to have earned a mandate for rebuilding political power and government. At that time, it seemed that the commonly achieved military success could be transformed into a common political agenda crossing clan affiliations.

With the flight of the Siyad Barre government in January 1991, the official Somali state openly collapsed. The national army and police, the state security apparatus, ministries and other institutions of state bureaucracy and the National Bank, dissolved as people who were known to have worked there fled

---

45 *Asharq Al-Awsat,* 16 March 1993.

for their lives. In a testament to the anger and frustration felt towards the defeated regime, most of the buildings and equipment were pillaged, looted or destroyed by young angry mobs.

USC forces finally succeeded in capturing Villa Somalia, the last retreat of the president and his family, on 26 January 1991. Only two days later, before the military leaders of the opposition movements could reach Mogadishu, the USC/Manifesto wing declared Ali Mahdi Mohamed as interim president. He was part of USC-Rome and supporter of the Manifesto-group, and as such represented those who had compromised longest with the old regime. As noted above, this group enjoyed high credibility among outside observers and foreign governments who were largely unaware of the details of the struggle against the Barre regime. An interim government was set up including some members of Siyad Barre's cabinet, such as the Prime Minister Omar Arteh Ghalib. Mohamed Abshir Musa, a Majertain, became vice-prime minister. Mahdi and his supporters claimed that all Somali clans were represented in the government, but the supposed clan balance did not reflect the actual power balance in the country. The argument of a clan-balanced distribution of government portfolios may have been appealing to outsiders, and a part of the Mogadishu middle class saw the Manifesto initiative and those behind it as a real alternative to the clan-based armed movements and their seemingly more radical approach to political change. However, most people considered the self-declared interim government yet another scenario by basically dishonest politicians. The Mahdi government was never accepted as legitimate within Somalia.

The military leaders involved, in particular Mohamed Farah Aideed from USC/Mustahil, felt cheated of their successes. The SNM and SPM also saw the October 1990 agreements broken and their decisive role in the war negated. SNM, in particular, saw the same pattern of political marginalisation, which it had experienced since independence being repeated. The victorious armed movements were thus denied the chance to pick up the few pieces of a Somali state structure, which were left after years of latent and weeks of open collapse.

Finally, the insensitivity of the USC/Manifesto wing in claiming a mandate to play the leading role in the re-establishment of a government led to the complete collapse of the state, the continuation of the civil war, and the fall of large parts of the country into anarchy. In the strong words of Salad Elmi (1992: p.46):

The felony was not only their clinging to imaginary power but it was also their insensitivity and inability to check the shameful occurring and destructive trends going before their own eyes or resign from their claim to power to disassociate themselves with the vandalism that added to their discredit. On the contrary, they never tried to relax the tension of animosity and take steps to resolve the disputes of the various sides but rather embarked on more negative steps of divide and rule tactics further complicating the situation from bad to worse.

The failure of various reconciliation conferences called by the Mahdi government can easily be understood in the light of these events. A conference of reconciliation to be held in Mogadishu on 28 February between all opposition groups that had fought against the Siyad Barre government was boycotted. Other conferences followed in Djibouti in March, April and July 1991, but none managed to gather together all the military factions.

The Impact of the State-Era on the Security of Somali Society – Some Preliminary Conclusions

In retrospect, Somali state policies threatened rather than secured the security of Somali citizens. The group of people who profited from the regime with regard to trading opportunities, land tenure policies, access to education and public employment, to food aid and other kinds of material support diminished while those who suffered from the regime steadily increased.

In reaction to these tendencies economic, social, legal and political security arrangements, which were rooted in pre-state Somali society, far from disappearing, were adapted to new circumstances. The clan system, especially, provided a strong organizational network capable of bypassing the state's institutional structure. The impact of state institutions, state laws, state territorial control and state ideology on the way in which people lived and survived diminished, except for the impact of physical violence and torture committed by state authorities. As state institutions lost their hold on security provision – lost *de facto* sovereignty – other social organizations, embedded in non-state networks gained importance. Although in a *de jure* sense, state sovereignty remained intact, and received backing from external powers, in a *de facto* sense it became more and more divided.

The head of state also activated sub-state mechanisms when he made use of political networks embedded in the clan-system in order to crush opposition. These sub-state tactics were combined with coercive policies by the national security apparatus that culminated in serious human rights violations throughout the 1980s (Amnesty International, 1988, 1990, 1992). Siyad Barre increasingly relied on *divide and rule* tactics, instigating conflict between clans, arming particular groups to fight against opposing clans or groups, buying loyalty through the allocation of development funds, and thereby dividing the opposition. The Manifesto Group noted one result of the tribalisation of politics in the decade before state collapse:[46]

> In addition, as a result of the regimes divide and rule policy, widespread tribal feuds and hooliganism have taken and are taking unlimited toll in almost every region throughout the country causing great losses to life and property, and disruption to trade, transport and communications as well as sowing seeds of disharmony among brotherly communities. Thus endangering the peaceful co-existence of Somali Communities.

Trans-state security arrangements were activated most prominently in the context of the two refugee crises: firstly, after the Somali defeat in the 1977/78 war against Ethiopia, when more than half a million Somali-Ethiopians (mostly from the Darod clan) fled into Somalia; and secondly, after the government's bombardment of the Northern towns of Hargeisa and Burao when approximately the same number of people (mostly from the Isaq clan) fled into neighboring Ethiopia. In the first case, the Somali state authorities turned the refugee crisis into their advantage, economically and politically. In the second case, the international provision of security benefited the Isaq opposition.

The move from a *state* to a *stateless* society was triggered by failed national reconciliation between the military factions in the early months of 1991. The final fall into statelessness made Somalia a unique case of a society without even a recognized *de jure* state sovereignty. The evolving transformation of the Somali polity after state collapse is the subject of the following chapter.

---

46 Manifesto No.1, 15 May 1990, printed in Brons (1991: p.101-114).

CHAPTER 8

Statelessness and After

After thirty years of Somali state rule, from independence in 1960 to the final breakdown of state authority and institutions in the early months of 1991, the Somali people found themselves in a situation of statelessness. The militarily powerful factions that had liberated the country from dictatorship failed to find common political ground but instead continued fighting over territory, power and resources. At the end of 1999, there is still no internationally recognized state authority in Somalia.

This chapter looks at how Somali society has functioned in this condition of statelessness, and at the social structures that have been used to deal with violence and to secure survival and economic and political stability. The situation after the collapse of the state differed from region to region. While the Central regions witnessed sporadic warfare, and the Northeast and Northwest were calmer and safer by comparison, people in the Southern region were faced by a complete breakdown of law and order and by continuous violence.

After a brief overview of the state of affairs in the different regions, the first part of the chapter concentrates on the situation in the Southern region. How did the continuation and even intensification of the civil war affect security arrangements at the sub-state and the trans-state levels? In this context, I will discuss the political economy of continuous violence in the Southern areas, the weakness and strength of sub-state arrangements dealing with this violence, and the performance of international security structures in the form of the UN involvement in Somalia.

The second part of the chapter discusses processes of political authority formation/state formation that took place in the years after the collapse. I will not cover the numerous international initiatives of reconciliation and top-down approaches to re-establishing a central government structure,[1] as these ultimately all failed to be implemented and did not prevent the outbreak of re-

---

[1] The most prominent of these agreements was the Addis Ababa Agreement that was signed at the Conference of National Reconciliation in Somalia, on 27 March 1993.

newed factional fighting. Instead, I argue that the peace and security of Somali society will best be served by strengthening those emerging political structures that already have the firm backing of their inhabitants. This can be done if external as well as internal political players accept that "Somalia goes regional" (*Horn of Africa Bulletin*, 10/6, 1998) for some time to come. In this connection I analyze the three cases of state formation/political authority formation: (1) the Republic of Somaliland, (2) the Digil Mirifle Governing Authority (Riverine State), and (3) Puntland (Map 5, Diagram 1). Terms of reference are the three pillars of the state: perceptions and problems with regard to territoriality, the emergence of a cohesive ideology, and the performance of political authorities with regard to the control of violence. My aim is not to reach definitive conclusions: the limited amount of written material and other sources of information, and the short lifespan of these social experiments in state formation, make this too difficult a task. However, general tendencies can be extrapolated that will aid the discussion on the political future of Somalia.

Before beginning the analysis of these aspects of the contemporary political landscape in Somalia, the following paragraphs provide a brief overview of political developments after the collapse of the Siyad Barre state.

In February 1991, the proclamation of a government by Ali Mahdi Mohammed (USC/Manifesto), with himself as the interim president of the country, antagonized not only the other Hawiye USC forces under Mohamed Farah Aideed but also the SNM Isaq faction in the Northwest of the country. This move by Ali Mahdi Mohamed confirmed the Northerners' suspicion of renewed political domination by Southern political forces. It was one of the factors that triggered off the May 1991 proclamation of an independent state in the Northwest of the country, the so-called Republic of Somaliland. A majority within the SNM finally opted for the suspension of the October 1990 coalition agreement with the Southern political factions, SPM and USC. Meanwhile, fighting in the Southern provinces and particularly in Mogadishu intensified. Shifting alliances marked a deepening rift between the USC wings led by Ali Mahdi Mohamed and Mohamed Farah Aideed, respectively. The capital became divided between the two Hawiye political factions.

The inter-riverine areas experienced fighting between various political factions, some of which had been created during the months of political turmoil in 1990/91. Among them was the Somali National Front (SNF), consisting of Marehan remnants of ex-president Barre's supporters, who tried to recapture the capital. Another new faction was the Somali Democratic Movement (SDM), founded by Rewin political leaders from the Southern farming communities. SPM/Ogaden forces were also present in the vicinity of the capital when the Siyad Barre state finally fell under the pressure of Hawiye forces.

Fighting in the inter-riverine lands in 1991/92 devastated farmland and destroyed the harvests and stores of the farming communities, bringing about the starvation and death of hundreds of thousands of people and a major wave of internal displacement from the inter-riverine lands. The Central region became a locus of fighting between the usc/Hawiye (Aideed) and the ssdf/ Majertain factions.

By mid-1992, mass starvation in Somalia became the focus of the international media. In January 1992, the un Security Council drafted a first resolution on the Somali crisis, calling for a ceasefire and a weapons embargo. In April 1992, the un became involved on the ground with a contingent of 50 un soldiers. In December 1992, Resolution 794 created the basis for peace enforcement, a humanitarian intervention that was allowed to use force in order to stop killings, starvation and the obstruction of aid delivery. "Operation Restore Hope" began in December 1992 as an American-led humanitarian intervention mission. With a changing mandate, unitaf was followed up by unosom, a un intervention unit, which included several European, Arab, Asian and African forces. The un intervention did achieve an improvement in food security for some parts of the country. However, the un failed to link the humanitarian with the political dimension of the Somali crisis. The un finally withdrew its contingents in March 1995.

After the un left, the situation in the South continued to be unstable with repeated fighting in Mogadishu. In 1996, there was a further split within the Hawiye factions in the capital. In Mogadishu North, Islamic forces, headed by Musa Sudi Yalahow, confronted Ali Mahdi Mohamed; in Mogadishu South, Mohamed Farah Aideed lost the support of his financially strong partner Osman Ali Atto, who built up his own forces. In August 1996 Mohamed Farah Aideed died and his son Hassan, a former us marine who grew up in America and had come back to Somalia in the context of the un intervention, took over the leadership of the usc/sna faction. Other centers of sporadically fierce fighting were: (1) the city of Baidoa in the heartland of the inter-riverine area where, from mid-1995, the Rahanweyn Resistance Army (rra)[2] fought against occupation by usc/Aideed forces; (2) the Gedo region bordering Ethiopia, where snf/ Marehan militia fought against the Islamic fundamentalist group Al-Itihad al-Islamiya, the snf being partially supported by Ethiopian troops who crossed the border into Somalia in order to push Al-Itihad units out of Ethiopia's own Southern territory; (3) Kismayo, the most Southern Somali port, and the adjacent Lower and Middle Juba regions where Majertain mili-

---

2 sdm had dissolved; in October 1995 the rra appeared as the new Rewin militia.

tias (under Mohamed Siad Hersi Morgan) and Ogaden militias (under Omar Jess/spm) competed for control; and (4) Merca, one of the most important export harbors after the closure of Mogadishu, some 150 km South of the capital, where Aideed's forces were in conflict with those of Osman Ali Atto who had formerly been Aideed's financial supporter.

These conflicts between political factions brought death, suffering and food insecurity for the civilian populations who became caught up in the fighting and who were plundered of their few belongings and food stores. Crime and the kidnapping of international and national aid agency staff formed another part of the picture of constant insecurity. Against this background, the return of thousands of internally displaced people and refugees, mostly from Kenya and Ethiopia, was extremely difficult, and the activities and programs of the aid agencies were severely disrupted.

In contrast to the violent power rivalries of the factions, many initiatives emerged at the local level, which established limited frameworks of relative security, and rudimentary localized mechanisms of peace and order. Besides the initiatives of lineage elders, Somali women and journalists were highly involved in local peace and reconciliation projects. The local press became less faction-controlled and more critically oriented.[3] Local women's NGOs in Mogadishu grew in strength and founded an umbrella organization, the *Coalition for Grassroots Women's Organizations* (cogwa).[4] Armed with a mandate to promote peace and women's rights in Somalia, representatives of cogwa attended workshops abroad, such as the conference on strategic initiatives for women in the Horn of Africa held in 1997 in Djibouti, where Somali women's organizations from the South met their counterparts from the North (Somaliland).[5] Women's initiatives for reconciliation and peace-keeping tend not to feature in the headlines of news coming out of Somalia, as they usually take place at the local level. But the following account, including the words of a woman from the Juba valley, illustrates the degree of determination of local

---

3 'Africa Confidential', 12 September 1997, in *Horn of Africa Bulletin*, Vol. 9, No. 5, Sept./Oct. 97. In April 1996, the Somali Independent Journalists Union held protest in memory of the forty-six journalists killed in Somalia since the overthrow of Siyad Barre, including seven foreigners.

4 The chairwoman of cogwa is Mariam Abdulle Qaawane. I am grateful to Faiza Jama Mohamed for her insights on this matter (interview, May 1998, The Hague, Netherlands).

5 The Northern women's umbrella organisation (negaad) is headed by Anab Omer Ileeye.

people, particularly women, to improve security and maintain peace in their localities:

> Two years ago we were a group of women in my region, which joined together and started discussing if there could be anything we could do to stop the violence. We formed a women's group of three women from each clan. As we have 22 clans in our region, we formed a group of a total of 66 women. I am the vice-president. When violence occurred in one of the areas, the women joined together and went there and stood in-between the fighting groups. Many women died, but successively our group gained more respect. If violence occurs today, the fighting groups decide to go outside town, not to injure innocent people. … Today we have come to the agreement that nobody is allowed to carry arms in our region, except for the guards and we check them every week. … Militiamen were given a plot of land by the community in order to earn their living by cultivating rather than robbing and looting. The general attitude is inclusive not exclusive, opening up in order to try to live together. Some years before, the same woman, who is a single mother, suffered from a violent attack committed by five men and supported by her two neighbour women, whereby her two little children were murdered in front of her house, and she was raped in front of her older daughter. Her strength and commitment to peace is shown in her comment that "one of the men and two of the women are still living in the same region. My brothers want me to tell them who the rapists were, but I do not want to tell them. It will only cause more violence, helping nobody (*Horn of Africa Bulletin*, Vol.9, No.6: p.20-21).

The situation in the Northwestern Somali region has stabilized since the proclamation of an independent state of Somaliland in May 1991. In 1991/92 there were power struggles and sporadic outbreaks of fighting between different sections within the SNM. These conflicts over the control over resources between Isaq sub-clans developed against a background of fear that those dominant in the new state framework would misuse their authority to capture state assets for their own clan constituencies. The conflicts were a test of the Somaliland government's commitment to achieving and maintaining peace within the country. Political reconciliation and stabilization was brought about by several peace conferences, such as in 1992 in Sheikh and in 1993 in Borama culminating in the election of a new president and the proclamation of a national charter and later in 1996 in Hargeisa. Success in achieving political stability was shown when the president was re-elected in 1996 for another term. In accordance with the National Charter, a constitution was drawn up, and it was approved in 1997. Progress was made in solving conflicts, keeping peace, and establishing an institutional framework, including police and army units and a legal system. Most of the (approximately) half million refugees who had fled to Ethiopia since 1988 returned to Somaliland. Although, as of 1999, international recognition has still not been achieved after eight years of relative peace and stability in the territory, the Somaliland government does run diplomatic missions in Ethiopia and in Djibouti.

Not only in the Northwest, but in other regions too, types of authority formation began to take shape that showed state-like features. In May 1995, the Digil Mirifle Governing Authority emerged in the South as a result of a pan-Rewin conference that lasted for five months and brought an end to intra-Rewin conflict. A few months later, however, this rudimentary state structure was destroyed when USC/Aideed forces occupied the regional capital, Baidoa, and most of the Bay and Bakol regions. It was not until June 1999 that the Rahanweyn Resistance Army – with the support of Ethiopian troops – regained control over Baidoa. More than 35,000 inhabitants who had fled the town under USC-siege returned home. It remains to be seen whether peace will prevail in Bay and Bakool and whether the Rewin elders will be able to revive the Digil Mirifle Governing Authority. In July 1998, Puntland regional state, comprising the Darod/Harti lands in the Northeastern region, was proclaimed at a conference in the town of Garowe, in Nugal region.

Insecurity in Statelessness

PATTERNS OF VIOLENCE IN THE SOUTHERN REGION

After the failure to establish a post-Barre government that was recognized as legitimate by all political factions, political and military alliances were reshuffled. New patterns of hatred emerged, encouraging continuous fighting, particularly in the Central and Southern region, in and around the capital Mogadishu.

In the aftermath of the flight of Siyad Barre from Mogadishu, many killings took place, motivated by hatred against all those that had profited from his rule and supported it to the end. Atrocities were committed by the liberating USC-forces, victims being selected according to their clan affiliation – Hawiye/ USC liberators against Darod (MOD) ex-government supporters. Violence ran out of control and was eventually directed against all non-Hawiye in the town, who were seen as collaborators or profiteers of the old regime (Compagnon, 1997). The few remaining Isaq and the indigenous clans of old Mogadishu

(*Xamar Weyn*) were chased out,[6] as were ex-Ethiopian Somali refugees, some of whom had settled in Mogadishu under the protection of a sympathetic government.[7]

In addition to clan-related revenge, another pattern of hatred emerged, related to the urban-rural divide, the conflict-ridden relationship between pasture and polis (Doornbos, 1993). Liberation fighters from pastoral rural backgrounds, who had never had a chance to profit from the glamour and high living standards of urban life, finally took their chance for revenge against townspeople who had prospered during the thirty years of independence.[8]

In the months that followed, heavy fighting over political power and claims to national leadership continued between the Ali Mahdi Mohamed Manifesto/Rome wing and the Mohamed Farah Aideed Mustahil wing of USC. The second war of Mogadishu[9] began in July/August 1991 with sporadic bombardments of each other's strongholds in the city. It reached its climax in November of that year, when most of the town was destroyed. More than 50,000 people died within six months. From that time on, the city was divided, the South being controlled by Aideed, the North by Ali Mahdi. The people of Mogadishu, who had survived the immediate post-liberation massacres and had stayed in the city, faced not only heavy bombardment and destruction but also lack of food, water, and health facilities. Those wounded by bombs or gunfire could not be helped, but died in the streets. Witnesses talked of a hell on earth in Mogadishu.[10]

The fight for political power and territorial control also continued in the inter-riverine region. In March 1991, supporters of President Barre (mainly Marehan) regrouped in the Somali National Front (SNF) and decided to launch

---

6   Gassem (1994) recalls several eyewitness reports of the ordeals that people went through.

7   In the process of liberating the Lower Shabelle region, in the months before reaching the capital, massacres of ex-Ethiopian Somali refugees by USC forces had already taken place.

8   The Somali novelist Nurradin Farah explains the Somali crisis as being driven by pastoral Somali who, for centuries, have been excluded from the wealth and comfort of town life, i.e. the "good life" in Mogadishu, and now finally are taking their revenge (Farah, 1997). (See also chapter 5.)

9   The first war of Mogadishu had taken place from November 1990 to January 1991; see p.216.

10   Coined by a journalist for his commentary on the Mogadishu war, M.M. Afrah (1993) used this phrase as the title of his book. The book gives a vivid account of the war in Mogadishu.

a military offensive in order to recapture Mogadishu and the farming areas then occupied by USC and SPM forces (Salad Elmi, 1992). On the side of the SPM and USC were the Somali Democratic Movement (SDM), representing the inter-riverine Rewin clans, and the Southern Somali National Movement (SSNM) whose members were mostly of the Dir/Biyamale clan family: they had fought within the ranks of the SNM in the North and continued to fight as the Southern Dir branch alongside USC and SPM. Both the SDM and the SSNM lacked military power of their own. This military alliance became the Somali National Alliance (SNA). In April 1992, SLA forces put an end to the "loyalist" threat. Mohamed Farah Aideed (USC) defeated the SNF forces in a battle 90 kilometers West of Mogadishu. The defeated fighters fled across the Kenyan border to Mandera. The SNF Barre loyalists were never again strong enough to try to reclaim control over the country.[11]

The Political Economy of War in the Fertile Lands

When the civil war reached the inter-riverine lands in 1990, USC/Aideed liberation forces were particularly eager to occupy the farmlands, which were under the control of the state or absentee landowners with good connections to government circles. The Somali Democratic Movement (SDM), the political organization of the Rewin at that time, was militarily weak, but had sided in this battle with USC forces, in the hope of an end to exploitation and landgrabbing. Nonetheless, the Rewin civilians suffered and, unlike the Marehan settlers in the area, had no clan safe haven to go to. In Elmi's description:

> Most of these military campaigns, which cress-crossed the agricultural sedentary areas of Shabelle, Middle and Lower Juba regions, Bay, Bakol and Gedo regions virtually destroyed almost all bases of life with massive human lives causing the greatest destitution and misery in the modern history of Somalia. The most effected were the farmers whose crops and plantations were completely laid waste and forced to flee with nowhere to seek refuge. Here not less than 50% of children and 40% of adults perished. ...
> They were subjected to indiscriminate mass genocidal, expropriation and destruction of urban property and homes, livestock and crops which resulted in the world famous Great Famine and Starvation that made Baidoa and its environs the number one disaster zone in the Somali disasters. This man-made calamity plus exacerbation of severe droughts

---

11 Until late 1997, SNF controlled an area bordering Kenya and Ethiopia.

claimed the lives of not less than 40% of children and 30% of adults (Salad Elmi, 1992: p.39-41).

In their hopes for liberation, the Rewin were dramatically let down by the Hawiye. Many analysts agree that the war in the fertile lands between the Shabelle and Juba rivers could be portrayed as a conflict between the Darod and the Hawiye for control of this precious resource, which originally did not belong to either of them (see Kusow, 1994; de Waal, 1994; Mukhtar and Kusow, 1993). In this context it is important to note that the inter-riverine lands are not only the single most fertile and agriculturally productive lands in the whole Somali region, but increasingly important for pastoral production, due to problems of desertification in the North (Kusow, 1994).

Thus, in addition to wanting control over the Southern inter-riverine areas for economic reasons, it was also important because of increasing environmental insecurity in the pastoral lowlands. The herding capacity of the pastoral lands was already diminishing during the 1980s, and more livestock was moved towards the Southern region. The trend of pastoralists moving into the Southern fertile lands was not a new phenomenon (see discussion of migration in chapters 4 and 7), although during the post-1991 faction war it did reach extreme dimensions. Before 1991, it was mostly Marehan who had profited, taking lands away from the Rewin, either by force or by claiming them according to the 1975 land laws designed by their government; after 1991, however, it was mainly Hawiye who occupied the cultivable lands. As mentioned earlier, many of the internally displaced persons in Mogadishu are farmers from these areas who were expelled from their lands.

For an understanding of the political economy of the inter-riverine lands it is important to remember that the Rewin are by number (although not by territory) one of the largest Somali clans, and not the Sab minority represented by long-held stereotypes.[12] A large number of the mostly Rewin farming communities were killed or starved to death by either the SNF or USC-SLA forces.[13] Interviews with various Somali reveal a perception that man-made starvation of the Rewin population in the triangle of death (Beled Weyne, Baidoa, Bardhere), in the most fertile area of Somalia, can be understood as an attempt to manipulate, once and for all, the population figures in Southern Somalia to the disadvantage of those who had originally settled there (*Africa Rights*, 1993). Seen in this light, the Rewin might have been considered a threat to Hawiye

---

12 In chapters 4 and 6 I referred to the political and social dominance of the nomadic clans (Samale) and their claim of superiority over the Sab settled communities.

political dominance – a dominance that, from the Hawiye perspective, was well deserved after three decades of Darod dominated central state leadership.

THE DISINTEGRATION OF SUB-STATE STRUCTURES

The period from mid-1991 to mid-1992 was characterized by increasing anarchy, rampant violence and the rule of the gun. By August 1992, more than two million people in Southern Somalia were reported to be directly threatened by starvation. Between a quarter and a third of the Somali population was at risk. Many people from the Southern countryside who had been caught up in fighting there had gone to Mogadishu in the hope of safe shelter and food aid. Like many inhabitants of the capital, they stayed in camps at the outskirts of the city.

The survival of the urban population depended mainly on the strategies and food policies of the two rival Hawiye clan forces, since they controlled the airport and the harbor. The factions made aid delivery a bargaining commodity, laying violent claim to a percentage of all food aid (sometimes up to 30% each) and medical supplies that were supposed to be distributed by the International Red Cross and other aid agencies.

Throughout the country many tribal factions were active. The militias of the factions, together with genuine criminals and bandits were creating chaos and insecurity in the city and in the country. These forces of greater darkness seemed to rejoice in causing unjustified killings and violence. In this incredibly tense climate it became impossible for almost anyone to provide normal delivery of humanitarian supplies (Gassem, 1994: p.113).

---

13 See Wiebe et al. (1995b). Kusow (1994) gives another account of atrocities committed against the Rewin people: "In 1990, Barre's troops fleeing from Mogadishu destroyed the Southern cities including Baidoa and Bardhere. They also indiscriminately wiped out rural villages, confiscating people's property and killing men between the ages of 15 and 30. Later, General Aideed's militia/clan finished off everything left by Siyyad Barre, to a point where the people could no longer sustain themselves. As late as September 13, 1992, the number of deaths was estimated to be more than 50 a day. The main reason for this tragedy is that Aideed's clan, who controlled the highways leading to the Southern cities, refused to allow food to pass through to the Rewin clans because of their cultural and linguistic differences and that Aideed wanted to starve them so that he could acquire their land" (ibid.: p.28).

Humanitarian aid delivery was threatened by uncontrollable violence. The movement of aid agency workers was hampered and only a minority of the people in need could be reached. Aid agencies paid large amounts of protection money in order to get food through the front lines. They found themselves forced into the role of indirectly financing the continuing war.

Flight, displacement and continuous warfare made it difficult for sub-state security structures to remain operational. Under the command of faction leaders, guerrilla forces conquered and re-conquered villages and farms in the countryside in a wave of humiliation, torture, violent death and starvation. A volatile combination of lack of discipline and control, the unleashing of clannish hatred, and the payment of fighters with the narcotic stimulant qaat and in seized bounty, meant that a large number of the urban and rural population in the Southern part of the country found itself at the mercy of the militias.

Besides militia fighters, who generally followed the orders of their superiors, there were also gangs of male youngsters, especially in Mogadishu; they had no close affiliation to political factions and secured their survival by looting and robbing. Known as *moryaan* (Marchal, 1997), the first group to be distinguished were a gang of urbanized youngsters who were largely responsible for the wave of revenge attacks against the wealthy people in Mogadishu, which took the form of looting, robbing and killing, and which are documented in several publications by Somali eye-witnesses (Afrah, 1993, Gassem, 1994). Many were drug addicts, mixing the stimulant qaat with amphetamines and tranquilizers (Marchal, 1997). They lived in relatively stable groups of young men, often together with kidnapped girls, and bound by personal friendship and age group rather than clan affiliation. These young looters developed their own code of conduct and logic of alliance, which borrowed some traditional Somali ways, such as post-feud compensation, but did not include the medium of the elders in their function of violence-control. For their survival they were entirely dependent on themselves; they felt accountable to nobody and were uncontrollable by authorities within the clan system. The result was anarchy, especially in the so-called Bermuda-triangle in Mogadishu, a no-go area controlled by neither of the two factions but by the *moryaans* (Afrah, 1993).

A second group of *moryaans* in the capital derived from young fighters with nomadic backgrounds who reached the city later in 1991. They were also regular drug users, although mainly of qaat, and were traumatized by the brutalities of the war (Marchal, 1997). These youngsters were more rooted in the traditional clan system, and as such were devoted to one or other of the sub-clans in the Aideed-Mahdi conflict. However, they were not fully disciplined or controlled by the faction leaders, and they secured their livelihood by using their control over firepower in order to loot. These youngsters faced a bleak future. They were disenchanted with pastoral life but had not yet settled in urban surroundings. In the civil war they were confronted with a culture of violence and disrespect for private or public property. Being paid in *qaat* rather than in money or food, their leaders could not keep them under control, and a culture of lawlessness developed.

Common to all those groups of young men was their lack of respect for traditional authority. I believe that this disintegration of the social fabric and its coherent moral value system as expressed in clan affiliation, religious identity and neighborhood solidarity, can be explained by several mutually-enforcing factors: (1) the scarcity of resources for daily survival; (2) a surplus of arms and ammunition captured from the stocks of the late Barre regime – in other words, the existence of non-controlled means of violence; and (3) mistrust and hatred between clans, sub-clans and lineages that had been sown a decade earlier by the policies of the head of state at the time, and that now created the grounds for acts of revenge. In this process, the categories of clan and class got intermingled as the differentiation between those clans who had supported the regime and those who had fought against it was more or less reflected in those groups who had profited under the regime and those who economically had been marginalized. That is why it is difficult to specify the degree of clannism in the motivation of the different moryaans. On top of all these, drug abuse and addiction almost certainly played a role (Marchal, 1997) in the carrying out of brutal crimes, such as the killing of children and parents and the rape of sisters, daughters and wives in front of family members, torture and mutilation, and the innumerable other ordeals which were experienced by a countless number of families in Somalia.[14]

During the state period, the state security institutions had been faced with an increasing resistance to their claimed monopoly of the use of force in the form of armed opposition. But the parties to this conflict had been relatively clearly defined. What made the stateless period in the South so extremely insecure for the civilian population was the disintegration not only of the state as dominant authority structure, but also of traditional structures within which violence had been organized and controlled. Although the sub-state security arrangements based on clan, family and neighborhood were not altogether destroyed; they failed to offer a stable framework of orientation. The civilian population was left in a situation of confusion, chaos and overall insecurity.

---

14 See Gassem (1994); see also the three documentary novels by Mohamoud. M. Afrah (1991, 1993 and 1994).

One reason for this was that the fighting in the capital and in the farming areas in the South involved continuously shifting coalitions. New military factions emerged, existing ones split apart and changed their objectives and, above all, the fighters of the respective factions were not continuously under the control of their leaders. This made it almost impossible for the civilian population to find protection from violent attack. Friend and enemy could hardly be identified. A second reason for the disintegration of sub-state security arrangements that prevailed during the early stateless years (1991-1992) was the weak position of the elders, traditionally the authorities responsible for political stability (see chapter 5, pp.119-123; table 1). Because the authority of the political factions was based on threat rather than on protection, they saw no need to accept any input from traditional leaders and elders in ending the fighting and finding a solution to the civil war.

Security from Trans-State Networks: The UN Involvement

In what follows we consider the UN humanitarian intervention (UNOSOM, 1992-1995), the work of the United Nations Development Office for Somalia (UNDOS) that emerged after 1995, and the role of UNHCR in the refugee aspect of the crisis.

The analysis of the UN intervention to Somalia has three main objectives. Firstly, the development of UN policy towards the Somali crisis is traced through the formulation of UN resolutions and mandates. Secondly, the achievements of the UN with regard to its defined goals of improving the security of the Somali population are assessed. Finally, space is given to some critical voices on the performance of UN troops *vis-à-vis* Somali people.

The UN involvement is perceived as one option for security provision available to Somali society and people, located at the trans-state level of the dynamics of relative security (see discussion at the end of chapter 1). The main problem that the UN faced in dealing with the Somali crisis was that there was no state authority in place. That was particularly difficult for UNOSOM and was one of the reasons why the peacekeeping mission turned into a peace-enforcement mission in Somalia. The activities of UNDOS are best portrayed as a caretaker function for an absent state, taking over aid co-ordination, data gathering and documentation. UNHCR, on the other hand, tackled the humanitarian problems deriving from the flight of Somalis into other countries; hence, UNHCR's work was less politicized than that of UNOSOM and UNDOS. In different degrees, these UN activities were based on political perceptions of the Somali polity. The following account focuses on some of the policies of

UNOSOM, UNHCR and UNDOS and their implementation.[15] In the process,
contradictions emerge that demonstrate the difficulties for international
agencies in dealing with a situation of divided sovereignty.

Our discussion will concentrate on the Southern part of the country, and
particularly on the events that took place in the capital, where the UN intervention had the most profound impact. The Northwest and Northeast proved
to be relatively stable and less conflict-ridden than the Southern and Central
regions. This was partly because the Barre regime had already been defeated in
the Northwest in mid-1990, while the Northeast had not experienced any major battles. After the state collapse, relative political security was established by
a return to sub-state pastoral clan arrangements. Internally displaced people
who had fled from the South to their original places of descent in the North
did cause temporary bottlenecks for housing, food and social services. However, relative political stability and – for the most part – the absence of fighting
had a positive impact on the operation of the harbors (Berbera and Bossasso)
and thus on the revival of trade and commerce, which in turn positively influenced food security. The UN therefore kept a low profile in these areas and
concentrated most of its efforts on the conflict-ridden South.

THE UN INTERVENTION IN SOUTHERN SOMALIA, 1992-1995

It took the UN a year to react to the collapse of the Somali state structure and
the human tragedy that was emerging from the continuing civil war. In January 1992, the first resolution on the Somali crisis was adopted. Three months
later, a small contingent of UN peacekeeping forces was stationed in Mogadishu. The decision to move from peacekeeping to peace-enforcement was
taken in early December 1992.

Peacekeeping missions, as referred to in Chapter VI of the United Nations
Charter, are in support of United Nations-sponsored negotiations between
warring sides. Peace-enforcement is included in Chapter VII of the Charter of
the United Nations. In the event that world peace and international or regional security is threatened, intervention by a multilateral UN force under UN
command is possible. Peace-enforcement is considered the last resort to secure world peace, the mandate led to the League of Nations and later the
United Nations.

---

15 The analysis cannot cover all UN programs in Somalia.

The UN humanitarian intervention in Somalia lasted from December 1992 to March 1995. The UNOSOM operation cost more than US$ 2.5 billion, of which 90% went to military operations. Only 4.5 % of this money flowed into the Somali economy through local staff, house rentals and vehicle leasing, while 85.5% of the military expenditure of the UNITAF/UNOSOM operation went to the different national armies seconded to the UN, and to Western contractors providing infrastructure such as catering.

UN Resolutions and the Mandate Discussion

The UN Security Council passed a first resolution on Somalia in January 1992 [733 (1992) 23.01.92] calling for a cease-fire and imposing a general and complete embargo on the delivery of weapons and military equipment to Somalia. Given the developments which had already taken place in Southern Somalia, this was clearly too little too late. Resolution 746 (17.03.1992) provided for a technical team to be dispatched to Somalia with the aim of developing a high priority plan to establish mechanisms to ensure the unimpeded delivery of humanitarian assistance. With Resolution 751 (24.04.1992), the United Nations Operation in Somalia (UNOSOM) was established under the authority of the Security Council, and it was decided that fifty UN observers should be sent to Mogadishu to monitor the latest cease-fire, which had just been proclaimed by the Aideed and Mahdi factions.

The UN approach was to maintain a low profile, to dispatch a minimal peacekeeping force, which partially controlled and operated the airport and harbor to protect food relief. At the same time the UN special representative focused on negotiations with the leaders of the military factions as well as the elders from different regions in Southern and Central Somalia. In the following months the special representative of the UN, Ambassador Sahnoun, was kept busy negotiating agreements between the military power holders in the country as well as with community, religious and clan leaders to improve on the delivery of humanitarian aid to the starving population (Sahnoun, 1994). The main question was how to involve the actual holders of military power without giving them full legitimacy, and at the same time to secure the involvement of those leaders within society who traditionally enjoyed the trust of their clans but were in no position to control the young fighters. This was a delicate task as the faction leaders in Mogadishu were concerned not to lose political ground to each other and not to give in to UN demands, which would have represented a loss of political authority.

The UN's approach was a pragmatic adaptation to the reality created by the breakdown of the central government authority and the disintegration of the whole country into clan-based power enclaves. There were two different kinds of authority in Southern Somalia: political authorities which were rooted in traditional forms of peace-making and reconciliation, but which, at that time, were powerless because unarmed; and military authorities whose credentials (gained from ending the dictatorship) had withered away as a result of the continuing war in Mogadishu and in the inter-riverine areas, but which nevertheless controlled different parts of the country in a reign of fear. Progress in this peace endeavor was slow, involving on the Somali side the precarious balance of local powers, and on the UN side the bureaucracy in New York and negotiators on the ground that were given limited room for bargaining (Sahnoun, 1994). Nonetheless, a continuation of this holistic approach, involving as many Somali authorities as possible, could ultimately have provided the necessary space for an empowerment of the traditionally accepted representatives of the various Somali communities and clans (Normark, 1994).

Toward the end of 1992, however, the UN approach to the Somali crisis changed fundamentally. This change was expressed in resolution 794 (3.12. 1992) which affected a shift from a peacekeeping mission to a peace-enforcement mission. The main argument for moving from peacekeeping to peace-enforcement was, according to the secretary-general's letter of 29 November 1992, that "there are at present very few authorities in Somalia with whom a peace-keeping force can safely negotiate an agreed basis for its operation". Resolution 794 provided that "action under Chapter VII of the Charter of the United Nations should be taken in order to establish a secure environment for humanitarian relief operations in Somalia as soon as possible". The Security Council authorized the member states that would be involved in that mission "to use all necessary means" in order to establish a "secure environment". Based on the threat to international peace and security, UN troops were thus authorized for the first time to use force in order to restore security in Somalia. The legitimacy for this mandate derived from the hundreds of thousands of helpless Somali who were held hostage by their own armed countrymen. A direct link was thus made between individuals in need of security and the international body of the UN, bypassing the state or those who claimed to represent a Somali government.

Successes and Shortcomings of the UN Mission

When the United Task Force (UNITAF) under American command landed in Somalia, the Somali population, although not necessarily the faction leaders welcomed it (Hirsch and Oakley, 1995). According to Gassem (1994), Somalis expected UNITAF to solve the root causes of insecurity in the country with the support of superior military power – in other words, to disarm the fighters and criminal youth gangs. It was hoped that reconciliatory dialogue, which had begun under the initiative of Sahnoun, would involve those men who enjoyed the trust and respect of Somali society, the heads of clans and village communities and the educated Somali.

The mass starvation of the Somali population, exposed by the media during August/September 1992, had made the need for speedy action clear, including the deployment of more UN troops in order "to establish as soon as possible a secure environment for humanitarian relief operations in Somalia". UNITAF forces controlled the airport and harbor and with them the major inlets and storage facilities of food aid. They accompanied food convoys and secured feeding stations in and around the capital. There were improvements in food delivery and medical care in the months following the initial intervention; feeding stations were operational in most major Southern and Central-Somali towns, and medical teams accompanying the UN soldiers opened field hospitals for local citizens. The immediate crisis was thus reasonably controlled. The extended UN mandate enabled it to save many lives, especially those of the internally-displaced farming communities who had fled to the capital when fighting intensified in the Southern Lower Juba and Shabelle regions. In many areas, the humanitarian mandate was fulfilled in a short span of time. Nevertheless, many undernourished people in the countryside, and even some in the capital, remained beyond the reach of the relief programs. Furthermore, the relief programs (*Africa Rights*, 1993) did not adequately address epidemic diseases that were among the main reasons for death.

Resolution 794 narrowly defined the Somali crisis as a purely humanitarian problem. Hence, the mandate did not address in detail other complementary objectives for a successful intervention, or the appropriate means for achieving these objectives. Initially there was a complete absence of discussion on issues such as disarmament and rehabilitation programs; the integration of Somali civilians into humanitarian operations as well as military control; confidence building between UN and Somali factions and the introduction of a UNOSOM code of conduct with regard to the imperative of UN-impartiality. The limitation of the UN mandate to the goal of providing humanitarian relief is the key to the difficulties that the UN experienced in its approach to the

Somali problem. The political dilemma was that, without tackling the problem of insecurity deriving from military and political instability, there could be no long-lasting humanitarian stability. Disarmament and demobilization were particularly important. The underlying problems of violence and the insecurity of food deliveries – the presence of armed fighters and bandits who were only partially controlled by faction leaders – were fundamentally neglected.

Although UNITAF won some credibility during the first weeks of its operations, this was subsequently lost through its inconsistency on disarmament. While heavy weapons remained more or less untouched, small arms were collected, leaving petty traders, drivers and farmers without protection. UNOSOM headquarters undermined some positive attempts at organized disarmament (Compagnon, 1997).

In 1993, a number of ambush attacks by faction fighters on UN personnel signaled a change in the relationship between Somali and the UN forces. On 5 June 1993, twenty-four Pakistani UN soldiers were ambushed and killed, and numerous others wounded. On 15 October, eighteen US servicemen were killed.[16] From that time on, UN forces were frightened of and became alienated from Somali society. In reaction to the 5 June killings, and the warrant against Mohamed Farah Aideed which followed on 17 June (with a US$ 25,000 reward for his arrest), the street patrols that had become so important for the safety of ordinary civilians came to a virtual halt while air strikes on supposed hideouts of Aideed and his supporters increased, causing the deaths of hundreds of uninvolved Somali people.[17] At the same time, UN-soldiers were coming under increasing criticism for their inhumane treatment of Somali civilians (Omaar and de Waal, 1994).

In numerous Somali-authored publications, UNOSOM has been criticized for not cooperating with Somali men and women to address the political situation in Somalia. The following extract is typical:

> Many concerned Somalis blame UNOSOM for not giving any consideration to their advice and not welcoming their practical assistance. This information gap was particularly damaging when it came to UNOSOM's lack of contacts with important personalities, Somali elders, politicians, intellectuals, religious dignitaries and women (Gassem, 1994: p.126-7).[18]

---

16 Similar, smaller scale ambushes took place until the very end of the UN mission in March 1995.

17 According to Dualeh (1994: p.165), UN-ordered aerial bombardments killed more than 9,000 Somali civilians, mostly women and children.

This attitude on the part of the UN played into the hands of the faction leaders. The military factions politically exploited feelings of anger and sorrow: public rallies against the UN should be seen in this light. In political slogans, radio and other communication, the UNOSOM mandate was portrayed as a quasi UN-trusteeship (Hirsch and Oakley, 1995). The inhabitants of Mogadishu increasingly perceived the UN soldiers as an occupation army (Gassem, 1994; Dualeh, 1994). This reawakened Somali pride as an independent nation, despite all the conflict.

Resolution 897 (4.2.1994) revised the UNOSOM mandate so that it no longer included the forcible disarmament of the various factions in Somalia.[19] With the departure of the "Western" UNOSOM troops in March 1994, leaving Asian, African and Arab troops with a minimum of modern military equipment, violence against UN units again escalated. The UN field of operation was increasingly restricted to guarding their own compounds. UN soldiers were repeatedly ambushed and killed, NGO workers and journalists were taken hostage or killed, frequently forcing the aid agencies to pull out their expatriate staff to Nairobi. Towards the end of 1994, UN troops stationed in other parts of the country were pulled back to bases in Mogadishu in preparation for their departure. The UN troops finally left Somalia altogether in March 1995.

The UN peace-enforcement mission in Somalia resulted in a death toll of 135 UN soldiers, and hundreds of Somali fighters and civilians, many of them women and children. In terms of its effectiveness in controlling violence, the overall record of the UN is poor. UNITAF and UNOSOM were not only incapable of interrupting the general cycle of violence which had developed in the anarchic period, but through their political misjudgments they even provoked additional violence directed against their own troops and installations, adding another dimension of conflict to the civil war arena.

---

18 In a chapter entitled "Suggestions to UNOSOM II" Gassem (1994) writes: "The second suggestion for UNOSOM is to emerge from its shell. UNOSOM people must come out of their detention-like offices and residences. Mogadishu is large and so is Somalia. They must establish offices and residences in other areas of the city whose population is not hostile to UNOSOM. To achieve the effectiveness UNOSOM people long for, they need to be able to interact and mix with Somalis, see them, talk with them and discuss their common issues of concern. In short, UNOSOM must be in serious contact with the local population without fear. It is important for UNOSOM personnel to become acquainted with Somali problems through normal Somalis, by engaging them in first hand dialogue in order to understand their way of thinking and real inner feelings."
19 See UN document SOM 53, 16 February 1994; in *Horn of Africa Bulletin* 2/94, p.15.

Reconstructing Political Security: The UNOSOM Political Division

In March 1993, under auspice of UNOSOM's political division,[20] the UN sponsored and organized a conference in Addis Ababa[21] that brought together political, military and community organizations from Somalia.[22] A Draft Transitional Charter was formulated that provided a framework for the re-establishment of a central government for Somalia, with a Transitional National Council as a first step towards the formation of a national government. Prior to the creation of such National Council, District and Regional Councils were to be created, an approach that was seen as grassroots oriented. UNOSOM's political division in accordance with the plans worked out in the Addis Ababa Agreement coordinated the establishment of District and Regional Councils.

Some of the first District Councils were established in Bay region in 1993. However, these political structures remained somewhat artificial bodies in the local political setting. Peace-building and the establishment of a secure political environment was undertaken by clan elders, while the councils were confronted with well-financed and powerful international organizations who had "assumed the role of social service providers in the absence of any effective government" (Wiebe et al., 1995b: p.20), and by rich, powerful local business people who influenced the power balance. The efforts of UNOSOM political division and other international agencies led to numerous local peace conferences. In March 1996, District Councils were in place in 68 of the 77 districts in Somalia (*Horn of Africa Bulletin* 2/96). However, the establishment of District Councils cannot be equated with the establishment of sustainable peace, political stability and an overall improvement in the provision of security, since the councils were not necessarily expressions of authority vested in them by the local community. In some cases, District Councils were set in place when local reconciliation had not fully matured. The motivation for people within the community to run for the position of Council member mainly derived from external sources, including the provision of training. Power and authority continued to lie with elders, and councilors admitted that they relied on elders for legitimacy and authority (Wiebe et al., 1995b). The functions of the councils in the local settings remained unclear, and their powers were per-

---

20 Besides the UNOSOM political division there was also a justice division that took responsibility for re-instituting the police, prisons and judiciary.

21 The text of the Addis Ababa Agreement of 27 March 1993 is printed in Brons (1993).

22 The majority of the delegates were from the various military factions. The SNM/ Somaliland refused to take part and sent an observer only.

ceived as very limited. As a result, relatively weak personalities were often given positions on these councils, while many of the former government administrators expected that "more prominent national positions would soon be on offer" (Wiebe et al., 1995a).

In many cases where rudimentary formation of political authority took place the process was hampered or completely undermined by the military factions who retained their monopoly of the means of violence and were able to transform their military superiority into political power. Two consequences of this power – forced migration and the occupation of territory by faction soldiers – provided additional reasons for skepticism with regard to the establishment of local administrative structures. A genuine reconstruction of political stability was impossible, given the continuation of widespread insecurity and military activity in Mogadishu and other parts of the country, such as in and around Kismayo and Baidoa. Goodwill and mutual trust, pre-conditions for reconciliation and political reconstruction, were lacking on all sides.

One imperative for political stability would have been the creation of a secure environment for the resettlement of Somali refugees and displaced persons. This would have included the difficult task of settlement of the land rights of farmers in the Southern region. In an UN-sponsored regional conference in March 1994, the so-called Jubaland conference, military factions in these areas were given the opportunity to settle this matter among them, marginalizing the Rewin farmers to whom the land originally belonged. The agreement that property should be returned to its owners implied the return of the land to those who had grabbed it under the Barre land registration laws. The UN hereby assisted in the implementation of injustice (de Waal, 1994).

Another dubious side effect of the various international conferences on reconciliation, such as the Addis-Ababa Conference in March 1993, was that the military faction leaders gained some sort of recognition and mandate. The international political players saw them as the main future power-holders in the country; furthermore, they had all been involved in politics before, in one way or another. The UN agencies seemed to be either incapable or unwilling[23] to find the right interlocutors in Somali society, people who could indeed

---

23 According to ex-ambassador Al-Azhari, it was very difficult to convince UNOSOM financially to support small-scale peace initiatives in regions such as the Mudug/Galgudud provinces. Statement at the international conference *"Crisis Management and the Politics of Reconciliation in Somalia"*, Uppsala, 17-19 January 1994, Nordiska Afrikainstitutet.

claim a mandate from the people and were therefore in a position to make a real contribution to reconciliation.

Misconduct of UN Troops in Somalia

During the UN peace-enforcement mission it became evident that UN contingents in Somalia enjoyed almost complete impunity for misconduct and crimes. A differentiation has to be made here between military decisions at a high command level, and abuses committed by individual soldiers. High command policies caused the UN mission to lose its moral superiority. Several UN operations were as neglectful of the safety of civilians as the operations of the faction fighters. The shelling of Digfer-hospital and recurrent searches of the building fall into this category, causing casualties and the destruction of building, infrastructure and equipment. USC sniper attacks from the roof of the hospital building were answered not by a withdrawal of the UN troops (which would have been the best option from the standpoint of civilian safety), but by a UN-attack on the hospital. Another example is the air-bombardment of a private house in which a political meeting of Aideed supporters was taking place. The UN did not act in defense but, during busy morning hours, bombed the house from the air; the attack cost the lives of 54 people, including children, women and a number of elders and religious leaders from various Hawiye clans. At least two incidents were reported in which Blue helmets opened fire on anti-UN demonstrations. Preventive detention of suspected Somali without trial for up to 45 days were recorded and admitted in press conferences. A less brutal category of abuse, nonetheless contravening the humanitarian mandate of the mission, was the demolition of government houses (some of the few which had survived the 1991 war in Mogadishu), and the relocation of inhabitants out of the areas surrounding military compounds for reasons of UN safety. The following extract from Omaar and de Waal (1994: p.134) highlights the way in which security provision paradoxically turned against the very group it was supposed to help, the civilian population:

> The commander of the UNOSOM base then proposed the demolition of the university residential compound: 61 houses, all intact, inhabited by former university lecturers and/or their relatives. The compound residents sent a delegation to the commander to protest and to offer alternative solutions to the security problems of the base, such as extending the defended perimeter to include the university residences. They reported an unsympathetic response: "These are government houses, not private ones. You have no government. So you can be kicked out."

The other category of human rights abuses, those committed by individual soldiers, resulted from lack of discipline, fear or inherent racist attitudes and the exploitation of UN authority and military superiority. These included the killing of unarmed civilians, physical abuse and harassment, careless demolition of ammunition without prior warning in the close vicinity of residential areas, unnecessarily brutal evacuation of houses, theft of money and looting and destruction of harvest (watermelons), and the humiliation of the local population during contacts.

UN Blue-helmets from different countries, including Belgians, Canadians, Italians, and Germans, were accused of human rights abuses. The ways in which the UN and the governments of the respective countries reacted to the allegations differed. In Somalia, only the American, Canadian and Australian forces had Complaints Offices: even then, Somali faced intimidation and sometimes threats when complaints were made. The few cases, which were followed up by UNOSOM, were apparently not taken very seriously, as they resulted in light punishments for offences such as the killing of unarmed civilians (Omaar and de Waal, 1994).

Mostly under pressure from press and opposition, several governments were forced to conduct criminal investigations. Several Canadians were brought to court, one of them convicted to five years' imprisonment for manslaughter, and others convicted of lesser offences. In Belgium, thirteen cases were investigated, including eight alleged offences of manslaughter. In Italy and Germany, too, military inquiries were conducted, including charges of ill treatment of detained Somali criminal suspects.[24]

In sum, the UN humanitarian intervention enhanced food security and enabled aid agencies to continue their programs in the health and other social sectors. However, its impact on the situation in Somalia was neither comprehensive nor long lasting, as it did not sufficiently take into account the root causes of the Somali crisis. Particularly the negative impact of the situation in the inter-riverine areas on food security, the occupation of farmland by faction soldiers that caused displacement of the farming communities and exploitation of those who remained on their lands, was not addressed. Political efforts to enhance the progress of reconciliation mostly involved the leaders of the military factions, who were thereby treated as quasi statesmen. After the

---

24 The evaluation report on human rights violations by UN forces on which most of this section is based, notes the remarkably positive conduct of the UN contingent from Botswana. This seems to support the argument that part of the reason for the behaviour of most other troops was inherent racism.

abrogation of the Sahnoun initiative, no serious efforts were undertaken by UNOSOM to respond adequately to the situation of divided sovereignty in Somalia and to empower those people who could have emerged as an alternative authority to represent Somali society. Disarmament and demobilization were neglected and finally dropped from the mandate. Misconduct of UN soldiers increased the insecurity of Somali people. Seen in this light, it can be argued that most of the UN efforts were counterproductive to peace and stability in the Southern region.

UNHCR: ASSISTANCE TO SOMALI REFUGEES

Flight is an extreme form of search for security. In the development of the Somali crisis, people fled first from state-induced violence committed by the army and police. Rather than protecting the lives of its citizens, the state authority had proved threatening to an increasing number of them. After the state collapsed, some groups who had the military means to control the use of force again neglected the security concerns of the civilian population. Many Somali civilians decided to flee, and many are in 1999 still forced to live in refugee camps and camps for internally displaced people with little hope of returning to their home areas.

UNHCR became involved in the Somali region in the late 1970s[25] when, in the aftermath of the Somali-Ethiopian war, Ethiopian Somali sought refuge in Somalia. The agency then became involved in caring for Somali fleeing from the civil war in 1988, when approximately half a million Northern Somali crossed the border into Ethiopia. From then on, UNHCR cared for Northern Somali refugees in camps located in the Ethiopian Haud areas, and for ex-Ethiopian Somali refugees who had settled in Somalia but because of the civil war returned to the Ogaden and other areas in the Ethiopian region (Brons et al., 1993). It is worth noting, however, that in the case of returnees into the Ethiopian Ogaden region, especially, self-help efforts within the Somali communities were at least as important as the officially organized repatriation programs.

Once the civil war had spread into the Southern region, and particularly during the 1991/92 wars in the inter-riverine region, Somali also found refuge in Kenya and in other countries in the region such as Tanzania, Yemen and

---

25 Although some Somali had already fled the country after the take-over of power by Siyad Barre in 1969, and applied for refugee status abroad.

Djibouti. On an international scale, UNHCR was also involved with Somali refugees who left for Canada and North America, and to various European countries, such as the Netherlands, Germany, Belgium, Italy, Scandinavia and Russia.

On their journey to supposed safety, Somali refugees often faced extreme danger, and many were killed. Refugees were forced overboard and drowned when trying to flee to Yemen or Tanzania in small wooden boats. Fleeing across land was also an ordeal. And reports of insecurity and crime in Kenyan refugee camps revealed that even under UN-protection, the safety of women, in particular, could not always be guaranteed.[26]

In 1992, during the peak of fighting in the South, about 420,000 Somali refugees were registered in Kenya. By April 1996, there were an estimated 275,000 Somali refugees remaining in Ethiopia, 129,000 in Kenya, 50,000 in Yemen, 20,000 in Djibouti and 1,350 in Eritrea. In 1995, UNHCR repatriated 42,000 Somalis from Kenya and expected to repatriate another 35,000 in 1996, and 20,000 in 1997. UNHCR assisted in the return of about 5,000 refugees from Yemen and 46,000 refugees from Ethiopia.[27] Transport and repatriation grants in cash and in non-cash items were provided. In the returning areas in the Southern regions to which many refugees returned, quick-impact projects were designed, integrating aspects of transport and rehabilitation of infrastructure, water, health, education and income-generating projects.[28] Whilst repatriation efforts progressed in the Northeast, the region for returnees from Yemen,[29] this was much more problematic in the South, because of the continuing insecurity deriving from warfare and the lack of functioning administrative structures.[30]

---

26 I do not deal extensively with the Somali refugees in Kenya. However, it is clear that physical security could not be guaranteed by UNHCR. Women, particularly, faced a second ordeal after flight in the form of rape, theft and harassment mostly at the hands of Kenyan police. See Omaar and de Waal (1993); Hamdi S. Mohamed (1997); Goldsmith (1997).

27 Figures provided by Mr. Nabil Musa, UNHCR cross-border operations (Nairobi, 8 October 1996).

28 *Humanitarian Aid to Somalia Evaluation Report* (1994) provides a detailed evaluation of UNHCR cross-border operations.

29 See publications of the War-torn Societies Project (WSP, 1998a, 1998b); also Heinrich (1998).

30 Interview with Mr. Nabil Musa (Nairobi, 8 October 1996).

Continuing International Involvement: undos

After the departure of the unosom military division in March 1995, un involvement did not come to an end. The un political division was transformed into a Nairobi-based office, the un Development Office Somalia (undos).[31]

With relatively limited resources,[32] undos took over a kind of caretaker role with regard to various functions usually provided by state authorities. These functions include data gathering, consultation with donor and aid organizations, and documentation. The undos documentation unit collects all available documents and articles on Somalia and the wider Somali region. With most former governmental documents having been destroyed or lost, and public educational institutions, ministries, schools and the national university having been looted; the efforts of the undos documentation unit are invaluable. A geographical information system (gis) is being developed, which includes an indication of health and educational facilities, price indices and other economic data; the gis is supposed to form part of an early warning system for Somalia with regard to food security. As part of this program, data collection surveys have been conducted under undos auspices.

The undos Local Administrative Structure Unit is involved in an assessment of local administrative structures in the various Somali regions and in the collection of population data. Indigenous capacity building with a focus on strengthening planning and management capacities, skills in administration, bookkeeping and accounting, budgeting, project identification, appraisal and monitoring, are carried out. Workshops and seminars are intended to strengthen the Somali capacity for self-administration while, in the meantime, surveys, planning and co-ordination are carried out by undos or its delegated agency.

In 1994, the Somalia Aid Co-ordination Body (sacb) was set up with the intention of enacting a code of conduct for international ngos in the context of increasing insecurity for their personnel, and extreme cases of kidnapping. Around sixty donor and aid organizations are members of the sacb, which is headed by the European Union Somalia Unit. undos functions as a secretariat to sacb and it's standing Committee. It also organizes multi-donor missions to Somalia, and provides sector or regional profiles and statistics to do-

---

31 undp, unicef, wfp, who, unctad and other un organisations still have programs in Somalia, though run from Nairobi.

32 undos is funded by undp, usaid, the eu, Italy, the Netherlands and Sweden; information collected in October 1996 in Nairobi.

nors for project-preparation purposes. UNDOS perceives its role as facilitative, enhancing the flow of information between UN agencies, donors and NGOs in order to improve the co-ordination of reconstruction and rehabilitation activities.

THE INTERNATIONAL FACTOR IN A NO-STATE SITUATION

The international approach to Somalia after the breakdown of the Siyad Barre regime in January 1991 was, until 1993 marked by neglect. By then the disastrous consequences of the collapse of the state and the continuation of civil war for the Somali population got the necessary attention and resulted in 'Operation Restore Hope'. UN policies, particularly in the early UNOSOM years, were aimed at the restoration of a central state within the territorial demarcations of 1960. The international order based on '*de jure*' sovereign states provided the conditions for this approach. Accordingly, the independence of Somaliland has not been recognized internationally, either by the UN-system at large, or by regional organizations such as the OAU, the Arab League or the IGAD.

The lack of a central government in Somalia provided a justification for international organizations, such as UNDOS and SACB, to "formulate joint policy and act as the primary forum for the exchange of information on developments in the country" (UNHCR/USAid/EUE, 1996: p.3). With a functioning state administration in place a bureau of national statistics, a ministry of planning or a ministry of economic co-operation would carry out these tasks. The involved international agencies are aware that choosing interlocutors in a no-state situation poses problems in terms of neutrality. One option is to wait for a central authority to appear, in other words, for state sovereignty to re-emerge. Another option asks for sensitivity and respect for the sovereign rights of people and a positive and supportive response to community-rooted processes of re-emerging political authority. It demands adaptation of the planning and processing of development aid according to the rhythm and speed of local community political processes.

At the trans-state level, the UNDP, the World Food Program, and other NGOs coordinated by the SACB, have established themselves as providers of basic securities in crisis situations; as such, they represent a kind of competition to the state as well as to sub-state structures. However, "multilateral institutions can neither replace the functions of the state nor reconstruct the state institutions they have directly or indirectly participated in destroying" (Mohamed Salih, 1999: p.137). An acknowledgement of the influence of aid on the political balance of power is not a new phenomenon (Prendergast, 1996).

In the situation of a society without a state – a situation where state formation processes might grow out of political collapse – it is even more important to be aware of the possible impact of security provision on socio-political balances within society.

Contemporary Dynamics of State Formation

By contrast with what has been described so far for the period of post-collapse statelessness in the South – continuous warfare, anarchy and a partial disintegration of sub-state security arrangements, and the UN involvement in alleviating the resulting humanitarian crisis – processes of political authority formation did evolve in some other parts of the country. I do not refer to mere assertion of state authority by political faction leaders, based simply on their superior military strength. I am rather referring to developments where political security provision was achieved by an integrated effort of political faction leaders and clan elders. In the process, new regional polities emerged reflecting, to a certain extent, consent between rulers and ruled.

We will examine three cases here (map 5, diagram 1): (1) Somaliland, in the Northwestern region, where political authorities proclaimed an independent state in May 1991, referring back to the territory of the colonial British Somaliland Protectorate; (2) the Digil and Mirifle Governing Authority in the inter-riverine region, which was formed in May 1995 and claims to represent the Rewin clans (Riverine State); (3) the Puntland regional state in the Northeastern region, established in July 1998 and basically comprising the Darod/ Harti (Majertain/Warsangeli/ Dulbahante) clan family.

Can we describe the emergence of these political entities as bottom-up state formation processes? It is difficult to assess with certainty the degree of involvement of the population living within these polities. What can be considered is in how far the political structures and mechanisms provided by the clan framework were integrated in the formation of these political entities. A second question is whether these entities can be considered states. To assess this, we will discuss them in the light of the conditions that define a state, that is, a coherent territory and population, a binding idea or ideology, and institutions that participate in security provision within this territory, in particular with regard to control over the use of force.

The underlying imperative for such an evaluation is that a state does not have an existence of its own. People create and use political structures and organizations and, according to the state-in-society approach, the state is one out of many alternative security-providing frameworks. Whether a state can be considered a sovereign political authority ultimately depends on whether people – the citizens living within a defined territory – accept and respect domination by this authority that is whether there is *de facto* sovereignty. Quite another question is *de jure* sovereignty, which is provided by international recognition. Somaliland, the only one of the three that makes a claim to international recognition, has not so far succeeded in achieving it.

The following accounts of Somaliland, the Riverine State and Puntland differ in length and depth. The case of Somaliland is dealt with in some detail, partly because the process has already been underway for eight years, and partly because this polity claims an independent '*de jure*' state status. The other two states perceive themselves as regional autonomous states within a broader federal or con-federal Somali political framework, which may come to exist in the future. As the formation of these latter polities is a relatively recent phenomenon and has not so far produced much literature or documentation, the presentation here is necessarily shorter and less detailed.

SOMALILAND

The Road to the Proclamation of Independence

The Somali National Movement (SNM) adhered to the option of a unified Somali state with guaranteed regional autonomy for the North until the beginning of May 1991 (see *Indian Ocean Newsletter*, 2 February 1991). From January to May 1991 it followed a course of reconciliation with those Northern Somali clans, which had fought against the SNM on the government side (*Indian Ocean Newsletter*, 9 February 1991). Numerous peace conferences took place between Isaq sub-clans on the SNM side and Warsangeli and Dulbahante (both Darod/Harti) and Gadabuursi and Issa (both Dir) on the other.[33] Although there had been support within SNM for the option of independence from Mogadishu, SNM official policy was in favor of keeping the union between North and South intact. What made the SNM change its view on this issue was an accumulation of political decisions from the USC/Hawiye, which suggested renewed tendencies towards Southern domination. Victory over the Siyad Barre regime, for instance, was claimed by USC, which had indeed

---

33 For the Sanaag region see: Somali Development and Relief Agency (SDRA); Mennonite Central Committee (MCC) (1994).

fought the final battle in Mogadishu in January 1991, but would not have been in a position to do so without logistical support from SNM in the preceding months. Another indication of Southern insensitivity was the discussion to take the 1960 constitution as a basis for the reconciliation process – a constitution which had been rejected by the North in the 1961 referendum (Drysdale, 1992) and which was considered an instrument of Southern domination (Madar, 1991).

It seems that pressure from within the Isaq (Hartisheik refugee) community (see chapter 7) was instrumental in making the SNM reconsider its position (ibid.). Peace-conferences in Berbera, Hargeisa and Burao brought together delegates from SNM, various Northern Somali clans, and many Somali refugees from Ethiopia, and paved the way to the proclamation of an independent state (*Indian Ocean Newsletter*, 6 April 1991).

The reconciliation initiative effected immediately after the defeat of the Government forces in Northern Somalia between the two sides of the civil war stands as a landmark for all other subsequent initiatives. It was a reconciliation between collective Dir and Darood clans with collective Issaq clans and was hosted and brokered by SNM. It started in Berbera on February 15-27, 1991 and culminated into the Burao historic May 1991 congress, where finally the hatchets of ten year civil war were buried and the independent Republic of Somaliland was proclaimed (Fadal, 1996: p.10).

Thus, from the very beginning of the process of reconciliation in the Northwest, clan elders from various backgrounds had been consulted. This was more or less a continuation and extension of the relationship that had existed during civil war times between SNM and Isaq elders. The political revival of these traditional political authorities in the region in so-called *guurti* assemblies had begun before the collapse of the central state. In traditional stateless Somali society, the maintenance of peace had been one of the obligations of the clan elders, particularly in the pastoral North (see chapters 4 and 5). The *guurti* are committees of elders from specific clans or lineages who meet in *shir*-conferences, which are called to settle conflicts between certain clan units. As Farah and Lewis (1993: p.18-19) note:

> In 1988, the repulsed massive offensive launched by the SNM against the government forces in Burao and Hargeisa, effectively undermined the capacity of the SNM as a military organization. This led to the formation of an Isaq Guurti, of 53 members, that took the responsibility of providing clan militias and logistical support [to] the impaired war effort. Held at Adarosh near the Ethiopian border, this important conference was organized by elders. Because of the vital collaboration between the elders, who had influ-

ence on Isaq groups, and military leaders, the Isaq Guurti was given recognition in the constitution of the SNM.

Traditionally, the heads of lineages and clans do not act as formally elected, independent representatives of their constituency but remain in constant consultation with the members of their lineage on how to assess and proceed in the process of conflict management. The structural framework for reconciliation and conflict management as based in the clan-system did not disappear during the central state period, in spite of attempts to replace it by socialist state institutions. It underwent some transformation through the establishment of the *aqils* as civil servants responsible for peace making, and the marginalisation of the role of the sultans. The Siyad Barre government used the *aqils* for its divide-and-rule policy by providing them with arms and inciting conflict between the lineages that they represented. The legacy of complicity with the former state followed some of the *aqils*. But in the peace conferences that led to the declaration of an independent Somaliland, these differences were overcome by fostering reconciliation between the formerly opposing clans and by restraining them from making any claims with regard to blood-compensation or reimbursement of property.

The conferences, which led in May 1991 to the proclamation of an independent Somaliland state, were therefore largely a continuation of the process of integrating elders into political decision-making. The new factor was the integration of all clans of the region, Isaq, Harti and Dir, in the process of creation of peace and political stability. This kind of authority formation that linked the sub-state level of political and legal security provision with faction politics probably came as close to being "bottom-up" as was possible under the circumstances.

On this basis, and with reference to the consent theory, I would argue that in the case of Somaliland a large majority of the Northwestern Somali population vested sovereignty in the political authorities that represented the new state. An analysis of the institutions, idea and territory of the Somaliland state further elucidates this hypothesis and sheds light on the strengths and weaknesses connected with the process of state formation.

Somaliland State Institutions: Political Stability and Control of Violence

The first government of Somaliland, the transitional government from May 1991 to May 1993, was based on the organizational structure of SNM. The SNM executive committee became the government, with the SNM president and vice-president becoming head of state and vice-president of the Republic of Somaliland, respectively. The former central committee functioned as national council or parliament. However, these formally erected state institutions did not immediately function in political practice. The transformation of the SNM from a liberation movement to a responsible and accountable government still had to be achieved.

What could be seen in the two years of the transition period was the increasing involvement and institutionalization of clan elders in peace making and reconciliation (Farah and Lewis, 1993). The country was still facing immediate post-war conditions: the clan-based SNM militia units were still carrying arms in their respective areas; feelings of mistrust and revenge were not far below the surface, and were easily aroused; and the population structure was dominated by the effects of forced migration, with about half the Somaliland people still resident in refugee-camps in the Ethiopian border area. Many conflicts arose over grazing rights and land disputes, which had partly been created as result of people returning from forced migration and flight. Various *guurtis* settled local resource conflicts and took over administrative functions within their respective communities.

There was also conflict over resources at higher levels in the political leadership of the country. These were rooted in a split within the SNM between Abdulrahman Ahmed Ali Tour (Garhajis/Habr Yonis), the chairman of SNM, and his predecessor Ahmed Silanyo (Habr Jaalo). After the establishment of the SNM interim government under President Abdulrahman Ahmed Ali Tour (Isaq/Garhajis/Habr Yonis) this split was transformed into support for or opposition to the country's political leadership.[34] The Burao conflict in 1991 marked the first outbreak of violence during the interim period that followed this pattern. The militant members of the clan constituencies of the political leaders from the Habr Jaalo and Garhajis fought in the town of Burao where the two communities live side by side.

The Berbera conflict in March 1992 evolved in reaction to government efforts to centralize authority and take over control of claimed state assets. Control over Berbera port – the main source of foreign exchange – was claimed by the Isaq/Habr Awal/Iisa Muse clan lineage. In their eyes, the Habr Yonis, who then held the presidency, were seeking to undermine the traditional rights of the Iisa Muse to control the port and its revenues. In this and similar cases, clans were suspicious and openly critical of the government's potential to

---

34 The SNM Khaakh faction was against, and the Shiish faction was for, the first interim government (Fadal, 1996: p.11).

exploit its powers in order to enrich its own clan base and monopolize state power, as had happened under the Siyad Barre state.

Neither of these intra-Isaq conflicts could be resolved through intervention by Isaq elders or from the government side. They were finally settled at a peace conference in Sheikh, through the efforts of the Gadabuursi *guurti*, the highest political authority of the Gadabuursi clan in Somaliland, which was neutral in the conflict (Farah and Lewis, 1993). The participants at the Sheikh peace conference, in October/November 1992, were the *guurtis* of the Habr Yonis and the Iisa Muse, the conflicting clans, and a forty-man arbitration group.

Of the forty man arbitration group selected among the large representative clan Guurtis, thirty six members came from the clans living in the following administrative regions: Awdal (Gadabuursi – nine members), Sool (Dhulbahante – nine members), Burao (Isaq – nine members) and Hargeisa (Isaq – nine members). The remaining four members were distinguished as religious men. In effect, the collective service of the Guurti in "Somaliland" was mobilized to arbitrate this relative serious internal Isaq upheaval, whose settlement evaded the ability of the Isaq elders. The Warsangeli Guurti was absent from this event because of involvement in important internal matters at the time (ibid.: p.53).

After settling the Berbera conflict, the Sheikh conference turned, in a second phase, to issues central to military and political security in the country. This marked a turning point in the process of state formation in Somaliland. As an inter-clan reconciliation initiative, it paved the way for an institutionalized National Guurti, which then took a leading role in the formulation of Somaliland's future as a state. Particularly with regard to the control of violence and the provision of internal law and order and external security, the Sheikh conference endorsed an overall legal framework, which was binding for all local *guurtis* in Somaliland. As the following excerpt from the proceedings of the Sheikh Reconciliation Conference (*Tawfiiq*), held from 28 October 1992 until 8 November 1992, shows (Farah and Lewis, 1993: p.84-87), a decentralized structure of security provision was introduced, which gave autonomy and full responsibility to the single, clan-defined communities.

A general framework for peace (law and order) in 'Somaliland' ... (1) To establish a hierarchical law and order mechanism, each local community shall establish its particular peace committee. Its mandate is to attend to the security affairs in its domain. However, the local peace committee works under the auspices of the general and constitutional Guurti of 'Somaliland'. (2) The local peace committees shall carry out their routine tasks independently. (3) Each community bears the responsibility for acts of aggression that take place in its sphere of influence. Thus, other groups have the right to exact compensation for homicide and other offenses that result in its area. It is the duty of the local Sultans and Akils to apprehend and exact compensation from members of their group that commit grievous offences. (4) Each community should keep its militias away from major towns, roads and public facilities. (5) Each community shall demolish the checkpoints manned by its militias in the area it controls. ... (8) Local groups have a legitimate right to establish particular legal law and order codes. Accordingly, they shall construct basic security apparatus, such as prison and police establishments as well as magistrate courts. ... (10) Unusual events that are found difficult to be effectively resolved by the local peace committee and Guurti of the lineage shall be resolved with the collaboration of the higher clan Guurti. The latter can also seek the support of the supreme Guurti of 'Somaliland' as need arises. (11) Each militia shall remain in the area controlled by its group, which must regulate and constrain its movements. Without permission from the concerned local peace committee, it must not trespass the boundary of a different group, regardless of intention. ... (13) Clan militias are proscribed to visit towns carrying weapons. Established security forces that are controlled by the local peace committees, are the only organs of security permitted to stay in the towns and carry guns as need arises. ... (18) If a district or a region in 'Somaliland' is attacked by an outside force, other local communities are obliged to support the attacked group.

These arrangements include the essential aspects of internal security provision and control of violence that characterize state institutions. The Sheikh-agreement was a fundamental step forward from the proclamation of independence of May 1991 and can be considered a first step toward the formulation of a Somaliland state.

In the transitional period (1991-93), dynamics of (in)security initiated a society-rooted process towards state formation. The business community and other relatively influential interest groups such as women supported the political structure of clan elders. These social organizations proved to be more reliable in establishing relative military/political security than the SNM faction, now that the civil war had been won.

The success of the Sheikh conference led to the Borama conference, the 'Grand Conference of the Communities in Somaliland' that was held from January to May 1993. In Borama, 150 elders representing the clan *guurtis* from all over the country met in order to discuss the political future of Somaliland. The Borama Conference endorsed a National Charter (25.4.1993) in which fundamental political and institutional structures of the Somaliland state were defined: (1) *Golaha Guurtida* (Council of Elders or first chamber); (2) *Golaha Wakiillada* (Constituent Assembly or second chamber); and (3) *Golaha Xukuumadda* (government or executive power). Parliamentary democracy was introduced in the form of a two-chamber system, but with paramount political security provided by the National *Guurti:* under politically stable circumstances, the National *Guurti* held an advisory role, but it was accorded extraordinary powers in the event of a serious government crisis.

In case of circumstances preventing the state bodies from performing their national duties, the Council of Elders has full authority to convene a conference, representing all the communities of Somaliland, to decide on political measures to solve outstanding problems (Warsame and Brons, 1994: p.24).

The Borama Conference elected Mohamed Ibrahim Egal president of Somaliland for a period of two years. This was later extended by eighteen months, to October 1996. Egal (Isaq/Habr Awal/Iisa Muse) had not been a member of snm, and in that sense was an outsider to the snm feuds. Ex-party leader of the Somali National League before unification with the South in 1960 (see p.153), and last prime minister of Somalia before the military coup by Siyad Barre (1967-69), he had been director of the chamber of commerce and trade in Mogadishu in the late 1980s. Egal was seen by many as one of the few respected prominent Somali politicians. People vested hope in him, firstly to bridge the differences within the Isaq and within the government in general and to foster political stability, and secondly as an internationally known ex-politician to promote international recognition of Somaliland, in the process enhancing regional peace and security.

During his three years in office President Egal failed to present a draft constitution for a referendum. Part of the problem was that the Garhajis, who had dominated the interim government, still opposed the Egal government for various reasons. They claimed that they had not been given a fair share in the distribution of portfolios. According to Farah (1995: p.2) "As the richest, most urbanized and sedentarised Isaq group, the rival Habr Awal [president Egal's clan] is associated with trade and wealth. The Garhajis fear that the Habr Awal are getting richer and more numerous and therefore may tend to translate these resources into political power." In addition, the attitude of former interim-president Abdulrahman Ahmed Ali Tour (Garhajis/Habr Yonis) towards Somaliland independence proved to be contradictory as, in 1995, he turned to align himself with Mohamed Farah Aideed in the South. This political conflict disturbed the process of consolidation. It led to the outbreak of violence when Garhajis militias engaged government forces in fighting over the control of Hargeisa airport. The conflict could partly be solved by a cabinet reshuffle, partly by a peace agreement in October 1995 between the government and the Garhajis/Eidegalla clans.

The Egal government was weakened through these events and partly criticized for not pushing hard enough to get the constitutional process going. In July 1996, the *Golaha Guurtida* – using its extra-governmental powers – called a national conference. The following resolution was adopted (broadcast on Radio Hargeisa, 6 July 1996; see *Horn of Africa Bulletin*, 8/4:p.24):

Having realized the impossibility of holding general elections in the Republic of Somaliland in order to present a constitution to a referendum, and having taken account of the stipulations of the national charter and its adjuncts on its expiry, the Council of Elders of the Republic of Somaliland today agreed on the holding of a congress of clans.

On 15 October 1996, the 'Congress of the Communities of the Republic of Somaliland' officially opened in Hargeisa. In his opening speech, the president handed over the leadership of the country to the National *Guurti*. In the conference (which lasted for 131 days), a final debate on the constitution took place and guidelines for qualifications for presidential elections were agreed upon (Radio Hargeisa, 7 December 1996; see *Horn of Africa Bulletin* 9/1, 1997). The new constitution finally became effective on 16 February 1997 for an interim period of three years, after which it is supposed to be ratified by public referendum (Radio Hargeisa, 24 February 1997; see *Horn of Africa Bulletin* 9/1). The same month, Mohamed Ibrahim Egal was re-elected president for a four-year term. The House of Elders was called in again in December 1998, following the unexpected resignation by President Egal that he explained with a general lack of energy to run the office of president (*Horn of Africa Bulletin* 10/1, 1998). In a joint session, the House of Representatives and the House of Elders voted 124 to 3 to reject Egal's resignation. The situation since 1997 reveals that there is potential political stability in Somaliland. The institutional framework of governance that is in place is functioning, also in times of crisis.

Somaliland's political stability derives from the fact that traditional authorities became integrated within a constitutional state framework that is thereby adapted to the existing social structure of the country. The constitutionally legalized extraordinary powers of the National Council of Elders provide a constant form of control over politicians in the legislative and the executive branches of government, and prevent the emergence of a political power vacuum in case of government crisis. Under this umbrella of relative political stability, other state institutions responsible for the control of violence, such as police and army, could be reformed and strengthened (Bryden, 1996). The re-integration of SNM units into a national army has largely been completed, including units that had been involved in anti-Egal government activities (*Indian Ocean Newsletter*, 1 February 1997). Demobilization efforts are underway; a police force is functioning.

In sum, in the eight years between the collapse of the central state in 1991, and the time of writing in late 1999, relative political and military security were established in Somaliland. New or revamped state institutions were able to function reasonably well with regard to conflict resolution and conflict prevention.

Somaliland State Institutions: The Need for Involvement in Economic, Social, Environmental and Legal Affairs

As the analysis of the pre-1991 period in the previous chapter showed, the Somali people in the Northwestern region had to cope with a situation of state-induced insecurity that forced them to look for survival mechanisms provided by sub-state economic, social and legal arrangements. In other words, people became accustomed to finding ways of securing their living, meeting their socio-economic needs and handling legal affairs, independently of state institutions and legal frameworks.

Against this background the question arises whether the citizens of Somaliland feel the need for their government to provide forms of security other than the basic prevention of conflict and implementation of general law and order. A second question is whether Somaliland state institutions have the capacity to provide these securities. These aspects of defining the role and function of the *state* for *society* are the subjects of an ongoing discussion in Somaliland. The following reflections offer a sketch of tendencies and discussions about the role that the Somaliland state institutions are expected to play in economic, social and legal affairs.[35]

Somaliland citizens generally do recognize and appreciate the function of the state in peace making and peacekeeping and particularly the important role that the House of Elders plays in that regard. The support that recurrently was provided by the business community in the form of the necessary funds for the peace and reconciliation endeavors of *guurti* at local, regional and national levels is a clear sign of their consent. The attempts of state

---

35 The following paragraphs are based on personal conversations with Somaliland citizens in 1997/98.

authorities to rebuild public administration, such as record keeping in land affairs, a public population register, etc., seem to be generally appreciated. Some services, such as water-provision, are government-administered and are fairly well done under the circumstances. Most other services which would be the responsibility of government in other countries and form part of economic and social security, are organized privately; these include electricity supply, postal and telecommunication services, air transport, local and regional bus services, and international banking (Fadal, 1996). In these fields, arrangements deriving from clan and/or family networks and private business connections seem to have an advantage over what the state could offer in terms of public services at the moment. However, there are those in Somaliland who would like to see the state more involved in fostering economic initiatives and actively creating a secure basis for foreign and Somaliland-Diaspora capital holders to invest confidently in the Somaliland economy – who are, in other words, in favor of a more developmental state (Grabowski and Shields, 1996:p.267-88).

A lack of public finances restricts the Somaliland state institutions from widening their scope of operation. The inability of state authorities to offer more services to the population must be seen in connection with the rudimentary taxation system operating in the country. Customs on import-export trade levied at Berbera port currently constitute the most significant public income, and a taxation system in the country is only slowly developing. The business sector is generally skeptical of taxation. Quoting one of Somaliland's biggest traders, Marchal (1996: p.82) notes:

> "Here, people will prefer to earn 5 USD without paying taxation than 10 USD paying it." There is a strong refusal of any commitment to the State's control; it will make very hard the establishment of any taxation system, except the one on the port.

The fact that states revenue through taxation is relatively low and unstable is only one aspect of the problem. An aggravating factor, particularly in the first few years after the proclamation of independence, was that the Somaliland state authorities were not successful in securing development aid. It has been argued that the lack of opportunities for borrowing money in bilateral credit agreements at least prevented Somaliland from becoming mired in debt, and strengthened its self-reliance and self-esteem.[36] Nonetheless, the social recon-

---

36 Comments of John Drysdale, according to Reuter (30.5.1997) quoted in an article by McFarlane, "Better times after the war", in *Horn of Africa Bulletin*, 9/3 (1997).

struction of war-torn Somaliland suffered from the fact that, *de jure*, the Somaliland state was and still is not recognized. This non-recognition has meant that the flow of bilateral development aid into Somaliland has been both slow and limited, as foreign governments hesitate before undertaking official dealings with a government which is still striving for international recognition. This, in turn, has hampered the reconstruction efforts in health- and educational infrastructure as well as the important task of demobilization, including the creation of alternative income opportunities for ex-fighters.

The lack of a recognized status in the international political and economic system also creates disadvantages for Somaliland traders who – in the world of international trade, where letters of credit and insurance certificates for trading commodities are obligatory – are left dependent on middlemen in other countries, to whom they must pay large portions of their profits (Shank, 1997; also Fadal, 1996). For Somaliland as a trading nation, dependent on livestock export and food and consumer commodity import, this is a great disadvantage.

While some parts of Somali society seem to manage quite well without socio-economic security provision by state institutions, there are others who fall through the social net provided by sub-state or trans-state security sources and are in need of publicly provided social security. In the economic context, impoverished pastoralists, petty traders with little capital of their own, people without relatives abroad, and those with no access to internationally financed programs face relatively more obstacles in finding resources in order to satisfy their basic needs.

Another area of concern is education, the basis of the economic, social and political life of future generations. Primary education has become more widespread within various communities, often in combination with Koran-schools. Higher education, however, including both secondary level and university education, cannot be made accessible to all students without state funding. International scholarships are limited and in the private sector only those who can afford it send their children to school or universities abroad.

At first glance, one might think that women in the new Somaliland state structure would be on the losing side. The revival of customary/sharia law and the recourse to political decision-making based on patriarchal sub-state institutions, such as the strengthening of the role of elders, means a reinforcement of their political marginalisation (Warsame, 1997). Nevertheless, the 1975 family law had provided women with legal equality and an improvement of fundamental rights with regard to inheritance, divorce and custody issues. The return to neo-traditional political forms in the intervening years did not mean that Somali women, who had grown strong in awareness of their equal rights and their social and economic importance, allowed their new social position to be taken away from them. Somali women's role in trade has always been significant. Nowadays, many female-headed households secure their living on their own, by farming and livestock trade, brokering and banking. Their double lineage affiliation through marriage (*hidid*) extends their networks as compared to those of male business competitors. Against this background, they now face the challenge of fighting for their place in politics.

Women are in the process of institutionalizing their important role in community peace building and the local provision of social, economic and legal security. The mushrooming of women's NGOs and support groups is clear evidence of this. In April 1997, the *Negaad* Women's Umbrella Organization was formed in the Somaliland capital Hargeisa, representing members of thirty women's groups and NGOs. Besides fostering capacity-building and training programs for women, they define their agenda as advocacy of women's rights and peace building. Seen in this light, women now have greater freedom and more socio-political space in the process of post-dictatorial state formation than ever before.

It is not only women who are featuring prominently well in contemporary Somaliland civil society. A thriving press, vigorously defending its right of critical analysis (*Indian Ocean Newsletter*, 20 September 1997), is another sign of the fresh wind that is accompanying the process of state formation in Somaliland.

It seems that, in Somaliland, people are in a process of finding a formula for combining the modern and the traditional in defining state-society relations.[37]

---

37 The convenor's report of the Uppsala Forum in January 1994, which was endorsed by the Forum participants, the vast majority of them Somali from different clan, regional and political background, states: "2. The question of state formation and state reconstruction has been raised. Two contradictory bases for restructuring the Somali state, or states, have been proposed: modernisation or traditionalism. It appears from the discussion that the social basis for a new Somali state, or states, has not transcended the age-old discussion about modernisation and traditionalism. The discussion is still rooted in either revivalist or radical transformation. Others prefer to leave the present process to take its own momentum, hoping that the genesis of the new state or states structures will emerge from within a post-war Somali society. It was submitted at the Forum that one key question requiring resolution is what alternative political framework will need to be developed, with what kind of institutional structures and for what purpose." Mohamed Salih and Wohlgemuth (1994b: p.105).

Territory of the Somaliland State

When looking at the territory of the Somaliland state, the legal relationship between North and South Somalia is of crucial importance. The territorial demarcation of Somaliland is based on the boundaries of the protectorate of British Somaliland, founded in 1887 (see chapter 6, maps 1 and 5). The union between Northern and Southern Somalia was established and the Somali Republic was proclaimed on 1 July 1960, following the independence of the former British Somaliland Protectorate and the Italian administered UN-trusteeship of Southern Somaliland. The main legal argument for an independent Somaliland is based on the claim that it became independent on 26 June 1960, five days before it joined the union with the South. There thus existed, before unification, a political entity that was territorially defined by colonial borders and recognized in international law.

A second important question is whether the Somaliland state authority can claim to control all its territory. As noted earlier, conflict between ex-president Abdurahman Ahmed Ali Tour (Isaq/Garhajis/Habr Yonis) and the Egal government developed into warfare in 1994, mainly concentrated on Burao and the wider Togder region (see maps 4 and 5). This region was therefore out of government control for some time (Fadal, 1996: p.26). However, the Garhajis community supported Somaliland's independence, as did ex-president Abdurahman Ahmed Ali Tour at that time. It seems that the Garhajis clan's problems with Somaliland were determined more by the loss of personal political power and influence of the ex-president and by loyalty of his clan towards him, than by a fundamental challenge of the Gerhajis population to the territorial integrity of Somaliland.

Another problem-spot within the territory of the Somaliland state is in the eastern part of Somaliland, the Sool and Sanag regions that are inhabited by the Harti clans, the Warsangeli and Dulbahante (see maps 3 and 5 and diagram 1). In early reconciliation meetings, there was a firm commitment by Harti clans to an independent Somaliland state. From as early as February 1991, and culminating in the Erigavo Peace Conference of August-November 1993, the four major sub-clans of the area, the Dulbahante and Warsangeli (Darod) and the Habr Yonis and Habr Jaalo (Isaq) were in agreement.[38] From the second transitional period (1993 onwards) the Harti became more integrated in the executive, legislative and juridical powers of the Somaliland state structure. In 1997, however, the Northern Somali Alliance (NSA) was formed,

---

38 See SDRA/MCC (1994); also Fadal, 1996 and Farah and Lewis, 1993.

made up of the United Somali Party (Dulbahante/Warsangeli) and the United Somali Front (Issa).[39] The NSA opposes the Egal government and the idea of independence for Somaliland (*Indian Ocean Newsletter*, 29 March 1997). The attitude, particularly of the Harti/Warsangeli and Harti/Dulbahante communities, thus, has a part to play in the unity of Somaliland state territory. This became even more evident after the formation of the Puntland regional state in July 1998, a development to which we will return later in this chapter.

    In summary, the colonial borders that were internationally recognized define Somaliland state-territory. Although there are members of the Issa/Dir, the Warsangeli/Harti/Darod and Dulbahante/Harti/Darod and the Isaq/ Gerhajis communities opposed to Somaliland independence, the issue is controversial in their own clan communities. The overall majority of Somaliland people seem satisfied with the state leadership that secured peace and political stability and thus the conditions for economic and social recovery. The National *Guurti*, which includes clan elders from every clan in Somaliland, embodies the supreme power of peacemaking and peacekeeping within the Somaliland state territory.

Idea of the Somaliland State

Besides state institutions and a defined territorial unit, the idea or ideology of the state is essential to the description of a political entity as a *state*. For Somaliland, there are three bases for the idea of independent statehood: (1) the '*de jure*' existence as a sovereign entity immediately after independence from Britain, (2) the recurrent economic neglect and political marginalisation by the various Southern-dominated central governments, and (3) the specific Isaq identity, the majority clan in the Northwest, which suffered particularly from persecution after 1982 and during civil war from 1988 to 1990.

    The first basis for the idea of the Somaliland state refers back to its existence as a British Protectorate, and to its four days of independence from 26 June to 1 July 1960. During the debate among Somali scholars that developed after May 1991, the point was stressed that the proclamation of an independent Republic of Somaliland was not secession but the *dissolution of the union* of 1 July 1960 (Mohamed Salih and Wohlgemuth, 1994a). Somaliland had joined the

---

39 The Issa is a sub-clan of the Dir and, in contrast to the Gadabuursi (the other Dir sub-clan) critical towards the Somaliland state (see diagram 1 and map 3).

union with the UN trusteeship territory, ex-Italian Somaliland, as an independent state.

With regard to the common Northwestern experience of continuous political and economic neglect since independence in 1960 (see chapter 7), the feelings of the minority clans are not necessarily the same as those of the Isaq. Members of the Isaq clan had particularly been targeted for discrimination by the Barre government. Nevertheless, the government's bombardment of the major towns in the Northwest had inflicted suffering on all clans in the region, including the Issa and Gadabuursi. Most problematic is the role of the Dulbahante in Somaliland who were among the supporters of the late Siyad Barre regime.

Hence, because of the clan mixture of the Somaliland population, the idea of the state faces a certain weakness. The Somaliland identity can easily be portrayed as Isaq-dominated. The Isaq collective memory is informed by the extreme violence and destruction committed by Southerners during the civil war of 1982-1990. All leading positions in the Barre state administration and army in the Northern part of the country were filled by people from Southern or non-Isaq clans. In that sense, the Isaq have never been governed by their own people but felt virtually occupied by increasingly alien and hated government officials that were sent from Mogadishu. State policies were mostly directed against Isaq people, and divide and rule policies lead ex-president Siyad Barre to furnish military and other support to non-Isaq clans such as the Gadabuursi and Dulbahante/Warsangeli. As noted above (chapter 7), Darod/Ogaden refugees as well as Darod/Dulbahante fought on Siyad Barre's side until shortly before the central state collapsed. To this common suffering of the Isaq population was added a common strength acquired through experience since 1988/89 in the Hartisheik refugee-camps.

Opposing the argument that the Somaliland national identity is an Isaq identity is the fact that, since 1991, Somaliland has gone through a period of crisis and reconciliation that has involved all clans and has largely succeeded in integrating the minority clans into the mainstream Somaliland state. I would therefore argue that the achievements of the eight years of claimed independent status makes up the core of contemporary Somaliland identity. Beside the efforts of peace making and peace-keeping that involved elders of all Somaliland clans, and united them in the institution of a National *Guurti*, there is a feeling of self-reliance which makes the Somaliland people proud and enforces their identification with the state (Warsame and Brons, 1994).

An important aspect of their identification with the state and strong pride in their own achievements is the Somaliland government's hesitant attitude towards external security-provision. The Hargeisa government consistently refused to allow its territory to be integrated into the UNOSOM framework, insisting on its independent state character and paying the price of receiving meager development and reconstruction aid. This political insistence on its independence paid off when, in November 1997, Djibouti recognized Somaliland (*Indian Ocean Newsletter*, 8 November 1997) as, *de facto*, did Ethiopia by signing bilateral agreements, maintaining diplomatic contact with the Hargeisa government and allowing a diplomatic mission to be established in Addis Ababa (*Indian Ocean Newsletter*, 18 October 1997).[40]

In short, the three pillars that make a *state*, territory, institutions and ideology, are recognizable in Somaliland and have consolidated since 1991. A common interest of the Somaliland population and government in sustainable peace, built on compromise, is prevalent. Citizens recognize the authority of the Somaliland state to secure peace by means of violence if necessary. Although all three aspects of statehood have their weaknesses, the government of Somaliland is aware of them and works toward the consolidation of territorial unity, the strengthening of state institutions and the integration of all parts of society in one Somaliland national identity.

THE DIGIL-MIRIFLE (REWIN) GOVERNING POLITICAL AUTHORITY – THE RIVERINE STATE

The inter-riverine areas in the South of the country witnessed the fiercest and most prolonged fighting in the post-1991 civil war. The Somali Democratic Movement (SDM) that had been founded in 1990 as a Digil Mirifle militia (see diagram 1), proved to be militarily weak and unable to protect the Rewin people from attack by the forces of both Siyad Barre and Mohamed Farah Aideed. In the course of events, SDM dissolved into two wings, one pro and one anti Aideed (the SDM and SDM/SNA).

The experiences of war, starvation and political deceit in 1991, 1992 and 1993 made the Digil and Mirifle clan families "more cognisant of being a distinct and cohesive community" (Wiebe et al., 1995b: p.43). As a result of that, a reconciliation process led by elders of the Digil and Mirifle clans managed to resolve a number of intro-clan conflicts. This led to the 'Boonka Conference' in

---

40 This is not the place to discuss in detail the international reactions to the declaration of independence of Somaliland (Brons, 1993), but it should be noted that the continuing non-recognition has the potential to cause internal as well as regional political instability.

March 1993 to which all Rewin clans were invited. Unfortunately, many of the Digil clan leaders could not attend because their territories were occupied by either Hawiye or Darod clans (see chapter 7) (Mukhtar and Kusow, 1993).

The Boonka meeting was extremely successful and represents a landmark in inter-riverine history. Unification was obtained between all the clans participating and a new Chairman of SDM was unanimously elected. The meeting also appointed a committee of clan leaders to be in charge of the daily affairs of the area under control.... This committee, known as 'The Supreme Committee' (*Guddiga Sare*) or, perhaps more correctly, 'The Committee of Clan Chiefs' (*Guddiga Malaqiiyada*), has since the Boonka meeting taken an unprecedented lead in the administration of the two regions (Helander et al., 1995: p.8-9).

The process of reconciliation and political unification of the Digil and Mirifle clans continued after the *Boonka* meeting and culminated in January 1995 in an overall Rewin conference, the 'Pan Digil and Mirifle Congress'.

Institutional Framework, Territory and Idea of the Riverine State

The *Pan Digil and Mirifle Congress* lasted for five months and ended on 25 May 1995 with an official ceremony inaugurating a supra-regional political authority of the Digil-Mirifle clans. It resulted in the establishment of state institutions, in a definition of what was considered to be the Rewin lands, and in a political awareness-building process that was formerly unknown for the Rewin clans.

A House of Elders and a House of Representatives was established. Out of the latter a Supreme Governing Council of seventeen members was chosen with government portfolios of economics, foreign affairs, social affairs, reconstruction/rehabilitation, interior and justice/religious affairs. Abdulkadir Mohamed Aden Zobbe was appointed titular head of state. The regional capital and seat of governance were located in Baidoa.

Malaq Haji Mukhtar, a highly respected Rewin politician from pre-independence times, was elected chairman of the House of Elders (*Guddiga Malaqiiyada*). In the hierarchical structure of the Rewin clan system the *Malaq* is considered the highest political and social authority. Malaq Mukhtar is the head of the Mirifle/Siyeed (see diagram 1), but is considered the leader of both the Siyeed and Sagaal of the Mirifle (Mukhtar and Kusow, 1993). Malaq Mukhtar had been a member of the first Territorial Council under the UN trusteeship administration in 1952 (see chapter 5). He was a member of the first Somali Legislative Assembly in 1959 and remained a Member of Parliament until the 1968 elections. During the same time-span he had been president of the Somali Independent Constitutional Party (HDMS) (see chapter 7).

According to Malaq Haji Mukhtar, the Rewin authorities were not guided by secessionist motives, but by the desire for a development towards regional autonomy and a federal Somali state (Wiebe et al., 1995b: p.44). The Rewin conference recommended the establishment of a federal state structure for Somalia: "A Riverine State in the South for the Reewin people; a Somaliland State in the North for the Issaq; a Central State for the Hawiye; and a Cape State in the North east for the Darood" (Mukhtar, 1996: p.552) (see maps 3 and 5). According to this proposal, the Rewin are considered the rightful majority in the overall Southern region, geographically defined to include Gedo, Lower Juba, Middle Juba, Bakol, Bay and Lower Shabelle regions.

It may be recalled that in pre-independence days, the Southern region was divided into three districts, Lower Juba, Upper Juba, and Benadir, with the capital Mogadishu (see map 1). In 1973, a regional reform by the Barre government had subdivided these three districts into eight (see map 4), whereby the Benadir region became Middle Shabelle, Lower Shabelle and the new Benadir that now comprised the capital and the outskirts of Mogadishu. Upper Juba had been split into Bay, Bakol, Gedo and Middle Juba, the last taking a small strip of the former Benadir region. Lower Juba had remained more or less unchanged. What is important to note here is that this regional reform had enabled clans other than the Rewin to claim a territory of their own. The Gedo region, for example, became a Marehan (Siyad Barre's clan) dominated administrative region. (See diagram 1).

This look back into the recent administrative history of the South reveals the problems that accompany the recommendations of the Digil Mirifle Governing Authority when asking for the recognition of the Southern region as a Rewin region. The Rewin's claim to a unification of all their indigenous territory in a *Riverine State* is weakened by the fact that the other clans in the region, particularly the Darod and Hawiye, would be minorities in such a state. The actual contemporary political situation leaves the inter-riverine region "the only one controlled by clans that are not indigenous to it" (Mukhtar, 1996: p.552). While the Shabelle valley and, since September 1995, the Bay and Bakol regions are controlled by the Hawiye/Habr Gedir (USC/SNA Aideed); the Juba valley (Lower Juba, Middle Juba and Gedo regions) is controlled by Marehan, Ogaden and Majertain (Darod) (see map 5).[41]

In the Digil Mirifle federal blueprint for Somalia, the Hawiye are returned to their own territory in Hiran, Galgudud and Mudug regions, as well as controlling Mogadishu/Benadir and Middle Shabelle. (See map 3). One can imag-

ine that the various Hawiye political factions that are the most militarily powerful group in the Southern region at the moment would not at all be satisfied
with such a share of the territorial cake. Given their current military strength,
the Hawiye adhere to the national approach to state formation with their own
leaders at the top of the state apparatus.[42]

The Riverine State territorial blueprint did not consider giving the Darod
population in the Lower and Middle Juba regions their own autonomous political authority. The Juba valley, with its major port at Kismayo, is a place
where Harti, Marehan and Ogaden Darod live beside people from the Digil
clans, and where pastoral and settled communities traditionally interacted.
Since the 1991 civil war, the territory has been under ever-shifting military
control, resulting in continuous warfare and violence against the civilian
populations.

The idea of a Riverine State lies in the Rewin identity: the identity of the
sedentary Somali against the people of nomadic background, the Sab against
the Samale, the *Maxaa*-speaking against the *May*-speaking Somali, those who
were suppressed and marginalized throughout the independence period
against the politically dominant groups of nomadic background. Although
the way to a Rewin reconciliation had its drawbacks, showed internal splits
and did not necessarily include all politically active Rewin,[43] one can still say
that the political revival of Rewin awareness created a strong ideology that has
the potential to nurture their struggle in the future.

In terms of the three pillars of the state, I would argue that one could justifiably speak of the establishment of the Digil Mirifle Governing Authority in
May 1995 as a rudimentary beginning of what could have developed into a
state formation process. But political developments did not allow this embryonic state structure to mature.

---

41 In June 1999, the military power balance shifted when the Rewin militias – with the
support of Ethiopian troops – recaptured parts of Bay and Bakool, while Hawiye militias – with support from Eritrea – ousted the Majertain out of the Lower Juba. It remains to be seen whether these changes are of long-term nature.

42 For one of many examples, see the interview with Hussein Aideed by Reuters, 30
August 1998; in *Horn of Africa Bulletin*, 10/4.

43 Some Rewin are members of militias other than the Rahanweyn Resistance Army
(RRA), others were not able to participate as they were internally displaced, impris-
oned, or resident in territories occupied by other military factions.

Obstacles on the Road to a Riverine State

There are three major obstacles blocking the path to a future Riverine state of the Digil Mirifle clans. The first is the continuing occupation of the inter-riverine lands by non-Rewin military factions, the Darod and Hawiye. The second, a result of the continuous violence and warfare, is the long-term displacement of the settled farming communities, which causes a disruption of the social, economic and political networks on which the Rewin social and political structure was based. The third factor militating against a future for a Riverine State is time. Political and economic realities are created on the ground; whether they are considered legally correct or not, circumstances become increasingly difficult to alter or correct the longer they exist.

As noted above, the process of political stabilization in the inter-riverine region during the years 1993-1995 did not occur in all indigenous Rewin areas. In the Bay and Bakol regions, where the regional capital Baidoa is located, the process was violently interrupted when forces of usc/sna Aideed attacked Baidoa in September 1995, occupying the town and its hinterland. Some members of the Digil Mirifle Governing Authority were killed and many were detained in Mogadishu (Mukhtar, 1996). In response, the Rahanweyn Resistance Army (rra) was formed in October 1995 under the leadership of Abdulkadir Mohamed Aden Zobbe, who had a few months earlier been announced head of the Digil Mirifle Governing Authority. A turning-point seemed to have been reached in the Baidoa conflict in October 1997, when an rra spokesman claimed the re-capture of Baidoa and its surroundings following an all-out offensive against the Aideed faction (Radio Mogadishu, 10 October 1997; see *Horn of Africa Bulletin*, 9/5). However, Baidoa was subsequently lost back to the Hawiye, won and lost again: no side could maintain the upper hand and fighting between usc/sna and rra in the Bay and Bakol regions continued throughout 1997 and 1998. In June 1999, the rra succeeded in recapturing Baidoa with the help of Ethiopian troops (*Horn of Africa Bulletin*, 10/1, 1999).

Widespread insecurity had already forced many Rewin people to flee their homes and fields in the years 1991/92, which as a secondary effect seriously threatened the food security and general economic security of the whole region. The uninterrupted fighting in the inter-riverine region between usc/sna forces and the rra caused new displacements of people. Some 22,000 families were reported to have fled Baidoa and parts of the Bay region after the sna invasion of the town in September 1995. This not only meant immediate insecurity for these families, but also rising food insecurity for the whole region and for Mogadishu, as

The ensuing insecurity also has resulted in a 67% reduction in food production from the pre-war annual average. Most economic activity has ceased and there is reportedly no sorghum in the markets in Bay Region, which is the country's largest producer of cereals (Report by Africa Horn, Nord Net, 16 April 1996; *Horn of Africa Bulletin*, 3/96: p.19).

At the beginning of 1996, there were an estimated 54,680 internally displaced people in Mogadishu, living in 109 camps. The majority of them were farmers and agro-pastoralists from the inter-riverine areas in the South. They were reported to be suffering from starvation (*Horn of Africa Bulletin* 8/1, 1996). Over the following years, the situation only worsened. In November 1998, the Africa News Services (27 November 1998, in *Horn of Africa Bulletin* 10/6: p.18) reported:

> Bay and Bakool, the traditional breadbasket districts of Somalia, are worst hit, with food shortages brought on by a civil war that has displaced a large number of people. Floods early in the year and the failure of recent rains have combined to worsen the crisis. ... Without more aid nearly 300,000 people, now subsiding on leaves and roots, will starve early next year. ... The situation is critical and wfp [World Food Program] has no option but to divert all available resources to saving lives in Bay and Bakool.

Continuing out-migration by farming communities from the Bay and Bakol regions was reported as late as January 1999 in a report by the United Nations Co-ordination Unit (*Africa News Online*, 14 January 1999):

> The number of Internally Displaced Persons (idps) in Luuq (Gedo region) and Wajid (Bakool region) increases. ... Almost all of these idps are from Bay and Bakool regions. The main reasons for displacement are shortage of food, lack of water and insecurity related to increased factional fighting. ... On the 25 December 1998, the Ethiopian tv reported on that, according to the Somali Regions Prevention and Preparedness Office, over 10,000 Somalis have crossed the border into Ethiopia, fleeing from the famine in Southern Somalia. The people are settling in Warder and Afder zones of the Somali region, which, according to the report, are already facing food shortages. ... In a related development, the Kenyan Broadcasting Corporation reported on 2 January that over 5,000 Somali displaced by the fighting in Bay and Bakool regions have arrived at the Kenya-Somali border town of Bulo Hawa. ... In the coastal town of Bossaso, there are idps coming from as far South as Bay and Bakool.

Whatever District and Regional Councils operate in occupied Baidoa and other towns in the Bay and Bakol regions, they lack the legitimacy of the Digil and Mirifle Governing Authority. In areas where the local Rewin population has fled and not yet returned, policies conducted by councils whose authority derives from the military power of an occupying faction cannot be considered legitimate. Long-term displacement creates new facts on the ground, particularly in the context of land tenure, and the time factor plays into the hands of those non-Rewin clans who control the inter-riverine lands by force.

The rift within Somali society between Samale and Sab continues to exist, and reflects the depth of the contemporary crisis of Somali identity. The settled population, who have mainly been farmers from the Digil and Mirifle clans, have up to now been the main losers in the political situation of statelessness in the Southern Somali region. Their insecurity derives from patterns of domination rooted within the socio-economic make-up of Somali society. This domination was state-induced under the dictatorial Barre regime, particularly in the context of the implementation of the 1975 land laws. After 1991, domination and exploitation still continued, and caused mass starvation during the Baidoa famine, this being portrayed by some as genocide against the Rewin (Salad Elmi, 1994; Mukhtar, 1996). The state leadership from 1960 to 1991 and the militarily powerful faction leadership after 1991, both belonged to the exploiting, dominating, oppressing groups within Somali society with regard to their relation to the Rewin clans.

Although they eventually got their own militia organized in the form of the Rahanweyn Resistance Army (RRA), which seems determined to free the region from other clan occupation and which enjoys the backing of the clan leadership within the Digil Mirifle clans, the RRA remains politically marginalized and militarily comparatively weak. Although the Digil Mirifle clans had their own party, the HDMS, as early as the 1950s, it was not until the development of the Digil Mirifle Governing Authority in 1995 that their self-identification was strengthened and gave an impetus to bottom-up political institutionalization. In that sense, the Rewin have never been as united, conscious of their plight and openly concerned about their future as they are now (Helander et al., 1995). Only a regional autonomous state for the Rewin clans and territories, however, would improve their overall political, economic and social security and the stability of the whole Southern region. The fact that, in terms of endowments, the inter-riverine lands are the most valuable resources in the whole Somali region, containing the only natural water sources and rich farm- and pasture-land, implies that the indigenous clans will have to continue facing the threat of exploitation and domination by other clans in the future.

PUNTLAND REGIONAL STATE

The formation of the Puntland regional state was officially solemnized in June 1998. However, the decision of the Somali Salvation Democratic Front (SSDF), the political faction that represents the Majertain/Harti/Darod sub-clan, to opt for a regional state formation process in the Northeast was born out of the failure in accomplishing a national solution. The Majertain political leaders had always preferred the latter option, the re-establishment of the Somali central state. As it is important to know about the processes that finally made SSDF take this decision in order to come to a solid evaluation of the statehood of Puntland, I first turn to the prelude to the formation of the Puntland state.

Prelude to the Formation of Puntland Regional State: The Failure of the Sodere Initiative

Since mid-1996, there have been serious efforts by various Somali (ex)politicians to begin a process of reconciliation, out of the limelight of international attention and deriving from Somali-rooted initiatives.[44] From August to October 1996 preliminary consultations took place in Addis Ababa and other venues in Ethiopia between all Southern Somali factions with the exception of USC/SNA, now led by Hussein Aideed after the death of his father Mohamed Farah Aideed in August 1996. These talks resulted into an invitation to all Somali factions for high-level consultations, which finally started in November 1996 at the resort site of Sodere, 150 kilometers Southeast of Addis Ababa.

As a result of the Sodere meeting, a National Salvation Council (NSC) was inaugurated on 3 January 1997, consisting of forty-one members: nine members from each of the main clans, Darod, Hawiye, Dir and Rewin, with five seats for smaller groups. Six seats were left open for the Isaq to join in. An eleven-person National Executive Committee headed the National Salvation Council with five rotating co-chairmen with the authority to act and speak on behalf of the NSC. The co-chairmen were Ali Mahdi Mohamed (Hawiye/Abgal; USC), Osman Ali Atto (Hawiye/Habr Gedir; since March 1996 in conflict with his ex-political partner Aideed), Abdulkadir Mohamed Aden Zobbe (Rewin; RRA), Abdulahi Yusuf Ahmed (Darod/Majertain; SSDF), Aden Abdullahi Nur Gebiyou (Darod/Ogaden, SPM).

---

44 These initiatives have had the guidance and support of the Ethiopian ministry of foreign affairs and the regional organisation, IGAD.

Following the example of the Somaliland experience, a Transitional National Charter was to be drafted and presented for approval to a national reconciliation conference in Bossasso, in Northeast Somalia (Darod/Majertain lands). By November 1997, it was reported that all Somali provinces had chosen their representatives for the Bossasso meeting, a total of 650 delegates who, according to the chairman of the NSC, represented all Somali groups and factions.[45] The intention was that in Bossasso, 183 members would be elected to form a transitional parliament, out of which a transitional government and a collective presidential council would be nominated.

The Bossasso/Sodere initiative was not dominated by one faction, one clan or one political clique, but included a relatively open and representative group of Somali politicians of former national standing. This was reflected in the fact that although, in the Sodere declaration, the unity, national sovereignty and territorial integrity of Somalia were reaffirmed, a reconciliatory and open attitude towards the Somaliland issue was taken. This was based on the realization that the South should first come to peace and stability, and bring its own house in order, before it could approach the North for a possible confederation.[46] The position of the Southern players had thus shifted from blaming the North for the continuation of conflict in the South,[47] to an acknowledgement of the political achievements in the North with regard to peace and stability. This was expressed in consultations held on an equal footing between Sodere members and the Egal government on the possible future options for co-operation. A meeting in summer 1997 had already resulted in preliminary agreements between representatives of the Sodere initiative and President Egal that once the South was free of conflict, Somaliland would consider the issuing of common passports, a framework of common foreign security and common tariffs and trade regulations.[48] The fact that Somaliland – the SNM/Isaq – faction was not involved in the Sodere initiative can be considered a sign of strength of this initiative rather than a weakness.

---

45 *Al-Hayat* (daily Arab newspaper), London, 31 October 1997.

46 Interview with Dr. Yusuf Omar Al-Azhari, November 1997: "It will never be as it has been before. Let the regions have their own development and loosely confederate."

47 Hashi (1991) states: "Therefore the SNM leaders designed their own plan to set the Hawiye and Darod clans against each other until the two have exterminated themselves. ... When the Republic of Somaliland was declared by its leaders, what they had in mind (and are now carrying out) was their subversive activities to make Southern Somalia remain in crisis and in a state of war" (p.50).

48 Interview with Dr. Yusuf Omar Al-Azhari, November 1997, Addis Ababa.

The Sodere group provided the following territorial blueprint for a future Somalia state.[49] Generally willing to respect the political developments in each region, the Sodere group had thought of a confederate system, including five regions: (1) Puntland (North-East), (2) Awdal (North-West), (3) Central (Hawiye), (4) Inter-riverine (Digil-Mirifle), and (5) Jubaland (West to Juba river). In this scheme, the Darod/Harti would have control over Puntland and thus over the largest area, including the Warsangeli and Dulbahante territories which now belong to Somaliland. North-Western Somaliland, which in the Sodere proposal was renamed Awdal,[50] would have contained an Isaq majority with a Gadabuursi/Issa minority, leaving out the Dulbahante and Warsangeli territories that were part of the British Protectorate and therefore part of the new Somaliland state (map 5). In the Central state, the Hawiye would have been restricted to their traditional territory in Central Somalia, Southern Mudug, Hiran, Galgudud and Middle Shabelle, and moved out of the inter-riverine lands. Leaving Jubaland as a sort of conglomerate region for a multitude of clans, the Darod (Marehan, Ogaden, Majertain), Hawiye and Rewin, would have provided the Darod with a second foothold in the confederation, in addition to their own Puntland region in the Northeast. This proposal therefore bears the hallmarks of a Darod/Harti/Majertain perspective.

One major weakness of the Sodere/Bossasso initiative lay in its failure to convince the Hussein Aideed (usc/sna) faction to participate. At the same time as the Sodere-initiative, Kenya took up the role of negotiator, concentrating primarily on the three Hawiye faction leaders fighting each other in the ex-capital Mogadishu and the surrounding Benadir areas. Hussein Mohammed Aideed, Osman Ali Ato and Ali Mahdi Mohamed had already met in Nairobi in October 1996 and declared in a joint communiqué their commitment to peace (*Horn of Africa Bulletin* 8/5, Sept/Oct 1996). In February and March 1997, committees of representatives from Hussein Aideed and Osman Ato and Hussein Aideed and Ali Mahdi, respectively, met for negotiations in the Kenyan capital. The Nairobi talks were Hawiye talks, supposed to bring peace to Mogadishu and find common ground among the Hawiye sub-clans.

Taking place in parallel to the Sodere talks, at which two of the three Hawiye military factions, Ali Mahdi and Osman Ato, were also involved, the Hawiye negotiations in Kenya could have been interpreted as preparatory

---

49 Interview with Dr. Yusuf Omar Al-Azhari, November 1997, Addis Ababa.
50 Awdal is the name of the most westerly of the former administrative regions in the Northwest, bordering on Djibouti. See map in Lewis (1994).

negotiations with Hussein Aideed, with the aim of involving him in the broader national approach designed by the Sodere/Bossasso group. An alternative interpretation, however, suggested a Hawiye unification in opposition to the Sodere approach, in reaction to the domination of Sodere by Darod/Harti/Majertain politicians, as reflected in the territorial blueprint of Sodere and the proposal of the town Bossasso in Northeast Somalia as conference-venue for the planned national reconciliation conference.

Another reason why the Hawiye, and particularly Hussein Aideed, might be opposed to Sodere lay in the fact that the RRA leadership, under Abdulkadir Mohamed Aden Zobbe, was involved in the Sodere/Bossasso initiative as an equal partner and as co-chairmen of the National Executive Council. For Hussein Aideed, supporting the Sodere option for national reconciliation and state formation would have implied a withdrawal from the forceful occupation of non-Hawiye lands in Bay and Bakol regions.

In May 1997, two peace declarations were signed, one in Sana'a (Yemen) between Osman Ali Ato and Hussein Aideed, and the other in Cairo (Egypt) between Ali Mahdi and Hussein Aideed. These led to the 1 December 1997 meeting in Cairo, at which members of the National Salvation Council of Somalia, as representatives of the Sodere group, met with the USC/SNA of Hussein Aideed. Although this gathering was first presented as a preparatory meeting for the Bossasso national reconciliation conference that was planned for the same month, the Cairo meeting turned out to be counterproductive to the Bossasso initiative and led finally to its collapse.

In Cairo, an agreement was reached to create a government of national unity to be chosen at a national conference in Baidoa. Of 465 participants at the conference, 80 seats would be preserved for the Aideed faction and 80 seats for the Ali Mahdi faction. But the political balance between militarily weaker and stronger clans that had characterized the Sodere/Bossasso initiative was undone by the Hawiye dominance, expressed in the Cairo accord. The choice of the town Baidoa, the regional capital of the Digil-Mirifle Governing Authority which had been under occupation by USC/SNA forces since September 1995, could only have been acceptable to the Rewin if accompanied by a military withdrawal of Hawiye forces from the town and area, and a political recognition of the sovereign authority of the Rewin over their territory.

Instead, the RRA (Rewin) and the SSDF (Darod/Majertain) opted out of the Cairo agreement. The conviction among the SSDF leadership grew that in the light of the disappointing results of their efforts in the Sodere initiative, the Northeast region should not invest any further in national approaches, but should concentrate on the formation of a political authority/state structure in their own region (WSP, 1998a).

The Formation of the Puntland State

The SSDF, the political and military faction operating in the Northeast, had been one of the first to act against the Siyad Barre regime in 1978 (see chapter 7). During the 1980s, however, it became divided, fell apart and almost ceased to exist as a political and military body.[51] SSDF regained importance in 1991 by successfully defending the Northeastern (Darod/Majertain) territory against the USC Mustahil militia (Hawiye/Aideed); in 1992, it defeated the al-Itihad al-Islamia fundamentalist militia in their attempt to establish Islamic rule in the port town of Bossasso.

SSDF was not able to build on these military successes, however, partly because of divisions within the leadership, which damaged their reputation within the Northeastern communities. The differences within the SSDF leadership, which centered on the two personalities of Abdullahi Yusuf Ahmed and Mohamed Abshir Musa, seemed to be solved when, in January 1997, parallel to the Sodere meetings, the two agreed on a power-sharing arrangement that gave Abdullahi Yusuf Ahmed the membership in the National Salvation Council and Mohamed Abshir Musa the chairmanship of the SSDF. Although the basic divisions within the SSDF were not completely resolved, the decision was made in 1997 that SSDF was in favor of a federal system for Somalia and that an all-inclusive participatory community conference should be held to decide on governance issues. The breakdown of the Sodere initiative, in which SSDF had played a leading role but became one of the two parties to reject the Cairo accord, provided the push for serious involvement in a regional state formation process covering the Northeastern part of Somalia.

Until that time, the SSDF had been disappointed in its efforts to provide consistent governance structures. District and Regional Councils that had been established in the UNOSOM period had only a nominal role and "were handicapped by a lack of effective authority and by internal dissent".[52] During these years of statelessness, clan elders in the region took the responsibility for resolving conflicts and administering internal affairs on an *ad hoc* basis by applying a combination of customary and Sharia law, as they had traditionally done.

---

51 In 1985, the chairman of SSDF, Abdullahi Yusuf, was arrested by the Ethiopian government and Mohamed Abshir became the new chairman. The 1990 tripartite agreement between SNM, SPM and USC had excluded the SSDF faction. See Bryden (1996); also WSP (1998b).

52 WSP (1998a: p.23); see also Wiebe et al. (1995a).

Coinciding with the shifting political agenda of ssDF in 1997 was the establishment of the War-torn Societies Project (wsp), a participatory action-
oriented project in the Northeast of Somalia, initiated by the United Nations
Research Institute for Social Development (unrisd) and the Program for
Strategic and International Security Studies (psis) of the Geneva Graduate Institute of International Studies.[53] Its first aim was to help clarify policy options
in societies that are emerging from major social and political conflict (wsp,
1998a: p.5). The project involved local researchers from Bari, Nugal and
Northern Mudug and aimed at facilitating dialogue within the communities,
including ssDF, elders, businessmen, women and local NGO staff, on post-war
socio-political reconstruction. Research notes on the main constraints and
potentials for reconstruction and development within the three regions were
combined into one report on the Northeastern zone, which, after several
rounds of revision within the communities, was finally presented at a meeting
in Bossasso on 15 March 1998. ssDF politicians, clan elders and traditional
leaders from the three Northeastern regions, women's groups and a number
of international agencies attended the meeting. Discussions that the three wsp
researchers had held at the local community level with elders, representing the
traditional authorities, and with the ssDF members, representing the authority of the single military faction in the territory, had a stimulating effect, and
became an integral part of the dynamics that finally led to the formation of the
Puntland state.

> For representational balance, it [the Zonal Project Group Meeting] was
> formally opened by Boqor Abdullahi Muse, the nominal traditional leader
> in the Northeast, and closed by Col. Abdillahi Yusuf Ahmed, the first chair-
> man of the ssDF, who referred to himself as a 'warlord in search of peace'.
> … Anticipating the establishment of a new government for the Northeast
> within the next few months, he stressed how this would need to translate
> wsp's research results into action (wsp, 1998a: p.28).

In May 1998, a constitutional conference began in Garowe, with more than
300 political and clan leaders participating. On 23 July 1998, after three months
of consultation, the meeting culminated in the proclamation of a regional

---

53 The unrisd War-torn societies project in Somalia is one of four projects, the others being located in Mozambique, Eritrea and Guatemala. The War-torn societies project (Somalia) had a preparatory phase from May 1995 to December 1996, and a first research phase from January 1997 to March 1998. The second research phase began in
August 1998. See wsp (1998a).

Puntland state with its capital based in Garowe. A presidential system was chosen for the regional state structure, comprising a president, a sixty-nine member parliament, and a nine-strong ministerial cabinet. Abdullahi Yusuf Ahmed was elected president of Puntland. The cabinet members were appointed in August 1998 (*Horn of Africa Bulletin* 10/4, July/Aug 1998). Although the council of elders is said to be in close consultation with the government, it was not transformed into a state institution in the form of a second chamber.

Puntland Institutions: Molding Traditional and Modern

Before the proclamation of Puntland, the role and function of the elders in a future state structure had been a controversial issue.

> A considerable number of the political elite, including members of the SSDF, quietly disapproves the increasing involvement of traditional leaders in political affairs. They consider governance and political affairs as their prerogative and the elders' involvement as a transgression (WSP, 1998b: p.16).

Although elders and SSDF politicians handled the stateless period in co-operation, it remains to be seen whether the reconciliatory function of the lineage elders in the predominantly pastoral society of the Northeast will be marginalized or further integrated in the future. It is too early to comment on the Puntland state institutions' performance or its acceptance by the Northeastern population. There had been some optimism before, as early as December 1991, over the establishment of an autonomous administration in the Northeastern Region (NER) under the leadership of Mohamed Abshir Musa; in practice, however, it had remained a non-functioning, empty structure.

> The main brains behind the administration were the traditional leaders, including elders chosen for their talent, *Ulema* (men of religion), intellectuals and politicians. They have established a functional administration at regional, district and municipal levels, with recognizable lines of responsibility and accountability (A.M. Mohamed, 1997: p.328).

The future will show whether Puntland state authority will succeed in securing overall control of the use of force in the territory. A demobilization of militias and the establishment of a regional state police are the first requirements. Since the Northeast is characterized by a strong urban-pastoral divide, one of the problems arising not only in terms of the use of force, but also with regard to the establishment of other institutional structures, is whether the pastoral countryside can be integrated into the overall state structure. This may be particularly important if the local and regional *guurti* are not integrated as an additional authority into the institutional framework of the regional state. So-called modern state structures might end up being superimposed on the clan structures of governance, as happened in earlier post-colonial state experiments. On this, the w s p research report (1998b: p.17) notes:

> The process of political reconstruction at the regional level also remains 'suspended', as in the past, from the population in the districts and rural area outside the regional capitals. To this silent majority the current political dynamic appears to be modeled on the discredited, rigid and centralized approach of past regimes. And the dismal performance of the regional administrations has further reinforced the legacy of public disillusionment.

At the same time, clan and lineage elders alone are unsuited to provide a sufficient and all-encompassing legal, political and military security. The *shir* meetings of reconciliation function as *ad hoc* problem-solving agencies in the pastoral areas, and – as a result of the absence or weakness of other institutions – increasingly also in the urban context. They are, however, not designed as preventive structures to ensure peace and order. Clan elders alone do not have the capacity to control the militias and young armed gangs; they are certainly not in a position to undertake their demobilization into organized units of police or army. Furthermore, while clan elders exercise authority within the Somali community, the political/military faction leaders do not see this as a superior authority. This is clear from discussions over whether clan elders are to be integrated into or excluded from government structures.

The dilemma is to find ways in which to mould the traditional and the modern institutions into one functioning body politic. Puntland authorities are still at an early stage of this process. In the constitutional conference the two worlds met, exchanged ideas, and opted for a regional state formation process rather than waiting for a national state to be established first. The challenge now is how to transform this consensus into one institutional framework. On the one hand, the traditional system of governance replaced modern institutions – even in urban settings – in the post-conflict era, and traditional rule proved indispensable in preventing a slide into total anarchy; but on the other hand, the traditional methods of conflict resolution are not adapted to cope with the complex needs of contemporary Somali society (w s p, 1998b).

Puntland Territory

The failure of the Puntland political authority to integrate the clan-based setting and the modern state order emerges again when reflecting on the territorial expansion of the Puntland territory.

There are contradictory versions of the territorial delimitation of Puntland.
Commonly, Puntland is seen as the equivalent of the territory traditionally belonging to the Majertain clan (*Migiurtinia*), an area that would approximately
comprise the administrative regions of Bari and Nugal (map 1, 4 and 5). Another territorial interpretation includes the provinces of Bari, Nugal, Mudug
and part of Galgudud (A.M. Mohamed, 1997). The UNRISD War-torn Societies Project took Bari, Nugal and Northern Mudug as its area of operation,
calling it the Northeastern *zone*. The rationale for dividing Mudug into *North*,
as part of the Northeastern zone, and *South*, as falling outside that zone, is
clan-affiliation: Darod/Majertain in Northern Mudug and Hawiye in Southern Mudug. This also takes account of the clan-divided character of the town
Galcaio. The Warsangeli and Dulbahante populations in the Western parts of
Bari and Nugal regions are also included in the Northeastern zone as they
form part of the administrative region.

To apply the criteria of Harti clan affiliation for a delimitation of Puntland
is rather problematic, as the territories inhabited by the Warsangeli and
Dulbahante stretch into the Sool and Sanaag regions that are an integral part
of Somaliland. While the War-torn Societies Project local research team refers
to the Bari and Nugal regional boundaries as delimiting their project area, the
Puntland authorities were not so clear-cut. This became evident during
preparations for the constitutional conference in Garowe in May 1998 when
some confusion arose over the question of whether invitations were being issued according to district or according to clan affiliation:

> Col. Abdillahi Yusuf and Mohamed Abshir have on May 15, 1998 stated that
> the conference is in session. However, the conference was not in progress
> on the second day (which was yesterday). It was said that the conference
> would be halted for some time as many of the delegates have not yet come.
> Other sources from Northeast Somalia indicate that there are disagree-
> ments on the way the representatives to the conference have to be chosen.
> Many delegates prefer the choice to be based on district. However, some of
> the leaders of the SSDF prefer to be chosen on clan basis. This results in
> many of the delegates not wanting to take part in the conference. The

sources further state that originally the plan was for presentation to be on district bases. This is believed to have changed at a latter stage.[54]

The intention of the Puntland authority was to include the areas that are inhabited by Dulbahante and Warsangeli in the Northeastern regional state territory, even though these lie in the Sool and Sanag regions. While the *Charter for Puntland State of Somalia*,[55] Article 1.3 left the territorial issue open, a press statement by Puntland State of Somalia on the *Principles and Position of Puntland State of Somalia*[56] notes:

> The Puntland State of Somalia informs the Somali people and the international community … That there is a major political development in Somalia: The Proclamation and successful establishment of a new regional state, the Puntland State of Somalia, composing of five former Somalia areas. Namely, Sool region, Eastern Sanaag region, Bari region North Mudug region, and Nugal region of Central, Northeastern and Northern Somalia.

This approach to the territorial question inevitably invites conflict with the neighboring Somaliland state. On 25 July 1998, two days after its proclamation of independent statehood, President Mohamed Ibrahim Egal of Somaliland launched a stinging attack on the Puntland state administration in Garowe:[57]

> Mr. Egal said that the administration could by no means extend into Somaliland territory, which was indivisible. He added that the borders of Somaliland territory were the same as those of British Somaliland. [He said:] 'We know the motives of the groups behind this issue and they should either refrain from blowing a non-existent administration out of proportion or take responsibility for any evil consequences arising from it.'

While the Somaliland government took a firm stand on the territorial issue, the clan elders of the Dulbahante clans in Sool and Sanag remained divided.

---

54 *Jumhuriya* (newspaper of Hargeisa, Somaliland), Sunday 17 May 1998 (vol.7, no.618). Title of Article: "The Garads of Sool Community (clan) are divided on the Gaowe Conference" (translated by A.M. Warsame).

55 "Charter for Puntland State Somalia" (undated), taken from web site: http://www.puntlandnet.

56 "Puntland State of Somalia: Principles and Position of Puntland State of Somalia" (undated), taken from web site: http://www.puntlandnet. The quotation is clause 1.1 (p.1).

57 Xog-Ogaal, Mogadishu: Somali 25 July 1998, Summary of World Broadcast-BBC, in *Horn of Africa Bulletin*, 10/4 (1998).p.22.

Some of them took part in the Garowe conference, others refused to go, arguing that "Dulbahante, both territorially and as inhabitants (people) are Somalilanders. Therefore it is not proper that the clan is confused with impossible matters i.e. the joining of another region".[58]

In early 1999, a Declaration on the Political Position of the People of Sool, Southern and Eastern Sanaag Regions and Buhoodle District of Somalia[59] appearing on the web site of Puntland, "puntlandnet", stated that:

[The *isimmada*, the traditional community leaders of the above-named districts] accept, therefore, the wish of the people of Sool, Southern and Eastern Sanaag regions and Buhoodle District, who freely decided through series of consultative and constitutional public conferences, to join with their brethren in the North-East Somalia, jointly forming the Puntland State of Somalia, a major partner of a future Somali federal system of government. We sincerely hope that the current position of the people we represent is perfectly clear to the international community, and that they will, thus, respect the new status of our regions; Consistent with the new status of our regions, we respectfully demand that all future humanitarian, reconstruction, development and national reconciliation matters concerning our regions are to be discussed with and conducted through the Government and community of Puntland State of Somalia. *No one else represents us.*

Ten clan elders from the areas/clans concerned signed the declaration. Although it remains to be seen how the matter of territoriality will be resolved in the future, the Puntland approach proved counterproductive to the consolidation of peace and stability in the North – the Northwest (Somaliland) and the Northeast (Puntland) – that had prevailed in that part of ex-Somalia for several years.

The Conflict-prone Idea of Puntland Regional State

The only coherent idea that seems likely to bind the people in Puntland to a Northeastern identity is the Harti sub-clan affiliation that is common to all of

---

58 Quote from Garaad Ismail Duale Gulaid, in *Jumhuriya*, 17 May 1998, vol.7, no.618. See also *Jumhuriya* 29 March 1998, vol.7, no.578.

59 "Declaration on the Political Position of the People of Sool, Southern and Eastern Sanaag Regions and Buhoodle District of Somalia" (undated), taken from web site: http://www.puntlandnet.

them. There was suffering under the dictatorial regime, but this applied mainly to the Majertain population, which was subjected to recurrent discrimination as silent supporters of the ssdf opposition. However, some Majertain politicians had also been won back into the political mainstream by the then head of state Siyad Barre. Dulbahante lineages from the Harti sub-clans, in particular, were very close to the Siyad Barre regime, which extended its political support base through marriage into the Marehan-Dulbahante-Ogaden (mod) sub-clan sections (see diagram 1).

An identification based on the Harti identity as a major Darod sub-clan would extend the Northeastern regional limits, as there are also Harti/ Majertain living in Middle and Lower Juba in the South. This might be one of the reasons for "the pervading sense of nationalism among the Majerteen" (wsp, 1998b: p.5), the desire to re-erect a national state. The Puntland state authority does not strongly promote Northeastern regional independence, but stresses that Puntland is considered an autonomous part of a future federal Somalia.[60]

According to the wsp research report (ibid.), however, the general population had rather different priorities:

Below the national level, the most important identity emanates from strong loyalty to the Northeast. The population in the Northeast regions (particularly the inhabitants of war-ravaged Mudug) staunchly supports the existence of the Northeast as an entity regardless of the shape the future Somali polity may eventually assume. And whenever the interest of the Northeast (which broadly coincides with the interest of the Majeerteen) is felt to be threatened, 'North-Easternism' overrides loyalty towards Somalia and the revival of the Somali State.

This observation provides quite a contrast to the involvement of the Puntland political leadership in political and military developments that continue to dominate the Southern region. Mobilization of Northeastern ssdf militia forces was reported in November 1998 (*Indian Ocean Newsletter*, 21 November 1998, in *Horn of Africa Bulletin* 10/6: p.15) in support of the Majertain/Ogaden side in the conflict around the Southern town of Kismayo, where General Mohamed Siad Hersi Morgan is trying to establish a Jubaland regional administration following the Puntland example. Puntland president Abdullahi Yusuf Ahmed was quoted as saying that "all military action against Kismayo was a declaration of war against Puntland" (ibid.). This must be seen in the wider

---

60 See "Charter for Puntland State Somalia" (undated), web site: http://www. puntlandnet.

context of the struggle for national leadership, which, after the collapse of the Sodere initiative and after the Cairo accord between the various Hawiye forces, is basically being fought between the Darod and the Hawiye. In the Hawiye long-term blueprint for Somalia, neither Somaliland nor Puntland are considered sovereign political entities, and the emergence of an autonomous Jubaland in the South is equally opposed (Hussein Aideed, quoted by Reuters 30 August 1998, in *Horn of Africa Bulletin* 10/4: p.19). The political agenda is still dominated by a top-down approach to state formation, backed by force if necessary. Given these political dynamics and the threat that Hawiye forces from the South might one day attack Puntland, President Abdullahi Yusuf Ahmed's political motivation in supporting Jubaland is to secure a Darod outpost in the South (as ally to Puntland in the Northeast) and not to allow the Southern region to become entirely Hawiye-dominated. The question remains, however, whether the Puntland population would support Puntland's integration into the national Somali blueprint.

Prospects for the Consolidation of State Formation Processes

In all three cases – Somaliland in 1991, the Riverine State in 1995 and Puntland in 1998 – the initiative to form a regional state structure derived from a deep frustration with the direction that 'national' politics had taken in Somalia. Generally speaking, the Isaq, the Rewin and the Majertain all felt threatened by political decisions and/or military actions undertaken by the Hawiye that were interpreted by the others as Hawiye claims to national leadership and attempts at political domination.

While the military factions, SNM, SDM and SSDF were initially incapable of overcoming the differences within their respective fronts, their negative experiences during periods of co-operation with Hawiye made them reconsider and finally put aside their own internal differences. The clan elders of the respective communities of the Isaq, the Rewin and the Majertain played an important role in this. Dialogue was initiated that included both the military faction leadership and the charismatic traditional political leadership in the three regions.

Somali people in general are very critical of state authority, an attitude born out of their negative experiences during three decades of Somali state rule after independence. Nevertheless, the years since 1991 during which Somalia has existed without an internationally recognized state identity have revealed some of the needs that a national government traditionally caters for:

The restoration of law and order to underpin public safety is one of the most commonly voiced needs. There is also ample grassroots recognition that traders need some minimum of regulation, that urban building activities require a basic plan, and that the provision of social services needs to be coordinated. Other common state functions "missed" by Somalis are the issuing of recognized travel documents, the establishment and regulation of financial institutions, a framework for international investment, and access to international assistance (w s p, 1998a:p.16).

These concerns, which were raised in the Northeastern region, are similar to those discussed in Somaliland. Although non-state institutions can satisfactorily manage internal and regional trade within the Somali region, on the international level the inescapable fact is that we live in a world of states. As long as the Somali people do not have an internationally recognized state, they participate in the world of international trade, finance, travel and aid on very unfavorable terms.

Peace and security can best be served in Somali society if those political entities, where the inhabitants consider themselves being represented in political decision making, are given the time to consolidate and adapt their governing institutions to their respective socio-political conditions. On the one hand, sub-state arrangements proved able to function well in the political, legal, economic and social realms and to respond to society's needs, during and even before the period of statelessness. On the other hand, it is the state that secures the international representation of people in the world community and enables the international mobility of people, goods and services.

The analysis of state formation in Somaliland, Puntland and the Riverine State has shown that the most promising basis for state formation in Somalia is that of regional clan-based units. We reach this conclusion particularly with regard to institutional stability (1) and identity (2). The demarcation of state territory (3) is rather more complicated.

1 In Somalia, the clan elders emerged as a medium for political stability and conflict resolution that enjoy the trust of their communities as legitimate representatives. However, as the means of violence are in the hands of faction leaders, the clan elders have no effective control over them. Political stability therefore depends on the willingness of the political factions to integrate clan elders committees in the political decision making process.

2 Under the present circumstances where most security derives from the non-state level, people in Somalia still identify first and foremost in clan terms. This implies that, in some respects, the Somaliland idea of state with reference to its colonial past is not satisfactory. The Isaq notion of common

suffering and resistance is still very strong in comparison to the sense of a 'Somalilander' identity. Whereas the Gadabuursi seem to be relatively well integrated in the political life of Somaliland, Harti clan elders are still divided on the issue of committing themselves fully to that state. The alternative option for the Harti (Warsangeli and Dulbahante) clans is to join Puntland that, then, would represent a Harti state in the Northeast. A Riverine State would also be based on clan identity, given the Rewin population's common experience of domination and exploitation.

3   The demarcation of clan territory is a difficult matter. Already in the stateless Somali society there emerged conflict between clans who both claimed the right over the use of grazing land and water in specific territories. In the contemporary setting we witness state-formation processes that are, on the one hand based on clan identity and on the other hand refer back to colonial boundaries. The drawing of borderlines does not only concern the settlement of resource conflict between clans, but impacts on past and future international and/or regional borders. That is what makes the so-far vocal dispute between Somaliland and Puntland difficult to resolve. The bottom-up consensus-driven approach to state formation that characterized both, Somaliland and Puntland recent political development demands from the political leaders a willingness to flexibility and compromise in order to maintain peace.

CHAPTER 9

Conclusions

In this book I have revisited Somalia's modern political history. I analyzed pre-colonial statelessness, the colonial and independent periods of Somali statehood and the experiences after the state collapse in 1991. *One major question that I intended to answer was whether the state in modern circumstances is a necessary and inevitable form of social organization, one that once it emerges in a given society, is a permanent fixture.* Let me answer this question by drawing from the Somali case. Various state structures were imposed on the Somali people without them having had much say in that matter. This process began with the colonial experience and continued uninterruptedly after independence. In the last few years, Somalia has been portrayed as a unique case of state collapse that brought chaos and anarchy to society. Not only did a dictatorial state leadership come to an end, state institutions also dissolved. The state ideology vanished and the state territory, although maintaining its external demarcations, did not maintain internal coherence. Although the state is the most prominent form of modern social and political organization and upheld by the international system of nation states, the Somali state, one can conclude, has so far not proven to be a permanent fixture of Somali life. With regard to the inevitability of the state the Somali experience has further revealed that, considering the matter internally, a society does not necessarily need a state in order to keep law and order, exercise a certain degree of control over the use of violence, achieve social security and economic recovery. Externally however, considering a society as a member of the world community, the state does seem to be inevitable. Furthermore, belonging to a state is part of the modern sense of national identity and pride and the Somali people are eager to regain their pride in this regard. This does not necessarily mean that they are eager to rebuild a central state.

What meaning can we ascribe to the state collapse against the background of Somali political history of the last hundred years? — The collapse of the Somali state did not suddenly erupt with the flight of the dictator, but had manifested itself in most parts of the country for some time before. It became evident in social disengagement, economic withdrawal, retreat to traditional legal processes wherever possible, and, since the mid-1980s, increasingly violent revolt against institutions of state repression (chapter 7). The groups or clans who controlled the state institutions in Somalia narrowed down until the point when they consisted merely of the relatives of the dictator. Others who had benefited from state assets lost ground, lost *de facto* power and influence. With reference to my definition of a 'weak state' in chapter 2, the Somali state was increasingly weakened, lost out against society and reacted with coercive measures in order to stay in control. The opposition movements that formed during the 1980s each represented particular group/clan with its own specific reasons to revolt against the regime. More and more clans denied the Barre regime their support. The timing of their change of mind from support or opportunism towards revolt played a significant role in their relation to the other opposition clan factions. Toward the end of 1990, the head of state controlled only the capital city. The rest of the country was under the control of armed opposition factions. The date of collapse of the Somali state is considered to be the day when Siyad Barre fled Mogadishu, 26 January 1991. In fact, since 1988, when SNM forces began to occupy parts of the Northern region, the government had failed to exercise jurisdiction over all its territory.

Although the option of reviving the 1960 Somali nation state has been kept alive by some of the Southern Somali factions, and in recent years to a lesser extent by the UN and other international bodies, this idea at the end of the 1990s no longer matches the realities of contemporary Somali society (chapter 8). The Somali state that existed at independence in 1960 turned out to be merely a formal shell which was empty long before 1991, and which seems further than ever from being refilled with empirical substance and political life. In retrospect, the Somali nation-state-formation project that was praised in the 1960s as being the most promising on the African continent, not only failed, but was on the wrong footing from the very beginning (chapter 7). The complete collapse of state structures that to a large extent had remained artificial and had become tools for repression rather than means of societal well-being and security is therefore not surprising.

This analysis of the Somali experience suggests that the state collapse of 1991 need not be understood as a rupture in Somali political history, but can be considered one step in the process of establishing political authority structures that are both adequately modern and rooted within the traditional set-up of Somali society. The most fascinating aspect of the Somali case is that, despite the state-oriented blueprint of the contemporary world structure, Somali society managed to free itself from state dictatorship, terror and persecution that had been exercised in the name of 'national security'. There came an end to hypocritical 'law and order' that, during most of the time after independence, was not upheld in the interest of the majority but to the advantage of a minority of clan elites. Although eight years after the collapse of the dictatorial state there is by no means everywhere in Somalia genuine 'law and order', and state terror was more often than not replaced by warlord terror, I still consider the collapse of the Somali state as a liberation for Somali society. Somalia now, at the beginning of the 21st century, is a showcase for the 'second liberation of Africa', the liberation from states and their leaders who have been superimposed on societies to the detriment of freedom and development. All this, however, does not imply that Somalis do not want to reconstitute some form of state structure.

What, then, can be the nature, purpose and future of a modern Somali state, considering that Somali society is faced both by globalizing dynamics of security provision and by localizing dynamics of political authority formation? — Localizing dynamics have their roots in the specific political history of Somalia. As I recalled in chapter 5, before colonialism the Somali people lived in political communities that in the sedentary setting were centered around the village, in the pastoral setting around descent and contract (*tol* and *heer*). We also came across localized city-state-formation in the coastal areas that were mostly initiated by immigrant communities from the Arabian Peninsula. These local political entities were not only influenced by local production patterns but also overlapped with clan identities (chapter 4). In the first decade of independence the parliamentary system tried to accommodate the various politicized clan groups. This project failed mainly because there were no decentralized political institutions in place. State power was not shared, as in a federal system, but centralized in Mogadishu (chapter 7). After the 1969 revolution, it seemed that decentralization under a socialist banner would take place but this turned out to be only a device for controlling citizens rather than one of handing over control to them. Opposition to the Siyad Barre state formed along clan political identity lines. It remained localized throughout the 1980s. It was particularly the Somali National Movement, the Northern opposition movement founded in 1981, which succeeded in integrating the traditional clan leaders into their struggle. Other movements remained relatively detached from traditional political authority structures. After the fall and flight of the Barre government in January 1991 the factions did not succeed in creating a united platform for a post-Barre state. In my view, however, the formation of a central state at that time would have failed sooner or later, as only the 'political elite in waiting' would have been involved – that is, faction leaders (warlords) of the various clan-based opposition movements, most of whom had been political opponents of Siyad Barre at one time or the other. Such a state again would not have integrated the traditional, society-based political authorities but would once again have been superimposed on Somali society.

Globalizing dynamics received less attention during my analysis than localizing dynamics. External political dynamics such as the superpower conflict had their impact on political developments in Somalia and the Horn of Africa in general. In chapter 7 I showed how Siyad Barre profited from the East-West confrontation. Somalia maintained one of the largest armies on the African continent, initiated a regional war and could fight internal opposition only because it could rely on a huge weaponry and continuous equipment and training delivered by its international partners from the East and later from the West. In other words, the weak state received the means to stay alive mostly through foreign support (chapter 2).

I have also referred to the global influence in the context of multilateral agents of security provision. Several UN organizations were involved in Somalia, in particular UNHCR since the late 1970s in the aftermath of the Ogaden war. The aid that flew into Somalia in the context of the refugee crisis mostly strengthened the state. Once the state collapsed the role of multilateral institutions became very critical. During the years 1991 and 1992 many people were desperately in need of help when faced by intensified war in the capital Mogadishu and in the Southern region. The withdrawal of UN organizations in 1991 reduced the options for coping with starvation and withdrew international attention from the Somali crisis. The UN intervention in December 1992 improved the situation for many Somalis although it strengthened the position of the faction leaders and did not succeed – some would say did not even try – to reach out to the traditional holders of authority, the clan elders.

The UN policy of the early 1990s that envisaged rebuilding the central Somali state as soon as possible has changed toward a bottom-up approach that focuses on local community reconciliation and rehabilitation. During the last few years, the UN, the EU and international NGOs have been involved in capacity building of local institutions. It is well known that aid can influence the balance of power in a community and a country at large. This is even more the case if – in a stateless setting – the power balance is unsettled. That is why international involvement in Somalia posed a special challenge to international aid agencies.

What kind of state formation took place in the 1990s and how are the prospects for its success in the future? — The period of statelessness that the Somali people went through created a political vacuum that made room for state formation attempts by force – as is still going on in Southern Somalia – and to state formation processes driven by consensus (chapter 1). In chapter 1 I referred to the social contract theory of Thomas Hobbes, in which he reminds us of the fundament of legitimate power, namely the agreement of people to give up part of their personal freedom in the name of security for all – the birth of political society. In Somalia, people literally sat under trees, trying to reconcile their different security concerns and needs in order finally to reach an agreement, a political contract establishing stability and security. This had been done before the advent of colonialism in the *guurti* meetings of the clan elders in response to conflict in the pastoral areas, and in the *aqiyaarta* meetings among the settled communities (chapter 5). After decades of marginalisation of the traditional leaders by the independent Somali state these clan elders proved to be the foundation of Somali political society. When the modern state collapsed and when attempts to rebuild the central state did not succeed but led the country into an intensified civil war, it was these local political structures and institutions that took a central role in the reconstruction of political authority.

In Somaliland, in Puntland and – for a short time –in the Riverine State we witnessed processes that started off from clan leadership as the foundation of political authority in Somali society. The *Sheikh* and the *Borama* Conferences in Somaliland in 1992 and 1993 were the cornerstones of state formation that engaged a large spectrum of society including minority clans, women and religious leaders alike. The *Boonka* meeting and the *Pan Digil and Mirifle Congress* in the Southern Rewin territory in 1993 and 1995 marked a new beginning of modern political Digil and Mirifle clan identity. In Puntland, the *Garowe Constitutional Conference* in 1998 integrated the various clan elders from the region in an effort to keep the peace in the Northeast, *vis-à-vis* the Somaliland/Isaq neighbor and the Hawiye communities, particularly those in the divided town of Galcaio. The principal condition for the success of such a process of state formation is the willingness of the political faction leaders, who are in control of force, to accept the authority of the clan elders who enjoy the trust and are at present the only reliable representation of the population.

Bottom-up political authority formation is not possible in those areas in the South where clan factions still occupy land of other clans and fight over territory and control of towns. There, the original population has been expelled from their properties and often enslaved as labourers, in other words ruled by the power of the gun. Those clan factions whose military control has expanded the limits of their own clan territories adhere to the blueprint of a united, centralized Somali state, with themselves claiming the leadership of such a state.

I conclude from the foregoing analysis that Somalia is a showcase for alternative, consensus-driven state formation. This is particularly true for those regions where reconciliation has had marked success and relative peace and stability have been established, such as in Somaliland and in Puntland. However, even in the Southern region localized civil society movements have gained ground and find themselves in alliance with traditional clan elders in the pursuit of peace against the prevailing violence and continuous clan warfare.

The state formation processes that we have witnessed in the 1990s in the Somali region show some similarities to but also fundamental differences from the *daraawiish* state of the early twentieth century (chapter 6). Similarities are first, the reliance on clan and lineage identity; second, the application of religious *sharia* and customary law; third, the problems of territorial demarcation that are encountered. Similarly like the Somaliland, Puntland and Riverine state formation processes the *daraawiish* state was a genuinely Somali polity, rooted in Somali traditional political realities. However, the *daraawiish* state was basically a theocracy that turned into dictatorship. The fundamental difference to the Somali states of the 1990s lies in the level of freedom and democratic participation structures that the new Somali states exhibit. Somaliland and to a lesser degree also Puntland are modern states in the sense that they attempt and partly succeed to integrate modern political institutions, international and national law with traditional political authority, clan identity and customary law.

In the light of the Somali experience, does a shift in the security debate from the conventional to a critical security approach seem promising and have we obtained insights that are relevant for the formulation of a theory of divided sovereignty? — The Somali experience confronts the analyst with unexpected political realities and challenges to conventional thinking. The conventional state-centred political science terminology of 'sovereignty' and 'security' is meaningless in Somalia since 1991. There are promising signs that the country will grow out of the era of modern statelessness as if newborn, embodying people's sovereignty in its original meaning. Voices from grassroots civic organizations are heard saying, 'If we are given a few more years without a centralized state and a government made up of clan factionist politicians, we will be strong enough to make ourselves heard in the future'. These voices encourage the attempt to re-interpret 'sovereignty' and 'security'.

In the introduction to this book I quoted Andrew Linklater who, in a review of the 20th century, said that the social sciences have been caught in state-centeredness and that in the future we should make more effort to theorize the world outside the state. My premise has been that security for its population is the main purpose of political organization. The means to reach this end can vary from case to case. Somalia has shown that the modern state is not the only source of security for society. Other social organizations provide social, economic, legal security. In the Somali case clan relations, built on descent, marriage and/or contract, dominate the social setting. With regard to military and political security the control over the means of violence and stability of the political system state control has declined steadily with the opposition forces' control rising (chapter 7). After the state collapse, the clan elders tried to provide political stability and to control the spread and use of guns among the young men in the respective clans. Somali society was and still is characterized by dispersed domination (chapter 2), a setting whereby a multitude of social organizations exercise control within society.

De facto divided security provision that challenged and finally dissolved the state as dominant institution, the *primus inter pares* within society, is what we have witnessed in Somalia. This has a direct impact on how to approach the idea of 'sovereignty'.

In pre-colonial times, Somalia was *de jure* stateless and consisted *de facto* of territorially divided sovereign political entities (chapter 5). At that time, the Somali concept of territoriality ameliorated harsh environmental conditions with economic adaptive strategies (chapter 3) and appropriate socio-political structures (chapters 4 and 5). This framework was undermined when the concept of undivided colonial state sovereignty was established in the Somali region (chapter 6). However, the fundamentals on which the pre-colonial Somali setting rested were not eradicated: in some cases they became dormant, in others they remained operational, albeit in changed form. In 1960, the independent Somali state inherited *de jure* sovereignty over its territory and people. Analysis of the independent period of Somali statehood, however, has revealed that the Somali state has never been the primary reference point for security provision for Somali society and people. In chapter 7 it became evident that national security concerns were upheld that allowed the persecution of an ever-growing number of citizens. This reveals the paradox that developed between the state's national security and actual security provision to society. Hence, the state was never socially or politically recognized by the Somali society as the one and only sovereign authority. Sovereignty remained *de facto* split between different authorities.

The Western notion of undivided state sovereignty is first and foremost founded in international law. It is the ideological underpinning of the contemporary world system of states. From a political science perspective, undivided state sovereignty is in need of critical review, as it is not necessarily a useful way of analysing political life in all states. The major outcome of our analysis of the Somali experience with regard to 'sovereignty' is that the term sovereignty must generally be linked to agents of security provision. In a socio-political analysis that starts from this premise the scale of *de facto* sovereignty extends from undivided to divided sovereignty.

The critical security approach starts from the three premises: First, the state is not the only agent of security; second, human beings rather than the state should be the object of security; and third, the focus of security studies must go beyond the military aspect and focus on all aspects of human security. International multilateral institutions as well as local agents intervene and infringe in the domain that was formerly left to the sovereign state. As a result of our findings it seems clear that research must focus on the security of people and can no longer take the state as the prime agent for security for granted. We cannot conclude, however, that the state has become redundant as a form of political organization.

The proponents of the critical security approach are clear that the issues that are central to conventional security studies – such as national security and arms control – remain important aspects also for critical security studies (chapter 2). A shift in the debate from conventional to critical security therefore implies a broadening of the agenda. The analysis of the Somali case has shown that we need to look beyond the state, not only in the context of economic and social security issues – aspects that would easily find support in liberal (anti-state regulation) circles – but also in the context of political security and stability, of legal and military security. Somalia has witnessed the strong and stabilizing impact of customary law. The elders have played a crucial role in reconciliation, peace making and arms control and in the reconstruction of political authority. While their role within society has remained significant throughout Somali political history it has become particularly crucial during the last nine years of statelessness. As long as there was a Somali state, the impact of traditional authority was marginalized and took place in a sphere parallel to the formal state sphere and sometimes in opposition to it. It is important to realize, however, that after the state collapse the efforts arising from the sub-state level of security provision were by no means anti-state, but intended to help re-establish state authority in Somalia. In my view the critical security approach offers ways to understand these processes. Bearing in mind the many cases of state weakness within Africa and the current debate on the role of the state, I do believe that the critical security studies will gain increasing importance.

Does a society-based theoretical approach to security and sovereignty provide a suitable framework for analyzing cases of hidden and open state collapse? — From the arguments that I have developed above so far it is evident that a society-based theoretical approach to security and sovereignty does provide a suitable framework for the analysis of state collapse. At the end of chapter 2 I developed a scheme for analyzing security provision based on the idea of divided sovereignty and critical security. It identifies six dimensions of security (legal, social, economic, environmental, political, military) and defines three layers of security providing agents, the sub-state (or stateless/non-state), the state and the trans-state (international community) levels. The scheme illustrates that sub-state and state security arrangements exist and operate side by side, complementary at times and competitive at others. In addition, international policies influence the security setting of the Somali state and society.

In chapter 6 I elaborated on the sub-state level of security provision and gave an overview of 'Relative Security Providing Social Arrangements'. Annexed to this conclusion the reader will find the full version of this overview summarizing the findings of my research in respect of the sub-state, the state and the trans-state level of security provision, differentiated for all six dimensions of security.[1] The table indicates that the provision of security is contested. There are various security arrangements operational at any given time. In my view, the scheme can be a useful tool for a society-based analysis of the weak-state and the collapsed-state scenario not only in Somalia but elsewhere.

The major conclusion that I draw from the Somali experience of statehood and statelessness is that it is society and people that come first. The most prominent political organization of modern times, the state, is nothing but one optional means for a people to achieve security and well-being. What has impressed me most during the years of research for this book is how determined Somalis were as they emerged from years of state collapse and civil war to shape their future in their own way. My hope is that the international community of nation states will allow the tender shoots of state formation to rise, prosper and grow strong and that the efforts of the Somali people to bring their house in order is honored and recognized in an appropriate way.

---

1   Comparison of sub-state (a), state (b) and trans-state (c) provision of political stability (vertical column 5) indicates the factor that is most pertinent to stability, conflict resolution, law and order in Somali society, is the elders in their respective pastoral and rural communities (column 5a). The various political systems that were supposed to bring stability after independence, i.e. the parliamentary and after that the socialist system (column 5b), both failed. Particularly under socialist rule the state instruments of control of the use of force (vertical column 6b) turned against the Somali people. International involvement (columns 5c and 6c) proved destabilizing first, during colonial rule, second, through superpower competition in the Horn and the continuous support of a government that had become dictatorial, and third, in the course of the political failure of the UN intervention in the 1990s.

RELATIVE SECURITY PROVIDING SOCIAL ARRANGEMENTS (II)

Variations of (In)Security	1 Legal	2 Social (Education, Health)	3 Economic (Incl. Food Security)	4 Environmental	5 Political (Stability and Conflict Resolution)	6 Military/Physical (Control of the Use of Force)
Levels of Security Provision						
SUB-STATE [PRE STATE STATELESS] ... indicates adapted sub-state (in)security mechanisms after state formation and/or state collapse	customary law, *Sharia law*	support by diya/mag-paying group, support by matrimonial relatives, prevalent for pastoral people; village community support; age groups traditional Koran schools [local (women) NGOS]	clan arrangements on pasture/ water; land-right allocation, trade-networks abban-system, exchange pastoral/ farming products livestock export trade; limited local production/ craftsmanship [remittances franco valuta system, all making use of tol+hidid]	pastoral adaptation (migration determined by availability of water/pasture); agricultural adaptation to soil variation by differing cultivation systems and crops, crisis: migration	council of elders (guurti or aqiyaarta) relatively open to all male adults, non-institutionalized character; ad-hoc reconciliation meetings. [re-emergence of guurti culture from local to national level in Somaliland]	among pastoral people limited control of elders over young warriors =defenders of clan assets and honor, widespread traditional inter-/intra-clan fighting, attack of caravan trade, village communities relatively defenseless. [mooryaans faction-fighters local clan-police]

B STATE	modern state law, (Italian/British style) 1975 family law adaptation to equality of women; land tenure laws trade laws security laws	social security youth/women organization; trade unions; educational system incl. national university	civil servant strata banking system state-farms/plantation economy nationalization of industries control of trade/licensing	drilling of wells poisoning of wells during civil war; mining	colonial administrations British/Italian; post-independence constitutions centralized parliamentary system (1960-69); socialist one-party system (1969-91); Somaliland (since 1991 two-chamber parliamentary system	national army including sub-sections: National Security Service (NSS) Red Berrets police regular National Army; arming of refugees
C TRANS-STATE (INTER-NATIONAL COMMUNITY)	refugee-convention, human rights convention, UN-Charter, chapter VI + VII	international development aid refugee related aid; UNHCR cross-mandate approach; role of SACB/Nairobi all with regard to poverty alleviation, health facilities educational facilities	international development aid related to agriculture and livestock.; IMF-policy; international livestock market; food aid; remittances from migrants and refugees abroad; illegal international trade of arms, ivory, qaat	international pirating with regard to plunder of fish stocks in Somali waters; de-mining projects in Somaliland	international political involvement in Somali region: (1) colonial partition (2) superpower political rivalry (3) UNOSOM political mandate, (4) UNDOS caretaker function	international arms trade; superpower conflict = militarisation of Somali state; increased accessibility to weapons intensified post-state conflict, UNOSOM military intervention

Bibliography

Adam, Hussein M. (1995) "Somalia: A Terrible Beauty being Born?" in Zartman, I. William (ed.) *Collapsed States. The Disintegration and Restoration of Legitimate Authority*, Boulder, London: Lynne Rienner.

Adam, Hussein M.; Ford, Richard (1997) (eds.) *Mending Rips in the Sky. Options for Somali Communities in the 21ˢᵗ Century*, Lawrenceville: Red Sea.

Afrah, Mohamoud M. (1991) *Target: Villa Somalia*, Mogadishu: The National Agency, 2ⁿᵈ ed. Karachi: Naseem Publishers.

Afrah, Mohamoud M. (1993) *Mogadishu: A Hell on Earth*, Nairobi: Copos Ltd.

Afrah, Mohamoud M. (1994) *The Somali Tragedy*, Mombasa: Mohamed Printers.

African Rights (1993) Somalia. Operation Restore Hope: A Preliminary Assessment, London: Africa Rights.

Africa Watch (1990) *Somalia. A Government at War with its own People. Testimonies about the Killings and the Conflict in the North*, New York, Washington, London: Africa Watch Committee.

Africa Watch (1993) "Seeking Refuge, Finding Terror: The widespread Rape of Somali Women Refugees in North Eastern Kenya" in *Africa Watch Women's Rights Project*, Division of Human Rights Watch, vol.5, no.13, London: Africa Watch.

Ahmed, Ali Jimale (1995b) "'Daybreak is near won't you become sour?' Going beyond the Current Rethoric in Somali Studies" in Ahmed, Ali Jimale (ed.) *The Invention of Somalia*, Lawrenceville: Red Sea Press, pp.135-155.

Ahmed, Ali Jimale (ed.) (1995a) *The Invention of Somalia*, Lawrenceville: Red Sea Press.

Ali, Mohamed Nuuh (1985) *History in the Horn of Africa, 1000 BC to 1500 AD*, PhD Dissertation, Los Angeles: University of California.

Al-Safi, Mahasin A. G. H. (1995) "Kenya Somalis: The Shift from 'Greater Somalia' to Integration with Kenya" in *Nordic Journal of African Studies*, vol.4, no.2, pp.34-41.

Amnesty International (1988) *Somalia. A long-term Human Rights Crisis*, London: Amnesty International.

Amnesty International (1990) *Somalia. Report on an Amnesty International Visit and Current Human Rights Concerns*, London: Amnesty International.

Amnesty International (1992) *Somalia. A Human Rights Disaster*, London: Amnesty International.

Anderson, Benedict (1983) *Imagined Communities: Reflections on the Origin and Spread of Nationalism*, London:Verso.

Asharq Al-Awsat, Daily Newspaper.

Aves, Maho A.; Bechtold, Karl-Heinz W. (1987) "The Effects of IMF Conditionality in Somalia" in Aves, Bechtold (eds.) *Somalia im Wandel. Entwicklungsprobleme und Perspektiven am Horn von Afrika*, Tuebingen: Institut f. wissenschaftliche Zusammenarbeit, pp.136-172.

Awad, M. H.; Boothman, I. M. (1975) "The Physical Geography and Water Resources of Somalia" in Lewis, I. M. (ed.) *Abaar: The Somali Drought*, London: International African Institute.

Ayele, Negussay (1980) "The socio-political Impact of semi-arid Ecology: The Case of the Horn of Africa" in Fassil G. Kiros (ed.) *The Development Problems and Prospects of semi-arid Areas in Eastern Africa*, Workshop Proceedings, 9-13 April 1980, in Nazareth, Ethiopia: Organization of Social Science Research in Eastern and Southern Africa (OSSREA), pp.295-321.

Ayoob, Mohammed (1992) "The Security Predicament of the Third World State: Reflections on State Making in a Comparative Perspective" in Job, Brian (ed.) *The Insecurity Dilemma. National Security of Third World States*, Boulder, London: Lynne Rienner, pp.63-80.

Azarya, Victor (1988) "Reordering State-Society Relations: Incorporation and Disengagement" in Rothchild, Donald; Chazan, Naomi (eds.) *The Precarious Balance. State and Society in Africa*, Boulder, London: Westview.

Azarya, Victor (1992) "Civil Society and Disengagement in Africa" in Harbeson, John W.; Rothchild, Donald; Chazan, Naomi (eds.) *Civil Society and the State in Africa*, Boulder, London: Lynne Rienner, pp.83-100.

Barth, Fredrik (1969) (ed.) *Ethnic Groups and Boundaries. The Social Organization of Cultural Difference*, London: Allen and Unwin.

Berki, R. N. (1986) *Security and Society*, London: Dent.

Besteman, Catherine (1995) "The Invention of Gosha: Slavery, Colonialism, and Stigma in Somali History" in Ahmed, Ali Jimale (ed.) *The Invention of Somalia*, Lawrenceville: Red Sea, pp.43-62.

Besteman, Catherine (1996) "Local Land Use Strategies and Outsider Politics: Title Registration in the Middle Juba Valley" in Besteman, C.; Cassanelli, Lee (eds.) *The Struggle for Land in Southern Somalia. The War behind the War*, Boulder, Col.: Westview, pp.29-46.

Besteman, Catherine; Cassanelli, Lee V. (eds.) (1996) *The Struggle for Land in Southern Somalia. The War behind the War*, Boulder Colorado: Westview.

Beyene, Taddesse; Tamrat, Taddesse; Pankhurst, Richard (eds.) (1988) *The Centenary of Dogali*. Proceedings of the International Symposium, Addis Ababa, Asmara, January 24-25, 1987, Addis Ababa: Institute of Ethiopian Studies, Addis Ababa University.

Booth, Ken (1991) "Security and Emancipation" in *Review of International Studies*, vol.17, no.4.

Booth, Ken (1997) "Security and Self: Reflections of a Fallen Realist" in Krause, Keith; Williams, Michael C. (eds.) *Critical Security Studies. Concepts and Cases*, London: UCL Press, pp.83-119.

Boutros-Ghali, Boutros (1992) *An Agenda for Peace*, printed as Appendix A in Roberts, Adam; Kingsbury, Benedict (eds.) (1993, 2nd edn.) *United Nations, Divided World. The UN's Roles in International Relations*, Oxford: Clarendon.

Bovin, Mette; Manger, Leif (eds.) (1990) *Adaptive Strategies in African Arid Lands*, Uppsala: Scandinavian Institute of African Studies.

Bratton, Michael (1989) "Beyond the State: Civil Society and Associational Life in Africa" in *World Politics*, vol.34, no.2, pp.407-414.

Braun, Gerald (1992) "Survival Strategies and the State in Somalia" in Raffer, Kunibert; Mohamed Salih, M. A. (eds.) *The Least Developed and the Oil-Rich Arab Countries*, New York: St. Martin's Press, pp.111-127.

Brons, Maria (1990) *Die Haltung der USA und der UdSSR zum Konflikt am Horn von Afrika bis 1987*, Bonn: Bonn University, Dept. of Political Science, unpublished MA Thesis.

Brons, Maria (1991a) Somalia im Buergerkrieg. Ursachen und Perspektiven des innenpolitischen Konflikts, Hamburg: Institut f. Afrikakunde.

Brons, Maria (1991b) *The Civil War in Somalia. Its Genesis and Dynamics*, Current African Issues 11, Uppsala: Nordiska Afrikainstitutet.

Brons, Maria (1992) "Some Political Factors influencing Food Security in Jijiga Awraja, Ethiopia" in Nett, B.; Wulf, V.; Diarra, A. (eds.) *Agricultural Transformation and Social Change in Africa*, Frankfurt/Berlin: Peter Lang, pp.1-16.

Brons, Maria (1993) *Somaliland. Zwei Jahre nach der Unabhängigkeitserklärung*, Hamburg: Institut für Afrikakunde.

Brons, Maria (1997) "The United Nations Intervention in Somalia" in Adam, Hussein; Ford, Richard (eds.) *Mending Rips in the Sky. Options for Somali Communities in the 21st Century*, Lawrenceville: Red Sea Press, pp.579-593.

Brons, Maria; Doornbos, Martin; Mohamed Salih, M. A. (1995) "The Somali-Ethiopians: The Quest for Alternative Futures" in *Eastern Africa Social Science Research Review*, vol.11, no.2, pp.45-70.

Brons, Maria; Elisa, Woldeyesus; Tegegn, Mandefro; Mohamed Salih, M. A. (1993) "War and the Somali Refugees in Eastern Hararghe, Ethiopia" in Tvedt, Terje (ed.) *Conflicts in the Horn of Africa: Human and Ecological Consequences of Warfare*, Uppsala: EPOS, pp.46-67.

Bryden, Matthew (1996) *Briefing Notes on Northeastern Somalia and "Somaliland"*, Addis Ababa: UNDP Emergency Unit for Ethiopia

Bryden, Matthew (1994) *Mission to Somaliland*, Addis Ababa: UN Emergency Unit for Ethiopia.

Bull, Hedley (1969) "Society and Anarchy in International Relations" in Butterfield, Herbert; Wight, Martin (eds.) *Diplomatic Investigations. Essays in the Theory of International Politics*, London: Allen & Unwin.

Burton, Richard F. (1894) *First Footsteps into East Africa: or an Exploration of Harar*, London: Tylson and Edwards.

Buzan, Barry (1983) *People, States and Fear. The National Security Problem in International Relations*, Brighton, Sussex: Wheatsheaf.

Buzan, Barry (1991, 2nd revised edition) *People, States and Fear. An Agenda for International Security Studies in the Post-Cold War Era*, London, New York: Harvester Wheatsheaf.

Cerulli, Enrico (1957-59) *Somalia: Scritti vari editi et inediti*, I-III, Rome: Istituto Poligrafico dello Stato.

Cervenka, Zdenek (1968) *The Organization of African Unity and its Charter*, London: C. Hurst Publishers.

Charter for Puntland State Somalia (undated) taken from website: http://www. puntlandnet.

Chazan, Naomi; Mortimer, Robert; Ravenhill, John; Rothchild, Donald (1988, 2nd ed.) *Politics and Society in Contemporary Africa*, Boulder Colorado: Lynne Rienner.

Chazan, Naomi; Rothchild, Donald (eds.) (1988) *The Precarious Balance: State and Society in Africa*, Boulder: Westview.

Clapham, Christopher (1990) "The Political Economy of Conflict in the Horn of Africa, in *Survival*, vol.32, Sept-Oct, pp.403-420.

Clapham, Christopher (1998) (ed.) *African Guerillas*, Fountain Indiana: James Currey.

Clark, Ian (1991, 2nd. ed.) *The Hierarchy of States. Reform and Resistance in the International Order*, Cambridge: Cambridge *University Press.*

Cohen, Roberta; Deng Francis (1998) *Masses in Flight. The Global Crisis of Internal Displacement*, Washington, Brookings Institution Press.

Compagnon, Daniel (1998) "Somali Armed Units. The Interplay of Political Entrepreneurship and Clan-based Factions", in Clapham, Christopher (ed.) *African Guerillas*, Fountain Indiana: James Currey, pp.73-90.

Conroy, Richard W. (1994) "From Peace-Keeping to Peace-Enforcement: Lessons from the Case of Somalia", Paper presented at the 7th *Annual Meeting of the Academic Council on the* UN *System: 'Approaching Fifty: The United Nations from Europe'*, The Hague, 23-25 June 1994.

Dalby, Simon (1997) "Contesting an Essential Concept: Reading the Dilemmas in Contemporary Security Discourse" in Krause, K.; Williams, M. C. (eds.) *Critical Security Studies. Concepts and Cases*, London: UCL Press, pp.3-31.

Davis, M. Jane (ed.) *Security Issues in the Post-Cold War World*, Cheltenham, Brookfield: Edward Elgar.

De Waal, Alex (1994) "Land Tenure, Famine and Peace in Somalia" in Wohlgemuth, L.; Mohamed Salih, M. A. (eds.) *Crisis Management and the Politics of Reconciliation in Somalia*, Uppsala: Nordiska Afrikainstitutet, pp.29-41.

Declaration on the Political Position of the People of Sool, Southern and Eastern Sanaag Regions and Buhoodle District of Somalia (undated) taken from website: http://www. puntlandnet.

Declich, Francesca (1995) "Identity, Dance and Islam among People with Bantu Origins in Riverine Areas of Somalia" in Ahmed, Ali Jimale (ed.) *The Invention of Somalia*, Lawrenceville; Red Sea, pp.191-222.

Deng, Francis Mading (1993) *Protecting the Dispossessed. A Challenge for the International Community*, Washington: The Brookings Institution.

Deudney, Daniel (1995) "Political Fission: State Structure, Civil Society and Nuclear Security Politics in the United States", in Lipschutz, Ronnie (ed.) *On Security*, New York; Columbia University Press, pp.87-123.

Dietz, Ton (1987) *Pastoralists in Dire Straits. Survival Strategies and External Interventions in a semi-arid Region at the Kenya-Uganda Border: Western Pokot, 1900-1986*, PhD Thesis, Amsterdam: University of Amsterdam, Netherlands Geographical Studies 49.

Dillon, Michael (1996) *Politics of Security. Towards a Political Philosophy of Continental Thought*, London, New York: Routledge.

Doornbos Martin; Markakis, John (1994) "Society and State in Crisis: What went wrong in Somalia?" in Mohamed Salih, M. A.; Wohlgemuth, Lennart (eds.) *Crisis Management and the Politics of Reconciliation in Somalia. Statements from the Uppsala Forum*, 17-19 January 1994, Uppsala: Nordiska Afrikainstitutet, pp.12-18.

Doornbos, Martin (1975) "The Shehu and the Mulah: The Jihads of Usuman dan Fodio and Muhammed Abd-Allah Hassan in Comparative Perspective" in *Geneva-Africa*, vol.14, no.2, pp.7-31.

Doornbos, Martin (1990) "The African State in Academic Debate: Retrospect and Prospect" in *Journal of Modern African Studies*, vol.28, no.2, pp.179-198.

Doornbos, Martin (1993) "Pasture and Polis: the Roots of Political Marginalisation of Somali Pastoralism" in Markakis, John (ed.) *Conflict and the Decline of Pastoralism in the Horn of Africa*, London: Macmillan & Institute of Social Studies, pp.100-121.

Drysdale, John (1992) *Somaliland 1991. Report and Reference*, Hove: Global States Ltd.

Dualeh, Hussein Ali (1994) *From Barre to Aideed. Somalia: The Agony of a Nation*, Nairobi: Stellagraphics.

Echete, Tibebe (1988) *A History of Jijiga Town 1891-1974*. Addis Ababa: Dept. of History, unpublished M.A. Thesis.

Ehret, Christopher (1995) "The Eastern Horn of Africa, 1000 BC to 1400 AD: The Historical Roots" in Ahmed, Ali Jimale (ed.) *The Invention of Somalia*, Lawrenceville: Red Sea, pp.233-256.

Eliasson, Jan (1994) "Conflict, Development and Peace-Making. Keynote Address" at the Conference on *Conflict, Peacemaking and Development: Research and Action*, Sigtuna, Sweden, 26 May 1994.

Eno, Umar Abdulkadr (1997) "The Untold Apartheid Imposed on the Bantu Jarer People in Somalia" in Adam, Hussein; Ford, Richard (eds.) *Mending Rips in the Sky*, Lawrenceville: Red Sea, pp.209-220.

Fadal, Mohamed (1996) *Rebuilding Somaliland. A Critical Appraisal of the Post-Conflict Reconstruction Process*, Ottawa/Geneva: IDRC/UNRISD War-Torn Societies Project.

Farah, Ahmed Yusuf (1994) *The Milk of the Boswellia Forests. Frankincense Production among the Pastoral Somali*, Uppsala: EPOS, University Uppsala.

Farah, Ahmed Yusuf (1995) *Prospects for Peaceful Solution to the Conflict in "Somaliland"*, Addis Ababa: UNDP/Emergency Unit Ethiopia, pp.1-5.

Farah, Ahmed Yusuf; Lewis, I. M. (1993) *Somalia: The Roots of Reconciliation. Peace Making Endeavours of Contemporary Lineage Leaders: A Survey of Grassroots Peace Conferences in "Somaliland"*, London: ActionAid.

Farah, Mohamed I. (1993) *From Ethnic Response to Clan Identity*, Uppsala: Almquist and Wiksell.

Farah, Nuruddin (1997) "Quarrelling over the Crumbs of Memory", Paper presented at the conference on *Identity and Conflict in Africa*, University of Leeds, 15-17 September 1997.

Fenet, Alain (1983) "Djibouti: Mini-State on the Horn of Africa" in *Horn of Africa. From 'Scramble for Africa' to East-West Conflict*, Analysen aus der Abteilung Entwicklungsländerforschung Nr.106/107, Bonn: Friedrich Ebert Stiftung, pp.59-69.

Fieldings, Lois E. (1994) "The Evolving Legal Parameters For Intervention by the Security Council under Chapter VII to Protect Human Rights", Paper presented at the *7th Annual Meeting of the Academic Council on the UN System: "Approaching Fifty: The United Nations from Europe"*, The Hague, 23-25 June 1994.

Fitzgibbon, Lewis (1982) *The Betrayal of the Somalis*, London: Rex Collins.

Forni, Elisabetta (1980) "Women's Role in the Economic, Social and Political Development of Somalia" in *Afrika Spectrum*, vol.15, no.1, pp.19-27.

Garthoff, Raymond (1985) *Détente and Confrontation. American-Soviet Relations from Nixon to Reagan*, Washington: Brookings Institution.

Gassem, Mariam Arif (1994) *Hostages. The People who kidnapped themselves*, Mogadishu/Nairobi: Central Graphics Services.

Goldsmith, Paul (1997) "The Somali Impact on Kenya, 1990-1993: The View from outside the Camps" in Adam, Hussein M., Ford, Richard (eds.) *Mending Rips in the Sky*, Lawrenceville: Red Sea, pp.461-483.

Grabowski, Richard; Shields, Michael P. (1996) *Development Economics*, Cambridge, Mass.: Blackwell.

Greenfield, Richard (1989) "The Somali-South African Connection", in: *Africa Events*, vol.5, April 1989, pp.32-35.

Grindle, Merilee S. (1996) *Challenging the State. Crisis and Innovation in Latin America and Africa*, Cambridge: Cambridge University Press.

Hall, Sir Douglas (1961) "Somaliland's lastYear as a Protectorate" in *African Affairs*, vol.60, no.1, pp.26-37.

Hamilton, Angus (1911) *Somaliland*, London: Hutchinson.

Hashi, Mohamed (1991) "Djibouti Conference and the Current Political Changes in Somalia" in Mohamed Salih, M. A. (ed.) *The Current Situation in the Horn of Africa. Statements from the Uppsala Forum*, 28-30 August 1991, Uppsala: Scandinavian Institute of African Studies, pp.49-53.

Hatchard, John (1993) *Individual Freedom and State Security in the African Context. The Case of Zimbabwe*, London: James Currey.

Heinrich, Wolfgang (1998) *Building the Peace. Experiences of Collaborative Peacebuilding in Somalia 1993-1996*, Uppsala: Life & Peace Institute.

Helander, Bernard, Mukhtar, M.H., Lewis, I.M. (1995) *Building Peace from Below? A Critical Review of the District Councils in the Bay and Bakool Regions of Southern Somalia.* Commissioned by the Life and Peace Institute, Uppsala (April 1995).

Helander, Bernhard (1996) "The Hubeer in the Land of Plenty: Land, Labour, and Vulnerability Among a Southern Somali Clan" in Besteman, Catherine; Cassanelli, Lee (eds.) *The Struggle for Land in Southern Somalia. The War behind the War*, London: Westview, pp.47-69.

Helander, Bernhard (1997) "Clanship, Kinship and Community among the Rahanweyn: A Model for other Somalis?" in Adam, Hussein M.; Ford, Richard (eds.) *Mending Rips in the Sky*, Lawrenceville: Red Sea, pp.131-143.

Held, David (1995) *Democracy and the Global Order. From the Modern State to Cosmopolitan Governance*, Cambridge: Polity Press.

Hersi, Ali Abdurahman (1977) *The Arab Factor in Somali History: The Origin and Development of the Arab Enterprise and Cultural Influences in the Somali Peninsula*, PhD Dissertation, Los Angeles: University of California.

Hirsch, John L.; Oakley, Robert B. (1995) *Somalia and Operation Restore Hope. Reflections on Peacemaking and Peacekeeping*, Washington DC: United States Institute of Peace Press

Hjort af Ornäs, A.; Mohamed Salih, M. A. (1989) (eds.) *Ecology and Politics: Environmental Stress and Security in Africa*, Uppsala: Nordiska Afrikainstitutet.

Hjort af Ornäs, Anders (1989) "Environment and Security of Dryland Herders in Eastern Africa" in Hjort af Ornäs, A.; Mohamed Salih, M. A. (eds.) *Ecology and Politics: Environmental Stress and Security in Africa*, Uppsala: Nordiska Afrikainstitutet, pp.67-88.

HLC [High Level Consultation of Somali Political Movements] (1997) "Solemn Declaration" of 3 January 1997 at Sodere, in: *Ethioscope*, vol.3, no.1, 1997, pp.15-17.

Hoerster, Norbert (1989, 6th ed.) *Klassische Texte der Staatsphilosophie*, München: dtv wissenschaft.

Holsti, K. J. (1992) "International Theory and War in the Third World" in Job, Brian (ed.) *The Insecurity Dilemma. National Security of Third World States*, Boulder, London: Lynne Rienner, pp.37-60.

Holt, Julius; Lawrence, Mark (1992) *The Price of Peace. A Survey of Rural Somaliland*, London; Save the Children Fund (UK), January.

Horn of Africa Bulletin (various issues).

Howard, Michael C. (1993, 4th ed.) *Contemporary Cultural Anthropology*, New York: Harper Collins.

Humanitarian Aid to Somalia (1994), Operations Review Unit; Netherlands Ministry of Foreign Affairs, The Hague.

Indian Ocean Newsletter (various issues)

Jackson, Robert (1992) "The Security Dilemma in Africa" in Job, Brian (ed.) *The Insecurity Dilemma. National Security of Third World States*, Boulder, London: Lynne Rienner, pp.81-96.

Jackson, Robert H. (1990) *Quasi-States: Sovereignty, International Relations and the Third World*, New York: Cambridge University Press.

Jackson, Robert H; Rosberg, Carl G.(1982) "Why Africa's Weak States persist: The Empirical and the Juridical in Statehood" in *World Politics*, vol.27, Oct. 82, pp.1-24.

Jamal, Vali (1992) "Somalia: The Gulf Link and Adjustment" in Raffer, Kunibert; Mohamed Salih, M. A. (eds.) *The Least Developed and the Oil-rich Arab Countries*, New York: St. Martin's Press, pp.128-152.

Janzen, Joerg (1984) "Nomadismus in Somalia" in *Africa Spektrum*, vol.19, no.2, pp.149-171.

Janzen, Joerg (1987) "Kennzeichen und Tendenzen laendlicher Entwicklung in Somalia", in Awes, Maho A.; Bechtold, Karl-Heinz (eds.) *Somalia im Wandel*, Tuebingen: Institut f. wissenschaftliche Zusammenarbeit, pp.16-43.

Jardine, D. (1923) *The Mad Mullah of Somaliland*, London: Herbert Jenkins Ltd.

Job, Brian (1992b) "The Insecurity Dilemma. National, Regime and State Securities in the Third World", in Job, Brian (ed.) *The Insecurity Dilemma. National Security of Third World States*, Boulder, London: Lynne Rienner, pp.11-36.

Job, Brian (ed.) (1992a) *The Insecurity Dilemma. National Security of Third World States*, Boulder, London: Lynne Rienner.

Jumhuriya, Daily Newspaper of Hargeisa, Somaliland.

Kaplan, Irving et al.(eds) (1969) *Area Handbook for Somalia*, Washington: Foreign Area Studies.

Kassim, Mohamed M. (1995) "Aspects of the Benadir Cultural History: The Case of the Bravan Ulama" in Ahmed, Ali Jimale (ed.) *The Invention of Somalia*, Lawrenceville: Red Sea, pp.29-42.

Keohane, Robert (1986) *Neo-Realism and its Critics*, New York: Columbia University Press

Korn, David (1986) *Ethiopia, the United States and the Soviet Union* 1974-1985, Carbondale: Southern Illinois University Press.

Krause, Keith; Williams, Michael C. (1997b) "From Strategy to Security: Foundations of Critical Security Studies" in Krause, Keith; Williams, Michael C. (eds.) *Critical Security Studies. Concepts and Cases*, London: University College London Press, pp.33-59.

Krause, Keith; Williams, Michael C. (eds.) (1997a) *Critical Security Studies. Concepts and Cases*, London: University College London Press.

Kusow, Abdi M. (1994) "Peace and Stability in Somalia: Problems and Prospects" in *Ufahamu Journal of the African Activist Association*, vol.XXII, nos I & II, pp.25-39

Kusow, Abdi M. (1995) "The Somali Origin: Myth or Reality" in Ahmed, Ali Jimale (ed.) *The Invention of Somalia*, Lawrenceville: Red Sea Press, pp.81-106.

Laclau, Ernesto (1994) (ed.) *The Making of Political Identities*, London, New York: Verso.

Laclau, Ernesto; Zac, Lilian (1994) "Minding the Gap. The Subject of Politics" in Laclau, Ernesto (ed.) *The Making of Political Identities*, London, New York: Verso, pp.11-39.

Laitin, David; Samatar, S. Said (1987) *Somalia. Nation in Search of a State*, Boulder, Colorado: Westview.

Legum, Colin (ed.) *African Contemporary Record*, Annual Survey and Documents, New York and London: Africana Publishing Company; vol.IX 1976-77, vol.XII 1979-80, vol.XIII, 1980-81, vol.XIV, 1981-82, vol.XIX, 1986/87.

Lewis, Herbert (1966) "Origins of Galla and Somali" in *Journal of African History*, vol.7, pp.27-46.

Lewis, I. M. (1955/56) "Sufism in Somaliland: A Study in Tribal Islam" in *Bulletin School of Oriental and African Studies*, vol.17, no.3, pp.581-602; vol.18, no.1, pp.146-160.

Lewis, I. M. (1961) *A Pastoral Democracy*, London: Oxford University Press.

Lewis, I. M. (1965) *The Modern History of Somaliland*, London: Weidenfeld and Nicolson.

Lewis, I. M. (1969/1994) *Peoples of the Horn of Africa: Somali, Afar and Saho*, London: International African Institute.

Lewis, I. M. (1980, 2nd edn.) (ed.) *Islam in Tropical Africa*, London: Hutchinson University Library for Africa.

Lewis, I. M. (1988, 3rd ed.) *A Modern History of Somalia. Nation and State in the Horn of Africa*, London, New York: Westview.

Lewis, I. M. (1990) "Somalia: Recent History" in *Africa South of the Sahara 1991*, London: Europa Publications, pp.894-911.

Lewis, I. M. (1994) *Blood and Bone. The Call of Kinship in Somali Society*, Lawrenceville: Red Sea.

Linklater, Andrew (1995) "Community", in Danchev, Alex (ed.) *Fin de Siecle. The Meaning of the Twentieth Century*, London, New York: Tauris Academic Studies, pp.177-197.

Lipschutz, Ronnie D. (ed.) (1995) *On Security*, New York: Columbia University Press

Luling, Virginia (1988) "The Man in the Tree. A Note on a Somali Myth" in Puglielli, Annarita (ed.) *Proceedings of the Third International Congress of Somali Studies*, Rome: Il Pensiero Scientifico Editore, pp.330-334.

Lyons, Terrence (1986) "The United States and Ethiopia. The Politics of a Patron-Client Relationship" in *North-East African Studies*, vol.8, no.2-3, pp.53-75.

Macpherson, C. B. (ed.) (1985) *Thomas Hobbes. Leviathan* (1651), London: Penguin Classics.

Madar, Yusuf Ali Sheik (1991) "The Republic of Somaliland: Its Declaration and Political Orientation" in Mohamed Salih, M. A. (ed.) *The Current Situation in the Horn of Africa, Statements from the Uppsala Forum*, 28-30 August 1991, Uppsala: Scandinavian Institute of African Studies, pp.45-48.

Makinda, Samuel (1987) *Superpower Diplomacy in the Horn of Africa*, London: Croom Helm.

Mansur, Abdalla Omar (1995) "The Nature of the Somali Clan System" in Ahmed, Ali Jimale (ed.) *The Invention of Somalia*, Lawrenceville: Red Sea, pp.117-134.

Marchal, Roland (1996) *The Post Civil War Somali Business Class*, Paris, Nairobi: European Commission Somalia Unit.

Marchal, Roland (1997) "Forms of Violence and Ways to control it: The Mooryaan in Mogadishu" in Adam, Hussein M.; Ford, Richard (eds.) *Mending Rips in the Sky*, Lawrenceville: Red Sea, pp.193-207.

Markakis, John (1987) *National and Class Conflict in the Horn of Africa*, Cambridge: Cambridge University Press.

Markakis, John (1989) "The Ishaq-Ogaden Dispute" in Hjort af Ornas, Anders; Mohamed Salih, M. A. (eds.) *Ecology and Politics*, Uppsala: Scandinavian Institute of African Studies, pp.157-168.

Matthies, Volker (1977) *Der Grenzkonflikt Somalias mit Äthiopien und Kenya*, Hamburg: Institut für Afrikakunde.

Menkhaus, Kenneth (1996) "From Feast to Famine: Land and the State in Somalia's Lower Jubba Valley" in Besteman, Catherine; Cassannelli, Lee (eds.) *The Struggle for Land in Southern Somalia. The War behind the War*, London: Westview, pp. 133-153.

Merryman, Nancy Hawk (1996) "Women's Welfare in the Jubba Valley: Somali Socialism and After" in Besteman, Catherine; Cassanelli, Lee (eds.) *The Struggle for Land in Southern Somalia. The War behind the War*, London: Westview, pp.179-198.

Meyers, Reinhard (1979) *Weltpolitik in Grundbegriffen, Band 1: Ein lehr- und ideengeschichtlicher Grundriß*, Bonn: Droste.

Migdal, Joel (1988) *Strong Societies and Weak States. State-Society Relations and State Capabilities in the Third World*, Princeton, New Jersey: Princeton University Press.

Migdal, Joel (1994) "The State in Society: an Approach to Struggles for Domination" in Migdal, J.; Kohli, A.; Shue, V. (eds.) *State Power and Social Forces. Domination and Transformation in the Third World*, Cambridge: Cambridge University Press, pp. 7-34.

Mohamed Salih, M. A. (1988) "Camel Production in the Arid Lands of the Sudan: National and Local Perceptions of the Potential" in Hjort af Ornäs, Anders (ed.) *Camels in Development*, Uppsala: Nordiska Afrikainstitutet, pp.19-29.

Mohamed Salih, M. A. (1992) *Pastoralists and Planners: Local Knowledge and Resource Management in Gidan Magajia Grazing Reserve, Northern Nigeria*, London: International Institute for Environment and Development, Paper no.32.

Mohamed Salih, M. A. (1999) "The Horn of Africa: Security in the New World Order" in Thomas, C.; Wilkin, P. (eds.) *Globalization, Human Security and the African Experience*, Boulder, London: Lynne Rienner, pp.127-143.

Mohamed Salih, M. A. (ed.) (1991) *The Current Situation in the Horn of Africa. Statements from the Uppsala Forum*, Uppsala: Scandinavian Institute of African Studies.

Mohamed Salih, M. A.; Wohlgemuth, Lennart (1994b) "Conveners' report to the Uppsala Forum" in: Mohamed Salih, M. A.; Wohlgemuth, Lennart (eds.) *Crisis Management and the Politics of Reconciliation in Somalia. Statements from the Uppsala Forum*, 17-19 January 1994, Uppsala, Nordiska Afrikainstitutet.

Mohamed Salih, M. A.; Wohlgemuth, Lennart (eds.) (1994a) *Crisis Management and the Politics of Reconciliation in Somalia. Statements from the Uppsala Forum*, 17-19 January 1994, Uppsala: Nordiska Afrikainstitutet.

Mohamed Salih, M.A. (1999) "The Horn of Africa: Security in the New World Order", in Thomas, Caroline and Wilkin, Peter (eds) *Globalization, Human Security and the African Experience'*, Boulder and London: Lynne Rienner, pp.127-143.

Mohamed, Abdi-Asis M. (1997) "How Peace is maintained in the Northeastern Region" in Adam, Hussein, Ford Richard (eds.) *Mending Rips in the Sky*, Lawrenceville: Red Sea, pp.327-332.

Mohamed, Hamdi S. (1997) "The Somali Refugee Women's Experience in Kenyan Refugee Camps and their plight in Canada" in Adam, Hussein M.; Ford, Richard (eds.) *Mending Rips in the Sky*, Lawrenceville: Red Sea, pp.431-440.

Mohamed, Mohamed-Abdi (1997) "Somalia: Kinship and Relationship derived from it" in Adam, Hussein M.; Ford, Richard (eds.) *Mending Rips in the Sky*, Lawrenceville: Red Sea, pp.145-159.

Morgenthau, Hans (1973 5th ed.) *Politics among Nations*, New York: Knopf.

Mubarak, Jamil A. (1997) "The 'Hidden Hand' behind the Resilience of the Stateless Economy of Somalia" in *World Development*, vol.25, no.12, pp.2027-2041.

Mukhtar, Mohamed Haji (1995) "Islam in Somali History: Fact and Fiction" in Ahmed, Ali Jimale (ed.) *The Invention of Somalia*, Lawrenceville: Red Sea Press, pp.1-27.

Mukhtar, Mohamed Haji (1996) "The Plight of the Agro-pastoral Society of Somalia" in *Review of African Political Economy*, vol.23, no.70, pp.543-553.

Mukhtar, Mohamed Haji (1997) "Somalia: Between Self-Determination and Chaos" in Adam, Hussein M.; Ford, Richard (eds.) *Mending Rips in the Sky. Options for Somali Communities in the 21st Century*, Lawrenceville: Red Sea, pp.49-64.

Mukhtar, Mohamed Haji; Kusow, Abdi Mohamed (1993) *The Bottom-up Approach in Reconciliation in the inter-river Regions of Somalia, A Visiting Mission Report*, 18 August to 23 September 1993, Nairobi: UNDOS/EU Somalia Unit.

Nelson Harald D. (1982) *Somalia. A Country Study*, Washington DC: US Government Printing Office.

Normark, Sture (1994) "Life and Peace Institute in Cooperation with UNOSOM Political Division", in Mohamed Salih, M. A., Lennart Wohlgemuth (eds.), *Crisis Management and the Politics of Reconciliation in Somalia. Statements from the Uppsala Forum*, 17-19 January 1994, Uppsala: Scandinavian Institute of African Studies, pp. 42-46.

OAU Doc. CM/2004 (LXVI) June 1997, in *Horn of Africa Bulletin* vol.9, no.3, 1997.

Olsson, Asha Ismail (1994) "Somali Women in Reconciliation and Ecological Recovery" in Mohamed Salih, M. A.; Wohlgemuth, Lennart (eds.) *Crisis Management and the Politics of Reconciliation in Somalia*, Uppsala: Nordiska Afrikainstitutet, pp. 73-75.

Olufemi, Kola (1983/84) "Sino-Soviet Rivalry in the Horn of Africa" in *Horn of Africa Bulletin*, vol.6, no.3, pp.16-24.

Olukashi, Adebayo O., Laakso, Liisa (eds.) (1996) *Challenges to the Nation-State in Africa*, Uppsala: Nordiska Afrikainstitutet/Institute of Development Studies, University of Helsinki.

Omaar, Rakiya, de Waal, Alex (eds.) (1993) *The Nightmare continues... Abuses against Somali Refugees in Kenya*, London: African Rights Report.

Omaar, Rakiya; de Waal, Alex (1994) Somalia: Human Rights Abuse by the United Nations Forces, in Mohamed Salih, M.A.; Wohlgemuth, Lennart (eds.) *Crisis Management and the Politics of Reconciliation in Somalia. Statements from the Uppsala Forum*, 17-19 January 1994, Uppsala: Scandinavian Institute of African Studies, Document V, pp.124-149.

Pankhurst, E. Sylvia (1950) *Ex-Italian Somaliland*, London: Watts & Co.

Patman, Robert (1982) "Ideology, Soviet Policy and Realignment in the Horn", in Adeed Dawisha, K. Dawisha (eds.) *The Soviet Union in the Middle East*, pp.45-61. Holmes and Meier Publishing.

Paulitschke, Phillip (1888) *Harar. Forschungsreise nach den Somal- und Galla-Laendern Ost-Afrikas*, Leipzig: F. A. Brockhaus.

Petrides, P.S. (1983) *The Boundary Question between Somalia and Ethiopia*, New Delhi: People's Publishing House.

Plant, Raymond (1991) *Modern Political Thought*, Oxford: Blackwell.

Porter, Bruce (1984) *The USSR in Third World Conflicts. Soviet Arms and Diplomacy in Local Wars. 1945-1980*, Cambridge: Cambridge University Press.

Prendergast, John (1994) *The Bones of our Children are not yet buried: The Looming Spectre of Famine and massive Human Rights Abuse in Somalia*, Washington: Centre of Concern.

Prendergast, John (1996) *Frontline Diplomacy. Humanitarian Aid and Conflict in Africa*, Boulder and London; Lynne Rienner.

Puntland State of Somalia: Principles and Position of Puntland State of Somalia (undated) taken from website: http://www.puntlandnet.

Rirash, Mohamed Abdillahi (1988) "Camel Herding and its Effects on Somali Literature" in: Hjort af Ornäs, Anders (ed.) *Camels in Development*, Uppsala: Nordiska Afrikainstitutet, pp.53-66.

Roberts, Adam; Kingsbury, Benedict (eds.) (1993, 2nd ed.)*United Nations, Divided World. The UN's Roles in International Relations*, Oxford: Clarendon.

Rubenson, Sven (1991, 3rd ed.) *The Survival of Ethiopian Independence*, Addis Ababa: Kuraz Publishing Agency.

Russett, Bruce; Starr, Harvey (1992a) *World Politics: The Menu for Choice*, New York: W.H. Freeman and Co.

Sahnoun, Mohamed (1994) *Somalia: The Missed Opportunities*, Washington, DC: United States Institute of Peace Press.

Salad Elmi, Omer (1992) *The Somali Conflict and the Undercurrent Causes*, Mogadisho: Beeldeeq Printing Press.

Samatar, Abdi Ismail (1989) *The State and Rural Transformation in Northern Somalia 1884-1986*, Wisconsin: University of Wisconsin Press.

Samatar, Ahmed (1988) *Socialist Somalia. Rethoric & Reality*, London, New Jersey: Zed Books and Institute for African Alternatives.

Samatar, Ahmed; Lyons, Terrence (1995) *Somalia. State Collapse, Multilateral Intervention, and Strategies for Political Reconstruction*, Brookings Occasional Papers, Washington: The Brookings Institution.

Samatar, Said S. (1982) *Oral Poetry and Somali Nationalism: The Case of Sayyid Mahammad Abdille Hasan*, Cambridge: Cambridge University Press.

Save The Children Fund (UK) (1993) *First Steps to Recovery. Urban Survey in Somaliland*. First and Second Round of Food Security Surveys, Hargeisa: Safe the children Fund.

Schlee, G.; Shongolo, A. A. (1995) "Local War and its Impact on Ethnic and Religious Identification in Southern Ethiopia", in *Geo-Journal*, vol.36, no.1.

Schlee, Guenther (1994) *Identities on the Move*, Nairobi: Gideon S. Were Press.

Schlee, Guenther (1995) "Regelmäßigkeiten im Chaos: Elemente einer Erklärung von Allianzen und Frontverläufen in Somalia" in *Afrika Spektrum*, vol.30, no.3, pp. 274-292.

Shank, Robert (1997) *Livestock Marketing and Cross Border Trade in the Southeast of Ethiopia*, Nairobi: UNDP-Emergency Unit for Ethiopia (EUE).

Sharif Hassan, Amina (1997) "Somalia: The Forgotten People" in Adam, Hussein; Ford, Richard (eds) *Mending Rips in the Sky*, Lawrenceville: Red Sea, pp.221-231.

Sheik-Abdi, Abdi (1993) *Divine Madness. Mohammed Abdulle Hassan (1856-1920)*, London, New Jersey: Zed Books.

Sicker, Martin (1991) *The Genesis of the State*, New York, Westport Connecticut, London: Praeger.

SIDA (1994) "What Relief for the Horn?" *SIDA Evaluation Report* (1995/3), prepared by ISSAS for SIDA.

Simons, Anna (1995) *Networks of Dissolution: Somalia Undone*, Boulder, London: Westview.

Somali Development and Relief Agency (SDRA), Mennonite Central Committee (MCC) (1994) *Proceedings of the Erigavo Peace Conference, Sanaag Region, Somalia*, Djibouti.

Statistisches Bundesamt Wiesbaden (1988) *Länderbericht Somalia 1988*, Statistik des Auslandes, Stuttgart, Mainz: Kohlhammer.

Steven, David (1979) "Realignment in the Horn: The Soviet Advantage" in *International Security*, vol.4, no.2, pp.69-90.

SWDO [Somali Women's Democratic Organisation] (1985) *Women in the Somali Democratic Republic. An Appraisal of Progress in the Implementation of the World Plan of Action of the United Nations Decade for Women 1975-1985*, Mogadishu: Somali Women's Democratic Organisation.

Thomas, Caroline (1987) *In Search of Security: The Third World in International Relations*, Boulder Colorado: Lynne Rienner.

Thomas, Caroline (1992) *The Environment in International Relations*. London: The Royal Institute of International Affairs.

Thomas, Caroline and Wilkin, Peter (1999) (eds.) *Globalization, Human Security and the African Experience*, Boulder, London: Lynne Rienner.

Tilahun, Takele; Hadj, Bashir; Barre, Bashir (1994) "From Communal Grazing to Privatised Enclosures: a Case Study of Changing Land Tenure in Region 5" in Rahmato, Dessaleng (ed.) (1994) *Land Tenure and Land Policy in Ethiopia after the Derg, Proceedings of the Second Workshop of the Land Tenure Project,* Working Papers on Ethiopian Development, no.8, Institute of Development Research, Addis Ababa University/ Centre for Environment and Development, University of Trondheim; pp.264-277.

Tilly, Charles (1992) "War Making and State Making as Organized Crime" in Evans, P. B.; Rueschmeyer, D.; Skocpol, T. (eds.) *Bringing the State back in,* (7ᵗʰ edn.) Cambridge: Cambridge University Press, pp.169-191.

Touval, Saadia (1963) *Somali Nationalism,* Cambridge, Mass.: Harvard University Press.

Turton, E. R. (1975) "Bantu, Galla and Somali Migrations in the Horn of Africa: A Reassessment of the Jubba/Tana Area" in *Journal of African History,* vol.16, pp.519-537.

UN Document SOM 53, 16 February 1994, in *Horn of Africa Bulletin* no.2/94, p.15.

UN Secretary-General report on Somalia of 16 September 1997

UNHCR/USAID/EUE (1996) *Somalia: Humanitarian Assistance and Development in Support of Peace and Stability,* Draft Proceedings of an Informal Meeting held in Addis Ababa on June 11, 1996.

Waever, O.; Buzan, B.; Kelstrup, M.; Lemaitre, P. (1993) (eds.) *Identity, Migration and the New Security Agenda in Europe,* New York: St. Martin's Press.

Waltz, Kenneth N. (1979) *Theory of International Politics,* Reading, Mass.: Addison Wesley.

Warsame, Amina Mahamoud (1997) *The Civil War in Northern Somalia (Somaliland): Its Impact on Pastoralists, especially Women and Children,* The Hague: Institute of Social Studies Research Report.

Warsame, Amina Mahamoud (forthcoming) *Resource Conflict in Somaliland,* The Hague: Institute of Social Studies.

Warsame, Amina; Brons, Maria (1994) "Somaliland: A State in Pursuit of Peace and Stability" in Wohlgemuth, Lennart, Mohamed Salih, M. A. (eds.) *Crisis Management and the Politics of Reconciliation in Somalia. Statements from the Uppsala Forum,* 17-19 January 1994, Uppsala: Nordiska Afrikainstitutet, pp.19-28.

Waterfield, Robin (ed.) (1998, 2ⁿᵈ ed.) *Plato, Republic,* Oxford, New York: Oxford University Press.

Weber, Max (1968) *Economy and Society. An Outline of Interpretive Sociology.* Edited by Günther Roth; Claus Wittick, New York: Bedminster Press.

Weizsäcker, Ernst Ulrich von (1994) *Earth Politics,* London and New Jersey; Zed Books.

Wiebe, Menno F.; Meshack I. Mwera; Ahmed M. Warfa (1995a) *Local Administrative Structures in Somalia. A Study of Nugal Region,* Nairobi: Life & Peace Institute / UNDOS.

Wiebe, Menno F.; Meshack L. Mwera; Ahmed M. Warfa (1995b) *Local Administrative Structures in Somalia. A Case Study of Bay Region,* Nairobi: Life and Peace Institute, Horn of Africa Program, UNDOS.

Wight, Martin (1978) *Power Politics*, Leicester: Leicester University Press.

Williams, Michael C.; Krause, Keith (1997) "Preface: Toward Critical Security Studies" in Krause, Keith; Williams, Michael C. (eds.) *Critical Security Studies. Concepts and Cases*, London: University College London Press, pp.vii-xxi.

Wood, J. (1984) "Unchartered Territory Between Relief and Development: A Comment on the Somali Emergencies" in Labahn, Thomas (ed.) *Proceedings of the Second International Congress of Somali Studies*, Studies on Humanities and Natural Sciences, vol.iv, Hamburg: Helmut Buske Verlag.

WSP (1998a) *War-torn Societies Project Somalia*, Geneva: UNRISD.

WSP (1998b) "Rebuilding Somalia: The Northeast Somalia Zonal Note", *War-torn Societies Project*, Geneva: UNRISD.

Wyn Jones, Richard (1995) "Message in a Bottle? Theory and Praxis in Critical Security Studies" in *Contemporary Security Policy*, vol.16, no.3, pp.299-319.

Wyn Jones, Richard (1996) "'Travel without Maps': Thinking about Security after the Cold War" in Davis, M. Jane (ed.) *Security Issues in the Post-Cold War World*, Cheltenham, Brookfield: Edward Elgar, pp.196-218.

Zartman, I. William (1995) (ed.) *Collapsed States. The Disintegration and Restoration of Legitimate Authority*, Boulder, London: Lynne Rienner.

Index